The European Union

D1561300

Thoroughly revised, the seventh edition of this accessible and highly respected text provides a rigorous yet digestible introduction to the European Union. Additionally, it authoritatively explains developments that continue to bring challenges to this powerful institution in times of great political change.

Key features:

- Clearly covers the history, governing institutions, and policies of the EU;
- Fully updated with new tables, figures, and photographs;
- In-text features such as Chapter Overviews, Questions to Consider, and Further Reading encourage deeper research and debate;
- Sustained discussion of transformative and historical change in the upheaval of Brexit and its ramifications, and the future relationship of the UK with the EU;
- Thorough reflection on destabilizing issues such as immigration and the years of refugee crisis in Europe, the continued crisis in the eurozone, tensions with Poland and Hungary, Euroskepticism, Russia, and the rise of populism;
- Increased coverage throughout of women or minorities within the EU.

Jonathan Olsen presents the EU as one of the world's economic and political superpowers, which has brought far-reaching changes to the lives of Europeans and has helped its member states to take a newly assertive role on the global stage.

Essential reading for students of European and EU politics, this book offers an up-to-the-minute look at both the opportunities and the existential threats facing the EU.

Jonathan Olsen is Professor and Chair of the Department of History and Political Science at Texas Woman's University, USA.

Two decades ago, when I began teaching an EU course, I assigned an early edition of this textbook. I then switched several times to other books, looking for the right balance of attention to the nuts and bolts of EU institutions and policies and an exploration of theoretical and substantive debates about integration. I love what this revised edition offers and am thrilled to adopt it again. Olsen emphasizes change – what drives it and why it matters – without sacrificing the original strengths of this text: accessibility and comprehensiveness.

Jennifer A. Yoder, Colby College, USA

Jonathan Olsen's book is an exceptional combination of updated erudite knowledge about the European Union based on decades of original research, outstanding simple story telling ability of the complex supranational multilevel governance system, and theoretical richness. It is an indispensable intelligent introduction to one of the most innovative contemporary transnational integration projects of the world.

José M. Magone, Berlin School of Economics and Law, Germany

Already a classic among introductory EU textbooks, this updated edition of *The European Union: Politics and Policies* covers a complex array of treaty revisions, institutional changes, new actors, crisis-management processes, and pro-active policy initiatives that have driven EU politics over the last ten years. Olsen packs a formidable amount of information into every chapter, using lucid prose, recrafted Boxes and everyday comparisons likely to push even US students beyond their national comfort zones.

Joyce Mushaben, University of Missouri-St. Louis, USA

Jonathan Olsen provides a highly readable account, combining historical narrative, political theory, and institutional analysis of the development and current state of the European Union. This is a book that is accessible to students and to the general reader and provides a valuable reference tool and review for the specialists and scholars in European history and politics.

Laura Gellott, University of Wisconsin-Parkside, USA

From environmental and social policies to trade and security politics, Olsen's *The European Union* demonstrates that the EU is a major force influencing the everyday lives of Europeans and people around the globe.

Stacy D. VanDeveer, University of Massachusetts Boston, USA

The European Union

POLITICS AND POLICIES

SEVENTH EDITION

Jonathan Olsen

Routledge
Taylor & Francis Group

NEW YORK AND LONDON

Seventh edition published 2021
by Routledge
52 Vanderbilt Avenue, New York, NY 10017

and by Routledge
2 Park Square, Milton Park, Abingdon, Oxon, OX14 4RN

Routledge is an imprint of the Taylor & Francis Group, an informa business

First edition published by Westview Press 1996
Sixth edition published by Westview Press 2017; Routledge 2018

Library of Congress Cataloging-in-Publication Data
Names: Olsen, Jonathan, 1959– author.
Title: The European Union : politics and policies / Jonathan Olsen.
Description: Seventh edition. | New York, NY : Routledge, 2021. | Includes bibliographical references and index.
Identifiers: LCCN 2020010834 (print) | LCCN 2020010835 (ebook) | ISBN 9781138340312 (hardback) | ISBN 9781138340329 (paperback) | ISBN 9780429440724 (ebook)
Subjects: LCSH: European Union.
Classification: LCC JN30 .M37 2021 (print) | LCC JN30 (ebook) | DDC 341.242/2–dc23
LC record available at https://lccn.loc.gov/2020010834
LC ebook record available at https://lccn.loc.gov/2020010835

ISBN: 978-1-138-34031-2 (hbk)
ISBN: 978-1-138-34032-9 (pbk)
ISBN: 978-0-429-44072-4 (ebk)

Typeset in Berling and Futura
by Wearset Ltd, Boldon, Tyne and Wear

Contents

Part I: History   9

Photos

Figures

Maps

Tables

Boxes

Preface and Acknowledgments

Although the financial and debt crisis that broke in Europe over a decade ago has given policy makers many sleepless nights, it also had the effect of drawing wider public attention to an entity about which many North Americans knew little: the European Union (EU). Since the early 1950s, Europeans have been working to remove the political, economic, and social barriers that have long divided them, and the result has been the development of the world's newest superpower, one of the wealthiest marketplaces in the world, and one of the world's leading trading powers.

Worries about the stability of the euro have combined with Brexit and an alarming migration crisis – as well as the EU's response to COVID-19 – to raise some concerning questions about the shape of the EU's long-term future, but it still remains a tremendously powerful actor in the world – one that is important for North Americans in particular to understand. The EU is one of the biggest trading powers in the world, it is our most influential and dependable ally in an uncertain world, and its emergence has been one of the defining events of the modern era, helping reorder the international system and bringing to Europe the longest spell of general peace that it has seen in centuries. Its achievements in this last regard were recognized in 2012 when it was awarded the Nobel Peace Prize. The EU has helped promote democracy and economic development throughout Europe, it has helped more than half a billion Europeans overcome many of their political, economic, and social divisions, and it stands as a prime example of how peaceful means can bring lasting change.

But in spite of all this, it remains – for most people – a mystery and an enigma. Few North Americans know much about it beyond the euro, and even Europeans are perplexed: many support the idea of "Europe" in principle – and even more support the EU's key achievements – but also admit that they know too little about how the EU works, or who makes the decisions, or how the EU has changed their lives. Enthusiasm for the EU is harder to find than ambivalence, indifference, or outright hostility. There are two reasons for the confusion:

- The EU is unique. There has never been anything quite like it before, and it fits few of our usual ideas about politics and government. Is it an international organization, a new European superstate, or some unique entity in between? How much authority does it have relative to its member states? How do its powers and structure differ from those of a conventional national government?
- The EU keeps changing. Just when we think we have begun to understand it, a new treaty comes along that gives it new powers, or its leaders agree to a new set of goals that give it a different character and appearance, new member states join (or in the case of Brexit, leave), changing its personality and its structure, or new crises arise,

demanding new EU action. Change is, of course, a core feature of politics and government everywhere, but the European target tends to move more quickly than most, with no certainty about where exactly it is headed.

Having taught courses on the EU and written on European politics for over two decades, I am very familiar with the challenge of explaining the EU. As the power and influence of the EU grows – and its future challenges become more visible – so does the importance of clear guidance through the complexities of the EU and detailed analysis that offers observers the context they need to better appreciate the implications of European integration. It was concerns such as these that prompted the initial writing of this book by John McCormick in 1993–1995. This was a period in which the EU was still adapting to the near completion of the single market, struggling with preparations for the single currency, and mired in the fallout from the serial foreign policy embarrassments of the Gulf War and the Balkan conflicts. John's first edition was a pathbreaker. At that time, the EU was simply not very well explained, much of it bogged down in a morass of treaty articles and arcane jargon, and sidetracked by inconclusive debates over theory. Moreover, there was relatively little public or political interest in the EU and few textbooks that provided a true *introduction* to the EU (and none written specifically for North American students). Publishing on the EU has been a growth industry in the last several decades – reflecting new levels of interest in the EU – yet there is still more than ever a need for a book such as this. The EU is one of today's most important and dramatic political and economic developments, full of fascinating characters and driven by conflicts, conspiracies, successes, crises, and failures, and yet much of the scholarly writing about the EU makes it sound dull, technocratic, and legalistic.

This seventh edition of *The European Union: Politics and Policies* retains its core goals of informing mainly North American students, explaining how the EU functions from first principles, and explaining how and why the EU matters for those of us on this side of the Atlantic. In the last two editions of this book I joined John as co-author. This new seventh edition continues John's legacy by keeping the presentation simple enough for the introductory student (who most often is exposed to the EU in a one-semester course on European politics and the EU) yet detailed enough to provide a comprehensive overview of the EU's history, institutions, and policies. Every chapter begins with a bulleted overview and ends with questions for discussion, along with a list of recommended readings that provides recent, readable, and enlightening Anglo-American sources. The book ends with a glossary of key terms, a chronology of events, and the best sources of accurate, current, and dependable information – indeed, the challenge in our internet age is less about finding online sources as it is accurately keeping up with new developments in the EU.

The EU changes so much and so quickly that texts on it date quickly, so this new edition – while keeping the same basic structure as its predecessors – has been significantly overhauled and updated:

- Aside from new substantive material concerning the impact of Brexit, the biggest change since the last edition has been its attempt to incorporate gender into its presentation of the EU. As I now teach at the US's largest public university intended primarily for women, it has become apparent in my classes on the EU that the book hitherto simply had not done enough to incorporate the importance of gender. Based on reviews of the book, it was clear that highlighting the important institutional roles that women play in the EU as well as policies that affect women were in need of particular attention.
- Given that this book is not a history of the EU, but recognizing that any book on the EU that did not discuss its history would be incomplete, writing a more condensed history

of the EU has always posed a challenge – especially as "history" never stops happening! Consequently, historical discussions in Chapters 2 and 3 have been slimmed down a bit, taking Chapter 2 through the Treaty of Rome and Chapter 3 through the Maastricht treaty. Meanwhile, Chapter 4 has been expanded to include more discussion of all the substantial developments since 2009, including the financial and debt crisis, the migration crisis, and – above all – the UK's departure from the EU ("Brexit").

- The chapters on institutions (5 to 10) have been revised to account for new developments – especially Brexit – since the last edition of this book and to inject new analytical material. Chapter 5 has been updated to include a discussion of the new 2019–2024 Commission. Chapter 6 has been both updated and reorganized to include the European Council along with the Council of Ministers (rather than leaving the former in a different chapter), since these two EU institutions have a natural connection to one another. Chapter 7 has been restructured for a similar reason and now includes a discussion of European parliamentary elections, including the 2019 European Parliament elections. Chapters 9 and 10 have been reorganized, expanded, and substantially updated in order to give a more comprehensive picture of EU agencies and bodies on the one hand, and public opinion and EU identities on the other.
- The chapters on policy (11 to 15) have been overhauled to include all the latest developments in the different policy areas, noting Brexit's impact where important. The discussion on agriculture and environment has been moved to Chapter 13 to capture its crucial importance in the policy history of the EU. Material dealing with the relationship between the US and EU has been moved to a new Chapter 16 in discussing the EU's relationship with the wider world, while Chapter 15 has been revised and expanded to include new developments in the Common Foreign and Security Policy, such as the EU's Global Strategy and Permanent Structured Cooperation. There is completely new material on topics such as monetary union and economic policy; regional development/ cohesion policy; social policy; justice and home affairs (otherwise known as the "Area of Freedom, Security, and Justice"); and the EU's relations with Russia, Turkey, China, and the global south.
- Many of the boxes have been replaced, new figures and tables added and existing ones updated, and the titles in the lists of Further Reading updated to reflect newer scholarship.
- Several of the Chapter Overview and "Questions to Consider" sections in each chapter (added in the fifth edition) have been edited and revised.

The biggest influence on this book has come from the students on the courses I have taught on European politics. It was their needs and concerns that have been the driving force in each new edition of this book. I would like to thank the anonymous reviewers drafted by my new publisher, Routledge, to comment on the plans for this seventh edition, and the editorial team at Routledge for their encouragement and their fine job on production. I would particularly like to thank Dr Joyce Mushaben (Professor Emeritus at the University of Missouri–St. Louis) for her patient and careful reading of the last edition, and her creative suggestions for the new edition. Many thanks to family, friends, and colleagues at Texas Woman's University for their continued support of this project and a special note of thanks to my fiancée, Carson Childress, who patiently read through the manuscript, gave me extensive stylistic advice, and last but not least provided her loving support. Finally, I owe a huge debt of gratitude to John McCormick – truly a pioneer and a consummate scholar of the EU – who brought me in as co-author for the fifth edition before departing to pursue other projects. I am deeply thankful for the opportunity to continue his fine work.

A Note on Terminology

Anyone writing a book about the EU is faced with the challenge of deciding when and where to use the terms European Economic Community, European Community, and European Union. I have opted for the third except in cases of specific references to historical events where it would not make sense. I have also occasionally used Europe where European Union would be more accurate, mainly for stylistic reasons but also to make the point that the two terms increasingly have the same meaning. Finally, I have used the term Eastern Europe to refer to all those countries that were once behind the iron curtain, conscious that many in those countries like to make a distinction between Eastern and Central Europe.

Acronyms and Abbreviations

ACP	African, Caribbean, and Pacific Program
AFSJ	Area of Freedom, Security, and Justice
BEU	Benelux Economic Union
BRIC	Brazil, Russia, India, China
CAP	Common Agricultural Policy
CCP	Common Commercial Policy
CF	Cohesion Fund
CFP	Common Fisheries Policy
CFSP	Common Foreign and Security Policy
CJ	Court of Justice of the European Union
CoR	Committee of the Regions
Coreper	Committee of Permanent Representatives
CSDP	Common Security and Defence Policy
DG	directorate-general
EAFRD	European Agricultural Fund for Rural Development
EAGF	European Agriculture Guarantee Fund
EAP	Environmental Action Programme
EBRD	European Bank for Reconstruction and Development
EC	European Community
ECB	European Central Bank
Ecofin	Economic and Financial Affairs
ECSC	European Coal and Steel Community
ECTS	European Credit Transfer and Accumulation System
ECU	European currency unit
EDC	European Defence Community
EEA	European Economic Area or European Environment Agency
EEAC	European Atomic Energy Community
EEC	European Economic Community
EESC	European Economic and Social Committee
EFTA	European Free Trade Association
EGF	European Globalisation Adjustment Fund
EGS	EU Global Strategy
EIB	European Investment Bank
EIONET	European Environmental Information and Observation Network
EMFF	European Maritime and Fisheries Fund
EMI	European Monetary Institute
EMS	European Monetary System

EMU	economic and monetary union
ENP	European Neighbourhood Policy
EP	European Parliament
EPC	European Political Community or European Political Cooperation
ERDF	European Regional Development Fund
ERM	Exchange Rate Mechanism
ESDP	European Security and Defence Policy
ESF	European Social Fund
ESM	European Stability Mechanism
EU	European Union
Euratom	(see EEAC)
EUSF	European Union Solidarity Fund
EU-15	the fifteen pre-2004 member states of the EU
EU-25	the twenty-five member states of the EU 2004–2007
EU-27	the existing twenty-seven member states of the EU
EU-28	the twenty-eight member states of the EU until Brexit
FDI	Foreign Direct Investment
G8	Group of Eight (industrialized countries)
GAC	General Affairs Council
GATT	General Agreement on Tariffs and Trade
GDP	gross domestic product
GNI	gross national income
GNP	gross national product
IGC	intergovernmental conference
IGO	intergovernmental organization
IMF	International Monetary Fund
IO	international organization
IR	international relations
JHA	justice and home affairs
MEP	Member of the European Parliament
MFF	Multiannual Financial Framework
MPCC	Military Planning and Conduct Capability
NAFTA	North American Free Trade Agreement
NATO	North Atlantic Treaty Organization
NGO	nongovernmental organization
OECD	Organisation for Economic Cooperation and Development
OEEC	Organisation for European Economic Cooperation
PESCO	Permanent Structured Cooperation
QMV	qualified majority vote
SAPARD	Special Accession Program for Agriculture and Rural Development
SEA	Single European Act
TEN	Trans-European Network
USMCA	US–Mexico–Canada Agreement
VAT	value-added tax
WEU	Western European Union
WTO	World Trade Organization

EU MEMBER STATES

AT	Austria
BE	Belgium
BG	Bulgaria
CY	Cyprus
CZ	Czech Republic
DE	Germany
DK	Denmark
EE	Estonia
EL	Greece
ES	Spain
FI	Finland
FR	France
HR	Croatia
HU	Hungary
IE	Ireland
IT	Italy
LT	Lithuania
LU	Luxembourg
LV	Latvia
MT	Malta
NL	Netherlands
PL	Poland
PT	Portugal
RO	Romania
SE	Sweden
SI	Slovenia
SK	Slovakia

Introduction

Why read a book about the European Union? Perhaps it is because you recognize the global political and economic importance of the EU. After all, the EU is the world's second-largest economy, one of its biggest trading powers, and its largest investor. The euro – used by nineteen of its member states – is one of the two leading currencies in the world, and many of the EU's member states are among the richest on the globe. And while the EU's military capacity is still modest, its global power is nevertheless notable, largely because of its ability to use economic carrots and sticks to influence and shape behavior around the globe. Indeed, the promise of access to the European marketplace or even – for the select few – of membership in the EU has arguably had a significant effect on promoting lasting democratic change and economic development. Overall, the EU's emergence has changed the character and definition of Europe, helped bring to the region the longest uninterrupted spell of general peace in its recorded history, and altered the balance of global power by helping Europeans reassert themselves on the world stage.

Perhaps, though, you are reading this book because the EU is particularly important for North Americans. In terms of economic significance, it is the US's largest – and Canada's second-largest – trading partner, the source of about two-thirds of all the foreign direct investment in the US and Canada; subsidiaries of European companies employ several million North Americans – more than the affiliates of all other countries combined – and account for a substantial percentage of all manufacturing jobs in the US and Canada; and US and Canadian corporations have made some of their biggest overseas investments in the EU. Historically, the US and Europe have also had one of the world's strongest and most enduring political relationships. During the Cold War, Western Europe relied on the US for security guarantees and economic investment, while the US could depend on its European allies to have its back. Although there was always some discord behind the scenes as the two partners disagreed over policy and over how to deal with the Soviet threat, these tensions were always contained within the larger sense of purpose and democratic values both sides championed. Of course, since the end of the Cold War, disagreements have spilled out into the open. The US and the EU are now both partners and competitors: the two have become increasingly aware of what divides them, differing not just over the use of military power and how to deal with many international problems (including global trade, terrorism, climate change, nuclear proliferation, and the Middle East) but on a wide range of social values and norms.

You might also be interested in reading about the EU because, as a European, you are a critic, or at least are trying to understand criticisms of the EU. Indeed, the European project has for decades lacked no shortage of doubters, no more vividly on display than in the United Kingdom's (UK) decision to leave the bloc, the so-called "Brexit." Many in the UK (but not only there) have questioned the wisdom of European states transferring authority to a joint system of governance that is often criticized for its elitism and its lack of account-ability and transparency. Others have felt that the EU overreached by creating a common currency (and feel their skepticism vindicated by the recent financial and debt crisis in the EU), complain about overregulation and a cumbersome bureaucracy, question its ability to reach common agreement on critical foreign and security policy issues, or simply doubt whether the EU really looks out for their interests.

You might, however, have more immediate and less abstract reasons for reading a book about the EU. You may have traveled to Europe sometime in your life – or want to do so sometime in the future – and simply wish to understand what the EU is. You may be aware of the differences between visiting Europe in, say, the 1970s – the decade I graduated high school – and today. If you were flying into West Germany at that time, your first stop, after passport controls, would be to change your dollars (or other currency) into deutschmarks (for a fee), mentally calculating the exchange rate between the two currencies and what prices you would be paying while you were in the country. Perhaps after some days spending your time sightseeing in Munich, Cologne, or possibly West Berlin, you took the train to Amsterdam or maybe to Paris. At the French or Dutch borders, you would have been asked to show your passport again, while your first stop in Paris or Amsterdam would have been a local currency exchange, where you could change your dollars – and perhaps your remaining deutschmarks – into French francs or Dutch guilders, paying a fee again and this time calcu-lating the exchange rate and prices twice, once for dollars to francs and once more for deutschmarks to francs or guilders If you took a multi-week trip through various European countries – perhaps even venturing behind the Iron Curtain to visit Prague or Krakow – this pattern would repeat itself: showing your passport at border control, changing money, paying the associated fees, and calculating exchange rates.

Flash forward to 2020. Today, you do not need to pull out your passport at every border you cross (including most of those once behind the Iron Curtain), nor do you have to exchange your dollars a second, third, or fourth time on your visit. There is little time spent calculating prices, little time worrying about producing a passport, and travel within most of the states which belong to the EU – now more likely to be done via budget airlines rather than long-distance trains – is relatively hassle free. If you are a European, the changes between now and the 1970s are even more profound. As a business person or entrepreneur, selling your products within Europe is vastly easier and less complicated than it was then; as a student today, studying or earning a degree in another member state is almost as easy as it is for Americans to transfer to another university; and as an employee, the ability to live and work in another EU member state poses few bureaucratic hurdles, unlike those encountered by a worker in the 1970s.

However, even if you grew up in an EU member state, you still may be puzzled about how the EU functions and uncertain how you feel about all the changes the EU seems to have made to your life. Non-Europeans are even more puzzled. Many are – or at least have been, until recently – only vaguely aware of its existence and do not yet fully understand what difference it has made to Europe or to relationships with their own countries. Political leaders are more attuned to its implications, as are corporate and financial leaders who have had to learn to deal as much with a twenty-seven-member regional grouping as with each of the individual states in the EU. But doubts remain about the bigger picture and about what difference the EU has made. To complicate matters, there is no agreement on just how we should define and under-stand the EU. It is not a European superstate, and suggestions that it might one day become a United States of Europe are greeted with equal measures of enthusiasm and hostility.

Whatever your reasons for picking up a book on the EU, they all raise some key questions: what were the driving forces behind changes to the EU and how did they come about? What does the EU do exactly? How does it work? What difference does it make? What do its supporters and critics say about it?

This book attempts to answer these questions.

The origins of the EU, and the motives behind European integration, are relatively clear. Frustrated and appalled by war and conflict, many Europeans argued over the centuries in favor of setting aside national differences in favor of a collective European interest. The first serious thoughts about a peaceful and voluntary union came after the horrors of World War I, but the concept matured following the devastation of World War II, when the most serious Europeanists spoke of replacing national governments with a European federation. They dreamed of integrating European economies and removing controls on the movement of people, money, goods, and services; they were driven by the desire to promote peace and to build a single European market that could compete with the US.

The first tangible step came in April 1951 with the signing of the Treaty of Paris, which created the European Coal and Steel Community (ECSC), set up at least in part to prove a point about the feasibility and benefits of regional integration. Progress in the 1950s and 1960s was quite modest, but then the European Economic Community (EEC) was launched, membership began to expand, and the goals of integration became more ambitious. Today, the EU is an entity with its own institutions and body of laws, twenty-seven member states and more than 450 million residents, a common currency used by more than two-thirds of its members, and increasing agreement on a wide range of common policy areas. The Cold War–era political and economic divisions between Western and Eastern Europe have almost disappeared, and it is now less realistic to think of European states in isolation than as partners in an ever-changing EU. The buzzword *integration* is used more often than *unification* to describe what has been happening, but some of those who champion the EU suggest that an even deeper political union of some kind is almost inevitable. It may not be a United States of Europe, and it may stay largely an association in which more power still rests with the member states, but it has been true for some time now that when one speaks of "Europe," this means "the EU."

Like it or not, the EU cannot be ignored, and the need to better understand how it works and what difference it makes becomes more evident by the day. In three parts, this book introduces the EU, dissects the steps in its development, explains how it works, and provides an overview of its policy activities.

Part I (Chapters 1 to 4) provides context by first surveying the most important theories and concepts of regional integration and then showing how and why the EU has evolved. Providing the background on the earliest ideas about European unification sets the scene for the creation of the ECSC, whose founding members were France, West Germany, Italy, Belgium, the Netherlands, and Luxembourg. This was followed in 1957 by the signing of the two Treaties of Rome, which created the EEC and the European Atomic Energy Community (Euratom). With the same six members as the ECSC, the EEC set out to build an integrated multinational economy among its members, to achieve a customs union, to encourage free trade, and to harmonize standards, laws, and prices among its members. It witnessed greater productivity, channeled new investment into industry and agriculture, and became more competitive in the world market.

By the late 1960s, the EEC had all the trappings of a new level of European government, based mainly in Brussels, the capital of Belgium. Analysts refused to describe it as a full-blown political system, but it had its own executive and bureaucracy (the European Commission), its own protolegislature (the European Parliament), its own judiciary (the Court of Justice), and its own legal system. Over time, the word *Economic* was dropped from the name, giving way to the European Community (EC). Its successes drew new members,

MAP 0.1 The EU.

starting with the UK, Denmark, and Ireland in 1973, and moving on to Greece, Portugal, and Spain in the 1980s, East Germany joining via German unification, and Austria, Finland, and Sweden joining in the 1990s. The most recent round of enlargement came in 2004–2007 with the addition of twelve mainly Eastern European member states – including Hungary, Poland, and the three former Soviet Baltic states. Another Eastern European state, Croatia, became the EU's newest member in 2013. The character and reach of integration have evolved along the way with revisions to the founding treaties:

- In 1987 the Single European Act led to the elimination of almost all remaining barriers to the movement of people, money, goods, and services among the twelve member states.

TABLE 0.1 The EU in Figures

	Area (Thousand Square km)	Population (Millions)	Gross Domestic Product (Purchasing Power Parity) ($ Billion)	Gross Domestic Product Per Capita (Purchasing Power Parity) ($)
Germany	357,022	80.1	4,199	50,800
France	643,801	67.8	2,856	44,100
Italy	301,340	62.4	2,317	38,200
Spain	505,370	50.0	1,778	38,400
Netherlands	41,543	17.2	924	53,900
Sweden	450,295	10.2	518	51,200
Poland	312,685	38.2	1,126	29,600
Belgium	30,528	11.7	529	46,600
Austria	83,871	8.8	441	50,000
Denmark	43,094	5.8	287	50,100
Greece	131,957	10.6	299	27,800
Finland	338,145	5.5	245	44,500
Portugal	92,090	10.3	314	30,500
Ireland	70,273	5.1	353	73,200
Czech Republic	78,867	10.7	376	35,500
Romania	238,391	21.3	483	24,600
Hungary	93,028	9.7	289	29,600
Slovakia	49,035	5.4	179	33,100
Croatia	56,594	4.2	102	24,700
Luxembourg	2,586	0.62	62	105,100
Bulgaria	110,879	6.9	153	21,800
Slovenia	20,273	2.1	71.2	34,500
Lithuania	65,300	2.7	91.4	32,400
Latvia	64,589	1.9	54.0	27,700
Cyprus*	9,251	1.2	31	37,200
Estonia	45,228	1.2	41.6	31,700
Malta	316	0.46	19.2	41,900
EU–28 Total (before Brexit)	4,479,968	518	20,850	40,900
United States	9,833,517	332	19,490	59,800
United Kingdom	243,610	65.1	2,925	44,300

Continued

TABLE 0.1 Continued				
	Area (Thousand Square km)	Population (Millions)	Gross Domestic Product (Purchasing Power Parity) ($ Billion)	Gross Domestic Product Per Capita (Purchasing Power Parity) ($)
China	9,596,960	1,394	25,360	18,200
Japan	377,915	125.5	5,443	42,900
Brazil	8,515,770	211.7	3,248	15,600
Russia	17,098,242	141.7	4,016	27,900
India	3,287,263	1,326	9,474	7,200
Canada	9,984,670	37.6	1,774	48,400
World	510,072,000	7,684	127,800	17,500

Source: CIA World Factbook, 2017, at www.cia.gov/library/publications/the-world-factbook/geos/fr.html. Eurozone states indicated in boldface.

Note
* Figures are for the entire island of Cyprus

- In 1993 the Maastricht Treaty on European Union committed the EC to the creation of a single currency, a common citizenship, and a common foreign and security policy, and imparted new powers over law and policy to the EC institutions. It also made the EC part of a broader new entity called the European Union.
- In 1998 and 2003 the treaties of Amsterdam and Nice built on these changes, fine-tuned the powers of the institutions, and helped prepare the EU for new members from Eastern Europe.
- An attempt was made in 2002–2004 to provide focus and permanence by replacing the accumulated treaties with a European constitution. But the finished product was lengthy, detailed, and controversial, and it had to be ratified by every EU member state before it could come into force. When French and Dutch voters turned it down in 2005, another brief "crisis" ensued before European leaders reached agreement in 2007 to draw up a new treaty based on much of the content of the failed constitution.
- The resulting Treaty of Lisbon fundamentally reformed several of the EU's institutions and attempted to give more coherence to the Union's policies, even while avoiding the language and trappings of a constitution that had been unpopular with many EU citizens.

Part I concludes with a discussion of the three crises – a financial and debt crisis, a migration crisis, and Brexit – which have buffeted the EU over the last decade, and how both its supporters and detractors have responded to each. As a result of these crises, the EU has created new policies and instruments in attempting to deal with these challenges while moving forward with plans for the future.

Part II (Chapters 5 to 10) looks at the EU institutions, explaining how they work and how they relate to each other. Their powers and authority have grown steadily since the 1950s, although their work is often misunderstood and analysts continue to disagree over their character and significance. There are five main institutions:

- *The European Commission.* Based in Brussels, this is the executive and administrative branch of the EU, responsible for developing new EU laws and policies and for overseeing their implementation.
- *The Council of the EU* (most often known as the *Council of Ministers*). Also based in Brussels, this is the major decision-making body of the EU, made up of government ministers from each of the member states. Working with the European Parliament, the Council makes the votes that turn Commission proposals into European law.
- *The European Council.* The EU's newest institution, it is less an institution than a forum, consisting of the political leaders of the member states. The Council meets at least four times per year to make broad decisions on policy, the details of which are worked out by the Commission and the Council of Ministers.
- *The European Parliament.* Divided among Strasbourg, Luxembourg, and Brussels, the members of the European Parliament are directly elected to five-year terms by the voters of the member states. Although it cannot introduce proposals for new laws, Parliament can discuss Commission proposals, and it has equal powers with the Council of Ministers over adoption.
- *The Court of Justice of the European Union.* Based in Luxembourg, the Court interprets national and EU law and helps build a common body of law that is uniformly applied throughout the member states. It bases its decisions on the treaties, which in some respects function as a constitution of the EU.

Part III (Chapters 11 to 16) provides an overview of the policy areas pursued by the EU, looking at what integration has meant for the member states and for Europeans themselves. Covering economic, monetary, regional development, agricultural, environmental, social, justice and home affairs, foreign, and security policies, this section examines the EU policy-making process, identifies the key influences on that process, and analyzes its consequences and implications. The final chapter focuses on relations between the EU and the wider world, and most especially its relationship with its most important partner, the US.

Today, the EU cannot simply be ignored, nor can we understand our world without understanding how the EU evolved, how it works, and what it does. Not everyone is convinced that the EU has been a good idea or that it has been able to fully capitalize on its assets and resources, but – like it or not – the changes it has wrought cannot be undone. The pace of global political and economic change is accelerating, and the results of the European experiment have fundamentally changed the way in which the world functions.

PART I

History

CHAPTER 1

What Is the European Union?

CHAPTER OVERVIEW

- Because the EU is a political arrangement that defies easy categorization, it has stirred a much more vigorous theoretical debate about how to understand it than there has been for conventional states, such as the US.
- How we approach the EU still depends in large part on how we think about the role of the state. Consequently, there are at least five ways to conceptualize the EU – as an international organization, a regional integration association, a political system in its own right, a unique entity, or something that exhibits and combines all four of these.
- Theories analyzing the EU can be divided into two broad categories: those explaining how the EU evolved and those explaining what it has become. While the first category – which includes the theories of neofunctionalism and intergovernmentalism – was long dominated by scholars of international relations, the second category has increasingly become the province of scholars of comparative politics. The latter see the EU as a political system with its own institutions, processes, procedures, and policies. In recent years the term *multi-level governance* has emerged as one way to understand the EU as a political system.

Numerous books have been published on national systems of politics and government, but rarely do they begin with a chapter defining their subject. No survey of the US, for example, would begin by asking "What is the United States?" We know that it is a country with an established and self-contained political system, with institutions bound together by laws and political processes, and for which there is a multitude of explanatory theories and an extensive political science vocabulary. But the EU is an animal of a different stripe: it is a unique political arrangement that defies easy definition or categorization and defies orthodox ideas about politics and government. It is clearly much more than a conventional international organization, but it is less than a European superstate. We do not even have a noun that comfortably describes the EU: for some it is an "actor," but for others it is simply *sui generis*, or unique.

This uniqueness has spawned a vigorous debate over theory, which plays a much greater role in the process of trying to understand the EU than it does in understanding other political systems. Initially, the debate was dominated by explanations generated by the subdiscipline of international relations (IR). The EU was approached as an international organization, driven by decisions made among the governments of the member states; European institutions were seen as less important than national institutions, although the supranational element of the European Economic Community – those aspects of its work and personality that rose above national interests – were not ignored. Since the 1990s there has been a reaction against the dominance of IR, and new studies of the EU have been influenced just as much by theories and analyses arising out of the subfields of comparative politics and public policy. In other words, rather than being portrayed as an international organization (albeit one with unique features and powers), the EU is now increasingly seen as a political system in its own right. A sharper spotlight is shining on the executive, legislative, and judicial features of its institutions, the channels through which EU citizens engage with the EU (such as elections, referendums, and the work of interest groups), and its public policy processes.

The field of EU studies remains fluid, however; no agreement exists among either scholars or political leaders about how best to classify and understand the EU, nor on the balance of power between EU institutions and member state governments. Although there is no shortage of competing theories of European integration, there is no single, generally accepted theoretical framework. Undaunted, this chapter introduces the EU by outlining a selection of the major concepts and theories of integration, divided into two broad categories: theories of how the EU evolved and theories of what it has become. It begins with a survey of the role of the state, then reviews attempts to understand how and why the EU emerged and developed. Finally, it examines different analyses of the structure of the EU, focusing in particular on its federal and confederal qualities.

THE ROLE OF THE STATE

The EU scholar Ben Rosamond once suggested four possible approaches to the study of the EU.[1] First, we could try to understand it as an international organization, tying it to the substantial literature on such organizations. Second, we could study it as an example of regionalism in the global economic system, and compare it to other regional blocs such as the North American Free Trade Agreement (NAFTA) or the Latin American free trade grouping named Mercosur. Third, we could approach it as an example of the dynamics of policy making in an attempt to better understand the crafting of interstate policy and how it is influenced by actors interested in the use of power. Finally, we could try to understand it purely on its own terms, as a unique organization that emerged out of a unique set of circumstances. But Rosamond's list overlooked a critical fifth option: trying to understand the EU as a political system in its own right, and comparing its structure and operating principles with those of conventional national political systems.[2] This approach to the EU figures prominently in the multilevel governance approach discussed below.

Of course, how we approach the EU depends in large part on how we think about the role of the state, which has for centuries dominated studies of politics and government. A state is usually defined as a legal and physical entity that (1) operates within a fixed and populated territory, (2) has authority over that territory, (3) is legally and politically independent, and (4) is recognized by its people and by other states. Most people – particularly when they cross international borders – identify themselves as citizens of a state and distinguish themselves from the citizens of other states by all the trappings of citizenship: legal residence, passports, allegiance to their national flag, protection by their home government, and a sense of belonging.

Just how long states have been important to an understanding of the ways in which societies are governed is debatable, but the 1648 Peace of Westphalia – which brought an end to two European wars and resulted in many territorial adjustments – is usually taken as a convenient starting point. Many states existed long before 1648, but Westphalia gave a new permanence to the idea of borders and sovereignty. As a result, the term *Westphalian* is often used as shorthand by political scientists to describe the international state system that has existed since then.[3]

In spite of its philosophical domination, the state has many critics. States are accused of dividing humans rather than uniting them and of encouraging people to place sectional interests above the broader interests of humanity. Identification with states is often associated with nationalism – the belief that every state should be founded on a nation and that national identity should be promoted through political action. But because few states coincide with nations, and most European states in particular consist of multiple national groups, nationalism can lead to internal instability, to a belief in national superiority, to ethnocentrism, racism, and genocide, and – in the worst cases – to war within and between states. Nationalism lay at the heart of many of the disputes and wars that destabilized European politics for centuries, reaching their nadir with World War I and World War II.[4] In the 1990s, nationalist violence tore the former Yugoslavia into several pieces, and even today several European states – the UK and Spain, for example – contain national minorities campaigning and agitating for greater self-government or even independence.

Americans have much less direct familiarity with the difficulties of nationalism than Europeans. The US for most of its history has been relatively stable and united, avoiding the kinds of nationalist pressures and jealousies that have long brought stress to European societies. It had a civil war, but the conflict centered primarily on the issue of slavery and was further fueled by economic pressures. Internal nationalist or ethnic divisions have rarely been an issue for Americans, who – as a result – often find it difficult to understand nationalism in Europe. But it has long formed the core of European political, economic, and social developments.

Criticisms of the state contributed to the growth of international cooperation in the twentieth century, particularly after 1945. Seeking to reduce tensions and promote cooperation, states signed international treaties, reduced barriers to trade, worked together on shared problems, and formed a network of international organizations (IOs). Usually defined as bodies that promote voluntary cooperation and coordination between or among their members but have neither autonomous powers nor the authority to impose their rulings on their members, IOs are mainly a product of the second half of the twentieth century. By one estimate, there were fewer than 220 IOs in 1909, about 1,000 in 1951, and about 4,000 in 1972. Then came the era of growth: by 1989 there were nearly 25,000 IOs in the world, and today there are more than 70,000.[5] They include intergovernmental organizations (IGOs) – which consist of representatives of national governments and promote voluntary cooperation among those governments – and international nongovernmental organizations – consisting of individuals or the representatives of private associations rather than states. The most prominent example of an IGO is the United Nations.

The growth of IOs has led to the building of institutions in which states can attend to matters of mutual interest, the agreement of international treaties, the reduction and removal of trade barriers, and – in some cases – regional integration. This does not mean that states surrender their separate legal, political, economic, social, or national identities, but rather that they pool authority in selected areas and set up shared institutions with restricted powers. The ultimate expression of integration would be full political union, where states would create a new level of joint government and surrender or transfer most of their existing powers. This outcome is what some hope will happen with the EU, while others regard it as the most dangerous risk of integration.

Integration involves the surrender, transfer, or pooling of sovereignty: the rights of jurisdiction that states have over their people and territory and that cannot legally be challenged by any other authority. Regional institutions are authorized to coordinate the making of new rules and regulations to which their member states are subject, although their work is restricted to the policy areas in which the member states have agreed that they should work together rather than separately, and the members collectively have the final say on the adoption of common rules and regulations. Regional institutions do not have powers of enforcement – they may be able to fine or embarrass members into action, but the execution of laws and policies is left to the governments of the member states.

HOW DID THE EU EVOLVE?

The underlying motive behind European integration has always been peace. Exasperated by the frequency with which Europeans had gone to war over the centuries, and determined after 1945 to create a permanent peace, a number of thinkers outlined what they saw as the necessary conditions. Federalists argued that postwar Europe needed to be rebuilt on the basis of a complete break with the past, replacing national states with a new European federation. Federalism was based on the idea that states had lost their political rights because they could not guarantee the safety of their citizens[6] and that political integration would beget economic, social, and cultural integration. The European Union of Federalists was created in 1946 with this view in mind, but their plan was too radical for the tastes of many, and by the time they met at their first congress in 1948, national political systems were being rebuilt and the moment (assuming there ever had been one) had passed. All they were able to agree on was the creation of the Council of Europe, which had the more modest goal of intra-European cooperation.

A contrasting philosophical option came from David Mitrany, a Romanian-born British social scientist. He was interested in the achievement of world peace more generally, not European integration – in fact, he opposed regional unification because he felt it would replace international tensions with interregional ones – and yet his ideas formed the starting point for discussions about the road to integration. Mitrany saw nationalism as the root of conflict and argued that states should be bound together by a network of international agencies that built on common interests and had authority in functionally specific fields.[7] In other words, the economic and functional ties would precede the political ties. These agencies would be executive bodies with autonomous powers and would perform some of the same tasks as national governments, only at a different level; governments would slowly find themselves living in a web of international agencies and less capable of independent action.[8]

The idea behind functionalism was to "sneak up on peace" by promoting integration in relatively noncontroversial areas such as postal services or a particular sector of industry, or by harmonizing technical issues such as weights and measures.[9] Success in one area would encourage cooperation in others, and national sovereignty would gradually decline, to be replaced by a new international community. But the story did not unfold as Mitrany had hoped because states did not give up significant powers to new international organizations.

American political scientists Ernst Haas and Leon Lindberg were among the first to try to understand European integration in particular, and their deliberations resulted in the adaptation of Mitrany's theories as neofunctionalism. Their thinking was in part a response to realism, then the dominant theory in IR, which argued that states were the most important actors in international relations, that domestic policy could be clearly separated from foreign policy, and that rational self-interest and conflicting national objectives spurred states to protect their interests relative to other states. Realists talked of an anarchic global system in which states used both conflict and cooperation to ensure security through a balance of power among states. By contrast, Haas tried to understand how and why states voluntarily mingled, merged, and mixed with their neighbors while acquiring new techniques for resolving conflict.[10] He saw territorially based governing organizations as important "agents of integration"[11] and argued that once governments had launched the process of integration, it would take on a life of its own (an "expansive logic") through the phenomenon of "spillover." Lindberg described this as a process by which "a given action, related to a specific goal, creates a situation in which the original goal can be assured only by taking further actions, which in turn create a further condition and a need for more action."[12] In other words, cooperation in one sphere (for example, in one area of the economy) would "spill over" to cooperation in other spheres, thus leading to greater economic, policy, and political integration of sovereign states.

Box 1.1 Spilling Over: Stages in Regional Integration

The concept of spillover has been applied to the process by which economic ties can move a group of states from limited economic integration to full political union. If there were a logical progression to this process in the EU, it might look something like this:

1   Two or more states create a *free trade area* by eliminating internal barriers to trade (such as tariffs and border restrictions) while keeping their own external tariffs against nonmember states. This happened in the European Economic Community (EEC) in the 1960s, and the US, Canada, and Mexico have been engaged in a less ambitious attempt since 1994 with NAFTA (now renamed "The US–Mexico–Canada Agreement" or USMCA).

2   The growth of internal free trade increases the pressure on the member states to agree to a *common external tariff*; otherwise all the goods coming into the free trade area from the outside would come through the country with the lowest tariffs. Agreement on a common external tariff creates a *customs union*. This happened in the EEC in 1968.

3   The reduction of internal trading barriers expands the size of the market available to agriculture, industry, and services, so these sectors want to expand their operations throughout the customs union. This increases investment in those countries and increases the demand for the removal of barriers to the movement of capital and labor, creating a *single market*. The European single market was more or less completed by the early 1990s.

4   With people moving more freely within the single market, pressure grows for coordinated policies on education, retraining schemes, unemployment benefits, pensions, health care, and other services. This in turn increases the demand for coordinated interest rates, stable exchange rates, common policies on inflation, and ultimately a *single currency*, thereby creating an *economic union*. A case in point: those EU states that have adopted the euro.

5   The demands of economic integration lead to growing political integration as the governments of the member states work more closely and more frequently together. The pressure grows for common policies in many other sectors, including foreign and defense policy, resulting in full *political union*. Although the EU has made progress in this direction, the idea of full political union remains controversial.

Consider the following specific examples which illustrate how spillover could explain the evolution of EU integration:

- *Functional spillover* implies that economies are so interconnected that if states integrate one sector of their economies (for example, coal and steel), it will lead to the integration of other sectors.[13] Functional IGOs would have to be created to oversee this process, the power of national government institutions would decline, and political union would eventually result (for further discussion of this, see Box 1.1).
- *Technical spillover* implies that disparities in standards will cause states to rise (or sink) to the level of those with the tightest (or loosest) regulations. For example, Greece and Portugal – which had few environmental controls before they joined the EU – adopted such controls because of the requirements of EU law, which in turn had been driven by pressures from states with tight environmental controls, such as Germany and the Netherlands.
- *Political spillover* implies that once different functional sectors are integrated, interest groups (such as corporate lobbies and labor unions) will switch from trying to influence national governments to trying to influence regional institutions, which will encourage their attempt to win new powers for themselves. The groups will appreciate the benefits of integration, and politics will increasingly play out at the regional rather than the national level.[14] Corporate lobbies and labor unions are already following this blueprint in the EU, although they remain very involved at the national level as well.

Joseph Nye added a new dimension to the debate in 1971 by taking neofunctionalism out of the European context and looking at non-Western experiences. He concluded that regional integration involved an "integrative potential" that depended on several conditions:

- The economic equality or compatibility of the states involved.
- The extent to which the elite groups that control economic policy in the member states think alike and hold the same values.
- The extent of interest group activity, or pluralism. (The extent of interest group activity at the European level shows that many corporate and public interest groups see Brussels as an important focus for lobbying.)
- The capacity of the member states to adapt and respond to public demands, which depends in turn on levels of domestic stability and the capacity – or desire – of decision makers to respond.[15]

On almost all of these counts, the EU has long had a relatively high integrative potential, in contrast to the NAFTA/USMCA parties. The US and Canada may act as strong forces for integration, but they are much wealthier than Mexico in both per capita and absolute terms. Elite groups in Mexico have historically been more strongly in favor of state intervention in the marketplace than are those in the US and Canada, labor unions in the US have been critical of NAFTA (and one of the drivers behind the renegotiated USMCA), and public opinion in Mexico is more controlled and manipulated than it is in the US and Canada. The agreement between the US, Mexico, and Canada has not had a significant impact on closing the gaps so far, and many obstacles remain to the development of the North American single market; not least of these is the fear north of the Rio Grande about immigration from Mexico (and from other countries in Central America using Mexico as a transit country), and the destabilizing effects of Mexican drug violence (see Box 1.2).

Box 1.2 What Makes NAFTA/USMCA Different from the EU?

Although Europeans have traveled far along the road of regional integration, North Americans are at a much earlier stage in the journey. NAFTA has been a more modest exercise in free trade that has raised some of the same economic and political questions in the US, Canada, and Mexico as have been raised in Europe by the EU.[16] An outgrowth of the Canada–US Free Trade Agreement, it was signed in 1988 and came into effect on January 1, 1989, aimed at reducing barriers to trade between Canada and the US. This pact evolved into NAFTA with the signing of a treaty in December 1992 that expanded free trade to Mexico, effective on January 1, 1994. After President Trump took office, he was highly critical of NAFTA and threatened a trade war with both Canada and Mexico. Consequently, he then negotiated a new agreement to supersede NAFTA, the USMCA. NAFTA and the USMCA are similar in their scope – although the terms of trade in the agreements vary – with most observers seeing the USMCA as a more narrowly circumscribed trade agreement than NAFTA.

The original goals of NAFTA aimed to

- Phase out all tariffs on textiles, apparel, cars, trucks, vehicle parts, and telecommunications equipment by 2004
- Phase out all barriers to agricultural trade by 2009
- Open up the North American advertising market
- Allow truck drivers to cross borders freely
- Allow banks, securities firms, and insurance companies total access to all three markets
- Loosen rules on the movement of corporate executives and some professionals.

But progress has been modest. Trade between the US and Canada is booming, yet they already had one of the world's biggest and most successful trade relationships before NAFTA was initiated. US–Mexican trade has grown, leading to the creation of more jobs in the US, but how much of this growth is due to NAFTA and how much would have happened anyway is hard to say. Despite some job losses in the US, as labor unions predicted, this trend was already discernible before NAFTA was signed. Moreover, there is no evidence that the overall unemployment rate in the US worsened as a result of NAFTA, and outsourcing has resulted in many more jobs moving to other parts of the world than to Mexico.

The opening of borders was slowed first by concerns about illegal immigration and international terrorism, and then by the drug war that broke out in Mexico in 2007. There is general political agreement in the US that NAFTA has helped promote economic growth in Mexico, but there has been only limited economic convergence between Canada and the US on the one hand and Mexico on the other; although significant progress has been made, Mexico still needs to do far more to free up its economy and to invest in education and infrastructure. Moreover, there has been little enthusiasm for working toward a common external tariff or customs union (see Box 1.1). Finally, there has also been no growth in common institutions. No institutions were initially created beyond two commissions that can arbitrate in disagreements over environmental standards and working conditions: NAFTA (and now USMCA) still has only small secretariats based in Washington, Ottawa, and Mexico City. In short, little evidence exists of neofunctionalism at work in North America.

Neofunctionalism dominated studies of European integration during the 1950s and 1960s but briefly fell out of favor during the 1970s, which Haas explained by arguing that it lacked strong predictive capabilities.[17] However, two additional problems stood out. First, the process of integrating Europe seemed to have ground to a halt in the mid-1970s, undermined in part by the failure of the European Commission (the Community's main executive body) to provide the kind of leadership that was vital to the idea of neofunctionalism. Second, the theory of spillover needed more elaboration. Critics of neofunctionalism argued that it was too linear, that it needed to be expanded or modified to accommodate different pressures for integration, and that it must be seen in conjunction with other influences.

One of the earliest responses to neofunctionalism was offered by Stanley Hoffmann, who in the mid-1960s countered that neofunctionalism concentrated too much on the internal dynamics of integration without paying enough attention to the global context. He instead argued that the process was best understood as intergovernmental, and while nonstate actors played an important role, the pace and nature of integration was ultimately driven by national governments pursuing national interests. They alone had legal sovereignty, they alone had the political legitimacy that came from being elected, and they alone ultimately determined the pace of integration.[18]

A variation on this theme is liberal intergovernmentalism, associated with scholars such as Paul Taylor, Robert Keohane, and Andrew Moravcsik. Emerging in the 1980s and 1990s, it combines the neofunctionalist view of the importance of domestic politics with recognition of the role of the EU member state governments in making major political choices; in other words, the positions of the governments of the member states are decided at the domestic level, and then European integration moves forward as a result of intergovernmental bargains reached at the European level.[19] As outlined by Moravcsik, integration advances as a result of a combination of factors such as the commercial interests of economic producers and the relative bargaining power of major governments.[20]

WHAT HAS THE EU BECOME?

Most of the early theoretical debates about the EU focused on trying to explain how it had evolved. With time, the focus began to shift to attempts to explain what the EU had become and how it worked. But here too there have been many disagreements and few generally accepted conclusions. On the one hand, the EU has some of the qualities of an international organization: its members are nation states, membership is voluntary, the balance of sovereignty lies with the member states, decision making is consultative, and the procedures used are based on consent rather than compulsion. On the other hand, the EU also has some of the qualities of a state: it has internationally recognized boundaries (even if these have changed quite dramatically over a short period of time as the EU has gone through cycles of enlargement), there is a European system of law to which all member states are subject, it has increasing authority to influence and control the lives of Europeans, in many policy areas the balance of responsibility and power has shifted to the European level, and in some areas – such as trade – it has become all but sovereign and is recognized by other states as an equal player.

However, it is neither one nor the other, and all we can say with any certainty – as noted earlier – is that the EU is more than a conventional international organization but less than a European superstate. The critical issues are (1) the relative powers of the member states and the EU institutions and (2) just where the EU sits on the continuum between intergovernmentalism (where key decisions are made as a result of negotiations among representatives of the member states) and supranationalism (the EU is a network of autonomous governing bodies that have the power and authority to make decisions above the level of the member states and in the interests of the EU as a whole).

Some have questioned the assumption that intergovernmentalism and supranationalism are two extremes on a continuum. Mitrany argued that governments cooperated out of need and that this was "not a matter of surrendering sovereignty, but merely of pooling as much of it as may be needed for the joint performance of the particular task."[21] Keohane and Hoffmann agree, arguing that the EU is "an experiment in pooling sovereignty, not in transferring it from states to supranational institutions."[22] Leon Lindberg and Stuart Scheingold believe that the relationship between the EU and its member states is more symbiotic than competitive.[23] Haas argued that supranationalism did not mean that EU institutions exercised authority over national governments but rather that it was a process or a style of decision making in which "the participants refrain from unconditionally vetoing proposals and instead seek to attain agreement by means of compromises upgrading common interests."[24]

For some critics, the key problem with the intergovernmental/supranational debate is that it treats the EU as an international organization and diverts attention away from looking at the EU as a political system in its own right. Instead of being so much influenced by the thinking of IR, they argue, perhaps we should be looking more at the methods of comparative politics.[25] In 1994, Simon Hix proposed that those methods could help us understand how governmental power was exercised in the EU, how Europeans related to EU institutions, and how European government was influenced by political parties, elections, and interest groups.[26] In other words, instead of studying the EU as a process, we should better understand how it actually works today.[27]

Hix was influenced by new institutionalism, an approach to the study of national and comparative politics that tried to revive the focus on the importance of institutions, superseded since the 1960s and 1970s by behavioralism, which had shifted attention away from institutions and toward political processes, such as the influence of interest groups. Behavioralists saw institutions as neutral arenas in which different groups competed for influence, but new institutionalists argued that structures and rules biased access to the political process in favor of some groups over others, and that institutions could be autonomous political actors in their own right.[28]

One of the handicaps faced by comparative politics approaches is the absence of a clearly identifiable European government. The term *government* typically applies to the institutions and officials (elected or appointed) that make up the formal governing structure of a state and have the powers to make laws and set the formal political agenda. But while the EU has a group of "governing" institutions and several thousand formally employed officials, there is no EU government as such. Instead, many prefer to use the term *governance* to describe the system of authority in the EU. This refers to an arrangement in which laws and policies are made and implemented without the existence of a formally acknowledged set of governing institutions, but instead as a result of interactions involving a complex variety of actors, including member state governments, EU institutions, interest groups, and other sources of influence. Taking this idea a step further, some use the term *multilevel governance* to explain how the EU is structured. This describes a system in which power is shared among the supranational, national, subnational, and local levels, with considerable interaction among them.[29]

In many ways, multilevel governance is just a more subtle and complex expression of the idea of federalism, which has received relatively little attention by scholars of the EU; as Rosamond notes, no famous names appear in the academic debate about European federalism to compare with Mitrany and Haas,[30] in spite of the controversy that surrounds public debates in Europe about federalism. For its supporters, Europe has stopped disappointingly short of becoming a federal union, while for its critics federalism has become a code word for fears of the dangers inherent in the surrender of national sovereignty. This aversion probably comes as a surprise to most Americans and Canadians, raised in federal systems that are at the core of an understanding of the American and Canadian political systems and are rarely seriously questioned (even if they are often misunderstood).

In addition to one of the most prominent federal states in the world – the US – there are about two dozen federations today, including Australia, Austria, Belgium, Brazil, Canada, Germany, India, and Nigeria.[31] In each of these countries, national and local units of government coexist within a system of shared and independent powers, but none has supreme authority over the other. The national (or federal) government usually has sole power over foreign and security policy; there is a single currency and a common defense force; a national system of law coexists with local legal systems; there is a written constitution and a court that can issue judgments on disputes between the national and local units of government; and there are at least two levels of government, bureaucracy, and taxation: national and local.

In the US system, federalism prohibits the states from having their own currencies, maintaining a military in peacetime, making agreements with other states or foreign nations, engaging in war, or – without the consent of Congress – levying taxes on imports or exports. The federal government cannot unilaterally redraw the borders of a state, impose different levels of tax by state, give states different levels of representation in the US Senate, or amend the Constitution without the support of three-quarters of the states. Meanwhile, the states reserve all the powers not expressly delegated to the federal government or prohibited to them by the federal government. A key feature of successful federalism in the US (and also in other strong democracies, such as Germany, Austria, and Australia) is the shared sense of identity of its citizens, the vast majority of whom place their primary loyalty to their country above their loyalty to the states, provinces, or regions in which they live.

Federalism is comparatively poorly understood by most Europeans, partly because they have had little direct experience with the concept: only three EU member states (Austria, Belgium, and Germany) are federations. The EU itself is not a federation because its member states can still do almost everything that the states in the US model (or provinces in the Canadian model) cannot do: they make treaties with other countries, make many independent decisions on interstate trade, operate their own currencies (in the case of the UK, Denmark, Sweden and – at the present time – most of the newer EU states), maintain their own armies, and go to war. The EU institutions, meanwhile, possess few of the powers of the American or Canadian federal governments: they cannot levy income taxes, they have a very thin common security policy and no real common military, and while they can negotiate with the rest of the world on behalf of the member states, these negotiations still do not cover all policy areas. And yet federalism remains an important analytical tool, because the EU has some of the features of a federal system of government:

- There is a system of European laws that coexists with national systems and is protected by the European Court of Justice.
- There is a directly elected European Parliament that coexists with national and subnational legislatures.
- There is a common budget, and a single currency in most of the member states.
- There is a common executive body (the European Commission) that has the authority to oversee external trade negotiations on behalf of all the member states and can sign international treaties on behalf of the member states.

- The member states of the EU are increasingly defined not by themselves but in relation to their EU partners.[32]

Federalism is not an absolute or a static concept, and it has taken different forms in different situations according to the relative strength and nature of local political, economic, social, historical, and cultural pressures. In the US, for example, while the balance of power originally favored the states, a gradual shift toward the center has resulted in both historical trends toward greater national unity and the growth of federal government programs that have made states more dependent. In India, by contrast, political fragmentation in recent years has seen the states develop greater self-determination and a new prominence in national politics, particularly through the influence of regional political parties.

A second idea, which appears with even less frequency in debates about the EU, is confederalism. If a federation is a union of peoples living within a single state, then a confederation is a union of states.[33] *Confederalism* describes a system of administration in which two or more states pool limited amounts of authority in a common supranational government. In a federal system, power is divided between national and local units of government, both of which exercise authority over – and are answerable directly to – the citizens. In a confederal system, by contrast, power rests with independent states, the central government derives authority from the states, and no direct link exists between the central government and the citizens. The states transfer specified powers to a higher authority for reasons of convenience, collective security, or efficiency. Where federalism involves the local units surrendering power over joint interests to a new and permanent national level of government, the units of a confederation are sovereign, and the higher authority is relatively weak; it exists at the discretion of the local units and can do only what they allow it to do.

Among the few examples of state confederalism in practice are Switzerland from the medieval era until 1789, and then again from 1815 to 1848; the Netherlands from 1579 to 1795; the US from 1781 to 1789; and Germany from 1815 to 1866.[34] In the case of the US, the assumption was that the original states might eventually cooperate enough to form a common system of government, but the 1781 Articles of Confederation created little more than a "league of friendship" that could declare war and conclude treaties, but could not levy taxes or regulate commerce, and the army depended on state militias for its support. There was no national executive or judiciary, and Congress (in which each state had one vote) rarely met.

For its part, Switzerland was more purely confederal until 1789, and although it now claims to be a federation, it has given up fewer powers to the national government than has been the case in the US. The Swiss encourage direct democracy by holding national and local referendums, have a federal assembly elected by proportional representation, and are governed by a federal council elected by the assembly. One of the members of the council is appointed to a one-year term as head of state and head of government.

The EU is confederal in several ways.

- Although the member states have transferred authority to the EU institutions, they still control the bulk of the power of negotiation and bargaining.
- The member states are still distinct units with separate identities, have their own national defense forces and policies, can sign bilateral treaties with other states, and can argue that the EU institutions exist at their discretion.
- It is a voluntary association. A member state could leave the EU if it wished, and its action would not legally be defined as secession (e.g., Brexit). Attempts to leave federations, by contrast, have almost always been defined as secession and have usually led to

civil war (as happened with the attempted secession of the Confederacy from the US in 1861, of Chechnya from Russia since 1994, and of Kosovo from Yugoslavia in 1998).

- The only direct link between citizens and the EU institutions is the European Parliament. With the Commission, the Council of the EU, and the European Council, authority derives mainly from the governments of the member states, and representation is indirect.
- There is no European government in the sense of Europe-wide elected leaders, such as a president (more on this in Chapter 6), a foreign minister, and a cabinet, and there exists only a variable sense of European identity among the inhabitants of the EU.
- The EU may have its own flag and anthem, but most citizens still hold a higher sense of allegiance toward national flags, anthems, and other symbols, and progress toward building a sense of European citizenship has been mixed.

Surprisingly little has been published on confederation as a general concept, let alone on the EU as a confederation. Perhaps part of the problem is that confederalism falls short of what the most enthusiastic European federalists envision for Europe, while still going too far for most Euroskeptics. Another part of the problem may be that, in those few cases where confederalism has been tried, it has either failed or has evolved ultimately into a federal system. One study of Europe as a confederation was offered in 1981 by Murray Forsyth, who argued that studies of federalism seemed to have little connection with the realities of European integration and that the study of historical examples of confederations revealed that the EEC was clearly an economic confederation in both content and form.[35] Frederick Lister agrees, describing the EU as a "jumbo confederation" whose member states and governments continue to dominate the EU's institutions.[36]

Through all the debate over how the EU evolved, and what it has become, this much is clear: there is little agreement among either scholars of the EU or European leaders about how best to understand the EU. Explanations coming out of IR still dominate, but it is clear that the EU has stretched far beyond being an international organization and that there is more to its character than a series of intergovernmental bargains. Although many now believe that the EU should be seen as a political system in its own right, comparable in many ways to a conventional state, it is unclear just how far the comparisons can go. Paul Magnette, for example, is certain that the EU cannot become a state because its budget is too small, because its institutions tend to perpetuate divisions rather than override them, and because it is not a military power.[37] Just what final form the EU will take is anyone's guess, especially given the uncertainty that the crisis in the eurozone and Brexit have engendered. It might remain a somewhat loose association of states, it might become a tighter United States of Europe with significant economic and political integration, or it might remain unique. The past offers little real certainty about the future.

QUESTIONS TO CONSIDER

1 In what ways does the EU today challenge traditional notions of the state and its importance to understanding the world of international politics? In what ways does the EU confirm the continuing importance of the state?
2 How might the proponents of neofunctionalism and the proponents of intergovernmentalism view the European debt crisis and the EU's response to it?
3 How helpful is the US model of federalism – or the earlier Articles of Confederation – in understanding the political system of the EU?

NOTES

1 Ben Rosamond, *Theories of European Integration*, 14–16 (New York: St. Martin's Press, 2000).
2 Rosamond only refers to comparative politics later in his book, particularly on pages 105–108 and 157–164.
3 For a discussion of the effects of globalization on the Westphalian system, see Robert J. Holton, *Globalization and the Nation State*, 2nd ed. (New York: Palgrave Macmillan, 2011). For examples of some of the debates involved, see James Caporaso, ed., *Continuity and Change in the Westphalian Order* (Malden, MA: Blackwell, 2000).
4 For a useful reader on the history and meaning of nationalism, see Anthony D. Smith, *Nationalism: Theory, Ideology, History*, 2nd ed. (Cambridge: Polity Press, 2010).
5 Union of International Associations at https://uia.org/, accessed December 12, 2019.
6 Altiero Spinelli, "The Growth of the European Movement Since the Second World War," in *Europe Integration: Selected Readings*, edited by Michael Hodges (Harmondsworth, UK: Penguin, 1972).
7 David Mitrany, *A Working Peace System*, 27 (Chicago: Quadrangle, 1966).
8 Mitrany, *A Working Peace System*, 27–31, 72.
9 Leon N. Lindberg and Stuart A. Scheingold, eds., *Regional Integration: Theory and Research*, 6 (Cambridge, MA: Harvard University Press, 1971).
10 Ernst B. Haas, "The Study of Regional Integration: Reflections on the Joy and Anguish of Pretheorizing," *International Organization* 24 (1970): 607–646.
11 Ernst B. Haas, *The Uniting of Europe: Political, Social, and Economic Forces, 1950–1957*, 29 (Stanford, CA: Stanford University Press, 1958).
12 Leon N. Lindberg, *The Political Dynamics of European Economic Integration*, 10 (Stanford, CA: Stanford University Press, 1963).
13 For examples, see Ian Bache, Stephen George, and Simon Bulmer, *Politics in the European Union*, 3rd ed., 15 (Oxford: Oxford University Press, 2011).
14 Bache, George, and Bulmer, *Politics in the European Union*, 17.
15 Joseph S. Nye, "Comparing Common Markets: A Revised Neofunctionalist Model," in *Regional Integration*, edited by Lindberg and Scheingold, 208–214.
16 See Gary Clyde Hufbauer and Jeffrey J. Schott, *NAFTA Revisited: Achievements and Challenges* (Washington, DC: Institute for International Economics, 2005); Stephen Clarkson, *Does North America Exist? Governing the Continent after 9/11 and NAFTA* (Toronto: University of Toronto Press, 2008); Sidney Weintraub, ed., *NAFTA's Impact on North America: The First Decade* (Washington, DC: Center for Strategic and International Studies, 2004).
17 Ernst B. Haas, *The Obsolescence of Regional Integration Theory* (Berkeley: Institute of International Studies, University of California, 1975).
18 Stanley Hoffmann, "The European Process at Atlantic Crosspurposes," *Journal of Common Market Studies* 3 (1964): 85–101, and "Obstinate or Obsolete? The Fate of the Nation State and the Case of Western Europe," *Daedalus* 95 (1966): 862–915.
19 A newer variation on intergovernmentalism ("deliberative intergovernmentalism") suggests that while EU states see the need for common action, they try to avoid simply ceding powers to supranational EU institutions and instead try to find new ways to achieve decentralized consensual decisions. See Uwe Putter, *The European Council and the Council: New Intergovernmentalism and Institutional Change* (Oxford, UK: Oxford University Press, 2014). For a discussion of other theories of integration beyond neofunctionalism and intergovernmentalism, see Sabine Saurugger, *Theoretical Approaches to European Integration* (New York and London: Palgrave Macmillan, 2014).
20 Andrew Moravcsik, "Preferences and Power in the European Community: A Liberal Intergovernmentalist Approach," *Journal of Common Market Studies* 31 (1993): 473–524, and *The Choice for Europe: Social Purpose and State Power from Messina to Maastricht* (Ithaca, NY: Cornell University Press, 1998).
21 David Mitrany, "The Functional Approach to World Organisation," in *The New International Actors: The UN and the EEC*, edited by Carol A. Cosgrove and Kenneth J. Twitchett (London: Macmillan, 1970).

22 Robert O. Keohane and Stanley Hoffmann, "Conclusions: Community Politics and Institutional Change," in *The Dynamics of European Integration*, edited by William Wallace, 277 (London: Royal Institute for International Affairs, 1990).

23 Leon N. Lindberg and Stuart A. Scheingold, *Europe's Would-Be Polity: Patterns of Change in the European Community*, 94–95 (Englewood Cliffs, NJ: Prentice Hall, 1970).

24 Ernst B. Haas, "Technocracy, Pluralism and the New Europe," in *A New Europe?*, edited by Stephen R. Graubard, 66 (Boston: Houghton Mifflin, 1964).

25 See Alberta Sbragia, "Thinking about the European Future: The Uses of Comparison," in *Euro-Politics: Institutions and Policymaking in the "New" European Community*, edited by Alberta Sbragia (Washington, DC: Brookings Institution, 1992).

26 Simon Hix, "The Study of the European Community: The Challenge to Comparative Politics," *West European Politics* 17, no. 1 (1994): 1–30.

27 Simon Hix and Bjørn Høyland. *The Political System of the European Union*, 3rd ed. (London: Palgrave Macmillan, 2011).

28 For details, see Bache, George, and Bulmer, *Politics in the European Union*, 28–29.

29 Gary Marks, "Structural Policy and Multi-Level Governance in the EC," in *The State of the European Community*, vol. 2, edited by Alan Cafruny and Glenda Rosenthal (Boulder: Lynne Rienner, 1993). For elaboration, see Lisbet Hooghe and Gary Marks, *Multi-Level Governance and European Integration* (Lanham, MD: Rowman and Littlefield, 2001).

30 Rosamond, *Theories of European Integration*, 23.

31 The study of comparative federalism has undergone significant growth in recent years. See, for example, Finn Laursen, ed., *The EU and Federalism: Polities and Policies Compared* (Aldershot: Ashgate, 2011); Michael Burgess, *Comparative Federalism: Theory and Practice* (London: Routledge, 2006); and Anand Menon and Martin Schain, eds., *Comparative Federalism: The European Union and the United States in Comparative Perspective* (Oxford: Oxford University Press, 2006).

32 Laursen, *The EU and Federalism*.

33 Frederick K. Lister, *The European Union, the United Nations, and the Revival of Confederal Governance*, 106 (Westport, CT: Greenwood, 1996).

34 Murray Forsyth, *Unions of States: The Theory and Practice of Confederation* (Leicester, UK: Leicester University Press, 1981).

35 Forsyth, *Unions of States*, x, 183.

36 Lister, *The European Union, the United Nations, and the Revival of Confederal Governance*, chapter 2.

37 Paul Magnette, *What Is the European Union?*, 195–98 (New York: Palgrave Macmillan, 2005).

BIBLIOGRAPHY

Bache, Ian, Stephen George, and Simon Bulmer, *Politics in the European Union*, 3rd ed. (Oxford: Oxford University Press, 2011).

Burgess, Michael, *Comparative Federalism: Theory and Practice* (London: Routledge, 2006).

Caporaso, James, ed., *Continuity and Change in the Westphalian Order* (Malden, MA: Blackwell, 2000).

Clarkson, Stephen, *Does North America Exist? Governing the Continent after 9/11 and NAFTA* (Toronto: University of Toronto Press, 2008).

Forsyth, Murray, *Unions of States: The Theory and Practice of Confederation* (Leicester, UK: Leicester University Press, 1981).

Haas, Ernst B., "Technocracy, Pluralism and the New Europe," in *A New Europe?*, edited by Stephen R. Graubard, 60–66 (Boston: Houghton Mifflin, 1964).

Haas, Ernst B., "The Study of Regional Integration: Reflections on the Joy and Anguish of Pretheorizing." *International Organization* 24 (1970) 24: 607–646.

Haas, Ernst B., *The Obsolescence of Regional Integration Theory* (Berkeley: Institute of International Studies, University of California, 1975).

Haas, Ernst B., *The Uniting of Europe: Political, Social, and Economic Forces, 1950–1957* (Stanford, CA: Stanford University Press, 1958; repr., Notre Dame, IN: University of Notre Dame Press, 2004).

Hix, Simon, "The Study of the European Community: The Challenge to Comparative Politics." *West European Politics* 17, no. 1 (1994): 1–30.

Hix, Simon and Bjørn Høyland, *The Political System of the European Union*, 3rd ed. (London: Palgrave Macmillan, 2011).

Hoffmann, Stanley, "The European Process at Atlantic Crosspurposes." *Journal of Common Market Studies* 3 (1964): 85–101.

Hoffmann, Stanley, "Obstinate or Obsolete? The Fate of the Nation State and the Case of Western Europe." *Daedelus* 95 (1966): 862–915.

Holton, Robert J., *Globalization and the Nation State*, 2nd ed. (New York: Palgrave Macmillan, 2011).

Hooghe, Lisbet and Gary Marks, *Multi-Level Governance and European Integration* (Lanham, MD: Rowman and Littlefield, 2001).

Hufbauer, Gary Clyde and Jeffrey J. Schott, *NAFTA Revisited: Achievements and Challenges* (Washington, DC: Institute for International Economics, 2005).

Keohane, Robert O. and Stanley Hoffmann, "Conclusions: Community Politics and Institutional Change," in *The Dynamics of European Integration*, edited by William Wallace, 277 (London: Royal Institute for International Affairs, 1990).

Laursen, Finn, ed., *The EU and Federalism: Polities and Policies Compared* (Aldershot: Ashgate, 2011).

Lindberg, Leon N. and Stuart A. Scheingold, *Europe's Would-Be Polity: Patterns of Change in the European Community* (Englewood Cliffs, NJ: Prentice Hall, 1970).

Lindberg, Leon N. and Stuart A. Scheingold, eds., *Regional Integration: Theory and Research* (Cambridge, MA: Harvard University Press, 1971).

Lister, Frederick K., *The European Union, the United Nations, and the Revival of Confederal Governance* (Westport, CT: Greenwood, 1996).

Magnette, Paul, *What Is the European Union?* (New York: Palgrave Macmillan, 2005).

Marks, Gary, "Structural Policy and Multi-Level Governance in the EC," in *The State of the European Community*, vol. 2, edited by Alan Cafruny and Glenda Rosenthal (Boulder: Lynne Rienner, 1993).

Menon, Anand and Martin Schain, eds., *Comparative Federalism: The European Union and the United States in Comparative Perspective* (Oxford: Oxford University Press, 2006).

Mitrany, David, *A Working Peace System* (Chicago: Quadrangle, 1966).

Mitrany, David, "The Functional Approach to World Organisation," in *The New International Actors: The UN and the EEC*, edited by Carol A. Cosgrove and Kenneth J. Twitchett (London: Macmillan, 1970).

Moravcsik, Andrew, "Preferences and Power in the European Community: A Liberal Intergovernmentalist Approach." *Journal of Common Market Studies* 31 (1993): 473–524.

Moravcsik, Andrew, *The Choice for Europe: Social Purpose and State Power from Messina to Maastricht* (Ithaca, NY: Cornell University Press, 1998).

Nye, Joseph S., "Comparing Common Markets: A Revised Neofunctionalist Model," in *Regional Integration: Theory and Research*, edited by Leon N. Lindberg and Stuart A. Scheingold, 208–214 (Cambridge, MA: Harvard University Press, 1971).

Puetter, Uwe, *The European Council and the Council: New Intergovernmentalism and Institutional Change* (Oxford, UK: Oxford University Press, 2014).

Rosamond, Ben, *Theories of European Integration* (New York: St. Martin's Press, 2000).

Saurugger, Sabine, *Theoretical Approaches to European Integration* (New York and London: Palgrave Macmillan, 2014).

Sbragia, Alberta, "Thinking about the European Future: The Uses of Comparison," in *Euro-Politics: Institutions and Policymaking in the "New" European Community*, edited by Alberta Sbragia (Washington, DC: Brookings Institution, 1992).

Smith, Anthony D., *Nationalism: Theory, Ideology, History*, 2nd ed. (Cambridge: Polity Press, 2010).

Spinelli, Altiero, "The Growth of the European Movement Since the Second World War," in *Europe Integration: Selected Readings*, edited by Michael Hodges, 43–68 (Harmondsworth, UK: Penguin, 1972).

Union of International Associations at https://uia.org/, accessed December 12, 2019.

Weintraub, Sidney, ed., *NAFTA's Impact on North America: The First Decade* (Washington, DC: Center for Strategic and International Studies, 2004).

FURTHER READING

David Mitrany, *A Working Peace System* (Chicago: Quadrangle, 1966).
> Arguably the grandparent of them all; one of the first modern expositions of the idea of building peace through cooperation.

Ernst B. Haas, *The Uniting of Europe: Political, Social, and Economic Forces, 1950–1957* (Stanford, CA: Stanford University Press, 1958; repr., Notre Dame, IN: University of Notre Dame Press, 2004).
> Still widely seen as the starting point for modern ideas about the mechanisms and motives of European integration.

Simon Hix and Bjørn Høyland, *The Political System of the European Union*, 3rd ed. (London: Palgrave Macmillan, 2011).
> An outstanding analysis of the EU as a political system using the methods of comparative politics.

Sabine Saurugger, *Theoretical Approaches to European Integration* (New York and London: Palgrave Macmillan, 2014).
> A critical analysis of theoretical perspectives on European integration including neofunctionalism and intergovernmentalism but also newer institutionalist, constructivist, and sociological approaches.

Anand Menon and Martin Schain, eds., *Comparative Federalism: The European Union and the United States in Comparative Perspective* (Oxford: Oxford University Press, 2006).
> A comparison of the European and US models of federalism, with chapters on concepts, institutions, and policies.

CHAPTER 2

Origins

The Road to Paris and Rome

CHAPTER OVERVIEW

- Although unity and cooperation were frequently suggested as a solution to Europe's long history of conflict, a peaceful European community was really only possible after World War II. The main legacy of the war was a fundamental reordering of the international system into a new bipolar world dominated by the US and the Soviet Union. American economic leadership ameliorated the continent's dire postwar economic needs and created the conditions for a prosperous Europe to emerge. At the same time, the security umbrella offered by the US provided Europe with the crucial space it needed to start addressing its long-term political problems.
- Meanwhile, recognition of the relative decline of Europe's power in the wake of frictions with the US in the 1950s led its governments to seek a greater degree of cooperation that would, some argued, lead eventually to political and economic integration and a common European identity. A first step toward these goals was the creation of the European Coal and Steel Community (ECSC), which dismantled some national tariff barriers and subsidies while creating a set of supranational governing institutions.
- Despite its importance as a stepping stone toward creating an economic union, the ECSC was limited in scope. Accordingly, leaders of the ECSC signed the Treaty of Rome, which sought to forge deeper economic integration among its member states. Rome also created institutions that continue to be used, in modified forms, in today's EU.

The roots of the EU lie in soil created by hundreds of years of conflict among the peoples of Europe. Many had long dreamed of unity as an answer to Europe's divisions and conflicts, and ideas for the creation of institutions and processes that might help bring Europeans together date back to medieval times. But it was only after World War II that a broader and more receptive audience emerged. Although Europe enjoyed military and economic dominance before the war, World War II dealt these a severe blow. Subsequently, Europe found itself both divided and threatened by a cold war in which the main protagonists were external powers: the US and the Soviet Union. The time was clearly ripe for Europeans to protect themselves from each other and to regroup in order to defend themselves from external threats potentially more destructive than any they had ever faced before.

The US created a recipe for the emergence of the EU by offering three essential ingredients that gave Europeans the luxury of more time and resources to address their internal problems. Ingredient one was the economic opportunity offered by US aid in the postwar reconstruction of Western Europe, embodied in 1948–1951 by the Marshall Plan, which invested billions of dollars in helping address the devastation caused by war. Ingredient two was the economic leadership offered by the Bretton Woods system, underpinned by US support for free trade and by the emergence of the US dollar as the linchpin of the international monetary system. Ingredient three was the security umbrella provided by the US in the defense of Western Europe against the Soviet threat, given heft in 1949 with the creation of the North Atlantic Treaty Organization (NATO).

Still, Europe's threats after World War II were not just external. Indeed, the largest threat to Europe remained nationalism, which had been at the heart of repeated conflict over the centuries, and had most recently been glorified, abused, and discredited by fascism and Nazism. Because the German brand fueled three major wars in seventy years, many now argued that peace was impossible unless Germany could be contained and its power diverted to constructive rather than destructive ends. It had to be allowed to rebuild its economic base and its political system in ways that would not threaten European security; France was particularly eager to ensure this outcome.[1] Perhaps if a new European identity could supersede multiple national identities, the cycle of conflict might be broken.

Unintentionally, the US helped push Western Europe toward this goal of European unity and identity by pursuing policies – particularly on the security front – that alarmed many Europeans. From the Korean War and continuing through the Suez crisis of 1956 and several major world events in the 1960s, transatlantic disagreements helped encourage Europeans to build stronger ties among themselves with a view to allowing Europe to build a stronger position as a global actor. Yet this goal demanded a concrete pathway to encourage a greater sense of unity and common purpose than they had ever been able to achieve before. The key would be to tamp down ambitions and develop a formula that could encourage Europeans to see the logic behind cooperation as well as produce tangible results as quickly as possible. The first move in this direction was taken with the creation in 1951 of the ECSC, designed to prove a point about the feasibility of European integration.

While the creation of the ECSC was an important first step toward unity, it was limited in its scope. Any move toward political integration and a common European identity would depend upon further economic integration. Accordingly, in 1957 members of the ECSC – France, West Germany, Italy, and the three Benelux countries – took matters further by creating the European Economic Community (EEC), which had the more ambitious goal of creating a single European market.

THE TAMING OF EUROPE

Americans sometimes think of Europe as a continent almost frozen in the past, a kind of cultural museum with centuries of history, timeless traditions, and relatively little social or political change. Nothing could be further from the truth. A long history it indeed has, but it is a history of constant change, of sometimes great political violence, and of almost unceasing social disturbance. Proposals for various kinds of international or regional bodies that might be the seeds of a European system of government, and thus the bridge to cooperation and unity, had often been put forward. But national, social, or religious divisions always won out, and it was only brute force that ever took Europe close to the goal of regional unity.

The term *European* was not generally used until 800, when Charlemagne was crowned Holy Roman Emperor by the pope and was described in poems as the king and father of Europe. Later champions of European unity were often motivated by their belief that a united Christian Europe was essential for the revival of the Holy Roman Empire and by concerns about Europe's insecurity in the face of gains by the Turks in Asia Minor.[2] Among those thinkers and philosophers who explored the theme of peace through unity several stand out: Jean-Jacques Rousseau favored a European federation; Jeremy Bentham in 1789 proposed a European assembly and a common army; Immanuel Kant in 1795 argued that peace could be achieved through integration; and the Comte de Saint-Simon published a pamphlet in 1814, *The Reorganization of the European Community*, arguing the need for a federal Europe with common institutions, but within which national independence would be maintained and respected. Meanwhile, Napoleon tried to unify the continent by force, a project that ultimately failed as Europe by the end of the nineteenth century descended into nationalism and military rivalry between states.

The horrors of World War I (1914–1918) resulted in an audience that was more receptive to the idea of European integration, the most enthusiastic proponents being smaller states that were tired of being caught up in big power rivalry. Yet prospects of a voluntary and peaceful European union were swept aside by economic recession and the rise of Nazi Germany, which was intent on correcting the "wrongs" of the Treaty of Versailles and creating a German *Lebensraum* (living space). Adolf Hitler spoke of a "European house," but only in the context of German rule over the continent.

The end of World War II in 1945 brought a fundamental reordering of the international system, which made the possibility of European unity appear more reachable. Before the war, the world had been dominated by "great powers" such as the UK, France, and Germany, which were distinguished from other states mainly by the size and reach of their militaries[3] but also by their large economies, their strong positions in international trade, and their deep investments in the international system. Since the war had resulted in the resounding defeat of Germany, the UK and France continued to act like great powers, even though Europe's global role was diminishing, and a new bipolar order was emerging, dominated by the US and the Soviet Union. Their power and reach were so formidable that they represented a new and unprecedented breed of "superpower."

In sharp contrast, Europe had to perform triage in the wake of its crushing defeat, with its chief task creating the conditions necessary for peacetime reconstruction. For some this meant a rethinking of their systems of government; for others it meant a new focus on social welfare; and for all it meant taking a new view of international cooperation. But each country had very different sets of priorities, and different ideas about what needed to be done.

ECONOMIC RECONSTRUCTION AND THE MARSHALL PLAN

As Western European governments worried about domestic postwar reconstruction and adjustment, changes were taking place at the global level that demanded new thinking. During the war economists on both sides of the Atlantic had discussed the best means of achieving a stable and prosperous postwar world. Their views were crystallized in July 1944, when representatives from forty-four countries met at Bretton Woods, New Hampshire, to plan for the postwar global economy. They agreed on an Anglo-American proposal to promote free trade, nondiscrimination, and stable rates of exchange – goals that were to be underpinned by American economic and political leadership, and by the creation of three new international organizations: the General Agreement on Tariffs and Trade (GATT, forerunner to today's World Trade Organization), the International Monetary Fund (IMF), and the World Bank.[4] More immediately, though, Europe's economies had to be rebuilt on a more stable footing.

World War II had spread through most of Europe, resulting in an estimated 40 million deaths and leaving behind gaping pockets of devastation. Major cities lay in ruins, agricultural production was halved, food was rationed, and communications were disrupted because bridges, harbors, and railroads had been primary targets of attack. Denmark, France, and the Benelux countries had suffered heavily under occupation. Many of the UK's major cities had been bombed, its exports had been cut by two-thirds, and its national wealth plummeted by 75 percent. Before the war, the UK had been the world's second-largest creditor nation; by 1945 it was the world's biggest debtor nation. Germany and Italy were left under Allied occupation, their economies in ruins. In all of Europe, only Finland, Ireland, Portugal, Spain, Sweden, and Switzerland were relatively undamaged or unchanged.

When an economically exhausted UK ended its financial aid to Greece and Turkey in 1947, President Harry S. Truman argued that the US needed to step into the vacuum to curb communist influence in the region. The Truman Doctrine confirmed a new US interest in European reconstruction as a means of containing the Soviets and discouraging the growth of communist parties in Western Europe.[5] At the same time, the US State Department had begun to realize that it had underestimated the extent of the wartime economic destruction in Europe. Despite an economic boom during the late 1940s, sustained growth was not forthcoming, food rationing persisted (raising the prospect of famine and starvation), and fears of communist influence spread like brushfire across a destabilized Europe.

Despite having already provided more than $10 billion in loans and aid to Europe between 1945 and 1947, the US needed something bigger and more structured.[6] Into the breach stepped Secretary of State George Marshall, who proposed a new and more structured program of aid to Europe. His calculations were mainly political (a strong Europe would be a buffer to Soviet expansionism), but he made his argument more palatable to Congress by couching it in humanitarian terms. "Our policy is directed not against any country or doctrine," he announced in a speech at Harvard in June 1947, "but against hunger, poverty, desperation and chaos." Marshall argued that the initiative should come from Europe and that "the program should be a joint one, agreed to by a number, if not all European nations."[7] Many in the State Department and elsewhere felt long-term stability demanded coordinated regional economic management that would prevent the breakdown of Europe into rival economic and political blocs.[8]

Clearly, Marshall's message struck the intended chord: the British and the French accepted the offer and approached the Soviets with the idea of developing a recovery plan. However, the Soviets suspected the US of ulterior motives and bowed out. In July 1947, sixteen European countries met in Paris and established the Committee on European Economic Cooperation. They listed their needs and asked the US for a whopping $29 billion in aid, much more than the US had envisaged. Still, with congressional approval the European Recovery Program (otherwise known as the Marshall Plan) ultimately provided roughly $12.5 billion in aid to Europe between 1948 and 1951.[9] In April 1948 the same sixteen states created a new body – the Organisation for European Economic Cooperation (OEEC), based in Paris – to coordinate the program.

Although the effects of the Marshall Plan are still debated even today, there is little question that it helped anchor the economic and political recovery already underway in Western Europe and bound the economic and political interests of the US and Western Europe more closely together. It was a profitable investment for the US, to be sure, but it also galvanized the idea of European integration; as Western Europe's first permanent organization for economic cooperation, the OEEC encouraged Europeans to work together and played a key role in showing them how much mutual dependence existed among their economies.[10] It also

MAP 2.1 Europe After World War II.

helped liberalize inter-European trade and ensured that economic integration would be focused on Western Europe. Yet the plan's focus on cooperation rather than true integration fell far short of promoting federalism or political unity.

SECURITY AND THE COLD WAR

Looming large alongside economic concerns were security concerns. US policy on Europe after 1945 had initially been driven by President Truman's desire to pull the military out as quickly as possible. American public opinion favored leaving future peacekeeping efforts to the new United Nations, so within two years the US military presence had been slashed by

95 percent. However, it was increasingly obvious to European leaders that Joseph Stalin planned to spread Soviet influence in Europe, and that the Nazi threat had been replaced by a Soviet threat. Winston Churchill helped spark a change in US public opinion with his famous March 1946 speech in Fulton, Missouri, in which he warned of the descent of an "iron curtain" across Europe.

The US had hoped to share responsibility for security with the Western European powers, but it soon became clear that the Europeans lacked the resources to maintain their end of the bargain, and the dangers that Europe still faced were intensified by events in Germany. Security concerns had propelled the UK, France, and the Benelux states in March 1948 to sign the Brussels treaty, creating the Western Union by which members would provide "all the military and other aid and assistance in their power" in the event of attack. In June, as a first step toward rebuilding German self-sufficiency, the Western Allies agreed to create a new West German state and a new currency for the three zones they were administering. In response, the Soviets set up a blockade around West Berlin. To counter this, in the next year a massive Western airlift was undertaken to supply West Berlin. The Soviet threat was now clear, and the Berlin crisis led to the arrival in the UK in 1948 of the first US bombers suspected of carrying nuclear weapons.

The US Congress was wary of any direct commitments or entanglements in Europe but saw the need to counterbalance the Soviets and to ensure the peaceful cooperation of West Germany. In 1949 the historic North Atlantic Treaty was signed, under which the US (entering its first ever peacetime alliance outside the Western Hemisphere) agreed to help its European allies "restore and maintain the security of the North Atlantic area." Canada also signed, as did the Benelux countries, the UK, France, Denmark, Iceland, Italy, Norway, and Portugal. The pact was later given more substance with the creation of NATO, headquartered in Paris until it was moved to Brussels in 1966. The US was now formally committed to the security of Western Europe.

Although NATO gave Europe more security and more space in which to focus on reconstruction, it soon became obvious that it was an unbalanced alliance: only 10 percent of NATO forces were American, but the US exercised most of the political influence over NATO policy. NATO members agreed that an attack on one would be considered an attack on them all, but each agreed to respond only with "such actions as it deems necessary." The creation of NATO sent a strong message to the Soviets, but at its heart was designed to make sure that the US would not immediately be drawn into in yet another European war.

Eager to encourage some kind of inter-European military cooperation, the UK invited its Brussels treaty partners to join with West Germany and Italy to create the Western European Union (WEU).[11] The WEU obliged each member to give all possible military and other aid to any member that was attacked. The WEU also reached beyond purely defensive concerns, and agreements signed by the seven founding members in Paris in October 1954 included the aim "to promote the unity and to encourage the progressive integration of Europe." Within days of the launch of the WEU in May 1955, and the coincidental admission of West Germany into NATO, the Soviet bloc created its own defensive alliance in the form of the Warsaw Pact. All of Central and Eastern Europe was firmly under Soviet control, and the lines of the Cold War were now clearly defined.

At the same time, two major events in the mid-1950s confirmed the new realities of the postwar international system, altered the self-perception of Western Europeans, and boosted supporters of European integration. The first occurred in French Indochina (now Vietnam, Laos, and Cambodia), which – except for its wartime Japanese occupation – had been under French colonial control since the late nineteenth century. Demanding independence, communist groups under the leadership of Ho Chi Minh launched an uprising in 1946, dragging the French into a bitter war. The end of the war came in May 1954 with the surrender of 12,000 French troops besieged in the village of Dien Bien Phu. The second defining event came in October 1956 when the Hungarian government of Imre Nagy announced the end of one-party rule and Hungary's withdrawal from the Warsaw Pact. As the UK and France were invading Egypt to reclaim the Suez Canal – built in 1856–1869 by the British and the French but nationalized by Egypt's new leader Gamal Abdel Nasser in July of 1956 – the Soviets responded to the Hungarian decision by sending in tanks. The US wanted to criticize the Soviet use of force and boast to the emerging Third World about the moral superiority of the West,[12] but it was hampered in doing so while British and French paratroopers occupied the Suez Canal. The UK and France were ostracized in the UN Security Council, the UK's prime minister, Anthony Eden, resigned, and the Suez invasion was quickly abandoned.

The combination of France's problems in Indochina, the Suez crisis, and the Hungarian uprising had tumultuous consequences.[13] The UK and France began steady military reductions, finally recognizing that they were no longer world powers capable of significant independent action. Both countries embarked on a concerted program of decolonization; the UK began looking increasingly to Europe for its economic and security interests; and it became obvious to Europeans that the US was the major partner in the Atlantic Alliance, a fact that particularly worried the French. Indochina and Suez left the French more doubtful than ever about American trustworthiness and more convinced of the vital need for European policy independence.[14] Meanwhile, Suez had the effect of drawing the UK's attention away from its traditional links with Australia, Canada, and New Zealand, and encouraging the UK to begin its slow turn toward Europe.[15] Indeed, for Walter Hallstein, later president of the European Commission, the Suez crisis helped foster greater European unity.[16] West Germany, meanwhile, worried about being caught in the middle of the Cold War, and many believed that a strong West German army would diminish the need for a nuclear defense strategy.

OPENING MOVES: COAL AND STEEL (1950–1953)

Support for the idea of European cooperation after the war found footing in the emergence (or reemergence) of several groups of pro-Europeanists. They included the United European Movement in the UK, the Europa-Bund in Germany, the Socialist Movement for the United States of Europe in France, and the European Union of Federalists. The spotlight shone particularly on the UK, which had led the resistance to Nazism and was still the dominant European power. In 1942–1943, Churchill had suggested the creation of "a United States of Europe" operating under "a Council of Europe" with reduced trade barriers, free movement of people, a common military, and a high court to adjudicate disputes.[17] Yet it was clear that he felt this new entity should revolve around France and Germany and would not necessarily include the UK, which he once said was "with Europe but not of it. We are interested and associated, but not absorbed."[18] This was not to be the last example of the UK's contradictory embrace of Europe (and the later EU) while at the same time keeping it at arm's length.

In an attempt to push the cause of European unity, pro-European groups organized the Congress of Europe in The Hague in May 1948. Within months the governments of the UK, France, Italy, and the Benelux countries had agreed to the creation of a new organization. The French and Italians hoped to call it the European Union, but the British insisted on the more ambiguous and noncommittal title Council of Europe.[19] It was founded in May 1949 with the signing of a statute in London by ten European states that agreed on the need for "a closer unity between all the like-minded countries of Europe." The Council of Europe made progress on human rights, cultural issues, and even limited economic cooperation, but it never amounted to anything more than a loose intergovernmental organization. It was far from the kind of organization that European federalists wanted.

Among those who sought something bolder were two Frenchmen: an entrepreneur and public servant named Jean Monnet and French foreign minister Robert Schuman (see Box 2.1). Both were ardent Europeanists, both felt something practical needed to be done that went beyond the noble statements of organizations such as the Council of Europe, and both believed that the logical point of departure should be the perennial problem of Franco-German relations. One way of promoting reconstruction in Germany without allowing it to become a threat to its neighbors (particularly France) was to let it rebuild under the auspices of a supranational organization, thereby tying it into the wider process of European reconstruction. The congresses of the European Movement in early 1949 had suggested that the coal and steel industries offered strong potential for common European organization, for several reasons:[20]

- Coal and steel were the building blocks of industry, and the steel industry had a tendency to create cartels. Cooperation would eliminate waste and duplication, dismantle cartels, make coal and steel production more efficient and competitive, and boost industrial development.
- The heavy industries of the Ruhr Valley had constituted the traditional basis for Germany's power, and France and Germany had battled before over coal reserves in Alsace-Lorraine. Monnet argued that "coal and steel were at once the key to economic power and the raw materials for forging weapons of war."[21] Forging a supranational coal and steel industry would help contain German power.
- Integrating coal and steel would ensure that Germany became reliant on trade with the rest of Europe, bolstering its economic reconstruction and calming French fears of German industrial domination.[22]

Monnet felt that unless France acted immediately, the US would become the focus of a new transatlantic alliance against the Soviet bloc, the UK would be pulled closer to the US, Germany's economic and military growth would burgeon, and France would hurtle towards its "eclipse."[23] As head of the French national planning commission, Monnet knew from personal experience that intergovernmental organizations tended to be hamstrung by the governments of their member states and to become bogged down in ministerial meetings. To avoid these problems, he proposed a new institution independent of national governments that would have a life of its own, one that would be supranational rather than intergovernmental. After discussing the proposal with West German chancellor Konrad Adenauer, Schuman announced it at a press conference at the French Foreign Ministry in Paris on May 9, 1950. In what later became known as the Schuman Plan, he argued that Europe would not be built at once or according to a single plan but only through a series of clearly identifiable achievements.

> The coming together of the nations of Europe requires the elimination of the age-old opposition of France and Germany.... With this aim in view, the French Government proposes that action be taken immediately in one limited but decisive point. It proposes that Franco-German production of coal and steel as a whole be placed under a common High Authority, within the framework of an organization open to the participation of the other countries of Europe.[24]

Concrete construction on European unity had begun.

PHOTO 2.1 & 2.2 The Founding Fathers of the EU: Jean Monnet and Robert Schuman.

Source: © European Union, 2018, EC – Audiovisual Service; © European Communities, 1958, EC – Audiovisual Service.

Box 2.1 Monnet and Schuman: The Fathers of Europe

The roll call of people throughout the centuries who have pondered the notion of European unity is impressive and includes William Penn, Jean-Jacques Rousseau, Jeremy Bentham, Immanuel Kant, Victor Hugo, and Winston Churchill. But it was two Frenchmen who outlined the ideas that led most immediately to the European Union as we know it today.

Jean Monnet (1888–1979) was an entrepreneur who spent many years in public service, notably during the two world wars. Born in Cognac in western France, Monnet worked for his family business before becoming an adviser to the French government during World War I, then working for the League of Nations. After the war he worked as a financier for an American investment bank, reentering public service during World War II. He was instrumental in postwar planning in France and was the architect of the Monnet Plan, a five-year strategy for investment and modernization. He became first president of the High Authority of the ECSC, from which he resigned in 1955.

Robert Schuman (1886–1963) had an altogether different career. Born to French parents in Luxembourg, he was raised in the province of Lorraine (which had been annexed by Germany in 1871 but was returned to France in 1918), attended university in Bonn, Munich, Berlin, and Strasbourg, and served in the German army during World War I. After the war he was elected to the French parliament and spent much of his time dealing with the legal problems of Alsace-Lorraine. He refused to serve in the French Vichy government during World War II, instead becoming an outspoken critic of German policy in Alsace-Lorraine. Schuman was imprisoned by the Gestapo, but he escaped and then worked for the French underground. Reelected to the new French legislature in 1945, he served as finance minister, briefly became prime minister, then served as French foreign minister from 1948 to 1952.[25]

Although the plan announced as the Schuman Declaration bears the name of the French foreign minister, it was actually Monnet's creation.[26] In fact, Monnet later claimed that Schuman "didn't really understand the treaty [the Treaty of Paris] which bore his name."[27] Nonetheless, the announcement of the plan was the spark that led to the European Union of today.

The plan, Schuman went on, would be "a first step in the federation of Europe" and would make war between France and Germany "not merely unthinkable, but materially impossible."[28] Few other governments were enthusiastic, however, and only four took up the invitation to join: Italy sought respectability and economic and political stability, and the three Benelux countries opted in because they were small and vulnerable, had twice been invaded by Germany, and felt their only hope for a voice in world affairs and a guarantee for security was to be part of a bigger unit. They were also heavily reliant on exports and had already created their own customs union in 1948.

Undeterred by a tepid response from other states such as the UK, the governments of the founding member states (the Six) opened negotiations and on April 18, 1951, signed the Treaty of Paris, creating the ECSC. The new organization began work in August 1952, following ratification of the terms of the treaty in each of the member states. It was governed by four institutions:

- A High Authority with nine members (nominated for six-year terms) who were expected to work toward removing all barriers to the free movement of coal and steel and to represent the joint interests of the ECSC rather than national interests.
- A Special Council of Ministers representing the member states which would have equal power of decision making for the ECSC.
- A Common Assembly with advisory responsibilities, chosen on the basis of population from the national legislatures of the member states.
- A Court of Justice tasked with settling conflicts between states and ruling on the legality of High Authority decisions.

The birth of the ECSC was a small step in itself, but it represented the first time European governments had transferred significant powers to a supranational organization. It was empowered to pull down tariff barriers, abolish subsidies, fix prices, and raise income by imposing levies on steel and coal production. Though it faced some national resistance, its job was facilitated by the fact that much of the groundwork had already been laid by the Benelux customs union. The creation of the ECSC showed that integration was feasible, and its very existence obliged the Six to work together. While ultimately failing to achieve many of its goals (notably the creation of a single market for coal and steel),[29] it had been established to prove a point about the feasibility of integration. In this respect, the ECSC was a great success.

FROM PARIS TO ROME (1955–1958)

Meanwhile, integrationists stumbled badly with two much larger and more ambitious projects. The first of these was the European Defence Community (EDC), which was intended to promote Western European cooperation on defense while binding West Germany into a European security system. Echoing ideas outlined by Churchill in a speech to the Council of Europe in August 1950, a draft plan for the EDC was made public in October of that year.[30] It argued the need for a common defense and "a European Army tied to the political institutions of a united Europe and a European Minister for Defense."[31] On that understanding, the six members of the ECSC signed a draft EDC treaty in May 1952. Although West Germany, Italy, and the Benelux countries all ratified the treaty, there was clear resistance in the UK – wary of any kind of supranational security arrangement – and, ironically, within France, which had first proposed it. Plans for the EDC were finally abandoned in August 1954, when the French National Assembly voted it down on the grounds that giving up the right to a national army would have a crippling effect on its sovereignty.

The second failed venture was the European Political Community (EPC), which was envisioned as the first step in the genesis of a European federation. A draft plan was completed in 1953, based around a European Executive Council, a Council of Ministers, a Court of Justice, and a popularly elected bicameral parliament. With ultimate power resting with the Executive Council, which would represent national interests, the EPC was more confederal than federal in nature.[32] With the collapse of the EDC, however, all hopes for an EPC died, at least temporarily, and the plans were shelved. The failure of these two initiatives dealt a sobering blow to the integrationists, sending shock waves through the ECSC; Monnet left the presidency of the High Authority in 1955, disillusioned by the political resistance to its work and impatient to move on with the process of integration.[33]

Nevertheless, it could be argued that the failure of the EDC created a much better opportunity for deeper economic integration to proceed. For EU historian Desmond Dinan, the EDC was not a lost opportunity but instead "rescued European integration from the political quagmire of an unworkable military commitment."[34] Indeed, while the six original members of the ECSC agreed that coal and steel had been a useful testing ground for economic integration, its scope was limited. Moreover, it was difficult to develop those two sectors in isolation. When the foreign ministers of the Six met at Messina, Italy, in June 1955, they decided to reach further by working "for the establishment of a united Europe by the development of common institutions, the progressive fusion of national economies, the creation of a common market, and the progressive harmonization of their social policies."[35] A committee chaired by Belgian foreign minister Paul-Henri Spaak (the driving force behind the conference) crafted what he himself admitted was a plan motivated less by economic cooperation than by a desire to take another step toward political union.[36]

The Spaak committee report led to a new round of negotiations and the signing on March 25, 1957, of the two Treaties of Rome, creating the EEC and the European Atomic Energy Community (Euratom). Following member state ratification, both came into force in January 1958. The EEC treaty committed the Six to several economic goals: the creation of a single

PHOTO 2.3 Signing of the Treaty of Rome.

Source: © European Communities, 1992, Source: EC – Audiovisual Service.

market within twelve years through the removal of all restrictions on internal trade; agreement on a common external tariff; the reduction of barriers to the free movement of people, services, and capital; the development of common agricultural and transport policies; and the creation of the European Social Fund and a European Investment Bank. The Euratom treaty, meanwhile – mainly of interest only to the French – aimed at creating a single market for atomic energy, but it was quickly relegated to focusing on research. When West Germany and Italy began developing their own nuclear power programs, Euratom funding was cut, and it rapidly dwindled to a junior actor in the process of integration.[37]

Although the EEC and Euratom inherited the same basic institutional framework as the ECSC, there were some notable changes:

- Instead of a High Authority, the EEC had an appointed nine-member quasi-executive Commission with less power to impose decisions on member states and whose main jobs were to initiate policy and to oversee implementation.
- The EEC Council of Ministers was granted greater power over decision making but still represented national interests. Though composed of six members, they shared seventeen votes (four each for France, Germany, and Italy; two each for Belgium and the Netherlands; and one for Luxembourg). Some decisions required unanimity, while others could be made by a simple majority or, more often, a qualified majority of twelve votes from at least four states. This system made it impossible for the larger states to outvote the smaller ones.
- A single Parliamentary Assembly was created to cover the EEC, ECSC, and Euratom, with 142 members appointed by the member states. It could question or censure the Commission of the ECSC, but had little legislative authority. The Assembly renamed itself the European Parliament in 1962.
- A single Court of Justice was created with seven judges appointed for renewable six-year terms. It was responsible for interpreting the treaties and for ensuring that the three institutions and the member states fulfilled their treaty obligations.

Desmond Dinan has argued that while the ECSC was "important politically and institutionally" it was economically insignificant.[38] Be that as it may, it was arguably the Treaty of Rome, more than the Treaty of Paris, which shaped the structure and ambitions of today's EU. Its institutional architecture has persisted to this day: a Commission that served as a quasi-executive, a Council of Ministers and a Parliamentary Assembly that performed legislative functions, and a Court of Justice that operated like a supranational constitutional court. Moreover, Rome set the stage for fuller economic integration and an accompanying logic of political integration which would take root, albeit slowly and fitfully, over the next several decades, as we shall see in the next chapters.

QUESTIONS TO CONSIDER

1 What were the major obstacles to progressing toward European unity and cooperation before World War II? What changed after World War II and what role did the US play?
2 Why did Jean Monnet and Robert Schuman emphasize the Franco-German relationship in their ideas about a future European community? Why was the integration of coal and steel chosen as the foundation for this community?
3 What were the factors which drove the Treaty of Rome and how did it further European integration?

NOTES

1 John Gillingham, "Jean Monnet and the European Coal and Steel Community: A Preliminary Appraisal," in *Jean Monnet: The Path to European Unity*, edited by Douglas Brinkley and Clifford Hackett, 131–137 (New York: St. Martin's Press, 1991).

2 Derek Heater, *The Idea of European Unity*, 6 (New York: St. Martin's Press, 1992).

3 Jack S. Levy, *War in the Modern Great Power System, 1495–1975*, 16–18 (Lexington, KY: University Press of Kentucky, 1983).

4 Armand Van Dormael, *Bretton Woods: Birth of a Monetary System* (New York: Holmes and Meier, 1978).

5 Michael J. Hogan, *The Marshall Plan: America, Britain, and the Reconstruction of Western Europe, 1947–52*, 26–27 (Cambridge: Cambridge University Press, 1987).

6 Alan S. Milward, *The Reconstruction of Western Europe 1945–51*, 46–48 (Berkeley: University of California Press, 1984).

7 Office of the Historian, *Foreign Relations of the United States*, vol. 3, 230–232 (Washington, DC: US Department of State, 1947).

8 Hogan, *The Marshall Plan*, 36.

9 Milward, *The Reconstruction of Western Europe 1945–51*, 94.

10 Derek W. Urwin, *The Community of Europe*, 2nd ed., 20–22 (London: Longman, 1995).

11 Ibid., 68–71.

12 Alan Sked and Chris Cook, *Post-War Britain: A Political History*, 135–136 (Harmondsworth, UK: Penguin, 1984).

13 See Albert Hourani, "Conclusions," in *Suez 1956: The Crisis and Its Consequences*, edited by William Roger Louis and Roger Owen (Oxford: Clarendon Press, 1989).

14 Geir Lundestad, *The United States and Western Europe Since 1945*, 115 (Oxford: Oxford University Press, 2003).

15 See Anthony Gorst and Lewis Johnman, *The Suez Crisis*, 151, 160 (London: Routledge, 1997).

16 Roger Morgan, "The Transatlantic Relationship," in *Europe and the World: The External Relations of the Common Market*, edited by Kenneth J. Twitchett (London: Europa, 1976).

17 Quoted in Michael Palmer and John Lambert, eds., *European Unity: A Survey of European Organizations*, 111 (London: George Allen and Unwin, 1968).

18 Quoted in Arnold J. Zurcher, *The Struggle to Unite Europe 1940–58*, 6 (New York: New York University Press, 1958).

19 Mark Gilbert, *Surpassing Realism: The Politics of European Integration Since 1945*, 34 (Lanham, MD: Rowman and Littlefield, 2003).

20 Milward, *The Reconstruction of Western Europe 1945–51*, 394.

21 Jean Monnet, *Memoirs*, trans. Richard Mayne, 293 (Garden City, NY: Doubleday, 1978).

22 Ibid., 292.

23 Ibid., 294.

24 Robert Schuman, "Declaration of 9 May 1950," in *Origins and Development of European Integration: A Reader and Commentary*, edited by Peter M.R. Stirk and David Weigall, 76 (London: Pinter, 1999).

25 Drawn largely from Sherrill Brown Wells, "Robert Schuman (1886–1963)," in *Encyclopedia of the European Union*, edited by Desmond Dinan (Boulder: Lynne Rienner, 1998).

26 François Duchêne, "Jean Monnet," in *Encyclopedia of the European Union*, edited by Dinan, 347.

27 Roy Jenkins, *European Diary, 1977–1981*, 220 (London: Collins, 1989).

28 Schuman, "Declaration of 9 May 1950," 76.

29 John Gillingham, *Coal, Steel, and the Rebirth of Europe, 1945–1955: The Germans and French from Rhur to Conflict to Economic Community*, 319 (Cambridge, UK: Cambridge University, 1991).

30 Sir Anthony Eden, *Memoirs: Full Circle*, 32 (London: Cassell, 1960).

31 Pleven Plan, reproduced in Peter Stirk and David Weigall, eds., *The Origins and Development of European Integration*, 108–109.

32 Urwin, *The Community of Europe*, 64–65.

33 Monnet, *Memoirs*, 398–404.
34 Desmond Dinan, "Crises in EU History," in *The European Union in Crisis*, edited by Desmond Dinan, Neill Nugent, and William E. Paterson, 16–32 (London: Macmillan, 2017).
35 Messina Resolution, cited in David Weigall and Peter Stirk, eds., *The Origins and Development of the European Community*, 94 (Leicester, UK: Leicester University Press, 1992).
36 Urwin, *The Community of Europe*, 76.
37 Ibid., 76–77.
38 Desmond Dinan, *Europe Recast: A History of European Union*, 4th ed., 63 (Boulder: Lynne Rienner, 2010).

BIBLIOGRAPHY

Dinan, Desmond, *Europe Recast: A History of European Union*, 4th ed. (Boulder: Lynne Rienner, 2010).
Dinan, Desmond, "Crises in EU History," in *The European Union in Crisis*, edited by Desmond Dinan, Neill Nugent, and William E. Paterson, 16–32 (London: Macmillan, 2017).
Duchêne, François, *Jean Monnet: The First Statesman of Interdependence*. (New York: W.W. Norton, 1995).
Duchêne, François, "Jean Monnet," in *Encyclopedia of the European Union*, edited by Desmond Dinan, 347 (Basingstoke, UK: Palgrave Macmillan, 1998).
Eden, Sir Anthony, *Memoirs: Full Circle* (London: Cassell, 1960).
Gilbert, Mark, *Surpassing Realism: The Politics of European Integration Since 1945* (Lanham, MD: Rowman and Littlefield, 2003).
Gilbert, Mark, *European Integration: A Concise History* (Lanham, MD: Rowman and Littlefield, 2012).
Gillingham, John, "Jean Monnet and the European Coal and Steel Community: A Preliminary Appraisal," in *Jean Monnet: The Path to European Unity*, edited by Douglas Brinkley and Clifford Hackett, 131–137 (New York: St. Martin's Press, 1991).
Gillingham, John, *Coal, Steel, and the Rebirth of Europe, 1945–1955: The Germans and French from Rhur to Conflict to Economic Community* (Cambridge, UK: Cambridge University, 1991).
Gillingham, John, *European Integration, 1950–2003: Superstate or New Market Economy?* (Cambridge: Cambridge University Press, 2003).
Gorst, Anthony and Lewis Johnman, *The Suez Crisis* (London: Routledge, 1997).
Heater, Derek, *The Idea of European Unity* (New York: St. Martin's Press, 1992).
Hitchcock, William I., *The Struggle for Europe: The Turbulent History of a Divided Continent* (New York: Anchor Books, 2004).
Hogan, Michael J., *The Marshall Plan: America, Britain, and the Reconstruction of Western Europe, 1947–52* (Cambridge: Cambridge University Press, 1987).
Hourani, Albert, "Conclusions," in *Suez 1956: The Crisis and Its Consequences*, edited by William Roger Louis and Roger Owen (Oxford: Clarendon Press, 1989).
Jenkins, Roy, *European Diary, 1977–1981* (London: Collins, 1989).
Judt, Tony, *Postwar: A History of Europe since 1945* (New York: Penguin, 2005).
Kaiser, Wolfram and Antonio Varsori, eds., *European Union History: Themes and Debates* (New York/London: Palgrave Macmillan, 2010).
Kershaw, Ian, *The Global Age: Europe 1950–2017* (New York: Viking, 2019).
Levy, Jack S., *War in the Modern Great Power System, 1495–1975* (Lexington, KY: University Press of Kentucky, 1983).
Lundestad, Geir, *The United States and Western Europe Since 1945* (Oxford: Oxford University Press, 2003).
Milward, Alan S., *The Reconstruction of Western Europe 1945–51* (Berkeley: University of California Press, 1984).
Monnet, Jean, *Memoirs*, trans. Richard Mayne (Garden City, NY: Doubleday, 1978).
Morgan, Roger, "The Transatlantic Relationship," in *Europe and the World: The External Relations of the Common Market*, edited by Kenneth J. Twitchett (London: Europa, 1976).

Office of the Historian, *Foreign Relations of the United States*, vol. 3 (Washington, DC: US Department of State, 1947).

Palmer, Michael and John Lambert, eds., *European Unity: A Survey of European Organizations* (London: George Allen and Unwin, 1968).

Schuman, Robert, "Declaration of 9 May 1950," in *The Origins and Development of European Integration: A Reader and Commentary*, edited by Peter M.R. Stirk and David Weigall, 76 (London: Pinter, 1999).

Sked, Alan and Chris Cook, *Post-War Britain: A Political History* (Harmondsworth, UK: Penguin, 1984).

Urwin, Derek W., *The Community of Europe*, 2nd ed. (London: Longman, 1995).

Van Dormael, Armand, *Bretton Woods: Birth of a Monetary System* (New York: Holmes and Meier, 1978).

Weigall, David and Peter Stirk, eds., *The Origins and Development of the European Community* (Leicester, UK: Leicester University Press, 1992).

Wells, Sherill Brown, "Robert Schuman (1886–1963)," in *Encyclopedia of the European Union*, edited by Desmond Dinan, 77 (Boulder: Lynne Rienner, 1998).

Zurcher, Arnold J., *The Struggle to Unite Europe 1940–58* (New York: New York University Press, 1958).

FURTHER READING

Alan S. Milward, *The Reconstruction of Western Europe 1945–51* (Berkeley: University of California Press, 1984); Michael Hogan, *The Marshall Plan: America, Britain, and the Reconstruction of Western Europe, 1947–52* (Cambridge: Cambridge University Press, 1987).

Two seminal studies of the Marshall Plan and its contribution to European integration.

William I. Hitchcock, *The Struggle for Europe: The Turbulent History of a Divided Continent* (New York: Anchor Books, 2004); Tony Judt, *Postwar: A History of Europe since 1945* (New York: Penguin, 2005); Ian Kershaw, *The Global Age: Europe 1950–2017* (New York: Viking, 2019).

Three excellent surveys of the history of postwar Europe.

Mark Gilbert, *European Integration: A Concise History* (Lanham, MD: Rowman and Littlefield, 2012); John Gillingham, *European Integration, 1950–2003: Superstate or New Market Economy?* (Cambridge: Cambridge University Press, 2003); Desmond Dinan, *Europe Recast: A History of European Union*, 4th ed. (Boulder: Lynne Rienner, 2010).

Three of the best general histories of European integration; Gillingham is particularly critical, writing of missed opportunities and bad decisions.

Wolfram Kaiser and Antonio Varsori, eds., *European Union History: Themes and Debates* (New York/London: Palgrave Macmillan, 2010).

An excellent overview of how historians and social scientists have conceptualized, written about, and debated the history of European integration.

François Duchêne, *Jean Monnet: The First Statesman of Interdependence* (New York: W.W. Norton, 1995).

A combined biography of Jean Monnet and history of European integration, written by Monnet's former speechwriter and press liaison officer.

CHAPTER 3

Stagnation and Renewal

The Single European Act and Maastricht

CHAPTER OVERVIEW

- After the Treaty of Rome the EU went through several rounds of enlargement, taking in the UK, Ireland, and Denmark in the 1960s, and Greece, Portugal, and Spain in the 1980s. Yet overall movement toward deeper economic and political integration stalled significantly during the 1960s and 1970s as member states sought to retain their own autonomy and prerogatives.
- The revitalization of the European project received its most significant impetus in more than a decade with the creation of the European Monetary System (EMS), which aimed to coordinate macroeconomic policies and regulate exchange rates, and the Single European Act (SEA), whose goal was the completion of the single market.
- Meanwhile, the sudden fall of communism in Eastern Europe and the Soviet Union from 1989 to 1991 caused a dramatic shift in direction for the EU. While the logic of economic integration embodied by the EMS and SEA was already propelling it toward a common currency, anxieties about the direction of Germany after the fall of the Berlin Wall moved the EU to take steps toward political union. The result was the historic Treaty on European Union – popularly known as the Maastricht treaty – which set a timetable for a common currency (the euro) and deepened political integration.

With the signing of the Treaty of Rome in 1958, the new European Economic Community (EEC) aimed to create a Western European internal market encompassing the free movement of people, goods, money, and services. Although in the 1960s and 1970s achieving this goal remained far in the future, the EEC nevertheless made tremendous progress in abolishing internal tariffs, building a single market for agricultural goods, and acting as a unified trade bloc in international trade negotiations. Rome's kick-start to economic integration also attracted new members: a first wave of enlargement added the UK, Denmark, and Ireland in the early 1970s, and a second wave in the 1980s added Greece, Spain, and Portugal.

However, moves toward fuller economic – not to mention political – integration were not as swift nor as straightforward as many European enthusiasts would have liked: the deepening of the European project appeared to stagnate during the 1960s and 1970s, plagued by member states' economic problems and reluctance to cede sovereignty on crucial economic issues. Yet economic risk created new opportunities and initiatives, and these materialized in the form of the EMS – designed to help coordinate the macroeconomic policies of member states – and the SEA, which sought the completion of a single market for the European Community by December 31, 1992. The SEA expanded the policy reach of European institutions and broke down some of the most difficult physical, fiscal, and technical obstacles to trade.

As economic integration continued to develop in the 1980s, the fall of communism across Eastern Europe and the Soviet Union galvanized greater political integration. The rapid implosion of communist power in the German Democratic Republic (East Germany) led inexorably to the question of German reunification, a prospect that alarmed many in Europe (including, most notably, the UK's Margaret Thatcher). Yet as a new unified Germany emerged, the German chancellor, Helmut Kohl, and French prime minister, François Mitterrand, took steps to anchor it more firmly in the West through the introduction of a common currency, the euro, and a fuller political integration with the creation of a "European Union." The result was the Treaty on European Union or Maastricht treaty, the most important EU treaty since Rome.

INTEGRATION TAKES ROOT (1958–1968)

Given the long history of inter-European hostilities and war, the integration of six Western European states under the auspices of the European Coal and Steel Community (ECSC), the EEC, and Euratom was a conspicuous achievement. There are barriers to the single market even today, but internal tariffs fell quickly enough in the early years of the EEC to allow the Six to agree on a common external tariff in July 1968 and to declare an industrial customs union. The single market expanded with the reduction of nontariff barriers to the movement of goods across borders (for example different technical or health and safety standards) during the 1960s and 1970s. Quota restrictions fell and huge gains in trade and productivity were made. It was, in economist Barry Eichengreen's view, "a golden age of growth" for the EEC.[1]

Other achievements burnished this "golden age":

- A fundamental goal of the Treaty of Rome had been agreement on a Common Agricultural Policy (CAP), which was achieved in 1968 with the acceptance of a watered-down version of a plan drawn up by the agriculture commissioner, Sicco Mansholt.[2] Its goals were to create a single market for agricultural products and to assure EEC farmers guaranteed prices for their produce. Although CAP initially encouraged both production and productivity, it was the largest single item in the budget and became enormously controversial (see Chapter 13).
- Under the Common Commercial Policy agreed to by the Treaty of Rome, the Six worked closely together on international trade negotiations and enjoyed influence they would not have had negotiating individually. The EEC acted as one, for example, in the Kennedy Round of General Agreement on Tariffs and Trade (GATT) negotiations during the mid-1960s and in reaching preferential trade agreements with eighteen former African colonies under the 1963 Yaoundé Convention (see Chapter 16).[3]
- Decision making was streamlined in April 1965 with the treaty establishing a Single Council and a Single Commission of the European Communities (the Merger Treaty). The decision-making process was fine-tuned further by the formalization in 1975 of regular summits of Community leaders coming together as the European Council (see Chapter 6). The EEC was finally made more democratic with the introduction in 1979 of direct elections to the European Parliament.

But there were serious problems as well. Even Jean Monnet had warned that "Europe will be established through crises and … the outcome will be the sum of the outcomes of those crises."[4] The failure of the European Defence Community and the European Political

Community had been early blows, but this was the result of a common core problem – excessive ambitiousness. Then came the "empty chair" crisis of 1965, whose structural implications were more worrying because they showed how far some member states were prepared to go to protect national interests.

At the heart of this crisis were French president Charles de Gaulle's attempts to discard the supranational elements of the Treaty of Rome and to build a Community dominated by France.[5] Several sparks set off the conflagration: demands from the European Parliament for more power, the fact that decision making by majority vote on certain issues in the Council of Ministers was scheduled to come into force on January 1, 1966 (thereby taking away the national veto), and a proposal by the European Commission that it replace its reliance on national contributions from EEC members with an independent source of income – seen as urgent to the challenges of financing CAP.

All these developments smacked of excessive supranationalism to the French, who insisted that EEC funding continue to come from national contributions, at least until 1970. The other five states disagreed, so in June 1965 France began boycotting meetings of the Council of Ministers, preventing any decisions from being made on new laws and policies. De Gaulle even went so far as to cast doubts on the future of the EEC unless the national veto was preserved. The crisis ceased only with the January 1966 Luxembourg Compromise (actually an agreement to disagree), by which the voting procedure in the Council of Ministers was changed. Unanimity remained the ideal, but members would be allowed to veto matters they felt adversely affected their national interests. This curbed the growth of the powers of the Commission, the European project's most ardent champion, and shifted more power into the hands of the member states (in the form of the Council of Ministers). This development, along with sagging economic fortunes and blows to the postwar welfare state across Europe in the 1970s, was to stall much of the forward momentum of the EU for well over a decade.

THE ROLE OF THE US

At the outset the US backed the idea of European integration. President John F. Kennedy announced in 1962 that the US looked on "this vast new enterprise with hope and admiration" and viewed Europe not as a rival but as "a partner with whom we can deal on a basis of full equality."[6] For the US, the Community not only promised valuable new trading opportunities, but might also help integrate West Germany into a peaceful Western Europe, improve Western Europe's prospects of standing up to the Soviets, and fortify the transatlantic community.[7] But in spite of the public show of transatlantic solidarity, there were transatlantic disagreements as well, and these sticking points contributed eventually in their own way to European integration. Western Europeans pondered the motives and implications of US foreign policy, and some were moved to question the prospects for real transatlantic agreement on key international problems.[8]

Early doubts had been raised by the Korean War. Europeans had initially been heartened at the US-led invasion to expel North Korean invaders from the South, but were then alarmed by the invasion of the North, which prompted an intervention by China and threatened to generate Soviet hostility. Following that came Suez, which saw the US at odds with the UK and France over the shape of the postwar international system. Then a series of events in the 1960s and 1970s rattled Europeans again, underscoring transatlantic policy differences and further convincing many Europeans of the need for the Community to develop policy independence from the US:

- When the Berlin wall was built in 1961, cutting off the Soviet-controlled east from the Allied-controlled west, Europeans were disappointed that the Kennedy administration did not take stronger action against the Soviets.
- In October 1962 the world teetered on the brink of the nuclear abyss during the Cuban missile crisis, when the US made decisions with little reference to their European NATO partners.[9]
- The mid-1960s saw an escalation of the war in Vietnam, and it was the US's turn to be disappointed in Europe: the Johnson administration hoped for political and military support from Europe but received none, and public demonstrations against the war were loud and vociferous in Western Europe; a 1967 poll found 80 percent of Europeans critical of US policy.[10]
- Finally, when the Nixon administration suspended the convertibility of the US dollar against gold in 1970 and then severed the link altogether in 1971 – in both cases without reference to the Europeans – even pro-American European leaders began to argue that Europe needed to unite in order to protect its interests.[11]

Despite these misgivings, however, and with the exception of anti-Vietnam demonstrations, European criticism of US policy was mostly muted. Still, Europeans wondered how much they could rely on the Americans, and the Americans felt slighted at how often the Europeans seemed unwilling to understand or support the American view of the world and its major threats. The disputes were to continue to grow – over the Middle East, over détente with the Soviets, and over nuclear weapons. The doubts sown in the 1960s and 1970s eventually exploded into the open in 2003, when the US invaded Iraq, and a newly assertive France and Germany made their opposition public (see Chapter 16).

Perhaps the most telling indicator of the changing transatlantic balance was the growing assertiveness of the Community as a global trading power. Progress on the single market may have been limited, there may have been difficulties with making agricultural policy work efficiently, and the road to economic and monetary union may have been bumpy, but on the trade front the Community was making great strides, and no country felt the effects more than the US. The Common Commercial Policy (CCP, see Chapter 15) meant strength through unity; the Six (and later, the Nine) wielded their combined powers and resources with considerable effect in the meeting chambers of GATT.[12] The Community and the US were each other's biggest trading partners and biggest sources of foreign investment, and they would ultimately become each other's biggest commercial competitors. Conflicts ignited between the two sides over agricultural exports, the steel industry, government subsidies, and concerns from the US about the rise of Fortress Europe, a unified trading bloc with external barriers working against US trade interests.[13]

ENLARGEMENT: LOOKING NORTH AND SOUTH (1960–1986)

The march toward progress in the European project received more momentum with a further growth in Community membership. The idea of enlargement was never far from the minds of its leaders since there was a limit to how much the EEC could achieve with just six members. The country most obvious by its absence was the UK – still Western Europe's major power – but although Churchill had been a champion of European integration during both the war and his years in opposition (1945–1951), neither the Labour government that ousted him in 1945 nor he, upon his return to office in 1951, took this philosophy any further. The UK still saw its interests lying with its empire and with the US, but the argument that joining the EEC might threaten its special relationship with the US was undermined by US support for the idea of a European Community.[14] Few in the UK government felt that the EEC had much potential;[15] but then came Suez, which finally shattered the UK's nostalgic idea that it was still a great power and shook the foundations of the Anglo-American relationship.

After being diverted briefly by its creation of EFTA, the European Free Trade Association (see Box 3.1), the UK began negotiating with the Six in early 1962, as part of a package deal that included Denmark, Ireland, and Norway. Denmark's motives for EEC membership were agricultural: it was producing three times as much food as it needed, and much of that was being exported to the UK. Furthermore, the EEC would be a big new market for Danish agricultural surpluses and foster Danish industrial development. Ireland saw the EEC as a potential boost for its industrial plans and as a means to reduce its reliance on agriculture and on the UK. Norway followed the UK's lead, owing to the importance of EEC markets.

Box 3.1 EFTA: An Escape Route for Brexit?

Dean Acheson, US secretary of state during the Truman administration, described the UK's decision not to negotiate on membership in the ECSC as its "great mistake of the postwar period."[16] Certainly it began a tradition of the UK dragging its feet on Europe and its overall ambivalent attitude toward the EEC and later the EU. But at this time it was not entirely alone in its reticence: several countries supported an early effort by the UK to organize an alternative to the EEC that would champion free trade without economic and political integration.

To that end, in January 1960, EFTA was founded with the signing of the Stockholm Convention by Austria, the UK, Denmark, Norway, Portugal, Sweden, and Switzerland. Membership in EFTA was voluntary (unlike the contractual arrangements set up for the EEC by the Treaty of Rome), and EFTA had no political goals and no institutions beyond a Council of Ministers that met two or three times a year and a group of permanent representatives serviced by a small secretariat in Geneva. Though EFTA helped cut tariffs it achieved relatively little over the long term. Several of its members did more trade with the EEC than with their EFTA partners, and questions surfaced about the UK's motives in pursuing the EFTA concept. It was a marriage of convenience, created to prove a point about the relative merits of a looser free trade arrangement with low tariffs.

It soon became clear that political influence in Europe lay with the EEC and that the UK risked political isolation if it stayed out. The continent had made impressive economic and political progress, and UK industry wanted access to the rich European market.[17] So in August 1961, barely fifteen months after the creation of EFTA, the UK applied for EEC membership at the same time as Denmark and Ireland. They were joined by Norway in 1962. With three of its seven members now trying to defect, EFTA lost much of its relevance, so the rest of its members – Austria, Portugal, Sweden, and Switzerland – all applied for associate membership in the EEC, followed by Malta and Spain. Today, EFTA comprises just four members: Iceland, Liechtenstein,[18] Norway, and Switzerland. However, in 1990, negotiations began on the creation of the European Economic Area (EEA), under which the remaining EFTA members would be extended the terms of the SEA (see below), in return for which they would accept the rules of the single market. The proposal made economic sense, given that 55 percent of EFTA exports went to the EC and 26 percent of EC exports went to EFTA.[19] All EFTA states joined the EEA, with the exception of Switzerland.

Curiously, EFTA has gained new visibility as a possible post-Brexit destination for the UK. For supporters, rejoining EFTA would keep the benefits of a single market, since EEA signatories enjoy a special trade relationship with the EU. Opponents have pointed out that joining EFTA and the EEA would continue to bind the UK to most EU rules (including those concerning the free movement of people) and require it to contribute money to support EU programs – all this without a seat at the EU decision-making table. Whether the UK will ultimately seek EFTA membership, after Brexit it will automatically be outside the EU, EFTA, and the EEA – for the time being, at least, an isolated trade partner within Europe.

UK membership seemed set for success, but then its application was tripped up by Charles de Gaulle, an Anglophobe who had plans for an EEC built around a Franco-German axis. He saw the UK as a rival to French influence in the EEC, and resented the UK's lukewarm response to the early integrationist moves of the 1950s. He also felt that UK membership would cede too much influence to the US in Europe, a concern that seemed to be confirmed at the end of 1962 when the UK accepted the US offer of Polaris missiles as delivery vehicles for the UK's nuclear warheads. For his part, Monnet was eager for UK membership and even tried to convince West German chancellor Konrad Adenauer by suggesting that he refuse to sign a Franco-German Friendship Treaty unless de Gaulle accepted the UK's application. But Adenauer thought that the development of the Franco-German axis was key, and had a close relationship with de Gaulle.[20]

In the space of just ten days in January 1963, de Gaulle vetoed the UK's application and signed the treaty with Germany. He upset the UK and some of his own EEC partners by reaching the veto decision unilaterally and making the announcement at a press conference in Paris. Since the UK's application was part of a package that included those of Denmark, Ireland, and Norway, they were turned down as well. Undeterred, the UK applied again in 1966 and was vetoed for a second time by de Gaulle, who was still worried about the influence within the EEC that UK membership would afford to the US, and also keen to ensure that French interests in the CAP were not undermined. Following de Gaulle's resignation as president of France in 1969, the UK applied for a third time, and this time its application was accepted, along with those of Denmark, Ireland, and Norway. Following membership negotiations in 1970 and 1971, the UK, Denmark, and Ireland finally joined the EEC in January 1973; Norway would have joined also, but a Norwegian public referendum in September 1972 narrowly went against membership, thanks mainly to the concerns of farmers and fishing communities. The Six had now become the Nine.

A second round of enlargements, which came in the 1980s, pushed the borders of the EEC farther south. Greece had made its first overtures to the EEC during the late 1950s but was turned down on the grounds that its economy was too underdeveloped. It was given associate membership in 1961 as a prelude to full accession, which might have come sooner had it not been for the Greek military coup of April 1967. With the return to civilian government in 1974, Greece applied almost immediately for full membership. Though the Commission felt that Greece's economy was still too weak, the Greek government responded that EEC membership would strengthen its attempts to rebuild democracy. The Council of Ministers agreed, negotiations opened in 1976, and Greece came aboard in January 1981.

MAP 3.1 Growth of the EU, 1952–1986.

Portugal and Spain had requested negotiations for associate membership in 1962, but both were dictatorships. Although the EEC treaty said that "any European State may apply to become a member of the Community," democracy was, in practice, a basic pre-condition. Spain received a preferential trade agreement in 1970 and Portugal in 1973, but only with the overthrow of the Marcelo Caetano regime in Portugal in 1974 and the death of Francisco Franco in Spain in 1975 was the possibility of EEC membership for the two states seriously considered. Despite their relative poverty, problems over fishing rights, and concerns about Portuguese and Spanish workers moving north in search of work, the EEC felt that membership would nurture democracy in the Iberian Peninsula and help link the two countries more closely to NATO and Western Europe. Negotiations opened in 1978 and 1979, and Portugal and Spain joined the club in January 1986, bringing EEC membership to twelve.[21]

The doubling of the membership of the EEC had several political and economic consequences: it increased the international influence of the EEC (which was now the largest economic bloc in the world), complicated the Community's decision-making processes, reduced the overall influence of France and Germany, and – by bringing in the poorer Mediterranean states – altered the internal economic balance. Rather than enlarging any farther, it was deemed time to strengthen the relationships among the existing twelve members. Applications ensued by Turkey (1987), Austria (1989), and Cyprus and Malta (1990) and although East Germany entered through the back door with the reunification of Germany in October 1990, there was to be no further enlargement until 1995.

TOWARD ECONOMIC AND MONETARY UNION (1969–1993)

The Treaty of Rome had mentioned the need to "coordinate" economic policies but had given the Community no specific powers to ensure this result, and coordination in practice meant little more than "polite ritualistic consultation."[22] Proposals to go further went head to head with concerns about loss of national sovereignty, and EEC leaders disagreed about whether to move first on economic union (the coordination of economic policies) or on monetary union (the creation of a single currency).[23] Following agreement on the principle of economic and monetary union (EMU) at a 1969 summit of EEC leaders at The Hague, it was decided to move on the economic and monetary fronts simultaneously, with the achievement of fixed exchange rates in stages by 1980.[24] The Six accordingly agreed to work to hold exchange rates steady relative to one another and to maintain the value of national currencies within ±2.25 percent of the US dollar in a structure colorfully known as the "snake in the tunnel" (a reference to the way values could go up and down within a defined band). They would meanwhile make more effort to coordinate national economic policies, with their finance ministers meeting at least three times annually.

The timing for this decision could not have been worse. The snake was launched in April 1972, just eight months after the Nixon administration took the US off the gold standard, ending the Bretton Woods era of fixed exchange rates. Nixon blamed the problems of Bretton Woods largely on the protectionism of the Community and its unwillingness to take more responsibility for the costs of defense, when in fact the inflationary effects on the US economy of the war in Vietnam were chiefly to blame.[25] The end of Bretton Woods brought international monetary turbulence, which was amplified in 1973 by an international energy crisis. In their anxiety to control inflation and encourage economic growth, several EC member states abandoned the snake: the UK, Denmark, and Ireland fled within weeks of joining; France refused to join, then joined, then left in 1974, then rejoined in 1975, then left again.[26]

A new approach emerged in March 1979, mainly on the initiative of the new West German chancellor, Helmut Schmidt, who was upset with the failure of the Carter administration in the US to take action to strengthen the dollar.[27] The EMS replaced the snake with an Exchange Rate Mechanism (ERM) (operating on a similar basis) founded on a European currency unit (ECU). The goal of the EMS was to create a zone of monetary stability, with governments moving to keep their currencies as stable as possible relative to the ECU, whose value was calculated on the basis of a basket of national currencies, weighted according to their relative strengths (the deutschmark made up nearly 33 percent, the French franc nearly 20 percent, the Dutch guilder 10 percent, and so on). The hope was that the ECU would become the go-to means of settling international debts between EC members, psychologically preparing them for the eventual introduction of a single currency.

EMU advanced further in 1989 with the elaboration by Commission president, Jacques Delors, of a three-stage plan:

1   The establishment of free capital movement and greater monetary and economic cooperation between the member states and their central banks
2   Greater cooperation among central banks, close monitoring of the EMS, and coordination of the monetary policies of the member states
3   The fixing of exchange rates and the creation of a single currency.[28]

European leaders approved the plan in June 1989, and it was later agreed that member states would have to meet several economic "convergence criteria" (including low inflation and interest rates) before they could adopt the single currency. If at least seven states met the criteria, a date would be set for stage three: the establishment of a European Central Bank responsible for setting monetary policy, thus paving the way for the single currency. The plan was easier said than done, however, and several member states found that the effort of controlling exchange rates caused their economies to overheat. Subsequently, several exchange rate realignments were made to help member states build monetary stability, but turbulence in world money markets escalated in the early 1990s, and the deutschmark came under pressure following German reunification in October 1990.[29] In 1992 and 1993, the ERM came close to collapse: the UK and Italy joined, then pulled out, and Ireland, Portugal, and Spain devalued their currencies. Clearly, monetary union was still a rough work in progress.

COMPLETING THE SINGLE MARKET: THE SINGLE EUROPEAN ACT (1983–1993)

At the heart of the Treaty of Rome lay the goal of building a single market that would pave the way for the "four freedoms": the free movement of people, money, goods, and services. Despite progress during the 1960s, nontariff barriers persisted, including different technical standards and quality controls, different health and safety standards, and different levels of indirect taxation. Progress in the 1970s was handicapped by inflation and unemployment and by the temptation of member states to protect their home industries.[30] European corporations also faced mounting competition from the US and Japan, particularly in new technology. As a counter measure, a decision was made in 1983 to revisit the single market project. A 1985 intergovernmental conference convened to discuss the necessary steps (see Box 3.2), and a Commission study (the *Cockfield Report*) listed 282 pieces of legislation that would need to be agreed to and implemented in order to remove all remaining nontariff barriers and create a true single market.[31]

The result was the SEA, which was signed in Luxembourg in February 1986 and came into force in July 1987. The first formal expansion of Community powers since the Treaty of Rome,[32] its goal was to complete the single market by midnight on December 31, 1992, by creating "an area without internal frontiers in which the free movement of goods, persons, services and capital is assured." As well as relaunching "Europe" and building the single biggest market and trading bloc in the world, the SEA brought many more specific changes:

Box 3.2 Outside the Lines: Intergovernmental Conferences in the EU

One of the key intergovernmental qualities of the EU can be found in the convening of summit meetings at which representatives of the member states discuss and reach decisions on broad strategic matters. Known as intergovernmental conferences (IGCs), these take place outside the institutionalized decision-making framework of the EU, typically over a period of weeks or even months. Depending on how they are defined, there have been as many as a dozen IGCs since 1950, but the most important have all been held since 1985.

The first IGC took place between June 1950 and March 1951 and focused on plans for the ECSC. Chaired by Jean Monnet, it led to the signing in April 1951 of the Treaty of Paris. The second IGC – which began in Messina, Sicily, in June 1955 and ended in Venice in May 1956 – led to the signing in March 1957 of the two Treaties of Rome, creating the EEC and Euratom. Several more IGCs were convened in the 1960s and 1970s, all dealing with more limited issues: a one-day IGC in April 1965 led to the Merger Treaty, another in 1970 discussed budgetary issues, and another in 1975 discussed the terms of the European Investment Bank.[33]

It was not until 1985 that the next substantial IGC was launched. Concerned about the lack of progress on integration and Europe's declining economic performance in relation to the US and Japan, representatives of the Nine met between September 1985 and January 1986, discussing and agreeing on the framework of the SEA. Two more IGCs took place during 1991 to examine political and monetary union, paving the way for the signature in 1992 of the Treaty on European Union.

Institutional reform and preparations for eastward enlargement were the top priorities of IGCs in 1996, 1997, and 2000, which resulted in agreement on the treaties of Amsterdam and Nice. Another IGC was convened in mid-2007 to discuss the content of the new Lisbon treaty in the light of the failure in 2005 of the Constitutional Treaty. In every case, the IGCs have been negotiated by national government ministers and permanent representatives, and so they continue to highlight the extent to which decision making on the EU's big initiatives still rests with the member states.

- The Community was given responsibility over new policy areas, such as the environment, research and development, and regional policy, and qualified majority voting in the Council of Ministers was extended to most areas of the single market.
- New powers were handed to the European Court of Justice, whose workload was eased by the creation of the Court of First Instance.
- Legal status was granted to meetings of heads of government under the European Council and to Community foreign policy coordination.
- Parliament was given more power relative to the Council of Ministers.
- Many internal passport and customs controls were eased or lifted and with the adoption of the separate Schengen agreement in 1985 (see Chapter 12) border checks were eliminated.
- Banks and companies enjoyed new freedoms to do business and sell their products and services throughout the Community.
- Protectionism was outlawed, and monopolies on everything from the supply of electricity to telecommunications were dismantled.

Despite the SEA's significant strides, a formidable challenge remained: addressing the problem of physical, fiscal, and technical barriers to trade was one thing, but economic disparities within the Community acted as additional handicaps. During the mid-1960s per capita gross domestic product in the Community's ten richest regions was nearly four times greater than that in its ten poorest regions. The gap closed during the early 1970s, but with the accession of the UK, Ireland, and Greece it grew to the point at which the richest regions were five times wealthier than the poorest.[34] The Commission-sponsored *Thomson Report* of 1973 concluded that these disparities presented an obstacle to a "balanced expansion" in economic activity and to EMU.[35] France and West Germany saw regional policy as a means of helping the UK integrate with its new partners, while the government of Prime Minister Edward Heath viewed it as a way of making EEC membership more palatable to Britons concerned about the potential costs of membership.[36] Reaching agreement in 1973, the Six launched the European Regional Development Fund (ERDF), designed to match existing national spending on the development of poorer regions, and aimed at projects that would create new jobs in industry and services or improve infrastructure.[37] While these structural funds accounted for only 18 percent of EC expenditures in 1984, they steadily moved up the budget and by 2007 still comprised about 46 percent of EU spending (about $62 billion). But despite the increased spending, regional disparities in the EU not only remained, they grew after 2004 as several relatively poor Eastern European states joined the EU.

With new attention focused in the 1980s on the reinvigoration of the single market, it became clear that social problems also required action, particularly those related to worker mobility, including industrial decline and long-term unemployment. The SEA now made "cohesion" a central part of economic integration, and new prominence was given to the Community's structural funds, including the ERDF, the European Social Fund, and the Cohesion Fund. Another boost for social policy came in 1989 with the Charter of Fundamental Social Rights for Workers (the Social Charter), promoting free movement of workers, fair pay, better living and working conditions, freedom of association, and protection of children and adolescents.

FROM COMMUNITY TO UNION (1970–1993)

The controversial idea of political integration received less attention from Community governments because of a prevailing feeling that there was little hope of building political union without first achieving economic union. A 1970 report authored by Belgian diplomat Etienne Davignon argued that foreign policy coordination would be a useful first step, especially given the growing divergence between US and Western European policies, made painfully obvious by Vietnam. He recommended quarterly meetings of the six foreign ministers, liaison among EC ambassadors in foreign capitals, and common EC instructions on certain matters for those ambassadors.[38] This so-called European Political Cooperation achieved some early successes, such as the 1970 joint EC policy declaration on the Middle East, the signing of the Yaoundé Conventions on aid to poorer countries, and collective European responses during the 1980s to the war in the Falklands, developments in Poland and Iran, and apartheid in South Africa.[39] But it was more reactive than proactive, its weaknesses illuminated during the 1990–1991 Persian Gulf crisis, when EC member states were divided over the US-led response to Iraq's invasion of Kuwait (see Chapter 6). Differences came to the fore as well in December 1991, when Germany unilaterally recognized Croatia and Slovenia without conferring with its EC partners.

Political union received renewed focus in 1984 by President François Mitterrand of France, who was determined to reassert the leadership of his country in the EC. It acquired special importance in the wake of the fall of the Berlin Wall and its resulting "German question" (that is, the consequences of the reunification of Germany for the EU). Mitterrand's goals for the EC now included a more thoroughgoing political union alongside its economic one so that reunified Germany would remain firmly tied to the fortunes of its western allies. West German chancellor Helmut Kohl, on the other hand, needed the French to sign off on his plan and timetable for unification (including the "4 + 2" agreement whereby the four allied powers and the two German states would negotiate the terms of the transition to unification) as well as securing the endorsement of the European Council for German unity. In return, Kohl agreed to move more quickly on monetary union and back a plan for a political union with more streamlined decision-making processes, a greater EU role in a number of policy areas, and a common foreign and security policy for the EU.[40]

The result was the 1990–1991 IGC on political union which led directly to the historic Treaty on European Union, agreed to at the Maastricht European Council summit in December 1991 and signed in February 1992. The many important changes enacted by the Maastricht treaty included the following:

- The creation of a new European Union, based on three "pillars" with their own rules: a reformed European Community which strengthened the European Parliament and European Council, a Common Foreign and Security Policy that would replace European Political Cooperation, and a third pillar which included new policy areas on justice and home affairs
- A timetable and conditions for the establishment of a single European currency
- The extension of EU responsibility to new policy areas such as consumer protection, public health, transportation, education, and social policy
- Increased cooperation on immigration and asylum, the creation of a European police intelligence agency (Europol) to combat organized crime and drug trafficking, and expanded regional funds for poorer member states
- New rights for European citizens and the formation of an ambiguous EU "citizenship" (with an EU passport), including the rights of citizens to live wherever they liked in the EU (subject to some limitations) and to vote in local and European elections.

Mark Gilbert argues that Maastricht represented an "unprecedented voluntary cession of national sovereignty," and that it was "less an international treaty than a tentative constitutional act."[41] The stakes were showcased by the debate over the wording of the draft treaty, which had originally mentioned the goal of federal union but was changed on the UK's insistence to "an ever closer union among the peoples of Europe, in which decisions are taken as closely as possible to the citizen." Problems also arose during ratification, when Danish voters caused political shock waves by rejecting the treaty in a June 1992 national referendum. Following agreement that Denmark could opt out of the single currency, common defense arrangements, European citizenship, and cooperation on justice and home affairs, a second referendum took place in May 1993, and Danes accepted the treaty. Following ratification in the other eleven states, the Maastricht treaty came into force in November 1993, nearly a year late.

Meanwhile, political agreement on the single currency was building in spite of doubts raised by the lessons of the ERM, and a decision was made in 1995 to call it the "euro." While supporters argued that a single currency would further economic integration by eliminating the cost of exchanging currency for both producers and consumers while removing exchange rate risks, critics charged that a common currency for the entire EU had a fatal flaw: national economies in the EU differed markedly from each other while labor flexibility and wage flexibility were too low, a situation that posed grave economic risks.[42] Essentially, this meant that unlike workers moving from one US state to another, if one country in the EU experienced a serious

PHOTO 3.1 Signing of the Treaty of Maastricht.

Source: © European Communities, 1992, EC – Audiovisual Service.

economic downturn (and therefore unemployment), workers would not willingly or easily move to those countries with more available, better-paying jobs.

Even more importantly, monetary policy (including the setting of interest rates and money supply) was to be directed by the EU through the European Central Bank, just as the US Federal Reserve Bank does. Consequently, individual countries would no longer be able to adjust their currencies to deal with the economic ups and downs of their economy. Yet in contrast to the US, fiscal policy (i.e., taxing and spending) was left in the hands of each of the member states of the EU, who oversaw their own budget surpluses or (crucially) deficits. In short, according to critics, monetary union had something of the worst of both worlds: member states had no power to set interest rates or devalue their currency to dig out of an economic hole, yet the EU as a collective had little power to ward off crises by controlling the spending and debt of its constituent parts. As would eventually become abundantly clear, few diagnoses could have been more accurate.

QUESTIONS TO CONSIDER

1 Two visions of European integration – widening, or EU enlargement, and deepening, or further economic and political integration of the existing members of the EU – are often seen as standing in tension with one another. How might this tension be illustrated in the development of the EU in the 1970s and 1980s?

2 Viewed from the perspective of today's EU, how important were the EMS and SEA? What did they do and what impact did they have on the European integration process?

3 What were Maastricht's most significant achievements? What internal and external developments drove the signing of this treaty?

NOTES

1 Barry Eichengreen, *The European Economy Since 1945: Coordinated Capitalism and Beyond*, 198 (Princeton, NJ: Princeton University Press, 2007).
2 See John Pinder, *European Community: The Building of a Union*, 78–86 (Oxford: Oxford University Press, 1991); Derek Urwin, *The Community of Europe*, 2nd ed., 132–135 (London: Longman, 1995).
3 Urwin, *The Community of Europe*, 131.
4 Jean Monnet, *Memoirs*, trans. Richard Mayne, 518 (Garden City, NY: Doubleday, 1978).
5 Don Cook, *Charles de Gaulle: A Biography*, 370–371 (New York: Putnam, 1983).
6 D.C. Watt, *Survey of International Affairs 1962*, 137 (London: Oxford University Press, 1970).
7 US State Department documents cited by Desmond Dinan, *Europe Recast: A History of European Union*, 4th ed., 91 (Boulder: Lynne Rienner, 2010).
8 For more details, see John McCormick, *The European Superpower*, chapter 2 (New York: Palgrave Macmillan, 2006).
9 See Frank Costigliola, "Kennedy, the European Allies, and the Failure to Consult," *Political Science Quarterly* 110, no. 1 (spring 1995): 105–123.
10 Richard J. Barnet, *The Alliance: America, Europe, Japan; Makers of the Post-War World*, 264 (New York: Simon and Schuster, 1983).
11 Roger Morgan, "The Transatlantic Relationship," in *Europe and the World: The External Relations of the Common Market*, edited by Kenneth J. Twitchett (London: Europa, 1976).
12 For details, see Sophie Meunier, *Trading Voices: The European Union in International Commercial Negotiations* (Princeton, NJ: Princeton University Press, 2005).
13 Klaus Heidensohn, *Europe and World Trade*, 133–138 (London: Pinter, 1995).
14 Dinan, *Europe Recast*, 70–71. For a detailed analysis of UK attitudes, see James Ellison, *Threatening Europe: Britain and the Creation of the European Community, 1955–58* (New York: St. Martin's Press, 2000).
15 Harold Macmillan, *Riding the Storm 1956–59*, 73 (New York: Harper and Row, 1971).
16 Dean Acheson, *Present at the Creation: My Years in the State Department*, 385 (New York: W.W. Norton, 1969).
17 Pinder, *European Community*, 46–47.
18 Liechtenstein is a principality between Austria and Switzerland with a population of 35,000. It is in a monetary and customs union with Switzerland, which also manages its diplomatic relations. It is one of several microstates within Europe that are independent but generally regarded as part of the larger states they border. (The others are Andorra, Monaco, San Marino, and Vatican City.)
19 Rene Schwok, "EC–EFTA Relations," in *The State of the European Community, Vol. 1: Policies, Institutions, and Debates in the Transition Years*, edited by Leon Hurwitz and Christian Lequesne (Boulder: Lynne Rienner, 1991).
20 See Charles Williams, *Adenauer. The Father of the New Germany*, chapters 10–12 (New York and Chichester: John Wiley & Sons, 2000).
21 In February 1985 Greenland became the first territory to leave the EEC. As a colony of Denmark, it had become part of the Community in January 1973, in spite of voting against membership out of concern for losing control of its fishing rights. In May 1979 it was granted self-government by Denmark, clearing the way for a vote to leave the Community.
22 Tommaso Paddoa-Schioppa, *Financial and Monetary Integration in Europe: 1990, 1992 and Beyond*, 18 (New York: Group of Thirty, 1990).
23 Urwin, *The Community of Europe*, 155.
24 Commission of the European Communities, "Economic and Monetary Union in the Community" (the *Werner Report*), *Bulletin of the European Communities*, Supplement 11 (1970).
25 Tony Judt, *Postwar: A History of Europe Since 1945*, 454 (New York: Penguin, 2005).
26 Eichengreen, *The European Economy Since 1945*, 248–249.
27 Mark Gilbert, *Surpassing Realism: The Politics of European Integration since 1945*, 138–152 (Lanham, MD: Rowman and Littlefield, 2003).
28 European Commission, *Report of the Committee for the Study of Economic and Monetary Union* (Luxembourg: Office of Official Publications, 1989).

29 Gilbert, *Surpassing Realism*, 227–261.
30 For details on the development of the single market program, see Kenneth A. Armstrong and Simon J. Bulmer, *The Governance of the Single European Market*, chapter 1 (Manchester, UK: Manchester University Press, 1998), and Gilbert, *Surpassing Realism*, chapter 6.
31 Commission of the European Communities, *Completing the Internal Market: The White Paper (the Cockfield Report)*, COM(85)310 (Brussels: Commission of the European Communities, 1985).
32 For an assessment of its initial results, see Michael Calingaert, "Creating a European Market," in *Developments in the European Union*, edited by Laura Cram, Desmond Dinan, and Neill Nugent (Basingstoke, UK: Macmillan, 1999).
33 Alfred Pijpers, "Intergovernmental Conferences," in *Encyclopedia of the European Union*, edited by Desmond Dinan, 294 (Basingstoke, UK: Macmillan, 1998).
34 Stephen George, *Politics and Policy in the European Community*, 3rd ed., 196 (Oxford: Oxford University Press, 1996).
35 Commission of the European Communities, *Report on the Regional Problems of the Enlarged Community (the Thomson Report)*, COM(73)550 (Brussels: Commission of the European Communities, 1973).
36 Dinan, *Europe Recast*, 149.
37 For an assessment of the ERDF and regional policy, see James Mitchell and Paul McAleavey, "Promoting Solidarity and Cohesion," in *Developments in the European Union*, edited by Cram, Dinan, and Nugent.
38 Urwin, *The Community of Europe*, 148.
39 Brian White, *Understanding European Foreign Policy*, chapter 4 (Basingstoke, UK: Palgrave Macmillan, 2001).
40 See Mary Elise Sarotte, *1989: The Struggle to Create Post–Cold War Europe*, 82–85 (Princeton: Princeton University Press, 1989). Also see Colette Mazzucelli, *France and Germany at Maastricht* (Routledge: London and New York, 1999).
41 Gilbert, *Surpassing Realism*, 212.
42 For a concise discussion, see Madeleine O. Hosli, *The Euro: A Concise Introduction to European Monetary Integration*, 15–16 (Boulder: Lynne Rienner, 2005).

BIBLIOGRAPHY

Acheson, Dean, *Present at the Creation: My Years in the State Department* (New York: W.W. Norton, 1969).

Armstrong, Kenneth A. and Simon J. Bulmer, *The Governance of the Single European Market* (Manchester, UK: Manchester University Press, 1998).

Barnet, Richard J., *The Alliance: America, Europe, Japan; Makers of the Post-War World* (New York: Simon and Schuster, 1983).

Calingaert, Michael, "Creating a European Market," in *Developments in the European Union*, edited by Laura Cram, Desmond Dinan, and Neill Nugent, 153–173 (London, UK: Palgrave, 1999).

Commission of the European Communities, "Economic and Monetary Union in the Community" (the *Werner Report*). *Bulletin of the European Communities*, Supplement 11 (1970).

Commission of the European Communities, *Report on the Regional Problems of the Enlarged Community (the Thomson Report)*, COM(73)550 (Brussels: Commission of the European Communities, 1973.).

Commission of the European Communities, *Completing the Internal Market: The White Paper (the Cockfield Report)*, COM(85)310 (Brussels: Commission of the European Communities, 1985).

Cook, Don, *Charles de Gaulle: A Biography* (New York: Putnam, 1983).

Costigliola, Frank, "Kennedy, the European Allies, and the Failure to Consult." *Political Science Quarterly* 110, no. 1 (spring 1995): 105–123.

Dinan, Desmond, *Europe Recast: A History of European Union*, 4th ed. (Boulder: Lynne Rienner, 2010).

Eichengreen, Barry, *The European Economy Since 1945: Coordinated Capitalism and Beyond* (Princeton, NJ: Princeton University Press, 2007).

Ellison, James, *Threatening Europe: Britain and the Creation of the European Community, 1955–58* (New York: St. Martin's Press, 2000).

European Commission, *Report of the Committee for the Study of Economic and Monetary Union* (Luxembourg: Office of Official Publications, 1989).

George, Stephen, *Politics and Policy in the European Community*, 3rd ed. (Oxford: Oxford University Press, 1996).

Gilbert, Mark, *Surpassing Realism: The Politics of European Integration Since 1945* (Lanham, MD: Rowman and Littlefield, 2003).

Heidensohn, Klaus, *Europe and World Trade* (London: Pinter, 1995).

Hosli, Madelin O., *The Euro: A Concise Introduction to European Monetary Integration* (Boulder: Lynne Rienner, 2005).

Judt, Tony, *Postwar: A History of Europe since 1945* (New York: Penguin, 2005).

Lundestad, Geir, *The United States and Western Europe Since 1945* (Oxford: Oxford University Press, 2003).

Macmillan, Harold, *Riding the Storm 1956–59* (New York: Harper and Row, 1971).

Mazzucelli, Colette, *France and Germany at Maastricht: Politics and Negotiations to Create the European Union* (London and New York: Routledge, 1997).

McCormick, John, *The European Superpower* (New York: Palgrave Macmillan, 2006).

Meunier, Sophie, *Trading Voices: The European Union in International Commercial Negotiations* (Princeton, NJ: Princeton University Press, 2005).

Mitchell, James and Paul McAleavey, "Promoting Solidarity and Cohesion," in *Developments in the European Union*, edited by Laura Cram, Desmond Dinan, and Neil Nugent, 174–192 (London: Palgrave, 1999).

Monnet, Jean, *Memoirs*, trans. Richard Mayne (Garden City, NY: Doubleday, 1978).

Morgan, Roger, "The Transatlantic Relationship," in *Europe and the World: The External Relations of the Common Market*, edited by Kenneth J. Twitchett (London: Europa, 1976).

Mulhearn, Charles and Howard Vane, *The Euro: Its Origins, Development and Prospects* (Northampton, MA: Edward Elgar, 2008).

Paddoa-Schioppa, Tommaso, *Financial and Monetary Integration in Europe: 1990, 1992 and Beyond* (New York: Group of Thirty, 1990).

Pijpers, Alfred, "Intergovernmental Conferences," in *Encyclopedia of the European Union*, edited by Desmond Dinan, 201 (Basingstoke, UK: Palgrave Macmillan, 1998).

Pinder, John, *European Community: The Building of a Union* (Oxford: Oxford University Press, 1991).

Sarotte, Mary Elise, *1989: The Struggle to Create Post–Cold War Europe* (Princeton: Princeton University Press, 1989).

Schwok, Rene, "EC–EFTA Relations," in *The State of the European Community, Vol. 1: Policies, Institutions, and Debates in the Transition Years*, edited by Leon Hurwitz and Christian Lequesne, 53–65 (Boulder: Lynne Rienner, 1991).

Stirk, Peter M.R. and David Weigall, eds., *The Origins and Development of European Integration: A Reader and Commentary* (London: Pinter, 1999).

Urwin, Derek W., *The Community of Europe*, 2nd ed. (London: Longman, 1995).

Watt, D.C., *Survey of International Affairs 1962* (London: Oxford University Press, 1970).

White, Brian, *Understanding European Foreign Policy* (Basingstoke, UK: Palgrave Macmillan, 2001).

Williams, Charles, *Adenauer. The Father of the New Germany* (New York and Chichester: John Wiley & Sons, 2000).

FURTHER READING

Peter M.R. Stirk and David Weigall, eds., *The Origins and Development of European Integration: A Reader and Commentary* (London: Pinter, 1999).

>Tells the history of European integration through Maastricht with documents, speeches, treaties, white papers, and excerpts from key texts.

Geir Lundestad, *The United States and Western Europe Since 1945* (Oxford: Oxford University Press, 2003).
> An excellent survey of transatlantic relations up until the Iraq war, showing clearly how and why the Americans and the Europeans could not always agree.

Barry Eichengreen, *The European Economy Since 1945: Coordinated Capitalism and Beyond* (Princeton, NJ: Princeton University Press, 2007).
> A detailed assessment of the impact of integration on European economic growth.

Colette Mazzucelli, *France and Germany at Maastricht: Politics and Negotiations to Create the European Union* (London and New York: Routledge, 1997).
> A riveting account of the negotiations between France and Germany on political and monetary union.

Charles Mulhearn and Howard Vane, *The Euro: Its Origins, Development and Prospects* (Northampton, MA: Edward Elgar, 2008).
> Provides a good overview of the euro against the backdrop of European integration and the steps leading to its introduction, including discussions of the ERM and EMU.

CHAPTER 4

Unity and Upheaval

The Eurozone, the Treaty of Lisbon,
and Crises in the EU

CHAPTER OVERVIEW

- The fall of the Berlin Wall and the end of the Cold War spawned an increasingly self-confident and influential EU. New rounds of expansion pushed the EU farther north and (most significantly) farther east. The initial post–Cold War era also brought significant deepening: a new joint currency (the euro), far-reaching institutional changes in the treaties of Amsterdam, Nice, and Lisbon, and a more independent and vigorous foreign policy.
- Yet these triumphs were followed by a severe financial and debt crisis in the eurozone and immediately after that an unprecedented migration crisis. Both exposed the limits of elite-led efforts to move the Union toward further integration as well as the inability of the EU to take quick and decisive action in the face of serious challenges.
- As a further blow, the UK has left the EU, the so-called "Brexit." Some analysts initially warned that Brexit might prove to be a final fatal wound to the EU and trigger the eventual breakup of the bloc. Yet despite the fact that it continues to suffer from serious concerns about its democratic accountability and ability to act decisively, the design flaws of its common currency, and the strong tailwind both of these have given to anti-EU populists across the continent, there are few signs of a fundamental weakening, as the EU has moved forward, garnering support from Europeans who acknowledge its important value and achievements. Whether the impact of the COVID-19 pandemic will change this balance is not yet clear.

With the fall of the Berlin Wall and the end of the Cold War, the European project gained new prestige and importance and the EU evolved in fundamental ways. It began to prepare for expansion to include the states of Eastern Europe (including the territory of the former East Germany) once under the Soviet imperium, a move that would stand as a potent symbol of the end of the Cold War. It also deepened with the signing of the 1992 Treaty on European Union – popularly known as the Maastricht treaty – seeking to further integrate the states of what was now to be known as the EU both politically and economically. Economic integration later found its most substantial, as well as symbolic, expression in the creation of a new joint currency, the euro. Successful enlargement also created its own challenges, as the institutional machinery designed for twelve states was not well suited for two dozen or more. Further tinkering with institutional arrangements in the treaties of Amsterdam and Nice were deemed insufficient, and thus a new European constitutional treaty was envisaged that could provide an institutional framework – and an overarching vision – commensurate with the importance and power of the EU. The rejection of the treaty by French and Dutch voters in 2005 indicated that EU elites may have reached too high; accordingly, a more modest, if not substantially different, framework emerged in the Treaty of Lisbon in 2009.

The EU today is a very different actor on the international stage than it was in its early years. It is a global powerhouse: the world's second-largest economy (after China but ahead of the US), its second-largest exporter and importer, and – with a population of almost 450 million – significantly larger than the US. It has also acquired newfound independence in foreign policy, however much it still punches below its economic weight. Both substantively and symbolically, the most recent rounds of enlargement have transformed the EU from a Western European economic club to one that includes most of Europe, such that "Europe" today is synonymous with the EU.

At the same time, a series of crises over the last decade have exposed serious problems in the European project:

- A global financial crisis beginning in 2007 soon after spilled over into a massive government debt crisis which demonstrated some of the weaknesses baked into the euro.
- A migration crisis beginning in late 2014 underscored the EU's inability to act quickly and decisively and highlighted serious east–west rifts among the member states.
- The UK's decision to leave the EU demonstrated the difficulty the EU has had in convincing a broad swath of Europeans (including of course the British people) that the EU works on their behalf – the most serious reminder of its longstanding "democratic deficit."

Although forecasts of the death of the euro (not to mention the EU as a whole) have not been merely premature but misplaced, these three crises gave succor to the increasingly loud voice of anti-EU populists across the continent. Whether the impacts of the COVID-19 pandemic – primarily the emboldening of a few increasingly authoritarian EU states (such as Hungary) and the virus's potential to fundamentally alter free movement within the EU – will be lasting is difficult to say. Nevertheless, it is clear that amidst all these crises, most Europeans back the EU

THE EURO ARRIVES (1995–2002)

Leaders of the member states met in May 1998 to decide which applicants met the criteria outlined under the Maastricht treaty to join the new common currency. It was decided that all but Greece were either ready or were making good progress,[1] but the UK, Denmark, and Sweden declined to adopt the euro, at least initially. In June 1998 the new European Central Bank took ownership for monetary policy in the eurozone, and in January 1999 the euro was launched when participating states permanently fixed their currency exchange rates relative to one another and to the euro.

The monumental task of preparing consumers and businesses in the eurozone for the physical switch to the euro proceeded, as did the printing of fourteen billion new euro banknotes and fifty-six billion euro coins. There was much discussion about the designs of the banknotes, which could not be tied to any one country but instead had to capture general European themes. The final decision was to use designs based on styles of architecture that were found throughout Europe. As for the coins, one side had a common design while the other featured designs peculiar to the participating states: so, for example, the Belgians, the Dutch, and the Spanish chose images of their monarchs, Ireland chose the Celtic harp, France used an image of Marianne (a mythical icon of liberty), and Germany used the German eagle.

With these distinct national emblems in place, the final switch to the euro began on January 1, 2002, as consumers and businesses turned in their old coins and banknotes for euros. The original plan was to make the transition in a period of six months, but the new currency found fast footing: within a month the euro was accounting for 95 percent of cash payments in participating countries, and the switch was largely complete by the end of February. After years of often heated discussion, the single currency was finally a reality. Gone were deutschmarks, drachmas, escudos, francs, guilders, lire, markkas, pesetas, punts, and schillings, and for the first time since the Roman era, much of Europe had a single currency. It was a remarkable achievement, standing as one of the most substantial steps yet taken in the process of European integration.

Not everyone climbed aboard the Euro train: Denmark and Sweden turned down membership in the euro in national referendums, so the focus of interest now switched to the UK, where debate about whether or not to join was heated. The government of Tony Blair set five criteria that would have to be met (including assurance that there would be no negative impact on jobs, financial services, or foreign investment) and insisted that a national referendum be held on the issue. Blair himself was in favor, but opinion polls regularly found a large majority opposed to adoption, and the referendum was repeatedly postponed. In January 2007, Slovenia became the thirteenth country to adopt the euro, with Cyprus and Malta following in 2008, Slovakia in 2009, Estonia in 2011, Latvia in 2014, and Lithuania in 2015.

With the single market almost complete and the euro circulating in the majority of EU member states, the core goals of economic and monetary union should have been close to fruition. Yet unresolved concerns about low productivity and high unemployment persisted, to which the EU responded with the launch in March 2000 of the Lisbon Strategy. This initiative was aimed at making the EU "the most competitive and dynamic knowledge-based economy in the world" within ten years, with the specific goals of liberalizing telecommunications and energy markets, improving European transport, and opening up labor markets.[2] But these high hopes did not anticipate the global financial crisis that erupted in 2007, followed by a government debt crisis in the eurozone in 2008, both of which sent policy makers reeling.

CHANGES TO THE TREATIES: AMSTERDAM AND NICE (1997–2001)

The ink had barely dried on the Maastricht treaty before EU leaders agreed that a new intergovernmental conference should be convened to take stock of the progress of European integration and to discuss the institutional and policy changes that many felt were vital in light of the projected growth of the EU to a membership of twenty countries or more. The result was the Treaty of Amsterdam, signed in October 1997 and enacted in May 1999.[3] Much was expected of the treaty, but it fell short of moving Europe closer to political union, and the leaders of the member states were unable to agree on substantial changes in the structure of EU institutions. Plans were confirmed for enlargement of the EU to the east, the goal of launching the single currency in January 1999 was cemented, and more focus was shifted to policies on gender equality (see Box 4.1), asylum, immigration, unemployment, social policy, health protection, consumer protection, the environment, and foreign affairs.

Box 4.1 Gendering the EU

The EU remained very much a "man's club" in its first several decades, barely glancing at the rights of women. Yet a key legal component for actions against nondiscrimination on the basis of gender in the EU was already articulated in Article 119 of the Treaty of Rome which stated that "Each Member State shall ... ensure and subsequently maintain the application of the principle that men and women should receive equal pay for equal work." It was not until a 1976 EU Court of Justice decision, *Defrenne* v. *Sabena*, however, that this provision became a tool to drive forward sweeping attempts to ensure gender equality. In this historic case, Gabrielle Defrenne, a flight attendant with the Belgian national airline, Sabena, had been forced into a lower paying job under a company policy that required female flight attendants, unlike their male counterparts, to retire at age forty. Defrenne argued that the lower pension rates she would subsequently receive violated Article 119. The Court of Justice agreed, affirming the principle of direct effect (see Chapter 8).

The introduction of direct elections to the European Parliament (EP) in 1979 raised women's share of seats from 1 percent to 16 percent, providing a new staging ground for efforts to extend and implement gender equality across all member states. Several major directives followed over the next decade, expanding the equal pay cause to include equal access to training, promotion, pensions and other labor market benefits, working conditions (including maternity leave), and protection against sexual harassment. In 1996 the Commission mandated the balanced participation of women and men during all stages of the policy process as well as in regard to policy substance, also known as "gender mainstreaming." The Treaty of Amsterdam elevated gender equality to a fundamental right of the EU, giving EU institutions new powers to monitor and fight discrimination on the basis of sex. Gender equality was also added to the EU's list of "chief tasks," along with securing high employment, sustainable economic development, and inclusive social protection.

Incorporated into the Charter of Fundamental Rights, the Treaty of Lisbon, and a host of recast directives over the last two decades, gender equality has become integral to the *acquis communautaire*, the body of EU laws, regulations, and jurisprudence that must be transposed into national law in all member states. However far nondiscrimination and full gender equality in the EU remain from full realization, it is nevertheless true that women have made enormous strides, a development symbolized by the selection of Ursula von der Leyen, former German defense minister and mother of seven, as the first female EU Commission President.[4]

Another set of changes to the treaties was agreed to by EU leaders at a summit meeting in Nice, France, in December 2000. Less radical and headline-making than either the Single European Act or Maastricht, the key goal of the Treaty of Nice was to make the institutional changes needed to prepare for eastward expansion of the EU, and to make the EU more democratic and transparent. It proved to be a disappointment, though, doing little more than tinkering with the structure of the institutions to anticipate future enlargement; hence the size of the Commission was to be increased, with no country having more than one commissioner, the distribution of votes in the Council of Ministers was to be changed, agreement was reached on a redistribution and capping of the number of seats in the EP, and changes were made to the Court of Justice and the Court of First Instance. Agreement was also reached on a Charter of Fundamental

Rights of the European Union (see Chapter 8, Box 8.1), including an early warning mechanism designed to prevent breaches of the rights of member states.

The Treaty of Nice was signed in February 2001, and like the earlier treaties was to come into force when ratified by all the member states. But a surprise landed in June 2001, when voters in Ireland – where the constitution requires a referendum on all new EU treaties – rejected the terms of Nice. Opponents argued that it required the surrender of too much national control, particularly concerning the implications for Irish neutrality. Part of the problem, however, was simply low voter turnout: just 33 percent of voters cast a ballot, and just 54 percent of those said no. A second vote took place in Ireland in October 2002, following assurances that Ireland's neutrality on security issues would be respected. This time turnout was a more respectable 48 percent, and the treaty sailed through with a 63 percent majority.

Nice came into force in February 2003, but it went largely unnoticed because there had already been broader discussions in the European Council in 2001 about the need to make the EU more democratic and to bring it closer to its citizens. At the Laeken European Council in December, a decision was made to establish a convention to debate the overall framework for the EU: to draw up a draft constitutional treaty designed to simplify and replace all the treaties, to determine how to divide powers between the EU and the member states, to make the EU more democratic and efficient, to determine the role of national parliaments within the EU, and to pave the way for more enlargement. With these aims in mind, a convention took place in 2002–2003 under the presidency of former French president Valéry Giscard d'Estaing. The result of its deliberations was a draft constitutional treaty,[5] published in July 2003. By the time this constitutional treaty was sent to the member states for consideration in 2004, the membership of the EU was up to twenty-five, and it was agreed that all twenty-five had to approve before it could take effect. Generally speaking, bigger countries were happier with the draft than were smaller ones, due to concerns that their voices would not be heard. Some countries declared that government ratification would be enough, while others opted for national referendums. Eight countries endorsed the treaty in late 2004 and early 2005, including Germany, Italy, and Spain, but then negative public votes in France and the Netherlands in May and June 2005 generated shock waves. By February 2007 eighteen member states had endorsed the treaty,[6] but in its existing form it was dead, and debates had already begun about where to go next. The end result was the Treaty of Lisbon.

MORE ENLARGEMENT: LOOKING EAST (1994–2013)

Perhaps nowhere was the new power and influence of the EU more obviously on show than in the attraction it held for its Eastern European neighbors, many of which were now anxious to join the club. Just as Community membership had helped bring stability to Greece, Portugal, and Spain, so there were hopes that extending membership to former Eastern bloc countries would promote their transition to capitalism and democracy, open up new investment opportunities, and pull Eastern Europe into a strategic relationship with the West that could be useful if problems in (or with) Russia worsened. But the challenge was substantial, and the hurdles to be jumped were high; *The Economist* argued that it was as though the US had agreed to welcome into the union several Mexican states, with a commitment to bring them up to American standards of infrastructure and social provision.[7] The EU nonetheless signed agreements between 1994 and 1998 with several Eastern European countries that allowed for gradual movement toward free trade and were designed to prepare its co-signatories for eventual EU membership, including their commitment to democratic norms (see Box 4.2). In 1997 the EU launched Agenda 2000, a program that contained a list of all the measures that the European Commission felt needed to be agreed to in order to bring ten Eastern European states into the EU.

Negotiations on membership began in 1998–2000 with Bulgaria, Cyprus, the Czech Republic, Estonia, Hungary, Latvia, Lithuania, Malta, Poland, Romania, Slovakia, and Slovenia. Following the completion of negotiations in December 2002, all but Bulgaria and Romania were invited to join the EU. All accepted, and all but Cyprus held referendums that came down in favor of membership. In May 2004 ten new members joined the EU, pushing membership up to twenty-five and for the first time assimilating former Soviet republics (Estonia, Latvia, and Lithuania). The population of the EU swelled by nearly 20 percent, but – given the relative poverty of the new members – its economic wealth grew by just 5 percent. In a second phase of eastern enlargement, Bulgaria and Romania joined the EU in January 2007, while Croatia completed negotiations for accession in 2011 and joined the EU in July 2013 (See Table 4.1 and Map 4.1.)

Eastward expansion was symbolically important in three ways: it provided final and emphatic confirmation of the end of the Cold War division of Europe, was a decisive step in the transformation of former Soviet bloc states from communism to liberal democracy, and gave new meaning to the word *European*. Until 2004 the EU had been a Western European league, and the absence of eastern neighbors from membership reflected the political, economic, and social divisions of the continent. By 2007, almost all of Europe had finally been brought together under the umbrella of the EU.

Today, Albania, North Macedonia, Montenegro, Serbia, and Turkey have been accepted as candidate countries, meaning that membership has been agreed to in principle, while Kosovo, and Bosnia-Herzegovina have applied for membership and have signed "stabilization and association" agreements with the EU. But the prospects for further enlargement any time soon are slim, given the difficulties it has had absorbing Eastern European states and the fact that these candidates face significant political and economic problems. Moreover, the Ukraine crisis and tensions with Russia (see Chapter 16) have made further eastward expansion all but politically impossible in the near future.[8]

TABLE 4.1 Development of the EU	
Year Member States	Cumulative Population (Millions)
1952 Belgium, France, Italy, Luxembourg, Netherlands, West Germany	160
1973 UK, Denmark, Ireland	233
1981 Greece	249
1986 Portugal, Spain	322
1990 East Germany (via German reunification)	339
1995 Austria, Finland, Sweden	379
2004 Cyprus, Czech Republic, Estonia, Hungary, Latvia, Lithuania, Malta, Poland, Slovakia, Slovenia	
2007 Bulgaria, Romania	500
2013 Croatia	504 (2020 = 513)
2020 UK (withdrawal after Brexit)	447

MAP 4.1 Growth of the EU, 1990–2013.

A CONSTITUTION BY ANOTHER NAME: THE TREATY OF LISBON (2001–2008)

With the failure of the constitutional treaty in 2005, EU governments pondered how best to move forward, eventually deciding to revive much of the content of the treaty in the form of what was ultimately named the Treaty of Lisbon. After an intergovernmental conference in 2007 in Lisbon, where it was signed the following December, its key provisions were:

- The creation of the positions of President of the European Council and a High Representative of the Union for Foreign Affairs and Security Policy – an EU foreign minister in all but name

Box 4.2 Democracy and the Free Market: The Copenhagen Criteria

With the institutional and policy change emanating from Maastricht, the time was ripe for new consideration of enlargement. The territory of the EU had expanded in 1990 as a result of German reunification, but this was a domestic matter rather than a broader issue of enlargement. Nonetheless, it added a new dimension to discussions about the eventual possibility of EU membership for Eastern European states, which was given new meaning by the end of the Cold War and the drawing aside of the iron curtain. It was always informally understood that countries applying for membership in the European Community should be European, although there was doubt about exactly what this meant. There was little question of rejecting an application from Morocco in 1987, while the eight remaining non-EU Western European countries all had strong prospects for joining. But further east the lines became fuzzy. Assuming that Europe's eastern border is marked by the Ural Mountains (deep inside Russia), eighteen more countries theoretically qualified for membership in 1992: seven in Eastern Europe, six former Soviet republics, and five former Yugoslavian states.

Focus sharpened in June 1993 when the European Council, meeting in Copenhagen, agreed on a set of terms for membership. The so-called Copenhagen criteria required that applicant states must:

- Be democratic, with respect for human rights and the rule of law
- Have a functioning free-market economy and the capacity to cope with the competitive pressures of capitalism
- Be able to take on the obligations of the *acquis communautaire* (the body of laws and regulations already adopted by the EU).

To ensure that it is meets these commitments, each candidate for membership is monitored by the Commission, including its application of EU legislation. Throughout the process, the Commission is tasked with informing the European Council and the EP on a candidate's progress through regular reports and strategy papers. In addition, the EU has to decide (as stated on the EU website for "Enlargement") whether it has "the capacity to absorb new members." As will be discussed in Chapter 16, a number of countries are currently candidates – even if most all are highly unlikely to be admitted anytime in the near future.

- Formal establishment of the European Council as an institution in its own right
- Abolition of the pillar structure of Maastricht and of the European Community
- A new formula for qualified majority voting within the Council of Ministers
- New powers for the EP, including giving it and the Council of Ministers equal power over proposals for almost all EU legislation
- Recognition of the rights laid out in the Charter of Fundamental Rights (see Chapter 13 for more details)
- A single "legal personality" for the EU (rights and duties within a single legal framework)
- Rights of action, consultation, recognition, support, and the secession of member states (Article 50, a clause first invoked with Brexit).

While every other state in the EU took the position that Lisbon was simply an amendment to past treaties (and therefore ratified it through parliamentary means), Ireland once again put the issue to the voters in a referendum, where it was rejected in June 2008. Its defeat owed much to false information propagated by the treaty's opponents, who claimed that Lisbon would endanger Irish neutrality, would mean radical changes in tax policy, and would legalize abortion in Ireland. To placate the Irish, new protocols to the treaty were added which not only attempted to assuage any fears that these things might happen but also retracted some institutional changes, such as the proposal to reduce the number of commissioners. A new vote on the treaty was held in Ireland in October 2009, and this time the result was an overwhelming 67 percent in favor. The following month, Czech president Vaclav Klaus (a well-known Euroskeptic who had held up ratification pending the Irish referendum and his own satisfaction as to the treaty's provisions) signed on to ratification and the treaty came into force.

THE FINANCIAL AND DEBT CRISIS (2008–2015)

Whatever residual concerns had existed about the way the Treaty of Lisbon had been designed and approved were swept aside when an economic crisis broke out in the eurozone. The roadmap to these problems can be traced back to (1) flaws in the design and execution of the euro,[9] (2) violation of the rules of membership in the euro by several states (above all, lax fiscal discipline), and (3) a global financial crisis that began in the US in 2007[10] and then migrated across the Atlantic, severely impacting a number of countries who were already dealing with their own domestic economic problems.

Although some European countries, such as Germany, appeared to initially weather the economic storm, others were hit hard, for a variety of reasons. Ireland and Latvia's property bubbles burst, leading to tremendous stress on the banking industry as defaults on loans (largely tied to the property boom) rose dramatically. Economic meltdown loomed as the economy fell into recession, tax revenues plummeted, and unemployment increased sharply. A housing bubble burst and reverberated throughout the Spanish economy, threatening to engulf its banking sector. Unemployment soared to almost a quarter of the population (with over 50 percent of young Spaniards unemployed); Spanish government debt rose and its borrowing costs skyrocketed.[11] Portugal was another country especially vulnerable to the global financial crisis: anemic economic growth throughout the early 2000s combined with rising budget deficits led to repeated violations of the rules set down for the common currency and a precarious economic situation by 2008. Meanwhile Cyprus sank into a deep economic recession, and its own banking sector virtually collapsed due to risky loans and entanglement with the Greek economy.

No country was harder hit by the recession than Greece, and its difficulties had synergistic effects on the entire eurozone. Greece's main industries were especially susceptible to economic downturns. Moreover, as it sought financial help from the EU it was revealed that Greek leaders had for years mismanaged the economy while underreporting Greece's debt load, fudging its balance sheet even as it adopted the euro. In the spring of 2010 the country's sovereign rating was downgraded to "junk" status. This meant that investors worried that putting money in the Greek economy was extremely risky; consequently, they demanded a high interest rate (up to 22 percent) if they were going to invest in Greek treasury bonds. Greece began a slide toward financial insolvency, given that servicing the interest and debt on high-interest treasury bonds would bankrupt it (imagine, for example, the difference in trying to pay off a huge credit card bill when the interest on your debt is

"DO YOU SEE ANY SIGNS OF IMPROVEMENT IN THEIR CONDITIONS?!"

PHOTO 4.1 Contagious Ward of Eurozone.

Source: Cartoonist: Pletch-Eldon Pletcher; www.cartoonstock.com.

2 percent – a more normal bond interest rate – versus 22 percent!). Fears spread that without a massive bailout it would be forced to leave the eurozone and re-adopt the drachma (even while remaining a member of the EU), the so-called "Grexit."

Supporters of Grexit argued that readopting the drachma would make Greek goods more competitive by making them cheaper on the world market, possibly sparking an economic revival (much like Argentina experienced after it severed its ties to the dollar in 2002). For opponents of Grexit, however, the cons were numerous. Reintroducing the drachma would take several months, and it was highly likely that without draconian measures Greeks would take their money out of the country, safeguarding their now more valuable euros. Goods from the eurozone would be much more expensive and the Greek government would find it hard to borrow from international markets. And Greece's foreign debt, still denominated in euros, would grow tremendously in relation to the devalued drachma-based economy. Moreover, the EU itself might suffer, with hard-to-calculate psychological effects on investors and lenders, as the euro would no longer be seen as an iron-clad currency union.

Despite the urgency, the EU's initial response to the crisis was slow and inadequate. Eventually, as the severity became clearer the EU responded more robustly: the European Central Bank stepped in to buy government bonds, thus lowering borrowing costs for countries at risk, and the EU agreed to bailouts for Ireland, Spain, Portugal, and Cyprus. However, as Greece's problems were to some extent self-inflicted, Germany (supported especially by the Netherlands and Finland) took an especially hard line, arguing that any financial assistance should be contingent upon Greece slashing its budget, cutting government spending dramatically, and agreeing to strict oversight from the EU.[12] Something of a north–south divide in the EU over Greece emerged, with northern, wealthier states arguing for stricter bailout terms while southern EU states urged more forgiving ones.

Eventually a series of loans to Greece from the so-called "troika" – the European Commission, the European Central Bank, and the International Monetary Fund – ensued. However, the troika's policy of forced austerity proved deeply unpopular in Greece. Several governments collapsed and political turmoil followed, with the radical-left party Syriza taking power in January, 2015. Syriza began a series of negotiations to soften the conditions of its bailout. Yet confronted with the very real possibility of a Grexit, it stepped back from the brink and surprisingly agreed to an even stricter bailout agreement.[13] Since that time, the Greek crisis has receded although it would be naive to suggest that all is well. Its debt load and fiscal balances have improved significantly, modest economic growth has returned, and unemployment is down from its peak in 2013 (albeit, still high at 18 percent). Still, it has been estimated that even with 2 percent annual growth, the Greek economy will not return to its pre-crisis size until the early 2030s. Moreover, Greeks are poorer now: while Greek GDP per capita was about 80 percent that of Germany before the crisis, in 2019 it stood at 55 percent.[14] Meanwhile, Syriza was ousted from power in the general election of July 2019. The new government led by the party "New Democracy" wants to lighten Greece's austerity burden. It does not, however, advocate any radical change in its relationship to the EU.

Measures taken by the EU since 2010 to address the economic crisis have stabilized the rest of the countries of the eurozone. These include a modest economic growth initiative, some steps toward a future banking union and bank oversight, a tightening of the criteria governing membership in the euro (known informally as the "Fiscal Compact"), and a new organization and procedure for administering EU bailout funds (the European Stability Mechanism) (see more discussion of all of these in Chapters 9 and 12). This has been especially true in Ireland, Latvia, Portugal, and Spain, where despite unemployment remaining uncomfortably high, borrowing costs/interest rates on government bonds have ctome down and economic growth has returned. Still, it remains to be seen whether measures taken by the EU will prove to be decisive enough in the long run to return the eurozone to robust growth and to ward off any future crisis. Indeed, a harsh critic of the Euro, Nobel prize–winning economist Joseph Stiglitz, has pronounced that the Euro was "flawed from birth" and that the EU should either abandon it as a common currency for the nineteen member states, or undertake significantly more far-reaching reforms than it has hitherto been willing to do.[15]

THE MIGRATION CRISIS (2015–2018)

On the heels of the financial and debt crisis came the largest refugee influx into in Europe since World War II. For some observers, the migration crisis illustrated the perils of the Schengen accords and a "borderless Europe," misjudgments on the part of EU leaders (chief among them Germany's Angela Merkel), and a woefully underfunded border control system. For others, the crisis was less a matter of EU failures (although there were certainly plenty of these) than a perfect storm of conditions in the wake of a civil war in Syria, the collapse of stable government in Libya (and very weak governments in other countries), and a rising level of antagonism between the EU and Turkey (a major smuggling route for migrants).[16] The increase in migration was sudden and dramatic: according to Europol, there were some 1.8 million irregular border crossings into the EU in 2015, an increase of 546 percent compared to 2014.[17] The human tragedy of the migration crisis was driven home by high-profile fatal incidents that claimed thousands of migrant deaths.[18] Although the number of border crossings into Europe declined slightly in 2016, Greece and Italy (and later, Spain[19]) saw sharp increases during that year. Because the vast majority of these migrants were not classic "economic migrants" (i.e., those simply seeking work, which the EU had dealt with for decades) but rather refugees seeking political asylum, the EU was required by international law to take them in and have their cases legally adjudicated. From 2015 onward such requests were overwhelming. In this respect, the EU's migration crisis paralleled later developments in the US from 2017 onward, where the sharp increase in illegal immigration could almost solely be traced to asylum seekers fleeing violence in Central America.

Initially the EU struggled with how to handle the scope and complexity of the migration crisis. Even though most migrants' ultimate destination was the wealthier, northern EU states (primarily Germany and Sweden), the southern, frontline EU states disproportionately bore the brunt of refugees, with Italy registering over 180,000 migrants in 2016.[20] Not surprisingly, with the collective temperature rising due to the strain of the crisis, sharp disagreements erupted among EU states, most often manifested in an east–west divide. Poland, the Czech Republic, Slovakia, and Hungary – the latter of which erected a fence along its borders to keep refugees out – fiercely resisted attempts to take in migrants, arguing that they were both economically unprepared and culturally unsuited to receive them. Xenophobic attitudes surfaced as well, with dark warnings of "Muslim invaders" or the dangers of migrants spreading disease. In contrast, Angela Merkel of Germany decided to unilaterally welcome hundreds of thousands of migrants, breaking agreed-upon EU rules (the "Dublin Regulation," discussed in Chapter 13) which mandated that migrants register and go through the asylum process in the state where they first entered the EU and remain in that country until a determination was made.

In the fall of 2015, the EU pushed through a plan to voluntarily redistribute some 160,000 refugees among all the EU states (see Chapter 13). Yet resistance was fierce, with qualified majority voting, rather than consensus, ultimately used to reach the agreement. So far the voluntary resettlement plan has been, in the words of EU scholar Laurie Buonanno, an "enormous flop,"[21] with only 272 refugees having been relocated by 2017. Indeed, in that same year the Commission sued the Czech Republic, Hungary, and Poland over their failure to accept the required quotas of refugees. As of this writing, the EU has been unable to force these three states to fulfill their obligations, which they argue was voluntary, not mandatory. Similarly, the EU has been unable to agree to rules harmonizing asylum procedures across the bloc[22] and new resistance to resettling migrants is now being echoed by right-wing populists in Italy.[23] Still, stepped-up border patrols under Frontex (discussed in Chapter 14) and the closing of migration routes, (much criticized) agreements struck with Turkey and Libya[24] to keep migrants in those countries, and the waning of political violence in Syria has led to a drop in irregular migrants coming into the EU. While almost 1.3 million applications for EU asylum protection were filed in 2016, this figure declined to 728,000 in 2017 and 634,000 in 2018.[25]

ANOTHER BLOW TO THE EU: BREXIT (2016–2020)

The ripple effects of the financial and refugee crises in the last decade sparked another consequence: the growth of EU-skeptic or EU-phobic parties, which managed to secure about one-third of the seats in European elections in the spring of 2014. However, EU skepticism was not limited to extreme right, anti-EU parties. Partly as a consequence of the financial crisis, partly as a result of backlash from immigration into the UK from other EU states, and partly, as we have seen in previous chapters, as a consequence of longstanding EU-skeptical attitudes among the UK public and within his own Conservative party, in 2013 Prime Minister David Cameron promised an "in-out" referendum on continued UK membership in the EU. Cameron wagered that he could secure a better deal for the UK (or as he called it, a "new settlement") vis-à-vis the EU while placating his Tory opponents with a referendum that, in light of this new deal, he thought could win.[26] Consequently, he would strengthen his position as prime minister – a woeful miscalculation as it turned out.

Despite an agreement reached between Cameron and EU leaders on the "new settlement," the Conservatives remained deeply split (as was the Labour Party), with prominent voices, such as former mayor of London Boris Johnson, supporting the "leave" campaign. While those in favor of "remain" argued that the UK benefitted enormously from the single market, Brexit supporters suggested that the UK could secure better trade deals on its own, that UK democracy was threatened by a European superstate, and that the country was being flooded by foreigners, refugees as well as legal migrants from other EU states. On June 23, 2016, the results of the "in-out" referendum surprised most observers, with almost 52 percent of voters opting to leave the EU. Cameron resigned shortly thereafter and the Conservatives voted in Theresa May as the new prime minister.

Though a supporter of "remain," May immediately assured Brexit hardliners that she would respect voters' wishes and set about trying to find ways to negotiate a divorce deal acceptable to Brexiters and to the EU. Yet a compromise solution seemed impossible to find: EU leaders were in no mood to agree to the UK cherry picking a favorable trade agreement while rebuffing EU rules on the free movement of people. After several deals she reached in negotiation with other EU leaders failed to pass the House of Commons, May announced her resignation in May of 2019 and Boris Johnson took over as prime minister. Although Johnson initially faced the very same problems as May – a House of Commons that simply could not agree on the terms of Brexit – he was able to cut the Gordian Knot by calling for an early election in December 2019. The Conservatives' overwhelming victory finally ended speculation that Brexit would be reversed while at the same time quieting (for the time being, anyway) Johnson's opponents in the Conservative Party who had been calling for a "no-deal" Brexit. The possibility of a no-deal Brexit was feared by both the EU and even most Tories. In the event of a "no deal," the UK and EU would not only, presumably, slap tariffs on one another's goods, but goods from either side would also be subject to customs inspections. The result could very well be gigantic traffic jams at the borders, as food rots (about one-third of the food consumed in the UK comes from the EU), medicines are not easily admitted, and manufacturing grinds to a halt.[27]

At the time of this writing, it remains to be seen exactly what kind of future economic relationship the UK will have with the EU. Boris Johnson hopes to conclude a new trade deal with the EU by the end of December, 2020 – although most observers think anything more than a "bare bones" trade agreement is highly unlikely by that time.[28] The most significant issue yet to be resolved in the wake of Brexit concerns the territorial integrity of the UK itself. Unlike the English, Scots voted overwhelmingly against Brexit, as did the Northern Irish. While Scotland has threatened to hold another referendum on Scottish independence in the wake of the Conservatives' election victory, Northern Ireland fears a renewed outbreak of sectarian violence – a return of "the troubles" – as a hard border returns between it and Ireland, the latter of which remains in the EU. As the *New York Times* notes, "to reimpose the border is like putting up the Berlin Wall again, after you've taken it down."[29] Theresa May's final negotiated deal with the EU addressed this issue through an "Irish backstop" which provided for a period in which the border would continue to be open while Northern Ireland (and the UK, in turn) remained aligned to many EU rules. Brexit supporters wanted none of this band-aid bartering and thus the deal collapsed. Johnson, in an attempt to avoid both redrawing the hard border as well as leaving the UK tied to EU rules, has proposed having Northern Ireland sit inside the EU's custom union, drawing the economic border (i.e., border checks) in the Irish Sea between it and the rest of the UK, at least for the time being.

In the immediate aftermath of Brexit, some feared (while others, of course, welcomed) a potential imminent collapse of the EU: it was thought that Brexit would have a "contagion" or domino effect, emboldening anti-EU populists across Europe to push for their own "Frexit" (France), "Nexit" (Netherlands), or even "Italeave." Yet this contagion has thus far failed to materialize. To be sure, right-wing populist parties have gained strength in many countries, are in power in Hungary and Poland, and have even governed, until recently, in coalitions in Italy and Austria, where they have pushed governments further to the right. Still, expected huge gains for anti-EU parties in the EP elections of 2019 largely failed to come to pass (see discussion in Chapter 7). EU-supportive parties performed well, even if some establishment parties did not. Public support for the EU across member states has risen by roughly 10 percent since the 2016 Brexit referendum, and right-wing populist parties no longer speak of leaving the EU (although their criticisms of it continue unabated).[30] Moreover, rather than contagion, EU member states appear more unified than ever on the question of the benefits of EU membership, while many countries outside the union continue to press for entrance into the club.

QUESTIONS TO CONSIDER

1   What effects has eastern enlargement had on the development of the EU in terms of its cohesion and identity?
2   In light of the EU's problems in dealing with recent economic crises, can the euro be considered a success or were early critics of the euro right after all?
3   Were the three crises the EU experienced over the last decade unavoidable or could they have been averted?

NOTES

1   For details, see Amy Verdun, "The Euro and the European Central Bank," in *Developments in the European Union 2*, 2nd ed., edited by Maria Green Cowles and Desmond Dinan (New York: Palgrave Macmillan, 2004).
2   See Anthony Wallace, "Completing the Single Market: The Lisbon Strategy," in *Developments in the European Union 2*, edited by Cowles and Dinan.
3   For an analysis of the origins, negotiation, and conclusion of the Treaty of Amsterdam, see Desmond Dinan, "Treaty Change in the European Union: The Amsterdam Experience," in *Developments in the European Union*, edited by Laura Cram, Desmond Dinan, and Neill Nugent (Basingstoke, UK: Macmillan, 1999).
4   See Birgit Locher, "Gendering the EU Policy Process and Constructing the *Gender Acquis*," in *Gendering the European Union: New Approaches to Old Democratic Deficits*, edited by Gabriele Abels and Joyce Marie Mushaben, 63–84 (New York and London: Palgrave Macmillan, 2015).
5   For details, see Desmond Dinan, "Reconstituting Europe," in *Developments in the European Union 2*, edited by Cowles and Dinan.
6   Those countries which had postponed or cancelled making a decision were the Czech Republic, Denmark, Ireland, Poland, Portugal, Sweden, and the UK.
7   "Europe's Mexico Option," *The Economist*, October 5, 2002, 36.
8   Alex Barker, "EU Offers Stronger Ties to Eastern Nations – But Cautiously," *Financial Times*, May 22, 2015, at www.ft.com/intl/cms.
9   Caroline De La Porte and Elke Heins, "The Aftermath of the Eurozone Crisis: Towards Fiscal Federalism?" in *The European Union in Crisis*, edited by Desmond Dinan, Neill Nugent and William E. Paterson, 149–166 (London and New York: Palgrave, 2017).

10 In the words of the historian Ian Kershaw, the economic crisis "was made in the United States, though with willing European accomplices." Ian Kershaw, *The Global Age: Europe 1950–2017*, 489 (London and New York: Viking, 2018).

11 "Going to Extra Time," *The Economist*, June 16, 2012, 26–28.

12 Regarding Germany's position on the euro crisis see for example Hans-Werner Sinn, "Why Berlin Is Balking on a Bailout," *New York Times*, June 13, 2012, A23; see also Nicholas Kulish, "Germany Is Open to Pooling Debt, with Conditions," *New York Times*, June 5, 2012, A1.

13 Peter Spiegel, "EU Frustration over Greece Hits Boiling Point at Eurogroup Meeting," *Financial Times*, April 24, 2015, at www.ft.com/content/962eac8a-ea83-11e4-a701-00144feab7de, accessed April 25, 2015.

14 Martin Wolf, "Greek Economy Shows Promising Signs of Growth," *Financial Times*, May 19, 2019, at www.ft.com/content/b42ee1ac-4a27-11e9-bde6-79eaea5acb64, accessed June 28, 2019.

15 See Joseph E. Stiglitz, *The Euro: How a Common Currency Threatens the Future of Europe* (New York and London: W.W. Norton & Company, 2016).

16 Laurie Buonanno, "The European Migration Crisis," in *The European Union in Crisis*, edited by Dinan, Nugent and Paterson, 100–130.

17 Europol, *Migrant Smuggling in the EU*, at www.europol.europa.eu/publications-documents/migrant-smuggling-in-eu, accessed July 1, 2019.

18 "EU Ministers Urged to Act after Hundreds of Migrants Feared Dead," *Financial Times*, April 20, 2015, at www.ft.com/content/716931fe-e673-11e4-afb7-00144feab7de, accessed April 27, 2015.

19 In 2018, 56,000 migrants crossed into Spain, about as much as in Italy and Greece combined. See Jon Henley, "What is the Current State of the Migration Crisis in Europe?" *Guardian*, November 21, 2018, at www.theguardian.com/world/2018/jun/15/what-current-scale-migration-crisis-europe-future-outlook, accessed July 1, 2019.

20 "Fewer Migrants at EU Borders in 2016," *Frontex News Release* at https://frontex.europa.eu/media-centre/news-release/fewer-migrants-at-eu-borders-in-2016-HWnC1J, accessed July 1, 2019.

21 Ibid., 116.

22 Jennifer Rankin, "EU Declares Migration Crisis Over as it Hits out at 'Fake News,'" *Guardian*, March 6, 2019, at www.theguardian.com/world/2019/mar/06/eu-declares-migration-crisis-over-hits-out-fake-news-european-commission, accessed on July 1, 2019.

23 Stephen Castle, "Brexit Plans Raise Fears of Food Shortages and Jammed Ports," *New York Times*, at www.nytimes.com/2018/07/30/world/europe/uk-brexit-shortages.html, accessed on August 1, 2018.

24 For a harsh assessment of the deals the EU struck with Turkey and Libya to curb migration, see Bret Stephens, "An Immigration Policy Worse than Trump's," *New York Times*, July 5, 2019, at www.nytimes.com/2019/07/05/opinion/immigration-trump-southern-border.html, accessed July 6, 2019.

25 "Asylum and Migration in the EU: Facts and Figures," *European Parliament News*, at www.europarl.europa.eu/news/en/headlines/society/20170629STO78630/asylum-and-migration-in-the-eu-facts-and-figures, accessed June 30, 2019.

26 Lee McGowan and David Phinnemore, "The UK: Membership in Crisis," in *The European Union in Crisis*, edited by Dinan, Nugent and Paterson, 77–99.

27 Amie Tsang, "What Would a No-Deal Brexit Look Like?" *New York Times*, April 2, 2019, at www.nytimes.com/2019/04/02/world/europe/brexit-no-deal-outcomes.html, accessed April 3, 2019.

28 See Mark Landler and Stephen Castle, "And You Thought Brexit Was Tough," *New York Times*, January 8, 2020, at www.nytimes.com/2020/01/08/world/europe/brexit-united-kingdom.html, accessed January 10, 2020.

29 Sarah Lyall, "On Irish Border, Worries that 'Brexit' Will Undo a Hard-Won Peace," *New York Times*, August 5, 2017, at www.nytimes.com/2017/08/05/world/europe/brexit-northern-ireland-ireland.html, accessed August 5, 2017.

30 Frank Langfitt, "Here's Why Brexit Wasn't Followed by Frexit, Swexit or Nexit," NPR, at www.npr.org/2019/04/26/715926169/heres-why-brexit-wasnt-followed-by-frexit-swexit-or-nexit, accessed July 11, 2019.

BIBLIOGRAPHY

Barker, Alex, "EU Offers Stronger Ties to Eastern Nations – But Cautiously," *Financial Times*, May 22, 2015, at www.ft.com/intl/cms.

Buonanno, Laurie, "The European Migration Crisis," in *The European Union in Crisis*, edited by Desmond Dinan, Neill Nugent and William E. Paterson, 100–130 (London and New York: Palgrave, 2017).

Castle, Stephen, "Brexit Plans Raise Fears of Food Shortages and Jammed Ports," *New York Times*, July 30, 2018 at www.nytimes.com/2018/07/30/world/europe/uk-brexit-shortages.html, accessed on August 1, 2018.

Dinan, Desmond, "Treaty Change in the European Union: The Amsterdam Experience," in *Developments in the European Union*, edited by Laura Cram, Desmond Dinan, and Neill Nugent, 290–310 (Basingstoke, UK: Macmillan, 1999).

Dinan, Desmond, "Reconstituting Europe," in *Developments in the European Union*, 2nd ed., edited by Maria Green Cowles and Desmond Dinan, 25–47 (New York and London: Palgrave Macmillan, 2004).

De La Porte, Caroline and Elke Heins, "The Aftermath of the Eurozone Crisis: Towards Fiscal Federalism?" in *The European Union in Crisis*, edited by Desmond Dinan, Neill Nugent and William E. Paterson, 149–166 (London and New York: Palgrave, 2017).

Economist, The, "Europe's Mexico Option," October 5, 2002, 36.

Economist, The, "Going to Extra Time," June 16, 2012, 26–28.

European Parliament, "Asylum and Migration in the EU: Facts and Figures," *European Parliament News*, at www.europarl.europa.eu/news/en/headlines/society/20170629STO78630/asylum-and-migration-in-the-eu-facts-and-figures, accessed June 30, 2019.

Europol, *Migrant Smuggling in the EU*, at www.europol.europa.eu/publications-documents/migrant-smuggling-in-eu, accessed July 1, 2019.

Financial Times, "EU Ministers Urged to Act after Hundreds of Migrants Feared Dead," April 20, 2015, at www.ft.com/content/716931fe-e673-11e4-afb7-00144feab7de, accessed April 27, 2015.

Frontex, "Fewer migrants at EU borders in 2016," *Frontex News Release*, at https://frontex.europa.eu/media-centre/news-release/fewer-migrants-at-eu-borders-in-2016-HWnC1J, accessed July 1, 2019.

Henley, Jon, "What is the Current State of the Migration Crisis in Europe?" *Guardian*, November 21, 2018, at www.theguardian.com/world/2018/jun/15/what-current-scale-migration-crisis-europe-future-outlook, accessed July 1, 2019.

Kershaw, Ian, *The Global Age: Europe 1950–2017* (New York: Viking, 2019).

Kulish, Nicholas, "Germany Is Open to Pooling Debt, with Conditions," *New York Times*, June 5, 2012, A1.

Landler, Mark and Stephen Castle, "And You Thought Brexit Was Tough," *New York Times*, January 8, 2020, at www.nytimes.com/2020/01/08/world/europe/brexit-united-kingdom.html, accessed January 10, 2020.

Langfitt, Frank, "Here's Why Brexit Wasn't Followed by Frexit, Swexit or Nexit," NPR, at www.npr.org/2019/04/26/715926169/heres-why-brexit-wasnt-followed-by-frexit-swexit-or-nexit, accessed July 11, 2019.

Locher, Birgit, "Gendering the EU Policy Process and Constructing the *Gender Acquis*," in *Gendering the European Union: New Approaches to Old Democratic Deficits*, edited by Gabriele Abels and Joyce Marie Mushaben, 63–84 (New York and London: Palgrave Macmillan, 2015).

Lyall, Sarah, "On Irish Border, Worries that 'Brexit' Will Undo a Hard-Won Peace," *New York Times*, at www.nytimes.com/2017/08/05/world/europe/brexit-northern-ireland-ireland.html, accessed August 5, 2017.

McGowan, Lee, and David Phinnemore, "The UK: Membership in Crisis," in *The European Union in Crisis*, edited by Desmond Dinan, Neill Nugent, and William E. Paterson, eds., 77–89 (London and New York: Palgrave, 2017).

O'Rourke, Kevin, *A Short History of Brexit* (London: Penguin UK, 2019).

O'Brennan, John, *The Eastern Enlargement of the European Union* (London: Routledge, 2006).

Pisani-Ferry, Jean, *The Euro Crisis and its Aftermath* (Oxford: Oxford University Press, 2011).

Poole, Peter, *Europe Unites: The EU's Eastern Enlargement* (Westport, CT: Praeger, 2003).

Rankin, Jennifer, "EU Declares Migration Crisis Over as it Hits out at 'Fake News'," *Guardian*, March 6, 2019, at www.theguardian.com/world/2019/mar/06/eu-declares-migration-crisis-over-hits-out-fake-news-european-commission, accessed on July 1, 2019.

Sinn, Hans-Werner, "Why Berlin Is Balking on a Bailout," *New York Times*, June 13, 2012, A23.

Spiegel, Peter, "EU Frustration over Greece Hits Boiling Point at Eurogroup Meeting," *Financial Times*, April 24, 2015, at www.ft.com/content/962eac8a-ea83-11e4-a701-00144feab7de, accessed April 25, 2015.

Stephens, Bret, "An Immigration Policy Worse than Trump's," *New York Times*, July 5, 2019, at www.nytimes.com/2019/07/05/opinion/immigration-trump-southern-border.html, accessed July 6, 2019.

Stiglitz, Joseph, *The Euro: How a Common Currency Threatens the Future of Europe* (New York: W.W. Norton & Company, 2016).

Stubb, Alexander, *Negotiating Flexibility in the European Union: Amsterdam, Nice and Beyond* (Basingstoke, UK: Palgrave Macmillan, 2003).

Tsang, Amie, "What Would a No-Deal Brexit Look Like?" *New York Times*, April 2, 2019, at www.nytimes.com/2019/04/02/world/europe/brexit-no-deal-outcomes.html, accessed April 3, 2019.

Verdun, Amy, "The Euro and the European Central Bank," in *Developments in the European Union*, 2nd ed., edited by Maria Green Cowles and Desmond Dinan, 255–275 (New York: Palgrave Macmillan, 2004).

Wallace, Anthony, "Completing the Single Market: The Lisbon Strategy," in *Developments in the European Union*, 2nd ed., edited by Maria Green Cowles and Desmond Dinan, 100–125 (New York and London: Palgrave Macmillan, 2004).

Wolf, Martin, "Greek Economy Shows Promising Signs of Growth," *Financial Times*, May 19, 2019, at www.ft.com/content/b42ee1ac-4a27-11e9-bde6-79eaea5acb64. Accessed June 28, 2019.

FURTHER READING

Alexander Stubb, *Negotiating Flexibility in the European Union: Amsterdam, Nice and Beyond* (Basingstoke, UK: Palgrave Macmillan, 2003).

> An assessment of the negotiations that led up to the treaties of Amsterdam and Nice by a Commission staff member who took part.

Peter Poole, *Europe Unites: The EU's Eastern Enlargement* (Westport, CT: Praeger, 2003); Neill Nugent, ed., *European Union Enlargement* (Basingstoke, UK: Palgrave Macmillan, 2004); John O'Brennan, *The Eastern Enlargement of the European Union* (London: Routledge, 2006).

> Three of the large number of assessments of enlargement that have been published in recent years.

Jean Pisani-Ferry, *The Euro Crisis and its Aftermath* (Oxford: Oxford University Press, 2011); Joseph Stiglitz, *The Euro: How a Common Currency Threatens the Future of Europe* (New York: W.W. Norton & Company, 2016).

> Two critical analyses of the origins of the eurozone crisis, the EU's responses, the possible long-range impacts, and what reforms to the euro should be made.

Kevin O'Rourke, *A Short History of Brexit* (London: Penguin UK, 2019).

> A critical analysis of the historical relationship between the UK and EU, and – despite its title – the long-term factors which impacted the Brexit vote, in addition to the challenges the question of the Irish border presents.

PART II

Institutions

CHAPTER 5

The European Commission

CHAPTER OVERVIEW

- The most supranational of the EU's institutions, the Commission performs executive and bureaucratic functions within the EU.
- The College of Commissioners operates much like a cabinet in a parliamentary system, with commissioners having significant authority over their portfolios, or areas of policy responsibility, and a president acting as the first among equals for the entire college.
- Although Euroskeptics have always had the Commission in their sights, seeing it as a powerful and unchecked institution, the reality is that the Commission's powers have never been as formidable as some critics have said they are. This has become all the more apparent in recent years as other EU institutions have gained power at its expense.

The European Commission is the executive-bureaucratic arm of the EU, responsible for generating new laws and policies and overseeing their implementation, managing the EU budget, representing the EU in international negotiations, and promoting the interests of the EU as a whole. Headquartered in Brussels, the Commission consists of a college of appointed commissioners who function collectively much like a national government cabinet in a parliamentary system, and several thousand full-time European bureaucrats assigned to one of the Commission's directorates-general (DGs), the functional equivalent of national government departments. There is a DG for each of the major policy areas in which the EU is active, and each is supported by services that provide policy advice, research support, and legal expertise. Confusingly, both the commissioners and the European bureaucrats are separately and collectively described as "the Commission."

As the most visible and supranational of the EU institutions, the Commission has long been at the heart of European integration. As a result, its powers are routinely over-estimated: Euroskeptics like to grumble about waste and meddling by the Commission, complain that commissioners are not elected, charge that the Commission has too little public accountability, and vent about an elite and distant bureaucracy working to centralize powers in Brussels. For some, "Brussels" is synonymous with the Commission and has thus become a code word for an out-of-touch political class, much like "Washington" figures in some American political discourse.

Yet the Commission has much less power than its detractors suggest, both because it takes its general directions from the intergovernmental European Council while at the same time final decisions on new laws and policies rest with the Council of the EU and the European Parliament (EP). With new initiatives and powers given to these institutions over the last several years, the argument could be made that there has been a decline in the

Commission's power. Furthermore, studies have shown that the women and men who make up the Commission bureaucracy, while highly educated, come from the ranks of national administrations and are overwhelmingly not career "Eurocrats" promoting a more centralized Europe.[1] Finally, the Commission is quite small given the size of its task; it had around 32,000 employees in 2019 (a ratio of about 1:15,000 EU residents), compared with over two million federal bureaucrats in the US (about 1:150 US residents).[2]

The Commission deserves credit for the leading role it has played in the process of European integration. It has not only encouraged member states to harmonize their laws, regulations, and standards in the interest of bringing down barriers to trade, but it has also been at the heart of some of the defining European policy initiatives, including the single market, efforts to create a single currency, efforts to build common foreign policy positions, and enlargement. Like all large institutions the Commission suffers occasionally from waste, mismanagement, and bureaucratic excess, but it is honest about its own shortcomings, and given the size of its task it has been remarkably productive.

EVOLUTION

The origins of the European Commission can be traced back to the High Authority of the European Coal and Steel Community. Based in Luxembourg, the nine members of the Authority were nominated for six-year terms by the national governments of the member states. Their job was to oversee the removal of barriers to the free movement of coal and steel, and their powers were checked by a Special Council of Ministers and a Common Assembly (the forerunners, respectively, of today's Council of Ministers and EP).

The Treaties of Rome created separate nine-member Commissions for the European Economic Community (EEC) and Euratom, which were nominated by national governments for four-year terms. Under the terms of the 1965 Merger Treaty, the three separate Commissions were merged in 1967 into a new Commission of the European Communities, more commonly known as the European Commission. As the Community expanded, the number of commissioners grew; today it stands at twenty-seven, one for each member state, after Brexit.

The Commission has always been at the heart of the debate over the balance of power between the EU and its member states. With its supra-nationalist tendencies, it has engaged in an ongoing tug of war with the intergovernmental Council of the EU. European federalism was championed by the Commission's first president – Walter Hallstein of Germany – in the face of Charles de Gaulle's preference for limiting the powers of the EEC. As noted in Chapter 3, the 1965 empty chair crisis began when de Gaulle challenged the right of the Commission to initiate the policy process as it tried to collect receipts from the Community's common external tariff.[3] This would have given the Commission an independent source of funds and would have loosened the grip of the member states. Although the Luxembourg Compromise obliged the Commission to consult more closely with the Council of Ministers, and de Gaulle was able to veto the reappointment of Hallstein in 1967, the crisis ironically confirmed the right of the Commission to initiate policies.

Despite this history, the Commission became less ambitious and aggressive and lost powers with the creation in 1965 of the Committee of Permanent Representatives (see Chapter 6), the creation in 1974 of the European Council (also Chapter 6), and the introduction in 1979 of direct elections to the EP. After enjoying a newly assertive phase under President Jacques Delors during the late 1980s and early 1990s, and winning responsibilities for developing laws in a growing range of new policy areas, the Commission saw its powers continuing to decline relative to those of the Council of Ministers and the EP.

Preparations for the 2004 enlargement of the EU forced a rethinking of the size and role of the Commission. The failed European constitution included a proposal that the Commission would be reduced in 2014 to seventeen voting members, with no more than one commissioner from each state. Reflecting the extent to which member states wanted to retain their own commissioners, and the extent to which national interests are still protected even in the Commission, the proposal was widely criticized, particularly by smaller member states. Consequently, Lisbon retained the current formula of one commissioner per member state and proposed capping the number of commissioners from 2014 on at no more than two-thirds of the number of member states (thus, if there are thirty member states, there will be twenty commissioners). Small states continued to balk at this idea, so one of the concessions made to Ireland as it looked for guarantees prior to its second referendum on Lisbon in October 2009 was confirmation of the rule of one commissioner per state. However, that decision by the European Council had a review clause and discussions continue on reducing the size of the commission in the future.

STRUCTURE

The European Commission is based in Brussels with a headquarters in the Berlaymont building, a distinctive piece of 1960s Belgian government architecture with a star-shaped floor plan that provided a strong visual image for the Commission. Most of the staff work in buildings sprinkled in and around the European Quarter in Brussels. When it was discovered in 1992 that the Berlaymont had high levels of asbestos, instead of the less expensive option of tearing it down, it was renovated at a cost of nearly $800 million. Commission staff were relocated to various new and existing buildings around the city until the new Berlaymont was ready in in 2004.

The Commission has five main elements: the College of Commissioners, the president of the Commission, the directorates-general and services, the Secretariat-General, and a network of committees.

The College of Commissioners

The European Commission is led by a group of twenty-seven commissioners who function something like a cabinet for the EU system, taking collective responsibility for their decisions. Each has a policy portfolio for which he or she is responsible (see Table 5.1), and each serves renewable five-year terms, which begin six months after elections to the EP. Commissioners are nominated by their national governments, which, in practice, usually means by the prime minister or the president. The nominations are made in consultation with the president of the Commission, and nominees must be acceptable to the president of the Commission (who has the power of veto), the other commissioners, other governments, the major political parties at home, and the EP.[4]

All nominees are required to attend hearings before the relevant committees of the EP, but Parliament does not have the right to accept or reject them individually; instead, it must approve or reject the College as a whole. Under the circumstances, it is unlikely to reject the College unless it has serious reservations about one or more of the nominees. Nevertheless, a disastrous performance in confirmation hearings by one country's candidate can lead to enormous pressure on the Commission president and the member state to put forward a new nominee. This happened in 2004 when the nominee from Italy – Rocco Buttiglione, who was to have been the new justice commissioner – commented before an EP hearing that homosexuality was a "sin" and that "the family exists in order to allow women to have children and to have the protection of a male who takes care of them."[5] The resulting outcry

TABLE 5.1 The European Commissioners, 2019–2024		
Name	Member State	Portfolio
Ursula von der Leyen	Germany	President
Josep Borrell	Spain	High Representative of the Union for Foreign Affairs and Security Policy
Frans Timmermans	Netherlands	Executive VP, European Green Deal
Margrethe Vestager	Denmark	Executive VP, Europe Fit for Digital Age
Valdis Dombrovskis	Latvia	Executive VP, An Economy that Works for People
Maros Šefčovič	Slovakia	VP, Interinstitutional Relations and Foresight
Věra Jourová	Czechia	VP, Values and Transparency
Dubravka Šuica	Croatia	VP, Democracy and Demography
Margaritis Schinas	Greece	VP, Promoting the European Way of Life
Johannes Hahn	Austria	Budget and Administration
Phil Hogan	Ireland	Trade
Mariya Gabriel	Bulgaria	Innovation, Research, Culture, Education, and Youth
Nicolas Schmit	Luxembourg	Jobs and Social Rights
Paolo Gentiloni	Italy	Economy
Janus Wojciechowski	Poland	Agriculture
Thierry Breton	France	Internal Market
Elisa Ferreira	Portugal	Cohesion and Reforms
Stella Kyriakdes	Cyprus	Health and Food Safety
Didier Reynders	Belgium	Justice
Helena Dalli	Malta	Equality
Ylva Johanson	Sweden	Home Affairs
Janez Lenarčič	Slovenia	Crisis Management
Adina-Ioana Vălean	Romania	Transport
Olivér Várhelyi	Hungary	Neighborhood and Enlargement
Jutta Urpilainen	Finland	International Partnerships
Kadri Simon	Estonia	Energy
Virginjus Sinkevičius	Lithuania	Environment, Oceans and Fisheries

led to Buttiglione being replaced as the Italian nominee by Franco Frattini. More recently, in 2019 the EP's judicial committee rejected two nominees for concerns about their personal finances and questionable links to Russia, leading to their withdrawal. Sylvia Goulard from France, embroiled in a past scandal over her role at an American think tank, also withdrew her name. Meanwhile, the nominee from Poland for agricultural commissioner – after a hearing in which he seemed to be unfamiliar with basic issues concerning the Common Agricultural Policy – did not, and was ultimately confirmed.[6]

Parliament also has the power to remove the College in midterm through a motion of censure, although it has never done this. The closest it came was in January 1999, when – after several years during which stories had circulated about fraud, nepotism, and cronyism in the Commission – Parliament tried to dismiss the College. It was unable to find the necessary two-thirds majority, but a committee was appointed to investigate the allegations, resulting in the surprise resignation of the College just hours after the committee report was published on March 16.

Despite the way they are appointed, commissioners are not expected to be national representatives; they must be impartial in their decision making and must swear an oath of office before the European Court of Justice agreeing "neither to seek nor to take instructions from any Government or body." In reality, it is difficult for commissioners to detach themselves completely from national interests, but it helps that (for now, at least) all member states are "represented" and that all commissioners have just one vote each. Their independence is also promoted by the fact that they cannot be removed in midterm by their home governments. However, they can be recalled at the end of their terms if there is a change of political leadership at home or a disagreement with their national leaders.

There are no formal rules on the qualifications of commissioners, but most tend already to have national political reputations at home.[7] At one time, many were political lightweights whose usefulness at home had ended, so they were "kicked upstairs" to the Commission. As the powers of the Commission increased and the EU became a more significant force in European politics, postings to the Commission became more desirable and important, and the quality of the pool of potential candidates improved.[8] Commissioners now tend to come to the job with senior national government experience, and they count among their number a host of former foreign ministers, finance ministers, labor and

PHOTO 5.1 The College of Commissioners, 2019–2024.
Source: © European Commission 2019.

trade ministers, deputy ministers, former Members of the European Parliament (MEPs), and even some former prime ministers.

At the beginning of each term, all commissioners are given responsibility for a policy area (a portfolio), distributed at the prerogative of the president. Just as in national cabinets, there is an internal hierarchy of positions: the key posts in the Commission are those dealing with the budget, agriculture, and trade. As the membership of the College has expanded, it has become more difficult to find significant portfolios; when the Bulgarian and Romanian commissioners arrived in January 2007, the best that could be found for them was – respectively – consumer protection and multilingualism. Modifying slightly a practice begun under former president Jean-Claude Juncker, Ursula Von der Leyen, the current president, has structured the 2019–2024 Commission to address the issue of not enough substantive portfolios for all member state representatives. In the new Commission, there are three "tiers" of commissioners – three executive vice presidents (for areas the president deems critical to the EU's future) and the High Representative; four "thematic" vice presidents (e.g., Democracy and Demography), and eighteen (regular) commissioners, with responsibility for one or more Commission DGs.

In making appointments, the president will be influenced by three main factors:

- The abilities, political skills, and professional backgrounds of individual commissioners.
- Lobbying by commissioners and their home governments.[9] The latter are obviously keen to see "their" commissioner win a good portfolio or one of particular interest to their country, so political influence is often brought to bear.
- Recognition and promotion in the case of returning commissioners. A commissioner with a strong reputation in a particular area will normally keep the same portfolio or at least be brought back for another term.

Every commissioner has a *cabinet* (French) – a small personal staff of assistants and advisers – which is headed by a *chef* (chief) *de cabinet* and provides advice and the basic information and services that help commissioners do their jobs. The quality of the *cabinet* staff can have a major bearing on the performance of a commissioner, and the *cabinets* collectively have become a key influence on the operations of the Commission.[10] The *chefs de cabinet* meet every Monday to prepare the weekly meeting of the College, which takes place every Wednesday. Most *cabinet* members once came from the same country as the commissioner and were usually recruited from the same national political party as the commissioner or from the national bureaucracy. But recent changes to the rules have required that every *cabinet* should include at least three different nationalities.

The President

The dominating figure in the Commission is the president, the person who – at least until the Treaty of Lisbon created a president of the European Council[11] – comes closest to being able to claim to be leader of the EU. The president is technically no more than a first among equals and can be outvoted by other commissioners, but he or she is one of the most visible of the leaders of the EU institutions, and – as with prime ministers in parliamentary systems – holds a trump card in the form of the power of appointment: the ability to distribute portfolios is a potent tool for patronage and political influence.

Serving a renewable five-year term, the president of the Commission oversees meetings of the College, decides on the distribution of portfolios, represents the Commission in dealings with other EU institutions (appearing regularly before the EP, for example), represents the

TABLE 5.2 Presidents of the European Commission			
Dates	Name	Member State	Ideology
1958–1967	Walter Hallstein	Germany	Christian Democrat
1967–1970	Jean Rey	Belgium	Centrist
1970–1972	Franco Maria Malfatti	Italy	Christian Democrat
1972–1973	Sicco Mansholt (interim)	Netherlands	Social Democrat
1973–1977	François-Xavier Ortoli	France	Conservative
1977–1981	Roy Jenkins	UK	Social Democrat/Labour
1981–1985	Gaston Thorn	Luxembourg	Socialist
1985–1995	Jacques Delors	France	Socialist
1995–1999	Jacques Santer	Luxembourg	Christian Democrat
1999–2004	Romano Prodi	Italy	Centrist
2004–2014	José Manuel Barroso	Portugal	Centrist
2014–2019	Jean-Claude Juncker	Luxembourg	Christian Democrat
2019–	Ursula von der Leyen	Germany	Christian Democrat

EU at meetings with national governments and their leaders, and is generally responsible for ensuring that the Commission gives impetus to the process of European integration. In these areas, the president has the same executive function as the president of the US, after 2010 even giving a similar "State of the Union" speech to the EP in Strasbourg. Still, Commission presidents have only a fraction of the powers of a US president, and in some ways have the same status as nineteenth-century US presidents, who had less of a role in government than either Congress or the states and were more clearly executives rather than leaders. However, the presidency of the Commission took on a new and more forceful character from the mid-1980s onward thanks mainly to one man: Jacques Delors.

The most productive, controversial, and well known of all Commission presidents, Delors came to the job in 1985 with experience as a banker, a labor leader, an MEP, and the economics and finance minister of France.[12] He was single-minded, hardworking, demanding, and sometimes short-tempered; a fellow commissioner once described his management style as a form of "intellectual terrorism," and a UK government minister described the Delors Commission as "practitioners of Rottweiler politics."[13] The Delors Commission will be remembered for at least four major achievements: the completion of the single market, the plan for economic and monetary union, promotion of the Social Charter, and the negotiations leading up to Maastricht. Delors left the Commission at the end of 1994 at age sixty-eight, and surprised many by turning down the opportunity to run for president of France.

There are few formal rules regarding how the president is appointed. Before the Treaty of Lisbon the selection process was labyrinthine, inasmuch as the successful nominee could be vetoed by any national leader within the EU. José Manuel Barroso was the product of just such a situation in 2004. Several names had been touted, including Belgian prime minister Guy Verhofstadt, Austrian chancellor Wolfgang Schuessel, and former NATO chief Javier Solana. Verhofstadt was the favored candidate of France and Germany but was opposed by the UK because he was considered too much a European federalist. In the end, Barroso – dismissed by some as a "lowest common denominator" compromise – was approved unanimously. For France and Germany he had sufficient pro-European credentials, and as a supporter of the war in Iraq he was acceptable to the UK and Italy.

The Treaty of Lisbon led to what might or might not be a significant change in this selection process: starting in 2014, Commission presidents were to be proposed by the European Council – "taking into account the elections to the European Parliament" – using the qualified majority vote (see Chapter 6). Candidates must be confirmed by the EP, a process not dissimilar to that used in the US Senate for presidential nominees to the cabinet, courts, and other offices. Whether this new process constituted a one-time development, a precedent, or something in between still remains a matter of confusion (see Box 5.1).

Box 5.1 *"Spitzenkandidaten"* and the Selection of the Commission President

In 2014 EP political groups put forward "lead candidates" (*Spitzenkandidaten*) for Commission president, citing language in the Lisbon treaty that the European Council must take EP elections into account when selecting a Commission president. Although a few heads of government (including David Cameron and Angela Merkel) initially resisted the EP's move, the European Council ultimately gave in, and former Luxembourg prime minister Jean-Claude Juncker – as the candidate of the European People's Party (EPP) (the EP's largest political group after the election) – was given the position.

Since then, however, things have gotten murkier. In 2019 EP political groups once again put forward their candidates for the election, chief among them Manfred Weber, a conservative from Germany (representing the EPP) and Frans Timmermans of the Netherlands (representing the Socialist group). However, the European Council president, Donald Tusk, indicated in February of 2018 that the European Council possessed the "autonomous competence" to nominate the Commission president and only needed to note the EP's wishes.[14] Moreover, Emmanuel Macron and Angela Merkel disputed the EP's literal reading of Lisbon and remained opposed to the *Spitzenkandidaten* system. EP election results in 2019 (see Chapter 7 for more details) brought no clarity: while the EPP and Socialists remained the largest parties in the EP, together they fell well short of a majority. Weber, a rival from Germany and never a favorite of Merkel's, was quickly brushed aside by the European Council, as was Timmermans, who remained largely disliked among states such as Poland as well as among conservatives across the bloc.

In the end, Ursula von der Leyen, the German defense minister and longtime supporter of Angela Merkel, was chosen for the post – but not without a fight. Sharply criticized in some EU states (as well as in her native Germany) for being, in the words of the *New York Times*, "too pious for feminists, too feminist for conservatives,"[15] von der Leyen endured especially sharp criticism from the Greens group, Socialists, and even some EPP members. Yet she won over enough MEPs to prevail with a razor-thin margin of nine votes – thirty-nine fewer votes than her predecessor. Given resistance on the part of the European Council to cede its right to choose its own candidate as well as the EP's insistence on the *Spitzenkandidaten* process, the manner of selecting a Commission president is likely to continue to be muddied.

As the reach of the EU has expanded, so competition for appointments to the presidency has strengthened, and the quality of the pool of nominees has deepened. Experience as a government minister was once enough, but four of the last five presidents have all been former prime ministers: Jacques Santer (Luxembourg), Romano Prodi (Italy), José Manuel Barroso (Portugal), and Juncker (Luxembourg). Until Ursula von der Leyen's selection in 2019, all Commission presidents had been men; the College itself, however, has made some strides in recent years in women's representation (see discussion below) and a number of top posts in 2019 went to women. As with most positions of leadership in government, the nature of the Commission presidency depends to a large extent on the character of the officeholders and the management style and agenda they bring to their task.[16] Like US presidents, incumbents have proven quite different in their styles, personalities, and abilities. Walter Hallstein, Roy Jenkins, and Jacques Delors are remembered as the most active, and the remainder as relatively passive. Still, while personality has been very important, institutional resources have also impacted the power of the Commission president. For example, Barroso and Juncker came to office after the Treaty of Amsterdam and Treaty of Nice, both of which invested the Commission president with more explicit authority over policy and procedural guidelines of the College, the portfolios of the Commissioners, and the Commission's internal organization.

Directorates-General and Services

Below the College, the European Commission is divided into thirty-one (excluding the Secretariat) DGs and a number of services (see Table 5.3). The DGs – each of which is headed by a director-general – are the equivalent of national government departments in that each is responsible for a specific policy area. (Although DGs are tied to commissioners, the list of policy areas does not exactly match.) Employees consist of a mixture of full-time bureaucrats known as *fonctionnaires*, national experts attached from the member states on short-term contracts, and supporting staff. The Commission is required to ensure balanced representation by nationality at every level, but nearly one in four Eurocrats is Belgian, mainly because of locally recruited secretarial and support staff. Although the people who eventually become directors-general theoretically work their way up through the ranks of the Commission, appointments at the higher levels are based less on merit than on nationality and political affiliation.

About two-thirds of Commission staff members work on drawing up new laws and policies or on overseeing implementation, while the rest are involved in research, translation, and interpretation; although the Commission mainly uses English and French in daily operations, all key documents must be translated into all twenty-three official EU languages. The Commission's services deal with a variety of external matters and internal administrative matters. They include the European Anti-Fraud Office (which fights fraud and corruption within EU institutions), the Internal Audit Service (which carries out audits of European agencies and other bodies that receive funding from the EU budget), and the Legal Service (which acts as an in-house source of legal advice for the Commission, most notably checking through legislative proposals before they are sent to the College of Commissioners for a decision). About three-fourths of Commission staff members work in offices in and around Brussels, the balance working in Luxembourg and other parts of the EU.

Recruitment is both complex and competitive. Several hundred new positions typically become vacant each year, for which there are literally thousands of applicants (a competition launched in May 2003 to recruit staff from the ten new, mainly Eastern European member states attracted nearly 38,000 applications).[17] A university degree and fluency in at least two

TABLE 5.3 Directorates-General and Services

Directorates-General

Agriculture and Rural Development	Health and Food Safety
Budget	Human Resources and Security
Climate Action	Informatics
Communication	Internal Market, Industry, Entrepreneurship and SMEs
Communication Networks, Content and Technology	International Cooperation and Development
Competition	Interpretation
Economic and Financial Affairs	Joint Research Centre
Education, Youth, Sport and Culture	Justice and Consumers
Employment, Social Affairs and Inclusion	Maritime Affairs and Fisheries
Energy	Migration and Home Affairs
Environment	Mobility and Transport
European Civil Protection and Humanitarian Aid Operations	Regional and Urban Policy
European Neighborhood Policy and Enlargement Negotiations	Research and Innovation
Eurostat	Taxation and Customs Union
Financial Stability, Financial Services and Capital Markets Union	Trade
	Translation

Services

Administration and Payment of Individual Entitlements	Infrastructures and Logistics – Luxembourg
Data Protection Officer	Internal Audit Service
European Anti-Fraud Office	Legal Service
European Personnel Selection Office	Library and e-Resources Centre
European Political Strategy Centre	Publications Office
Foreign Policy Instruments	Structural Reform Support Service
Historical Archives	Taskforce on Article 50 negotiations with the United Kingdom
Infrastructures and Logistics – Brussels	

EU languages are minimum requirements, and specialist professional training (in law, business, finance, or science, for example) is increasingly required. Entrance exams (the *concours*) are held in all the member states, but the overall process is so convoluted and detailed that applicants may have to wait as long as three years to find out whether or not they have been accepted. Once appointed, Commission staff in "The Capital" (see Box 5.2) are well paid, and redundancies are rare.[18]

A concerted effort to improve women's representation in the Commission in the mid-1990s and especially after enlargement in 2004 and 2007 resulted in an increase both at the lower levels of the Commission and in the College. Historically, there has been a gender disparity: from 1958–2019, only thirty-five women (compared to 147 men) had served as commissioners, with the College ceasing to be exclusively male in 1989 with the appointments of Vasso Papandreou of Greece and Christiane Scrivener of France. The 1995–1999 and 1999–2004 Colleges both had five women members, the 2009–2014 College had nine, and the 2019–2024 Commission has twelve, above the national average of women ministers in member state national governments (27 percent in 2019). Though the gender imbalance in the bureaucracy of the Commission has also greatly improved over the years, women remain concentrated in lower grades, with only a small number of women in middle and senior management posts.[19]

Box 5.2 "The Capital": A Satirical Novel about the EU

To write a riveting potboiler-cum-farce about the bureaucratic machinations of Brussels is not easy to do. But Robert Menasse's *The Capital* is just that.[20] Part murder mystery, part dark comedy, *The Capital* tells the story of Fenia Xenapoulou, a Cypriot Eurocrat stuck in what she considers a dead-end job in the DG for culture. Hoping to burnish the image of the Commission through a splashy "Jubilee Project," she enlists her colleague Martin Susman in brainstorming ideas for the commemoration. Susman proposes using Auschwitz as the "birthplace of the EU" – an inspired idea, given the EU's role in making another tragic European war a virtual impossibility. Yet their idea soon ascends to absurdist heights, such as staging the EU's fiftieth anniversary party on the grounds of the former concentration camp and using Auschwitz survivors as props for the Jubilee. Meanwhile another plot of the novel centers on an assassination in a Brussels hotel, a police inspector's attempt to solve it (despite serious obstacles thrown up by his superiors), and the assassin who realizes too late that his victim was the wrong target. Along the way, there are other minor sub-plots involving the EU's agricultural lobby (personified by Martin's pig-farmer brother), a disillusioned official at an EU think tank, and Auschwitz survivors who worry that the historical lessons of the Holocaust are slowly being lost.

The Capital is of course satire: Menasse pokes fun at the thought processes, language, and ambitions of bureaucrats in the EU – actually bureaucrats everywhere – as well as the conflicts between member states and their interests. But its resonance and popularity – Menasse, an Austrian, won Germany's top literary prize for the 2017 novel, which is now available in English – testify to its more complex and profound message. That message is that, despite its linguistic, cultural, and ethnic complexity (as well as deep political differences), Europeans share an enduring connection, both historical tragedies and optimism and renewal. And for Menasse, despite its shortcomings and comical layers of bureaucracy, the EU remains the primary vehicle for this renewal.

The Secretariat-General

The administration of the Commission is overseen by a Secretariat-General with a staff of about 700. The job of the Secretariat-General is to provide technical services and advice to the Commission, prepare the annual work program of the Commission, and organize and coordinate the work of the DGs and services. The secretary general chairs the weekly meetings of the *chefs de cabinet*, sits in on the weekly meetings of the commissioners, directs Commission relations with other EU institutions, and generally makes sure that the work of the Commission runs smoothly.[21] The position was held for nearly thirty years by Emile Noël of France. In 2018 Martin Selmayr, an uncharacteristically controversial figure, was tapped for the post.[22]

Committees

Most of the work of discussing and sorting out the details of proposed laws and policies is left to a series of advisory, management, and regulatory committees, participating in a phenomenon known as "comitology." There are several hundred such committees and subcommittees, chaired by the Commission and made up of small groups of officials from government departments in the member states. The committees have no formal powers to prevent the Commission from taking action, but the Commission is expected to take seriously the opinions of advisory committees in particular.

In addition, the Commission will work with expert committees consisting of national officials and specialists appointed by national governments, and consultative committees consisting of members with sectional interests, set up and funded directly by the Commission.[23] For example, if the Commission is thinking about a proposal for a new law on air pollution, it might have a meeting at which representatives from interest groups, the transport lobby, vehicle manufacturers, energy producers, consumer organizations, and other interested parties are invited to share their thoughts. Members are typically nominated by EU-wide organizations, but any interest group or lobbyist seeking to influence EU policy is well advised to give testimony before one of these committees.

HOW THE COMMISSION WORKS

The core responsibility of the Commission is to be the "guardian of the treaties," meaning that it must ensure that EU policies are advanced in light of the treaties. It does this in four ways.

Powers of Initiation

The Commission is legally obliged to make sure that the principles of the treaties are turned into practical laws and policies. In this respect it is sometimes described as a think tank and policy formulator, and it is expected to provide leadership for the EU.[24] It has the sole "right of initiative" on new European legislation and can also draw up proposals for entire new policy areas (as it did with the Single European Act and the Delors package for economic and monetary union) and pass them on to Parliament and the Council of Ministers for consideration. About 90 percent of Commission proposals become law. Compare this to the US Congress, where in the last legislative session the success rate was only 4 percent, even less if things like naming post offices or designating a week in May 2019 as "National Police Week" are excluded![25]

The Commission can take any initiative that it considers appropriate for advancing the principles of the treaties, but in reality most of its proposals are responses to either legal obligations or technical issues that need to be addressed. The Commission can also be prompted into action by other institutions; although neither Parliament nor the Council can formally initiate the lawmaking process, informal pressure and influence are brought to bear on the Commission. A proposal may also come from a commissioner or a staff member of one of the DGs, or may come as a result of a ruling by the Court of Justice. Member state governments, interest groups, and even corporations can exert direct or indirect pressure on the Commission. Increasing numbers of policy suggestions have also come from the European Council (see the section on agenda setting in Chapter 11), which gives general direction to the Commission in its policy agenda.

At the beginning of its term, the president of the Commission issues a document entitled "Political Guidelines for the Next Commission," which sets out the broad strategic objectives for the next five years. After this is given even more concrete form in the president's "State of the Union" speech to the EP, the "Political Guidelines" are formulated into discrete actions in an annual "Commission Work Programme" (CWP). Implementation of the CWP in specific Commission proposals often starts life as a draft written by middle-ranking Eurocrats in one of the DGs. It will then be passed up through the ranks of the DG, referred to other interested DGs, vetted by the Commission's Legal Service, presented at various stakeholder forums for consultation, and discussed by *cabinets* and advisory committees (for example, the European Economic and Social Committee or the Committee of the Regions, see Chapter 9). The draft law will be amended or revised along the way, before eventually reaching the College of Commissioners, which meets at least once each week to go through different proposals. Meetings usually take place on a Wednesday in Brussels, or in Strasbourg if Parliament is in plenary session. Meetings are not open to the public, but agendas and minutes are posted on the Commission website.

By a majority vote, the College can accept a law, reject it, send it back for redrafting, or defer making a decision. Once passed by the College, it will be sent to the EP and the Council of Ministers for a decision. It may take months or even years for the process to be completed, and Commission staff members will be involved at every stage, consulting widely with national bureaucrats and interest groups, working with and making presentations to the Council of Ministers and the EP, and carrying out their own research into the implications of the new law (see Box 5.3).

Powers of Implementation

Once a law or policy has been accepted, the Commission is responsible for ensuring that it is implemented by the member states. It has no power to do this directly but instead must work through national bureaucracies. The Commission has the power to (1) collect information from member states so that it can monitor progress on implementation; (2) take to the Court of Justice any member state, corporation, or individual that does not conform to the spirit of the treaties or follow subsequent EU law; and (if necessary) (3) impose sanctions or fines if a law is not being implemented. Every member state is legally obliged to report to the Commission on the progress it is making in meeting deadlines and incorporating EU law into national law, but detection can be difficult; governments and industries have been known to collude to hide the fact that they are breaking the law or not implementing a law. For this reason, the Commission also relies on whistle-blowing: individuals, corporations, and interest groups will occasionally report to the Commission that laws are being broken or that there are failures in implementation.

Box 5.3 EU Law

The foundation of the EU legal order is provided by nine major treaties: Paris (now expired), the two Treaties of Rome, the Merger Treaty, the Single European Act, Maastricht, Amsterdam, Nice, and Lisbon. Each results in changes to the one that came before, and cumulatively they set out the basic goals and principles of European integration and describe – as well as place limits on – the powers of EU institutions and of member states in their relationship with the EU. They have also spawned thousands of individual laws, which come in five main forms.

Regulations. Usually fairly narrow in intent, they are often designed to amend or adjust an existing law. A regulation is binding in its entirety on all member states and directly applicable in the sense that it does not need to be turned into national law.

Directives. These are binding on member states in terms of goals and objectives, but it is left up to the states to decide how best to achieve those goals. Most focus on outlining general policy goals, while some are aimed at harmonization. The governments of the member states must tell the Commission what they plan to do to achieve the goals of a directive.

Decisions. These are also binding and can be aimed at one or more member states, at institutions, and even at individuals. They are usually fairly specific in intent and have administrative rather than legislative goals. Some are aimed at making changes in the powers of the EU, and others are issued when the Commission must adjudicate disputes between member states or corporations.

Recommendations and Opinions. These have no binding force. They are used mainly to persuade or to provide interpretation on the application of regulations, directives, or decisions.

The Commission has also relied on two additional tools for the development of policies. *Green papers* are discussion papers on specific policy areas, addressed to interested parties and designed to elicit their input. *White papers* contain official proposals for Community policies and actions, and they usually follow a green paper.

The Commission adds to the pressure on member states by publicizing progress on implementation, hoping to embarrass the slower states into action. It was particularly busy in the two to three years leading up to the 2004 enlargement, checking to make sure that the Eastern European states were keeping up with the schedule to implement the large body of EU law. A report issued by the Commission just months before enlargement warned that all ten countries faced problems and were running the risk of fines, export bans, and losses of EU subsidies unless their records improved. Poland had the worst record, being criticized for its performance in areas as diverse as farm subsidies, inadequate standards at meat and dairy plants, corruption, and its fishing industry. At the other end of the scale, the Commission announced that Lithuania and Slovenia had made the most progress.[26]

If a member state falls behind schedule, the Commission can issue a warning (a Letter of Formal Notice) giving it time to comply – usually about two months. If the member still fails to comply, the Commission can issue a Reasoned Opinion explaining why it feels there may be a violation. If there is still noncompliance, the state can be taken to the Court of Justice for failure to fulfill its obligations. In 2018 for example, the court found that Greece, Italy, Spain, and Poland had failed to implement or fulfill various environment obligations.[27] Most cases of noncompliance come less from a deliberate avoidance by a member state than from differences in interpretation or differences in the levels of efficiency of national bureaucracies; the latter accounts, for example, for many of Italy's infringements because its national bureaucracy is notorious for delay, inefficiency, and corruption.

Managing the EU Budget and Finances

The Commission ensures that all EU revenues are collected, plays a key role in drafting and guiding the budget through the Council of Ministers and Parliament, and administers EU spending, especially under the Common Agricultural Policy and the structural funds. Collection involves working with national agencies to make sure that they understand where income is to be generated and ensuring that the member states make their required contributions. The administration of EU spending is undertaken in cooperation with the Court of Auditors (see Chapter 9); the Commission is involved in authorizing spending, ensuring that it has gone for the purposes intended, and evaluating the effectiveness of spending.[28] Finally, the "European Semester," a kind of initial vetting of member states' budgets, was introduced in 2010 as the financial and debt crises were gathering steam. It enables the Commission to undertake an analysis of each country's plans for its national budget, including any structural or macroeconomic reforms. While the Commission does not mandate specific steps to be taken by member states, its recommendations are treated seriously.

External Relations

The Commission acts as the EU's main external representative in dealings with international organizations such as the United Nations, the World Trade Organization, and the Organisation for Economic Cooperation and Development.[29] Discussions on global trade are overseen by the Commission acting on behalf of EU member states; thus the Commission has increasingly become the most common point of contact for US and Japanese trade negotiators. The Commission has also been a key point of contact between the EU and the rest of the world. As the power and significance of the EU have grown, more than 140 governments have opened diplomatic missions in Brussels accredited to the EU, and until the creation of the new European External Action Service (see Chapter 15) the Commission operated more than 130 offices in other parts of the world. The growing significance of the EU and the Commission can be seen in the numbers of foreign leaders who regularly visit Brussels (which is also the headquarters of NATO).

The Commission oversees the process by which applications for full or associate membership in the EU are considered. Although the applications initially go to the Council of Ministers, the Commission examines all the implications and reports back to the Council. If the Council decides to open negotiations with an applicant country, the Commission oversees the process.

QUESTIONS TO CONSIDER

1 What are the significant changes Lisbon made to the Commission? What effect, if any, have these changes had on the Commission's power?
2 What are the arguments for or against having the Commission president nominated by the winning (or even largest) party group in the EP?
3 What effect might the changing gender balance in the College and in the DGs have on Commission policies? Should more be done to ensure balanced gender composition in the Commission? If so, what?

NOTES

1 See Hussein Kassim et al., *The European Commission of the Twenty-First Century* (Oxford: Oxford University Press, 2013).

2 Commission figures are from the EU's official website. See "EU Administration – Staff, Languages and Location" at https://europa.eu/european-union/about-eu/figures/administration_en, accessed on July 13, 2019. US figures are from the Congressional Research Service at https://fas.org/sgp/crs/misc/R43590.pdf, accessed July 13, 2019. The number of federal employees in the US is at its lowest level since 1966. However, by some estimates, the size of the US federal bureaucracy – when contract employees are taken into account – is actually much bigger. See Paul C. Light, *The True Size of Government* (Washington, DC: Brookings Institution Press, 1999).

3 See Derek W. Urwin, *The Community of Europe*, 2nd ed., 107–113 (London: Longman, 1995).

4 For details of the nomination and appointment process, see David Spence, "The President, the College and the Cabinets," in *The European Commission*, 3rd ed., edited by David Spence, 34–38 (London: John Harper, 2006).

5 BBC News, "EU Panel Rejects Justice Nominee", October 11, 2004, at http://news.bbc.co.uk/2/hi/europe/3734572.stm, accessed April 27, 2020.

6 See "Ursula von der Leyen's Bumpy Start," *The Economist*, October 17, 2019, at www.economist.com/europe/2019/10/17/ursula-von-der-leyens-bumpy-start, accessed October 18, 2019; Matina Stevis-Grindneff and Milan Schreuer, "The Best and Brightest? Not Always for EU Leadership Jobs," *New York Times*, October 6, 2019, at www.nytimes.com/2019/10/06/world/europe/brussels-european-union.html., accessed October 6, 2019.

7 For more details, see Andrew MacMullen, "European Commissioners: National Routes to a European Elite," in *At the Heart of the Union: Studies of the European Commission*, 2nd ed., edited by Neill Nugent (New York: St. Martin's Press, 2000).

8 Neill Nugent, *The European Commission*, 88–91 (Basingstoke, UK: Palgrave Macmillan, 2001).

9 Ibid., 105–106.

10 Spence, "The President, the College and the Cabinets," 60–72.

11 Interestingly, former Commission president Juncker in his State of the Union speech in 2017 proposed that the presidencies of the Commission and the European Council be combined, arguing that "Europe would be easier to understand if one captain was steering the ship." As of this writing, however, there seems to be limited appetite for such a move. See Daniel Boffey, "Juncker Says EU Will 'Move On' from Brexit in State of Union Speech," *Guardian*, September 13, 2017, at www.theguardian.com/politics/2017/sep/13/jean-claude-juncker-plays-down-brexit-in-eu-state-of-union-speech, accessed September 18, 2017.

12 For a short assessment of the Delors presidency, see Helen Drake, "The European Commission and the Politics of Legitimacy in the European Union," in *At the Heart of the Union*, edited by Nugent, 238–244. See also Helen Drake, *Jacques Delors: Perspectives on a European Leader* (London: Routledge, 2000).

13 George Ross, *Jacques Delors and European Integration*, 51 (New York: Oxford University Press, 1995).

14 Laura Tilindyte, "Election of the President of the European Commission. Understanding the *Spitzenkandidaten* Process," *Briefing*, 6 (Brussels: European Parliamentary Research Service, February 2019).

15 Katrin Bennhold, "EU's Top Pick: Too Pious for Feminists, Too Feminist for Conservatives," *New York Times*, July 5, 2019, at www.nytimes.com/2019/07/05/world/europe/eus-top-pick-too-pious-for-feminists-too-feminist-for-conservatives.html, accessed July 6, 2019.

16 Michelle Cini, *The European Commission: Leadership, Organization and Culture in the EU Administration*, 109 (Manchester, UK: Manchester University Press, 1996).

17 European Commission press release, July 1, 2003, europa.eu/newsroom/index_en.htm.

18 See Antonis Ellinas and Ezra Suleiman, *The European Commission and Bureaucratic Autonomy* (Cambridge: Cambridge University Press, 2012).

19 See Kassim et al., *The European Commission of the Twenty-First Century*.

20 Robert Menasse, *The Capital*, trans. Jamie Bulloch (New York: Liveright, 2019).

21 For more details see Hussein Kassim, "The Secretariat General of the European Commission," in *The European Commission*, edited by Spence.

22 Selmayr, the former chief of staff to Commission President Juncker, was appointed to the post of deputy secretary general in 2018. Shortly thereafter, the secretary general unexpectedly resigned. Despite having made a number of enemies in Brussels, Selmayr was handed the top job by Juncker, already on his way out as he made way for the new Commission. Moreover, Selmayr – who resigned in the late summer of 2019 – compiled a list of confidants to be promoted before von der Leyen took office in what some see as a preemptive "coup." See Steven Erlanger, "A Sudden Promotion Raises Questions in the Brussels Bubble," *The New York Times*, March 11, 2018, at www.nytimes.com/2018/03/11/world/europe/eu-martin-selmayr-commission.html, accessed March 12, 2018 and "Selmayr Prepares New 'Coup' against Ursula von der Leyen," *Euractiv*, July 28, 2019, at www.euractiv.com/section/future-eu/news/selmayr-prepares-new-coup-against-ursula-von-der-leyen/, accessed July 29, 2019.
23 Nugent, *The European Commission*, 244–245.
24 Cini, *The European Commission*, 18–22.
25 The percentage of bills enacted in the US Congress in 2019 can be found at www.govtrack.us/congress/bills/statistics, accessed July 14, 2019. For commemorate holidays enacted in 2019, see Congressional Research Service, *Commemorative Days, Weeks, and Months: Background and Current Practice*, at https://fas.org/sgp/crs/misc/R44431.pdf, accessed July 14, 2019.
26 "Stark Warning to New EU Members," *BBC News*, November 5, 2003, at http://news.bbc.co.uk/2/hi/europe/3242941.stm, accessed November 6, 2003.
27 See Court of Justice of the European Union, *Annual Report 2018. The Year in Review*, at https://curia.europa.eu/jcms/upload/docs/application/pdf/2019-04/ra_pan_2018_en.pdf, accessed July 15, 2019.
28 Nugent, *The European Commission*, 287–288.
29 See Michael Smith, "The Commission and External Relations," in *The European Commission*, edited by Spence, chapter 12.

BIBLIOGRAPHY

BBC, "Stark Warning to New EU Members," *BBC News*, November 5, 2003, at http://news.bbc.co.uk/2/hi/europe/3242941.stm, accessed November 6, 2003.

Bennhold, Katrin, "EU's Top Pick: Too Pious for Feminists, Too Feminist for Conservatives," *New York Times*, July 5, 2019, at www.nytimes.com/2019/07/05/world/europe/eus-top-pick-too-pious-for-feminists-too-feminist-for-conservatives.html, accessed July 6, 2019.

Boffey, Danile, "Juncker Says EU Will 'Move On' from Brexit in State of Union Speech," *Guardian*, September 18, 2017, at www.theguardian.com/politics/2017/sep/13/jean-claude-juncker-plays-down-brexit-in-eu-state-of-union-speech, accessed September 18, 2017.

Congressional Research Service, "Federal Workforce Statistics Sources: OPM and OMB," at https://fas.org/sgp/crs/misc/R43590.pdf, accessed July 13, 2019.

Congressional Research Service, *Commemorative Days, Weeks, and Months: Background and Current Practice*, at https://fas.org/sgp/crs/misc/R44431.pdf, accessed July 14, 2019.

Cini, Michelle, *The European Commission: Leadership, Organization and Culture in the EU Administration* (Manchester, UK: Manchester University Press, 1996).

Court of Justice of the European Union, *Annual Report 2018. The Year in Review*, at https://curia.europa.eu/jcms/upload/docs/application/pdf/2019-04/ra_pan_2018_en.pdf, accessed July 15, 2019.

Drake, Helen, "The European Commission and the Politics of Legitimacy in the European Union," in *At the Heart of the Union: Studies of the European Commission*, edited by Neill Nugent, 226–244 (London and New York: Palgrave Macmillan, 1997).

Drake, Helen, *Jacques Delors: Perspectives on a European Leader* (London: Routledge, 2000).

Economist, The, "Ursula von der Leyen's Bumpy Start," October 17, 2019, at www.economist.com/europe/2019/10/17/ursula-von-der-leyens-bumpy-start, accessed October 18, 2019.

Ellinas, Antonis, and Ezra Suleiman, *The European Commission and Bureaucratic Autonomy* (Cambridge: Cambridge University Press, 2012).

Erlanger, Steven, "A Sudden Promotion Raises Questions in the Brussels Bubble," *New York Times*, March 11, 2018, at www.nytimes.com/2018/03/11/world/europe/eu-martin-selmayr-commission.html, accessed March 12, 2018.

Euractiv, "Selmayr Prepares New 'Coup' against Ursula von der Leyen," July 28, 2019, at www. euractiv.com/section/future-eu/news/selmayr-prepares-new-coup-against-ursula-von-der-leyen/, accessed July 29, 2019.

European Union, "EU Administration – Staff, Languages and Location," at https://europa.eu/european-union/about-eu/figures/administration_en, accessed on July 13, 2019.

Hartlapp, Miriam, Julia Metz, and Christian Rauh, *Which Policy for Europe? Power and Conflict inside the European Commission* (Oxford: Oxford University Press, 2014).

Kassim, Hussein, John Peterson, Michael W. Bauer, Sara Connolly, Renaud Dehousse, Liesbet Hooghe, and Andrew Thompson, *The European Commission of the Twenty-first Century* (Oxford: Oxford University Press, 2013).

MacMullen, Andrew, "European Commissioners: National Routes to a European Elite," in *At the Heart of the Union: Studies of the European Commission*, 2nd ed, edited by Neill Nugent, 28–50 (London and New York: Macmillan/St. Martin's Press, 2000).

Menasse, Robert, *The Capital*, trans. Jamie Bulloch (New York: Liveright, 2019).

Nugent, Neill, *The European Commission* (Basingstoke, UK: Palgrave Macmillan, 2000).

Ross, George, *Jacques Delors and European Integration* (New York: Oxford University Press, 1995).

Smith, Michael, "The Commission and External Relations," in *The European Commission*, 3rd ed., edited by David Spence, 39–50 (London: John Harper, 2006).

Spence, David, "The President, the College and the Cabinets," in *The European Commission*, 3rd ed., edited by David Spence, 34–38 (London: John Harper, 2006).

Stevis-Grindneff, Matina, and Milan Schreuer, "The Best and Brightest? Not Always for EU Leadership Jobs," *New York Times*, October 6, 2019, at www.nytimes.com/2019/10/06/world/europe/brussels-european-union.html, accessed October 6, 2019.

Tilindyte, Laura, "Election of the President of the European Commission. Understanding the *Spitzenkandidaten* Process," *Briefing* (Brussels: European Parliamentary Research Service, February 2019).

Urwin, Derek W., *The Community of Europe*, 2nd ed. (London: Longman, 1995).

FURTHER READING

Miriam Hartlapp, Julia Metz, and Christian Rauh, *Which Policy for Europe? Power and Conflict inside the European Commission* (Oxford: Oxford University Press, 2014).
>   An empirical and theoretical study of the dynamics of the Commission, opening the "black box" of internal Commission decision formation and decision making.

Neill Nugent, *The European Commission* (Basingstoke, UK: Palgrave Macmillan, 2000).
>   Although it is now showing its age, this is still the most thorough single-authored study of the structure and workings of the Commission.

George Ross, *Jacques Delors and European Integration* (New York: Oxford University Press, 1995); Helen Drake, *Jacques Delors: Perspectives on a European Leader* (London: Routledge, 2000).
>   Two studies of the Commission under Delors, the first written by a scholar who was given unparalleled access to its meetings and documents.

Hussein Kassim, John Peterson, Michael W. Bauer, Sara Connolly, Renaud Dehousse, Liesbet Hooghe, and Andrew Thompson, *The European Commission of the Twenty-first Century* (Oxford: Oxford University Press, 2013).
>   By far the best recent study of the women and men who make up the Commission bureaucracy, using a comprehensive survey, semi-structured interviews, and employment data.

Antonis Ellinas and Ezra Suleiman, *The European Commission and Bureaucratic Autonomy* (Cambridge: Cambridge University Press, 2012).
>   An in-depth study of the workings of the bureaucracy of the Commission and its attempts to sustain its independence, based on interviews with 200 top officials.

CHAPTER 6

The Council of Ministers and The European Council

CHAPTER OVERVIEW

- The Council of the European Union, or Council of Ministers, is one of the most intergovernmental of the EU's institutions and the forum in which government ministers from the member states meet to make decisions on EU policies. It performs legislative functions (as well as some executive ones) and can be considered akin to an upper house of parliament for the EU.
- The European Council – often confused with the Council of the EU – is the meeting place of the leaders of the EU member states and acts like a board of directors for the EU. Although the day-to-day management of EU business is still left with the Commission, the Council of Ministers, and the European Parliament (EP), the European Council sets the broad direction of policy and can be considered, along with the Commission, the quasi-executive branch of the EU.
- Recent treaties have formalized the institutional power of the European Council while changing the Council of Ministers' organizational structure. The Treaty of Lisbon in particular reduced the number of standing councils in the Council of Ministers, redefined the wrole of the General Secretariat, altered the future method of voting within the councils, and – while retaining a presidency for most of the councils – now has a foreign policy council chaired by the EU's High Representative of the Union for Foreign Affairs and Security Policy, who also sits in on meetings for the European Council when foreign affairs issues are discussed.

The Council of the European Union (often known as the Council of Ministers, as it will mostly be referred to here) is the forum in which national government ministers meet to make decisions on EU law and policy. It is one of the primary champions of national interests and one of the most powerful of the EU institutions. Once the Commission has proposed a new law, the Council of Ministers, in conjunction with the EP, is responsible for accepting or rejecting the proposal. The Council of Ministers also approves the EU budget, a responsibility it shares with the EP; coordinates the economic policies of the member states; champions the Common Foreign and Security Policy; helps coordinate police and judicial cooperation on criminal matters; and concludes international treaties on behalf of the EU. In short, it has a mix of mostly legislative and some executive functions. In many ways, its legislative power makes the Council of Ministers comparable to the US Senate, with the EP playing the role of the US House of Representatives.

Yet while all its decisions are credited to "the Council" (singular) its formal name – *Council of the European Union* – is misleading, because it actually consists of several different groups of ministers, membership depending on the topic under discussion. Thus, economic and finance ministers will meet to deal with economic issues, environment ministers to discuss proposals for environmental law and policy, and so on. Despite its powers, the Council of Ministers is less well known and more poorly understood than either the Commission or Parliament. Its meetings are closed (although most are broadcast on the internet), there has been less scholarly study of its structure and processes, and when most Europeans think of the EU, they think of the Commission, forgetting that the Commission can achieve little without the support of the Council of Ministers.

The European Council, meanwhile, is the meeting place for the leaders of the EU member states. This group convenes periodically at short summit meetings and provides strategic policy direction for the EU. Like a steering committee or a board of directors for the EU, the European Council sketches the broad picture and usually leaves it to the other institutions (particularly the Commission and the Council of Ministers) to fill in the details. It was created in 1974 in response to a feeling among European Community (EC) leaders that the Community needed stronger leadership to clear blockages in decision making and to give it a sense of direction. It gained legal recognition with the Single European Act, and Maastricht confirmed that the European Council would "provide the Union with the necessary impetus for its development and shall define the general political guidelines thereof." Since the Treaty of Lisbon, it has had an appointed president.

While intergovernmental at heart, the European Council by no means ignores general European interests. It has been an important motor for integration, launching major new initiatives (including every new EU treaty), issuing key declarations on international crises, generating EU institutional changes, and giving new momentum to EU foreign policy. It has been argued that without European Council summits the Community would not have survived the economic problems of the 1970s, launched the single market program during the 1980s, nor adjusted to changes in the international environment during the 1990s.[1] However, the European Council has also had its failures, including its inability to speed up agricultural and budgetary reform and to reach agreement on common EU responses to the two Gulf wars, the Bosnian conflict, the crisis in Kosovo in 1998 and 1999, and to respond more quickly and vigorously to the debt crisis in the eurozone and the migration crisis when they first emerged.

Before Lisbon, the Council of Ministers and the European Council were both chaired by government representatives occupying the presidency on a six-month rotation. But Lisbon created a new position of president of the European Council, so now only meetings of the Council of Ministers (excepting foreign policy) are chaired through the rotating presidency. This rotation has the advantage of providing member states with the opportunity to bring their pet issues to the agenda, put their stamp on the work and direction of the EU, and to lead the EU in its dealings with other countries. Meanwhile, the day-to-day work of the Council of Ministers is overseen – and most of its key decisions mapped out – by the Committee of Permanent Representatives (known by its French acronym, Coreper). Made up of the permanent representatives of the member states, Coreper is one of the most influential institutions in the EU system of governance, and yet most Europeans are barely aware of its existence.

EVOLUTION OF THE COUNCIL OF MINISTERS

The Council of Ministers grew out of the Special Council of Ministers of the European Coal and Steel Community (ECSC), which was created at the insistence of the Benelux countries to defend their national interests in the face of the dominance of France, Germany, and Italy.[2] Because its members consisted of national government ministers, the ECSC Council provided an intergovernmental balance to the supranational qualities of the High Authority (precursor to today's European Commission).

A separate Council of Ministers was created for the European Economic Community (EEC) in 1958, where the idea of defending national interests was taken a step further with a weighted system of voting designed to prevent the bigger member states from overwhelming the smaller ones. The EEC Council had only six member states, but among them they had seventeen votes: four each for the three largest countries, two each for Belgium and the Netherlands, and one for Luxembourg. In the case of simple majority voting, the big three could easily outvote the small three, but some votes required a qualified majority, meaning that a measure needed twelve votes from at least four states to pass. This stipulation not only protected small states and large states from each other, but also encouraged them to work together. As a result of the Merger Treaty, a single Council of Ministers was created in 1967. Its name was formally changed to Council of the European Union in 1993 following the passage of the Maastricht treaty, but this is still interchangeable with the "Council of Ministers."

Speaking at the first session of the ECSC Council of Ministers in September 1952, West Germany's Chancellor Konrad Adenauer argued that the Council stood:

> at the crossroads of two kinds of sovereignty, national and supranational.... While it must safeguard the national interests of the member states, it must not regard this as its paramount task ... which is to promote the interests of the Community.[3]

The Council has been torn ever since between these two goals, which some see as compatible and others as contradictory. It is dominated by national government ministers with their own parochial concerns, so its work is ultimately the sum of those particular interests. But the search for compromise can also encourage ministers to reach decisions that promote the broader interests of the EU.

It was assumed that as Europe integrated and the member states learned to trust one another, the Council would become less important, and the Commission would be able to initiate, decide, *and* implement policy. Yet in fact the power and influence of the Council expanded because member states hesitated to give up powers to the Commission. The result was a perpetuation of the idea of the EEC as an intergovernmental organization, which displeased those who supported a federal Europe. Several other developments reinforced the power and influence of the Council at that time:

- It increasingly adopted its own nonbinding agreements and recommendations, which the Commission found difficult to ignore.
- As the interests and reach of the EU spread, both the Commission and the Council of Ministers became involved in new policy areas not covered by the original treaties.
- The presidency of the Council of Ministers became integral to the EU decision-making system and the source of many key initiatives on issues such as economic and monetary union, and foreign policy.[4]

Since Lisbon, however, both the European Council and the EP have made inroads into the power of the Council of Ministers. The former – which is similarly torn between European and national pressures – has more power in deciding the broad goals of the EU, and the latter has demanded and won an equal say with the Council of Ministers in decision making. Even though the Luxembourg Compromise introduced the power of veto into the Council, it was rarely used, and decision making grew increasingly consensual and less nationalistic. More of its decisions have also been subject to qualified majority voting, which has obliged member states to put EU interests above national concerns. Thanks to changes introduced since the Single European Act – and most especially Lisbon – the Council of Ministers has had to share its decision-making authority with Parliament, and the two have effectively become the co-legislatures of the EU.

STRUCTURE OF THE COUNCIL OF MINISTERS

For many years, the Council of Ministers was based in the Justus Lipsius building in the European Quarter of Brussels (and still used today for offices and additional meeting rooms for the Council). It moved, as did the European Council, in 2017 to a newly renovated (and renamed) building, the Europa building, also in the European Quarter of Brussels. Inside those doors it has four main elements: the Councils of Ministers themselves, the Committee of Permanent Representatives, the presidency, and the General Secretariat.

The Councils

While there were once nearly two dozen different so-called technical councils (or "configurations") that were grouped under the general heading of the Council of Ministers, the number has now been reduced to ten:

- Agriculture and Fisheries
- Competitiveness
- Economic and Financial Affairs (Ecofin)
- Education, Youth, Culture and Sport
- Employment, Social Policy, Health and Consumer Affairs
- Environment
- Foreign Affairs
- General Affairs
- Justice and Home Affairs
- Transport, Telecommunications and Energy

Although supposedly equal in terms of their status and powers, two of the councils – the General Affairs Council and the Foreign Affairs Council – have defined roles in the treaties.[5] While the General Affairs Council prepares and ensures follow-up meetings of the European Council, the Foreign Affairs Council deals with external relations and trade and development issues. Other important councils include the Economic and Financial Affairs Council (Ecofin), the Justice and Home Affairs Council, and the Agriculture and Fisheries Council. These five councils meet most often (monthly for General Affairs, Foreign Affairs, Agriculture, and Ecofin), while the other councils meet three to four times per year or on an ad hoc basis. The number of meetings is determined by the country holding the presidency, and altogether the councils now meet about fifty to sixty times each year. Brussels is normally the gathering point for meetings, but during April, June, and October they are held in Luxembourg. Sessions usually last no more than one or two days, depending on the agenda, the volume of work, and the level of formality.

In a perfect world, each of the councils would consist of the relevant and equivalent ministers from each member state, but this does not always happen, for two main reasons. First, member states sometimes send deputy ministers or state secretaries instead of their ministers;

PHOTO 6.1 A Meeting of the Employment, Social Policy, Health and Consumer Affairs Council in May 2015.

Source: © European Union, 2015, EC – Audiovisual Service.

the relevant minister may have more urgent problems to deal with at home, may want to avoid political embarrassment on some issue, or may not think the meeting is important enough to attend. However, by the terms of the Lisbon treaty, every delegate to a Council meeting should be authorized to act on behalf of his/her member state. Second, not every member state has an identical set of ministers, and each divides policy portfolios differently. For example, some member states have ministers of women's affairs, while others do not. The result is that Council meetings are often attended by a mixed set of ministers with different responsibilities. The Commission and the European Central Bank are invited to send representatives to relevant meetings, but the Council may decide to meet without either institution being present. Another informal group, the Eurogroup, acts as something of a liaison between the Council of Ministers and the European Council on economic questions for eurozone members. It consists of ministers of the euro area member states, a president selected by the members (for a two-and-a-half-year term) and meets once a month immediately before Ecofin meetings.

Permanent Representatives

The ministers may be the most visible element of the Council hierarchy, but its heart and soul is the powerful and secretive Committee of Permanent Representatives (Coreper). Undoubtedly the most underrated and most often overlooked part of the entire EU decision-making process, Coreper is the meeting place for the permanent representatives – the heads of the Permanent Representations (much like embassies) of the member states in Brussels. Thanks to Coreper, as much as 90 percent of the work of the Council is resolved before the ministers even meet.[6] Only the most politically sensitive and controversial proposals normally go directly to the ministers without a decision having been reached by Coreper. One former UK government minister, Alan Clark, put it colorfully (if not entirely accurately) when he noted in his diaries that it makes not the slightest difference to the conclusions of a meeting what Ministers say at it. Everything is decided, and horse-traded off by officials at Coreper.... The ministers arrive on the scene at the last minute, hot, tired, ill, or drunk (sometimes all of these together), read out their piece and depart.[7]

Though no mention of Coreper was made in the Treaty of Paris, a Coordinating Committee helped prepare ministerial meetings in the ECSC, and member states began to appoint permanent representatives to the EEC in 1958.[8] Coreper was finally recognized in the 1965 Merger Treaty, by which time the growing workload of the Council had led to a decision to create two committees: permanent representatives constitute Coreper II and grapple with broad issues coming before General Affairs, Ecofin, and Justice and Home Affairs, while their deputies constitute Coreper I and concentrate on the work of the other councils.[9]

The permanent representatives act as a valuable link between Brussels and the member states, ensuring that the views of the member states (or at least their governments) are expressed and defended and that the capitals stay informed of what is happening in Brussels. Because they interact with each other so much and come to know each other well, the representatives are occasionally torn between defending national positions and trying to ensure that their meetings lead to successful conclusions.[10] At the same time, they know each other better than do the ministers and so are more apt to reach compromises and to negotiate deals, often informally over lunch. They also play a key role in organizing Council meetings by preparing agendas, deciding which proposals go to which council, and determining which of the proposals are most likely to be approved by the Council with or without discussion.

Much like a national legislature, the Council of Ministers also has a complex network of committees and working parties that does most of the preparatory work and tries to reach agreement on proposed legislation before it goes to the Council. There are several committees established by the treaties or by acts of the Council – including those on employment, trade, and agriculture – each made up mainly of national government officials but occasionally including representatives from interest groups (for example, the Committee on Employment includes representatives from industry). Working parties are organized along policy lines (so, for example, the working party on social questions will look at various sociocultural proposals, many with a gender dimension) and bring together policy specialists, national experts, members of the Permanent Representations, and staff from the Commission. They usually meet several times each week to review Commission proposals and try to identify points of agreement and disagreement. (Working parties are not to be confused with political parties; see Chapter 7.)

The Presidency

As mentioned earlier, while Lisbon placed the European Council under the direction of an appointed president, it did not fundamentally alter the structure of the presidency of the Council of Ministers: each such presidency continues to be held not by a person but by a country, with every EU member state taking a turn for a term of six months, beginning in January and July each year. The only exception to this rule, again courtesy of Lisbon, is that the Foreign Affairs Council is chaired by the High Representative of the Union for Foreign Affairs and Security Policy (who is also a member of the College of Commissioners), except when trade is on the agenda, in which case the rotating presidency takes up the chair. The presidency has several responsibilities:[11]

- It prepares and coordinates the work of the Council of Ministers, and sets the agendas for about 2,000 meetings, the most important of which are those of the ministerial councils.
- It arranges and chairs meetings of the Council of Ministers and Coreper and represents the Council in relations with other EU institutions. An active presidency will lean heavily on Coreper to push its favorite proposals and to ensure that agreement is reached.[12]
- It mediates, bargains, and promotes cooperation among member states and ensures that policy development has consistency and continuity. To that end, presidencies are measured according to the extent to which they are able to encourage compromise and build a consensus among the EU members, and by how many agreements they fail to broker.

At one time, the rotation among member states was alphabetical, but as membership of the EU grew, a more complex arrangement emerged to ensure a balanced work load and a mix of big and small countries. Lisbon formalized the practice whereby the Council uses a troika system in which ministers from the incumbent presidency work closely with their predecessors and their successors. This system has in effect created an eighteen-month, three-state "team presidency," albeit with one of the member states chairing all meetings for a six-month period and formally holding the position of president. Each troika should reflect the diversity and geographical balance of member states within the Union (see Table 6.1). Just how much one member state (or the troika) can actually achieve is debatable, because despite the importance attached to the job by the holder, and the grand plans that each member state typically has for its turn at the top, much of what happens is outside the control of the presidency. As *The Economist* once put it:

> Holding the presidency for six months lets a country and its leader host a few summits, chair a lot of meetings and enjoy an unusual share of the international spotlight. But it is rare that six-month presidencies decisively affect the Union's direction.[13]

So is the presidency much ado about nothing? Not quite. The main advantage of holding the presidency is that it allows a member state to convene meetings and launch strategic initiatives on issues of particular national interest, to try to bring those issues and initiatives to the top of the EU agenda, and to earn prestige and credibility (assuming the president does a good job). The presidency also allows the leaders of smaller states to negotiate directly with other world leaders – which they might otherwise rarely be able to do – and contributes

TABLE 6.1 Rotation of Presidencies of the Council of Ministers

Year	First Half	Second Half
2020	Croatia	Germany
2021	Portugal	Slovenia
2022	France	Czechia
2023	Sweden	Spain
2024	Belgium	Hungary

Source: European Council and Council of the European Union, at https://eur-lex.europa.eu/legal-content/en/TXT/PDF/?uri=CELEX:32016D1316&from=EN.

to European integration by making the EU more real to the citizens of that country; it helps them to feel more involved and to see that they have a stake in the development of the EU.

The main disadvantage of the job is the sheer volume of work involved, a burden that is especially onerous on member states with limited resources and small bureaucracies. Different states have different approaches to the presidency, depending upon a combination of their national administrative and political cultures, their attitudes toward the EU, and their policy priorities. This drawback was described in colorful terms by *The European* when it likened an Italian presidency to "a bus trip with the Marx brothers in the driver's seat," while the subsequent Luxembourg presidency was more like "being driven by a sedate couple who only take to the road on Sundays and then infuriate other motorists by respecting the speed limit."[14] Presidencies, in short, illustrate the often contrasting styles and priorities different member states bring to the job, as well as the frustrations they experience in really achieving their goals.

The General Secretariat

This is the bureaucracy of the Council, consisting of about 3,000 staff members based in Brussels, most of whom are translators and service staff. The office is headed by a secretary general appointed for a five-year term. The General Secretariat prepares Council meetings, advises the presidency, provides legal advice for the Council and Coreper, briefs every Council meeting on the status of each of the agenda items, keeps records, manages the Council budget, and generally gives the work of the Council some continuity. In 1999, the secretary general received new powers when the position was combined with the new office of the High Representative for the Common Foreign and Security Policy, and in so doing became a hub for the development of the EU's foreign and security policies.[15] But Lisbon reworked this; with the High Representative now chairing the Foreign Affairs Council (and serving as a vice president in the Commission as well) the role of secretary general is similar to its pre-1999 incarnation.

HOW THE COUNCIL OF MINISTERS WORKS

The Council of Ministers has a cluster of specific responsibilities, including overseeing attempts to coordinate the economic policies of the member states, working closely with the Commission on international treaties, approving (in conjunction with the EP) the EU budget, promoting the Common Foreign and Security Policy of the EU (through the High Representative and the Foreign Affairs Council), and coordinating cooperation between national courts and police forces on criminal matters. Its primary responsibility, though, is to decide – in conjunction with Parliament – which proposals for new European laws will be adopted and which will not. The European Commission may have a monopoly on proposing new laws and policies, but the Council and Parliament can encourage it to investigate an issue and to submit proposals for new policies or laws. The Council has exploited loopholes in the treaties to expand this power over the years, and the struggle between the Council and the Commission for power and influence has become one of the most important internal dynamics of EU decision making.[16]

What happens to a Commission proposal when it reaches the Council of Ministers depends on its complexity and urgency, and on the extent to which problems have already been ironed out in discussions between Council and Commission staff. The more complex proposals usually go first to one or more of the Coreper working parties, which examine the proposal in detail and identify points of agreement and disagreement.[17] The proposal then goes to Coreper itself, which considers the political implications and tries to clear up as many of the remaining problems as it can, ensuring that meetings of ministers are as quick and painless as possible before it moves on to the relevant Council.

The method of voting in the Council of Minister has changed dramatically over the years: although unanimity was once the rule it is now the rare exception, and while a simple majority continues to be used for some procedural or narrow policy issues, most issues are decided by qualified majority voting, or QMV. The idea behind QMV in its various forms is to prevent big states from having too much power and to encourage states to form coalitions. It also reduces the tendency toward nationalism inherent in the way the Council of Ministers is structured. Under the rules of QMV devised by the Treaty of Nice, each EU member state (or more properly, minister in the council) was allotted several votes roughly in proportion to its population for a total of 352 votes. To be successful, a proposal had to win a triple majority: a majority of states had to be in favor, they had to have a total of 260 votes, and those votes had to come from states whose cumulative population represented 328 million people (at that time, around 62 percent of the EU population). This form of QMV was criticized as setting the bar for approval too high. Lisbon has revised these rules to a double majority: to win approval a proposal must receive 55 percent of the vote from a minimum of fifteen member states home to at least 65 percent of the population. A blocking coalition must have at least four states representing 35 percent of the population of the EU. This formula stays the same post-Brexit but large states, according to some analyses, will gain voting power at the expense of smaller states.[18] Nevertheless, because small states have disproportionate representation in the EP in terms of population-to-MEP ratios (see Chapter 7), Brexit will have little effect on member state power dynamics in the EU.

Since the Luxembourg Compromise, each member state has possessed an implied national veto. Although rarely used, its very existence can be employed as a threat, and governments can use it to convince their citizens that national sovereignty has not been compromised by EU membership. A number of attempts since the 1980s to invoke the veto, usually in connection with votes on agricultural prices, failed for lack of political support. Typically, a vote will not be called if the threat of veto exists.[19]

Once the Council is faced with having to make a decision, three main options exist:

- Under the *consultation procedure* – once the most common method of decision making – the Council asks Parliament for its opinion, and Parliament can either accept or reject the proposal, or ask for amendments. If amendments are needed the Commission makes them and the new proposal advances to the Council, which then decides whether to accept or reject the proposal, with additional changes if desired.
- Under the *ordinary legislative procedure* – once known as the codecision procedure and now by far the most common method – the Council shares legislative powers with Parliament. Both institutions read and discuss the proposal twice and must agree on a common final draft. If they fail, a Council–Parliament conciliation committee is formed to develop agreeable wording and the proposal goes back to both institutions for a third reading and a vote. The proposal is either rejected or becomes law.
- Under the *consent procedure*, Parliament must agree before passing a proposal. Unlike the consultation procedure, where it can suggest amendments, the consent procedure requires acceptance or rejection of the proposal.

Because the Council of Ministers is a meeting place for national interests, the keys to understanding how it works lie in terms such as *compromise*, *bargaining*, and *diplomacy*. The ministers are often leading political figures at home, so they are clearly motivated by national

---

Box 6.1 Peeking Behind the Curtain: Meetings of the Council of Ministers

Meetings of the Council can often seem chaotic and unwieldy, with national delegations of perhaps half a dozen members each, delegations from the Commission and the General Secretariat, and a phalanx of interpreters. The number of participants was high even before the 2004–2007 enlargement, and it has only continued to climb since then.

The delegations sit at a table in order of the rotation of the presidency, with the Commission delegation at one end and the delegations from the presidency and the General Secretariat at the other. The member state holding the presidency not only chairs the meeting but also has separate national representation. The relevant minister leads the national delegations, backed up by national officials and experts. Several factors influence the performance of individual ministers, including national interests, the ideological leanings of the minister, public opinion at home (especially if an election is imminent), and the individual personalities and relationships in the room.[20]

In addition to general discussions, typical meetings include regular postponements and adjournments, huddles of delegates during breaks, periodic communication with national capitals, and a constant flow of ministers and officials coming and going. When negotiations stall, the president might use a device known as a *tour de table*, during which the heads of delegations are asked in turn to give a brief summary of their positions on an issue. Though often time consuming, this procedure gives every delegation the chance to take part in discussions, focuses the discussion, and helps raise possible new points of agreement and compromise.

However, Council meetings are not the only engine for discussion and decision making. In addition to the preparatory committee and working party meetings, Council meetings also break for lunches attended only by ministers and translators, and consensus often transpires over a meal. Meetings of the Council are not open to the public except when Commission proposals are sufficiently important that the Council decides to allow the public to watch and listen.

---

political interests.[21] Because they are also ideologically driven, Council decisions will be influenced by the relative weight of left-wingers, right-wingers, and centrists. The authority of different ministers will also depend to some extent on the stability of the governing party or coalition in their home states. All of these factors coalesce to pull ministers in many different directions and to deny the Council the kind of consistency and regularity enjoyed by the Commission.

EVOLUTION OF THE EUROPEAN COUNCIL

Although in contrast to the Council of Ministers the European Council was not institutionalized until well after the EU's founding treaties, the idea of holding formal high-level meetings among Community leaders can be traced back to Charles de Gaulle's ideas about political union. In July 1960 he broached the idea of a European political union that would include periodic summit meetings of heads of state or government and foreign ministers.[22] Although his motives were distrusted by many of his EEC partners, the idea survived, and the first formal summits were held in 1961 (Paris in February, Bonn in July). At the Paris meeting, a committee was formed under the chairmanship of Christian Fouchet, French ambassador to Denmark, which produced a draft treaty for a "union of states," including a suggestion for a council of heads of government or foreign ministers that would meet every four months and make decisions on the basis of unanimity. But because the Fouchet plan was an attempt to build a Community dominated by France, it met with little support outside that country.[23]

No more summits were convened until 1967 and 1969, by which time it was becoming increasingly obvious to many that the EC had no clear sense of direction and that conflicts over national interests in the Council of Ministers were blockading the Union's decision making. The effective end of the Bretton Woods system in 1971 emphasized Europe's inability to respond quickly and effectively to major external crises, as did the Community's halfhearted response to the 1973 energy crisis, which prompted French foreign minister Michel Jobert to declare that Europe was a "nonentity."[24] What was needed, Jean Monnet argued, was "a supreme body to steer Europe through the difficult transition from national to collective sovereignty"; he suggested calling it the "Provisional European Government."[25] Agreement was reached at a summit in Copenhagen in December 1973 to arrange more frequent meetings among heads of government.

Changes in leadership in the UK, France, and West Germany formed the background for the December 1974 summit of heads of government in Paris, where it was decided to formalize the links among them. President Giscard d'Estaing of France and Chancellor Helmut Schmidt of Germany argued for the need to bring leaders together regularly to provide policy direction and to clear logjams. A declaration was issued committing heads of government to meet at least three times annually and emphasizing the need for "an overall approach" to the challenges of integration and the importance of ensuring "progress and overall consistency in the activities of the Communities and in the work on political co-operation."[26]

The wording of the declaration was kept deliberately vague; it said nothing about the exact powers of the new body or its relationship to the other institutions, gave it no legal standing, and was careful not to allow the new body's creation to disturb or complicate the existing EC decision-making system. Concerns among the Benelux states that the summits would weaken the supranational qualities of the Community were offset in part by an agreement to hold direct elections to the EP.[27] The new body even lacked a name until Giscard's announcement at a press conference at the close of the meeting that "the European summit is dead; long live the European Council."[28] Outweighing suggestions that a new secretariat be created for the Council were desires not to expand the European bureaucracy or weaken the work of existing institutions. This is why the Council – which has been institutionalized to the extent that it exists and follows increasingly routine patterns of functioning – is the only branch of the EU without a secretariat or a sizable, salaried body of staff.

The first meeting of the Council was held in Dublin in March 1975 under the lumbering title "the Heads of Government Meeting as the Council of the Community and in Political Cooperation." It met more or less three times a year throughout the 1970s and 1980s, but a decision was reached at the December 1985 summit to hold just two regular summits each year, in June and December, with additional extraordinary meetings as needed. Legal recognition of the Council finally came with the Single European Act, which confirmed the membership of the Council and reduced the number of annual meetings from three to two. The most recent round of changes occurred with the Treaty of Lisbon, under whose terms a president was appointed to manage meetings of the Council and move its members toward a consensus, and a new pattern of four regular annual meetings in Brussels was set.

STRUCTURE OF THE EUROPEAN COUNCIL

The European Council brings together the heads of government of the EU member states (and the head of state in presidential and semi-presidential systems, such as Cyprus and France), the president of the European Council (created by the Treaty of Lisbon), the president of the European Commission (and a deputy commissioner if needed), the High Representative of the Union for Foreign Affairs and Security Policy (when foreign affairs are discussed), the secretary general of the Council of Ministers, and small retinues of staff and advisers. They convene at regular summits lasting no more than two days, under the direction of a full-time president. Historically, the membership of the European Council has been overwhelmingly male; in 2020 it included four women: Sophie Wilmès (Belgium), Sanna Marin (Finland), Angela Merkel (Germany), and Mette Frederiksen (Denmark).

The Council elects a president using a qualified majority vote for a term of two and a half years, renewable once. He or she cannot also be a sitting leader of a member state but, like the Commission president, will almost certainly come from the ranks of existing or former national leaders. According to Lisbon, the president's responsibilities include chairing the European Council and "driving forward its work," overseeing much of its preparatory work along with the president of the Commission and the General Affairs Council, and acting as an external representative for the EU. Despite some sentiment for choosing a strong and highly visible personality for the initial president, European leaders ultimately choose Herman van Rompuy, a former Belgian prime minister known for his ability as a facilitator and negotiator. He assumed the position in November 2009 and was succeeded by Donald Tusk, a former Polish prime minister, in 2014. Charles Michel, a former prime minister from Belgium, was elected in 2019.

European Council summits once took place either in the capital of the member state holding the presidency of the Council of Ministers or in a regional city or town, such as Cardiff, Venice, Strasbourg, or – in December 1991 – Maastricht in the Netherlands, where the Treaty on European Union was agreed. In order to ensure less cost and greater efficiency, all European Council meetings now take place in Brussels.

PHOTO 6.2 EU Bureaucracy.

Source: Cartoonist: RGJ – Richard Jolley; www.cartoonstock.com.

TABLE 6.2 Key Summits of the European Council

Date	Venue	Highlights
1975	Dublin	First meeting of the Council
1985	Luxembourg	Signing of the Single European Act
1991	Maastricht	Signing of the Maastricht treaty
1995	Madrid	Naming of the euro
1997	Amsterdam	Signing of the Amsterdam treaty
1998	Brussels	Selected member states adopt the euro
2000	Nice	Signing of the Treaty of Nice
2002	Copenhagen	Agreement for 2004 Enlargement
2007	Lisbon	Signing of Treaty of Lisbon
2009	Brussels	Appointment of first president and merger of High Representative responsibilities
2010–2011	Brussels	Various summits addressing the eurozone crisis
2014	Brussels	Conflict in Ukraine
2015	Brussels	Migration crisis
2016	Brussels	Brexit, migration crisis
2019	Brussels	Brexit

The Council has multiple personalities. It can be seen as the decision maker of last resort, as a collective presidency of pooled sovereignty, as a body that parallels other EU institutions by dealing with issues outside their competence, or as a true "council" that can engineer broad package deals.[29] Three keys unlock the way the Council works and fits into the EU system:

- *Flexibility.* The relative lack of rules, regulations, and attendant bureaucrats gives the Council a level of freedom and independence enjoyed by none of the other EU institutions.
- *Informality.* European Council summits are built on advance preparation, but agendas remain general, summits avoid formal votes, and meetings are kept as small and informal as possible.
- *Delegation.* Any signs that the Council is becoming bogged down in the routine day-to-day business of the EU are usually resisted. The Council instead focuses on the big picture, leaves other institutions to work out the details, and acts akin to a court of appeal if attempts to reach agreement at a lower level fail.[30]

The major goal of each summit meeting is to agree to a set of formal conclusions, an advanced draft of which usually awaits the leaders at the beginning of the summit, and provides the focus for their discussions (see Box 6.2).

Box 6.2 All in the Family: European Summits

Meetings of the European Council usually run for a period of two days; emergency or informal summits will normally last no more than a day. They begin with discussions over breakfast and move into the nuts and bolts at plenary sessions during the morning and afternoon. Overnight, officials will work on the draft set of conclusions, which are discussed at a second plenary on the morning of day two, and – if necessary – at a third in the afternoon. The summit then normally ends with a press conference and publication of the conclusions.

During summit plenaries, the prime ministers of the member states (and the presidents of Cyprus and France) sit around a table like a typical family at dinner, along with the president of the Commission, the European Council president, the secretary general of the Council, invited guests when appropriate (e.g., the president of the EP), and the High Representative (when foreign affairs are discussed). In an adjacent room (the "kids' table," to carry the analogy further) are representatives from Coreper, diplomats, assistants, and translators, most of whom are not allowed into the main meeting room, with the exception of translators and delegates (two per member state) relaying messages.

The Council makes its decisions on the basis of consensus (except where the treaties say otherwise), although some member states may want to attach conditions or reservations to the conclusions. In addition to the formal plenary sessions, summits usually break out into subsidiary meetings, including those of foreign ministers, and regular bilateral meetings of prime ministers over breakfast or coffee. This has become more common as membership in the EU has grown – it is sometimes easier to negotiate in smaller groups than in meetings of the whole.

Major media attention often shines on these summits, and great symbolism is attached to the conclusions, which are assessed according to the extent to which they represent breakthroughs or show EU leaders to be bogged down in disagreement. The headline-making nature of the summits is sufficient to focus the minds of participants and to foster agreement. A "family photo" of the national leaders, European Council president, and the president of the Commission commemorates the meeting, symbolizing the process of European integration. The smiles on their faces would look shallow if major disagreements had not (at least to some extent) been resolved.

HOW THE EUROPEAN COUNCIL WORKS

Preparation is the key to the success of European summits.[31] Officially, the Council has no set agenda, but needs some direction. Before Lisbon, much of the preparatory work for the summits was done by the member state holding the presidency: senior officials from the presidency worked with the Council of Ministers to identify agenda items which were then channeled to the Committee of Permanent Representatives. The monthly meetings of the foreign ministers under the General Affairs and External Relations Council would then try to resolve potential disagreements.[32] With the advent of a presidency of the European Council much of this preparatory work has now fallen to it. According to Lisbon, however, the president works "in close cooperation" with the member state holding the rotating presidency in the Council of Ministers as well as the president of the Commission.

Items on the agenda depend on circumstances: national delegations normally have issues they want to raise, continuity from previous summits is essential, and leaders must often deal with a

PHOTO 6.3 The European Council, 2019.
Source: © European Union, 2019.

breaking problem or an emergency that requires a decision. Some issues (especially economic ones) are routinely discussed at every summit, the Commission may promote issues it would like to see discussed, and an active presidency in the Council of Ministers might use the summit to bring items of national or regional interest to the attention of the heads of government.[33] Summits may also occasionally launch or finalize a major policy initiative, such as the June 2012 summit, which advanced some major initiatives to deal with the eurozone crisis. Some summits are routine and result in general agreement among leaders; in others, deep fissures arise, with some member states perhaps refusing to agree to a common set of conclusions.

The exact role of the European Council has been kept deliberately ambiguous by its members, the early statements of EU leaders suggesting that the purpose of the Council was to exchange views, give political impetus to the development of the EU, guarantee policy consistency, and reach common positions on foreign policy matters.[34] The Treaty of Lisbon describes its mission as follows:

> [to] provide the Union with the necessary impetus for its development and … define the general political direction and priorities thereof. It shall not exercise legislative functions.

More specifically, the Council makes the key decisions on the overall direction of political integration, internal economic matters, foreign policy issues, budget disputes, treaty revisions, new member applications, and institutional reforms. The summits achieve these outcomes through a combination of brainstorming, intensive bilateral and multilateral discussions, and bargaining. The mechanics of decision making depend on a combination of the quality of organization and preparation, the leadership skills of the president, the ideological and personal agendas of the individual leaders, and the strength of their political bases at home. Also, most European governments are coalitions, meaning that national leaders have to please a broader constituency and are somewhat hobbled in following the courage of their convictions.

The interpersonal dynamics of the participants also play a key role:

- The political significance of the Franco-German axis has always been critical, given additional influence by the strong personal relations that have usually existed between the leaders of the two states (Brandt and Pompidou, Schmidt and Giscard, Kohl and Mitterrand, Schröder and Chirac, and Merkel and Macron).

- Leaders who have held office for a relatively long time or who have a solid base of political support at home will be in different negotiating positions from those who have not. The June 2007 European Council suffered from a virtual leadership and experience vacuum: the leaders of Austria, France, Germany, the Netherlands, and Sweden were all relatively new, and the leaders of several other countries – including Bulgaria, the Czech Republic, Finland, Poland, and Romania – governed in uneasy coalitions. Greece, Hungary, Ireland, Latvia, and Spain were among the few EU countries at the time whose governments enjoyed stable majorities and some longevity.
- Some leaders have respect and strong credibility, while others do not. For example, German chancellor Helmut Kohl became a towering presence on the EU stage, holding on to office for sixteen years (1982–1998) and becoming a kind of elder statesman of European integration (helped, of course, by the dominating economic power of Germany). By 2002–2003 there was no longer a single dominant leader on the European scene, although the tripartite relationship among Tony Blair, Jacques Chirac, and Gerhard Schröder was playing an influential role on several issues, notably defense matters and European foreign policy. Since 2013 Angela Merkel has been the dominant figure in the European Council but as her political fortunes have fallen in Germany and she is now a "lame duck" chancellor, Emmanuel Macron has taken on much more of a leadership role.

In addition to the regular summits, special meetings of European leaders have also been convened to deal with a breaking issue or a persistent problem. Examples include the November 1989 summit in Paris to discuss rapidly changing events in Eastern Europe, the October 1992 summit in Birmingham to discuss the crisis in the Exchange Rate Mechanism, the July 1994 summit convened to choose a successor to Jacques Delors, the March 1999 summit to negotiate reforms to the EU budget, and the February 2003 summit held to try to heal rifts among the member states over the impending invasion of Iraq.

QUESTIONS TO CONSIDER

1 How has the relationship between the EP and the Council of Ministers changed over the years, and what difference has this made to how the EU operates?
2 How does QMV – and the different ways in which it is calculated – affect the balance of power within the Council? Could something similar work for the US Congress, and if so, would it be a good idea?
3 What role does the European Council play in the politics of the EU? Could any of its functions be compared with US institutions, and if so, which one(s)?

NOTES

1 Desmond Dinan, *Ever Closer Union? An Introduction to European Integration*, 4th ed., 235 (Boulder, CO: Lynne Rienner, 2010).
2 Desmond Dinan, *Europe Recast: A History of European Union*, 2nd ed., 159 (Boulder: Lynne Rienner, 2014).
3 Quoted in Jean Monnet, *Memoirs*, trans. Richard Mayne (Garden City, NY: Doubleday, 1978).
4 Thomas Christiansen, "The Council of Ministers: Facilitating Interaction and Developing Actorness in the EU," in *European Union: Power and Policy-Making*, 3rd ed., edited by Jeremy Richardson, 155–159 (New York: Routledge, 2006).

5 See Fiona Hayes-Renshaw and Helen Wallace, *The Council of Ministers*, 2nd ed., 34ff. (Basingstoke, UK: Palgrave Macmillan, 2006).

6 Fiona Hayes-Renshaw and Helen Wallace, "Executive Power in The European Union: The Functions and Limits of the Council of Ministers," *Journal of European Public Policy* 2, no. 4 (1995): 559–582.

7 Alan Clark, *Diaries* (London: Weidenfeld and Nicholson, 1993).

8 Fiona Hayes-Renshaw, Christian Lequesne, and Pedro Mayor Lopez, "The Permanent Representations of the Member States of the European Communities," *Journal of Common Market Studies* 28, no. 2 (December 1989): 119–137.

9 For more details on the work of Coreper, see Hayes-Renshaw and Wallace, *The Council of Ministers*, 72–82.

10 Hayes-Renshaw, Lequesne, and Mayor Lopez, "The Permanent Representations of the Member States of the European Communities."

11 See Ole Elgström, "Introduction," in *European Union Council Presidencies: A Comparative Perspective*, edited by Ole Elgström, 4–7 (London: Routledge, 2003).

12 Guy de Bassompierre, *Changing the Guard in Brussels: An Insider's View of the EC Presidency*, 48 (New York: Praeger, 1988).

13 "Turbulence for Silvio Berlusconi, at Home and Abroad," *The Economist*, July 5, 2003, 42.

14 *The European*, 28–30 December 1990.

15 Christiansen, "The Council of Ministers," 164–167.

16 See Hayes-Renshaw and Wallace, *The Council of Ministers*, chapter 8.

17 For a more detailed explanation of the process, see Hayes-Renshaw, Lequesne, and Mayor Lopez, "The Permanent Representations of the Member States of the European Communities."

18 European Parliament, "The Impact of the UK's Withdrawal on the Institutional Set-Up and Political Dynamics within the EU," Policy Department for Citizens' Rights and Constitutional Affairs, April 2019, at www.europarl.europa.eu/RegData/etudes/STUD/2019/621914/IPOL_STU (2019)621914_EN.pdf, accessed June 1, 2019; Werner Krisch, "The Brexit and the Distribution of Power in the Council of the EU," at www.researchgate.net/publication/304998986_The_Brexit_and_the_distribution_of_power_in_the_Council_of_the_EU, accessed July 16, 2019; Cian McCarthy, "EU Decision-making after Brexit: QMV and the Balance of Power," The Institute of International and European Affairs, at www.iiea.com/publication/eu-decision-making-after-brexit-qmv-and-the-balance-of-power/, accessed January 14, 2020.

19 Philippa Sherrington, *The Council of Ministers: Political Authority in the European Union*, 63–65 (London: Pinter, 2000).

20 On public opinion's influence on the Council see Sara Hagemann, Sara B. Hobolt, and Christopher Wratil, "Government Responsiveness in the European Union: Evidence from Council Voting," *Comparative Political Studies* 50, no. 6 (2017): 850–876.

21 B. Guy Peters, "Bureaucratic Politics and the Institutions of the European Community," in *Euro-Politics: Institutions and Policymaking in the "New" European Community*, edited by Alberta Sbragia, 79 (Washington, DC: Brookings Institution, 1992).

22 Annette Morgan, *From Summit to Council: Evolution in the EEC*, 9 (London: Chatham House, 1976).

23 Mary Troy Johnston, *The European Council: Gatekeeper of the European Community*, 2–4 (Boulder: Westview Press, 1994).

24 Philippe Moreau Defarges, "Twelve Years of European Council History (1974–1986): The Crystallizing Forum," in *European Council 1974–1986: Evaluation and Prospects* edited by Jean-Marc Hoscheit and Wolfgang Wessels, eds., 38–39 (Maastricht: European Institute of Public Administration, 1988).

25 Jean Monnet, *Memoirs*, 502–503.

26 Communiqué of the Meeting of Heads of Government of the Community (Paris, 10 December 1974), *Bulletin of the European Communities* 12 (December 1974): 7–12.

27 Johnston, *The European Council*, 14.

28 Morgan, *From Summit to Council*, 5.

29 Wolfgang Wessels, "The European Council: A Denaturing of the Community or Indispensable Decision-Making Body?" in *The European Council 1974–1986*, edited by Hoscheit and Wessels, 9–11.

30 Guy de Bassompierre, *Changing the Guard in Brussels*, 78.
31 See de Bassompierre, *Changing the Guard in Brussels*, 80–87, for more detail on the organization and outcomes of the European Council.
32 See Johnston, *The European Council*, 27–31.
33 Uwe Puetter, "Europe's Deliberate Intergovernmentalism: The Role of the Council and the European Council in EU Economic Governance," *Journal of European Public Policy* 19, no. 2 (2012): 161–178.
34 Paris Declaration 1974, in *European Parliament, Committee on Institutional Affairs, Selection of Texts Concerning Institutional Matters of the Community from 1950 to 1982* (Luxembourg: European Parliament, 1982); Statement of the European Council London 1977, in Commission of the EC, Bulletin 7 (1977); and Solemn Declaration of Stuttgart 1983, in Commission of the EC, Bulletin 6 (1983).

BIBLIOGRAPHY

Christiansen, Thomas, "The Council of Ministers: Facilitating Interaction and Developing Actorness in the EU," in *European Union: Power and Policy-Making*, 3rd ed., edited by Jeremy Richardson, 155–159 (New York: Routledge, 2006).

Clark, Alan. *Diaries* (London: Weidenfeld and Nicholson, 1993).

de Bassompierre, Guy, *Changing the Guard in Brussels: An Insider's View of the EC Presidency* (New York: Praeger, 1988).

Defarges, Philippe Moreau, "Twelve Years of European Council History (1974–1986): The Crystallizing Forum," in *The European Council 1974–1986: Evaluation and Prospects*, edited by Jean-Marc Hoscheit and Wolfgang Wessels, 38–39 (Maastricht: European Institute of Public Administration, 1988).

Dinan, Desmond, *Ever Closer Union? An Introduction to European Integration*, 4th ed. (Boulder, CO: Lynne Rienner, 2010).

Dinan, Desmond, *Europe Recast: A History of European Union*, 2nd ed. (Boulder: Lynne Rienner, 2014).

Economist, The, "Turbulence for Silvio Berlusconi, at Home and Abroad," July 5, 2003, 42.

Elgström, Ole, "Introduction," in *European Union Council Presidencies: A Comparative Perspective*, edited by Ole Elgström, 4–7 (London: Routledge, 2003).

The European. 28–30 December 1990.

European Communities, "Communiqué of the Meeting of Heads of Government of the Community (Paris, 10 December 1974)," *Bulletin of the European Communities* 12 (December 1974): 7–12.

European Council, "Statement of the European Council London 1977," Commission of the EC, Bulletin 7 (1977).

European Council, "Solemn Declaration of Stuttgart 1983," Commission of the EC, Bulletin 6 (1983).

European Parliament, "Paris Declaration 1974," in *European Parliament, Committee on Institutional Affairs, Selection of Texts Concerning Institutional Matters of the Community from 1950 to 1982* (Luxembourg: European Parliament, 1982).

European Parliament, "The Impact of the UK's Withdrawal on the Institutional Set-Up and Political Dynamics within the EU," Policy Department for Citizens' Rights and Constitutional Affairs, April 2019, at www.europarl.europa.eu/RegData/etudes/STUD/2019/621914/IPOL_STU(2019)621914_EN.pdf, accessed June 1, 2019.

Foret, François and Yann-Sven Rittelmeyer, *The European Council and European Governance: The Commanding Heights of the EU* (New York: Routledge, 2013).

Hagemann, Sara, Sara B. Hobolt, and Christopher Wratil, "Government Responsiveness in the European Union: Evidence from Council Voting," *Comparative Political Studies* 50, no. 6 (2017): 850–876.

Hayes-Renshaw, Fiona, and Helen Wallace, "Executive Power in The European Union: The Functions and Limits of the Council of Ministers," *Journal of European Public Policy* 2, no. 4 (1995): 559–582.

Hayes-Renshaw, Fiona, and Helen Wallace. *The Council of Ministers*, 2nd ed. (Basingstoke, UK: Palgrave Macmillan, 2006).

Hayes-Renshaw, Fiona, Christian Lequesne, and Pedro Mayor Lopez, "The Permanent Representations of the Member States of the European Communities," *Journal of Common Market Studies* 28, no. 2 (December 1989): 119–137.

Johnston, Mary Troy, *The European Council: Gatekeeper of the European Community* (Boulder: Westview Press, 1994).

McCarthy, Cian, "EU Decision-making after Brexit: QMV and the Balance of Power," The Institute of International and European Affairs, at www.iiea.com/publication/eu-decision-making-after-brexit-qmv-and-the-balance-of-power/, accessed January 14, 2020.

Monnet, Jean, *Memoirs*, trans. Richard Mayne (Garden City, NY: Doubleday, 1978).

Morgan, Annette, *From Summit to Council: Evolution in the EEC* (London: Chatham House, 1976).

Peters, B. Guy, "Bureaucratic Politics and the Institutions of the European Community," in *Euro-Politics: Institutions and Policymaking in the "New" European Community*, edited by Alberta Sbragia (Washington, DC: Brookings Institution, 1992).

Puetter, Uwe, "Europe's Deliberate Intergovernmentalism: The Role of the Council and the European Council in EU Economic Governance," *Journal of European Public Policy* 19, no. 2 (2012): 161–178.

Puetter, Uwe, *The European Council and the Council. New Intergovernmentalism and Institutional Change* (Oxford: Oxford University Press, 2014).

Sherrington, Philipa, *The Council of Ministers: Political Authority in the European Union* (London: Pinter, 2000).

Veen, Tim, *The Political Economy of Collective Decision-Making: Conflicts and Coalitions in the Council of the European Union* (Berlin: Springer, 2011).

Werts, Jan, *The European Council* (London: John Harper, 2008).

Wessels, Wolfgang, "The European Council: A Denaturing of the Community or Indispensable Decision-Making Body?" in *The European Council 1974–1986*, edited by Jean-Marc Hoscheit and Wolfgang Wessels (Maastricht: European Institute of Public Administration, 1988).

Westlake, Martin and David Galloway, *The Council of the European Union*, 3rd ed. (London: John Harper, 2004).

FURTHER READING

Fiona Hayes-Renshaw and Helen Wallace, *The Council of Ministers*, 2nd ed. (Basingstoke, UK: Palgrave Macmillan, 2006); Martin Westlake and David Galloway, *The Council of the European Union*, 3rd ed. (London: John Harper, 2004); Tim Veen, *The Political Economy of Collective Decision-Making: Conflicts and Coalitions in the Council of the European Union* (Berlin: Springer, 2011).

    The first two, older, texts present very good overviews but do not completely convey the political drama of Council operations; the third uses a (rather dense) theoretical model to explain policy outcomes for different member states within the Council.

Uwe Puetter, *The European Council and the Council. New Intergovernmentalism and Institutional Change* (Oxford: Oxford University Press, 2014).

    Using a theoretical model of "deliberative intergovernmentalism," the author shows how the European Council and the Council of Ministers have become the dominant institutional players in the EU through policy coordination and intergovernmental agreements.

Jan Werts, *The European Council* (London: John Harper, 2008); François Foret and Yann-Sven Rittelmeyer, *The European Council and European Governance: The Commanding Heights of the EU* (New York: Routledge, 2013).

    The first is a book-length study focusing solely on the European Council, tracing its evolution and changing institutional rules; the second examines the European Council as the primary institutional actor in a new EU political model which combines intergovernmental cooperation and supranational integration.

CHAPTER 7

The European Parliament

CHAPTER OVERVIEW

- The European Parliament (EP) is the only directly elected transnational legislature in the world, one of two legislative bodies of the EU and similar to a lower house in parliamentary systems or the US House of Representatives.
- The EP consists of 705 Members of the European Parliament (MEPs) elected to renewable five-year terms, with seats divided among the member states based on population. It is headed by a president elected by its members, and has a number of standing and special committees. While still lacking some of the defining features of a legislature, changes in the treaties have made it an equal legislative partner to the Council of the EU.
- Although the direct election of the EP remains the most visible of ways in which citizens across Europe can directly engage with the EU, turnout historically has been significantly below those of national elections. And ironically, recent EP elections have witnessed the growing power of EU-skeptical or EU-hostile parties in this most democratic of EU institutions.

As one of the legislative bodies of the EU, the EP shares responsibility with the Council of the EU for debating, amending, and voting upon proposals for new EU laws. Splitting its time between Strasbourg in France and Brussels, it has 705 members elected from the twenty-seven EU member states on a fixed five-year electoral rotation. Although possessing the moral authority inherent in being the only directly elected EU institution, it lacks three of the typical defining powers of a legislature: it cannot directly introduce proposals for new laws, cannot decide alone on the content of laws, and cannot raise revenues. However, the EP is far from powerless: it can ask the Commission to propose a new law or policy, shares powers with the Council of the EU on the approval of legislative proposals and the EU budget, must approve and can remove the Commission, and can veto membership applications from aspirant EU members.

Most of the EP's handicaps stem from the unwillingness of the governments of the member states to completely surrender their powers of lawmaking or to loosen their grip on decision making in the Council of Ministers. The idea that national legislatures – to which most voters have stronger psychological attachments – should be losing their lawmaking powers is a cause for concern among those who worry about growing EU powers and has figured prominently in the rhetoric of right-wing populists. Parliament also has a credibility problem: few Europeans know (or much care) what it does. In addition, European party groups still compete in European elections on national platforms and have not yet developed a strong European identity. The result of this is that many voters in EP elections make their choices on the basis of domestic rather than European issues, although the last EP election may portend a change in this trend. The EP's powers and credibility have been further undermined historically by low voter turnout: in a frustrating catch-22, few voters are interested in what it does because of its limited powers, but its powers are limited in part because so few voters are interested in what it does.

In fairness, Parliament is a much more substantial body than most Europeans realize. With increasing confidence, it has used arguments about democratic accountability to win more powers and to be taken more seriously. Instead of simply reacting to Commission proposals and Council votes, the EP has launched its own initiatives and forced the other institutions to pay more attention to its opinions. As well as winning more powers to amend legislation and to check the activities of the other institutions, it has been a valuable source of ideas and new policy proposals, and it has acted as the democratic conscience of the EU. The use of direct elections since 1979 has provided the EP an advantage over the other institutions, giving it a critical role in building bridges across the chasm that still separates EU citizens from EU institutions. Ironically, however, the 2014 EP elections brought a record number of anti-EU and EU-skeptical MEPs/political groups, a trend that increased slightly in the recent 2019 EP elections.

EVOLUTION

The EP began life in September 1952 as the Common Assembly of the European Coal and Steel Community (ECSC). The Assembly met in Strasbourg in northeastern France, and although the Treaty of Paris held out the possibility that the Assembly's members could eventually be directly elected, it initially consisted of seventy-eight members appointed by the national legislatures of the six ECSC member states. The Assembly had no power to make law for the ECSC, nor could it even influence the lawmaking process, which rested with the Council of Ministers. Its only significant power was the ability to force the High Authority of the ECSC to resign through a vote of censure, but it never exercised this power and ended up being little more than an advisory forum for the discussion of High Authority proposals.[1] Still, its very creation and existence broke ground for what would later become the European Parliament.[2]

More substantive changes came later. The Treaties of Rome did not create separate assemblies for the European Economic Community (EEC) and Euratom, but instead transformed the ECSC Common Assembly into the joint European Parliamentary Assembly. Its powers were expanded to give it joint responsibility with the Council of Ministers over the budget, but its suggestions for amendments to EEC law and policy were nonbinding. In 1962 the Assembly was renamed the European Parliament, but despite the symbolism of the change, it still consisted of members appointed by national legislatures from among their own numbers, an arrangement that had two important effects. First, only pro-European legislators volunteered for appointment to the Parliament. Second, since MEPs were also members of national legislatures, they placed national interests above European interests, mainly because their jobs at home depended on the support of voters. As a result, the EP was seen as a junior European institution.

Parliament was a keen supporter of the idea of direct elections, provision for which had been made by the Treaty of Rome, but the Council of Ministers remained opposed throughout the 1960s and early 1970s. At stake were concerns about the tendency toward supranationalism and the determination of the Council (and of national leaders such as Charles de Gaulle) to keep a firm grip on decision-making powers. It was only in 1976 that the

European Council finally reversed its thinking, and elections were held for the first time in June 1979. This event was a turning point: now that MEPs were directly elected and met in open session, they could argue that as the elected representatives of the citizens of the EU, they should be allowed to represent the interests of the voters.

More watershed developments followed. As new countries joined the EEC/EU, membership of the EP grew (see Table 7.1). And as membership increased, so did Parliament's powers. Changes in the 1970s gave it shared responsibility with the Council of Ministers over the Community budget, meaning that – within certain limits – it could raise or lower Community spending, redistribute spending across different budget sectors, reject the annual budget altogether, and determine how the Commission spent money already approved for the budget.[3] Although this was the first instance of Parliament receiving real legislative power, it was a 1980 Court of Justice decision that really helped expand the EP's legislative boundaries. In *SA Roquette Frères* v. *Council* (Case 138/79), a French company challenged a Council regulation limiting production of isoglucose (a starch-based sweetener used in a variety of food products), partly on the basis that it had been adopted without an opinion from Parliament. The Court agreed, thereby recognizing the right of Parliament to be consulted on draft legislation and giving Parliament standing to bring cases to the Court of Justice.[4]

TABLE 7.1 Growth of the European Parliament

Year	Membership	Details
1952	78	Common Assembly of the ECSC
1958	142	Parliamentary Assembly of the European Communities
1973	198	56 seats added for the UK, Denmark, and Ireland
1976	410	Membership increased in anticipation of first direct elections
1981	434	24 seats added for Greece
1986	518	84 seats added for Portugal and Spain
1994	567	Adjustments made to account for German reunification
1995	626	59 seats added for Austria, Finland, and Sweden
2004	732	Seat distribution reconfigured, and 162 seats added for Cyprus, Czech Republic, Estonia, Hungary, Latvia, Lithuania, Malta, Poland, Slovakia, and Slovenia
2007	785	Seats added for Bulgaria and Romania
2009	736	Reconfigured for 2009 elections
2011	754	Reconfigured under terms of Treaty of Lisbon
2013	766	Seats added for Croatia
2014	751	Reconfigured for 2014 elections and Treaty of Lisbon
2020	705	Reconfigured after Brexit

As Parliament took itself more seriously, it was taken more seriously by other institutions (notably the Commission). It used parliamentary questions to hold these institutions more accountable and published reports that were designed to promote new legislative ideas. The Single European Act (SEA) and the Maastricht treaty also handed Parliament more powers over a greater number of policy areas, and greater input into the lawmaking process generally. Under the SEA, for example, the consultation procedure (under which proposals for new laws were subject to a nonbinding opinion from Parliament) was joined by a cooperation procedure under which all laws relating to the single market had to be sent to the EP for two readings. With changes made under Maastricht and the Treaty of Amsterdam, a codecision procedure – now renamed the "ordinary legislative procedure" by the Treaty of Lisbon – was introduced and then widened, giving Parliament the effective right to veto new legislation.

The EP today is thus considerably closer to being the main legislative body of the EU. It has more powers over lawmaking, over the budget, and over the other institutions. Its credibility has increased in particular since the institution of direct elections, because it can claim to be the only EU institution with a direct mandate from EU citizens. However, until it can introduce new legislation, it will not have the kind of independence of action associated with national legislatures. And it still suffers from the lack of a strong psychological link with voters that would give it the credibility it needs to fully exploit its advantages.

STRUCTURE

The EP is the only elected international assembly in the world, and the only directly elected body in the network of EU institutions. It consists of a single chamber, and its members are elected by universal suffrage for fixed, renewable five-year terms. It divides its time among three cities:

- The parliamentary chamber is situated in Strasbourg, France. This is where the EP holds its plenary sessions (meetings of the whole), but it meets there for just four days each month (except in August, when much of Europe goes on vacation). Plenaries achieve relatively little, can become bogged down in procedure, and can last late into the night. Accommodation in Strasbourg is also at a premium, often obliging MEPs and their staff to stay in distant hotels. As a result, plenaries are not often well attended, and the sight of empty seats and the occasional dozing legislator does little to help the credibility of Parliament. But the siting in Strasbourg is less the fault of MEPs than of the French government (see Box 7.1).
- Parliamentary committees meet in Brussels for two weeks every month (except August). This is where most of the real bargaining and revising takes place, and since additional plenaries can be held in Brussels and a third week is set aside for meetings of political groups, committee meetings are relatively well attended, and MEPs spend most of their time there.
- The administrative Secretariat resides in Luxembourg. This is where most of Parliament's 3,500 support staff work, more than one-third on translation and interpretation. Few MEPs need to visit or spend time here, so the Secretariat is relatively isolated.

Parliament has four main elements: the president, parliamentary committees, the MEPs, and the political groups to which they belong.

Box 7.1 If it's Tuesday, This Must Be Belgium: Parliament's Multisite Dilemma

The image problems suffered by the EP are worsened by its rather absurd division among three sites, which not only forces a tiring and time-consuming travel schedule on MEPs but also encourages many to skip the Strasbourg plenary sessions because they are the least important. The division, moreover, inflates the parliamentary budget; in 2017 it was estimated that the EU spent $124 million moving MEPs, staff, and records back and forth, and it costs more than $25 million annually just to lease the EP building in Strasbourg for roughly sixty days of annual business.[5] The absurdity of this "travelling circus" (as one MEP described it) reflects poorly on Parliament and is galling to the many MEPs who favor holding plenaries in Brussels.[6]

It would make sense to move Parliament to Brussels (not least because most meetings of parliamentary committees take place there), but Luxembourg has refused to surrender the Secretariat, and France has refused to give up the parliamentary chamber.[7] The European Council decided in December 1992 that the EP Secretariat would remain in Luxembourg permanently and that the seat of the EP would remain in Strasbourg, but that additional plenaries could convene in Brussels. The EP responded by arguing that the decision violated its right to determine its own working methods and to carry out its tasks in the most effective manner, and signed a lease on a new $1.2 billion Brussels building complex. Not to be outdone, the French built a new and larger $520 million home for the EP in Strasbourg, described by one British journalist as feeling "like a huge new airport, built by a third world government in the middle of a jungle, and totally pointless."[8] Finally, a protocol was added to the Amsterdam treaty confirming that the seat of Parliament would remain in Strasbourg.

While most MEPs are in favor of extending Parliament the right to decide the location of its seat and its meetings, the governments of the member states have refused. Meanwhile, the extent to which governments can engage in petty territorial squabbles (and spend considerable money to defend those squabbles) is symbolized by the large and architecturally impressive – but usually almost empty – EP building in Strasbourg.[9]

The President

The EP is overseen by a president, who must be an MEP and is elected by other MEPs for a renewable term of two and a half years. He or she presides over debates during plenary sessions, signs the EU budget and all legislative proposals decided by the ordinary legislative procedure, passes proposals to committees, and represents Parliament in its relations with other institutions and internationally. The president also presides over meetings of the Conference of Presidents and the Bureau of the EP (see later in this chapter). To help deal with the many different political groups in Parliament, the president has fourteen vice presidents, who are also elected, for terms of two and a half years and can substitute for the president at meetings.

The president is elected by a majority vote of the EP. If Parliament actually had a majority political group, then the president would almost inevitably come from that group, but in the absence of this presidents to date have been appointed as a result of interparty bargaining. In 1989 the two largest political groups – the Socialists and the conservative European People's Party (EPP) – struck a deal whereby they would take turns holding the presidency. However,

PHOTO 7.1 Ursula von der Leyen Addresses the European Parliament.
Source: © European Union, 2019, EC – Audiovisual Service.

since 2014 the process has grown murkier as both the Socialists and EPP have lost significant seats in the last two EP elections. David-Maria Sassoli, an Italian socialist, was chosen as the new president in 2019.

Though parallels exist between the offices of the president of the EP and the Speaker of the US House of Representatives, the comparisons go only so far. The lack of majorities in the EP means that the president is less political than the Speaker, who comes from the majority party and works to ensure that the party's political goals succeed in the House. The Speaker also has a strong political role emanating from his or her relationship with the president of the US; speakers either oversee presidential legislative programs (if the two people are from the same party) or act as the focus of opposition to the president (if they are from opposing parties). EP presidents have been known to be partisan, and even nationalistic, but they are held in check by the need to build support across many different party groups.

Organizational matters in the EP are addressed by four groups:

- *Conference of Presidents*. Meeting bimonthly, this brings together the president and the heads of all of the political groups (and one non-attached member without voting rights) in Parliament. It decides the timetable and agenda for plenary sessions and manages the system of committees, establishing their size and their agendas.
- *Bureau of the EP*. Made up of the president of the EP, the vice presidents, and five "Quaesters" (advisers of MEPs elected from within the EP), this functions much like a governing council and is responsible for administrative, organizational, and staff issues, and for the EP budget.
- *Conference of Committee Chairs*. This meets monthly and assembles the chairs of parliamentary committees to discuss organizational issues and help draft plenary agendas. It keeps a close eye on the progress of proposals and brokers deals between the political groups regarding the parliamentary agenda.[10]

- *The Conference of Delegation Chairs.* This body oversees the running of interparliamentary delegations and delegations to the joint parliamentary committees, and often receives specific tasks from the Bureau and Conference of Presidents.

Parliamentary Committees

As with the US Congress, most of the detailed work of the EP is done in a series of committees in which MEPs gather to discuss and amend legislative proposals. The number of standing (permanent) committees has grown in concert with the work and the size of the EP, and today totals twenty. The committees usually meet in Brussels, where they consider all new legislation relevant to their areas. The titles of the committees offer a clue to the priorities of European integration: they include Foreign Affairs; International Trade; Economic and Monetary Affairs; Environment, Public Health and Food Safety; Regional Development; Agriculture and Rural Development; and Women's Rights and Gender Equality (see Table 7.2). They range in size from twenty-five to seventy-three full members.

Just as in the US Congress, there is strong competition among MEPs to win appointment to a committee, especially those with a higher political status than others. Seats are divided on the basis of a balance of party affiliations, the seniority of MEPs, and national interests. (For example, member states such as Poland and Ireland have a particular interest in agriculture and less interest in foreign and defense issues.) Once appointed, committee members select their own bureaus (a chair and three vice chairs), who hold office for half a parliamentary term. In the US Congress, committee leadership rarely changes, committee chairs are appointed out of the majority party, and an unspoken rule ensures that senior members will get prime consideration. In the EP the opposite is true: because there is no majority party, the chair positions are divided among political groups roughly in proportion to the size of their representation in Parliament, and there is more turnover.[11] An increasingly important role in the legislative process is that of the rapporteur, an MEP appointed by a committee to draw up a legislative recommendation for the full EP to vote on. Rapporteurs

TABLE 7.2 Standing Committees of the European Parliament	
Agriculture and Rural Development	Foreign Affairs
Budgetary Control	Human Rights
Budgets	Industry, Research and Energy
Civil Liberties, Justice and Home Affairs	Internal Market and Consumer Protection
Constitutional Affairs	International Trade
Culture and Education	Legal Affairs
Development	Regional Development
Economic and Monetary Affairs	Petitions
Employment and Social Affairs	Security and Defence
Environment, Public Health and Food Safety	Transport and Tourism
Fisheries	Women's Rights and Gender Equality

Source: European Parliament, at www.europarl.europa.eu/committees/en/parliamentary-committees.html.

consult with the relevant committee, policy specialists, and other interested stakeholders in drawing up these recommendations.

In addition to the standing committees, Parliament also has a continuous carousel of temporary committees and committees of enquiry. Those formed in recent years have looked at issues such as the foot and mouth disease crisis (2002), allegations of illegal CIA activities in Europe (2006–2007), climate change (2007–2008), the global economic crisis (2009), and organized crime, corruption, and money laundering (set up in 2012). Finally, there is the Conciliation Committee, in which representatives of the EP and the Council of Ministers meet to try to reach accord whenever the two sides have disagreed on the wording of a legislative proposal. There are twenty-eight members from each side; representatives of the Commission also attend.

Members of the European Parliament (MEPs)

The EP in 2019 had 751 elected members but after Brexit was completed in 2020 the EP shrunk to (a still quite large) 705 members, with some of the UK's former seats held in reserve for future enlargement and twenty-seven of the seats reallocated to remaining member states – France and Spain being the largest beneficiaries (see Figure 7.1).[12] Seats are distributed among the member states roughly on the basis of population, with the bigger

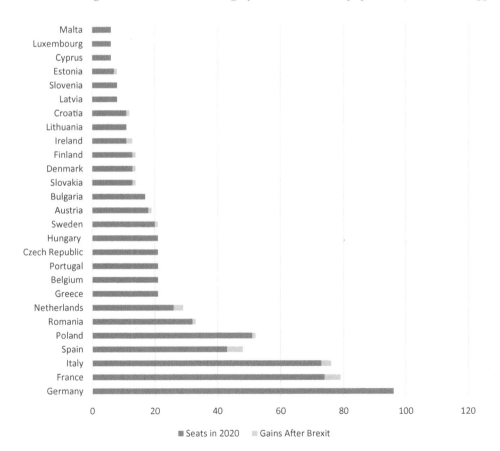

FIGURE 7.1 European Parliament after Brexit, 2020.

Source: European Parliament, *News*, January 31, 2020, at www.europarl.europa.eu/news/en/press-room/20200 130IPR71407/redistribution-of-seats-in-the-european-parliament-after-brexit.

states (e.g., Germany at ninety-six) underrepresented and smaller states (e.g., Luxembourg at six) overrepresented. Taking an average for the EU as a whole, there should be one MEP per 669,000 Europeans. But German and French residents are underrepresented (around 860,000 and 850,000 people per MEP, respectively), while the Maltese are greatly overrepresented (with 73,000 people per MEP).[13] A similar mathematical imbalance can be found in the US, where the population per district in the US House of Representatives averages over 710,000 people, but there is a high of 1:984,000 in Montana and a low of 1:527,000 in Rhode Island. The imbalances are even greater in the US Senate, where California's two senators share some forty million constituents, while those from Wyoming share just over 572,000.

In the past, MEPs were elected members of national parliaments who were also appointed to the EP, holding a so-called dual mandate. But as the workload of Parliament grew, the dual mandate became increasingly impractical; several member states (including Belgium and Spain) made it illegal, and it has been effectively eliminated. The result has been a weakening of the links between national legislatures and the EP, and greater independence and credibility for MEPs. Candidates for elections are chosen by their national parties, but once in office they have an independent mandate and cannot always be bound by those parties.[14] Turnover is fairly high: typically just under half of the MEPs who win election to the EP are newcomers.[15] In stark contrast, in the US (where the advantages of incumbency are well known) more than 90 percent of members of Congress typically win reelection. MEPs are paid by their home governments; because salary levels had varied significantly by member state, in 2005 it was agreed that all MEPs would be paid the same.

By socioeconomic makeup, the EP is similar to most national legislatures in the member states; it is dominated by white, middle-aged, middle-class professional men from urban backgrounds. Nonetheless, women are increasingly better represented with the percentage climbing steadily from 16 percent in 1979 to 41 percent today. This is around the average of the national legislatures of Scandinavian countries (39–45 percent), and well above that of the US (23 percent).[16] The increased levels of women's representation, however, has coincided with decreases in voter turnout (see Box 7.2).

Many MEPs already have political experience at the national level, but the EP – once seen as a haven for also-rans – is no longer an easy option for those who have failed to win office in national elections or who have been temporarily sidelined in (or have retired from) national politics. The quality of candidates has therefore improved over the years: among its members, the EP has counted senior national leaders, including former German chancellor Willy Brandt, former French president Valéry Giscard d'Estaing, former Italian prime ministers Emilio Colombo and Silvio Berlusconi, and former Belgian prime minister Leo Tindemans. Emphasizing the increasing role of Parliament as a stepping stone to office elsewhere, several MEPs have gone on to be appointed to the European Commission, including presidents Jacques Delors and Jacques Santer and commissioners Ray MacSharry, Viviane Reding, Carlo Ripa de Meana, Karel van Miert, and Antonio Vitorino. Several MEPs have also advanced to high national office, including French prime minister Jean Pierre Raffarin, UK defense minister Geoff Hoon, and Spanish foreign minister Ana Palacio.

Political Groups

MEPs do not sit in national blocs but together with elected MEPs (see Box 7.2) from other member states with whom they share similar goals and values. Although these clusters are formally known as "political groups," they have roles and structures similar to national parties: they have common ideologies and policy preferences, come together under a shared label in order to maximize their power and influence, and tend to vote together on issues before the EP. The number and makeup of groups have changed through time, partly in response to enlargement and the arrival of MEPs from new member states, and partly in response to changed political circumstances and opportunities. Some groups are marriages of convenience, bringing together MEPs with different policies,[17] but generally the groups have refined their focus, and they cover a wide array of ideologies and policies, from left to right, from pro-European to anti-European.[18]

Box 7.2 Power to the People: European Elections

Elections to the EP have been a fixture on the European political calendar since 1979. Held on a fixed five-year rotation, in years ending with a four or a nine, they give European voters a direct link with the work of the EU. The logistics of the elections are impressive: the electorate consists of some 400 million voters, many more than in the US. Voters must be eighteen years old and citizens of one of the EU member states. At one time, member states restricted voting to their own citizens, but EU citizens have been allowed since Maastricht to vote in their country of residence, and even to run for the EP wherever they live, regardless of citizenship. They must make a declaration to the electoral authority of the member state in which they reside, and they must meet local qualifications if they want to vote, and qualifications in their home state if they want to run. Member states have different rules on the minimum age for candidates (which range from eighteen to twenty-five) and also have different rules on how candidates qualify; some do not allow independent candidates, some require candidates to pay deposits, others require them to collect signatures, and so on.

Voter turnout figures vary from one member state to another, but are lower than those at national elections and are decidedly not impressive with a noticeable gender gap (women's turnout has been significantly lower). Overall turnout fell steadily from 62 percent in 1979 to around 57 percent in 1994, then took a relatively sharp fall to

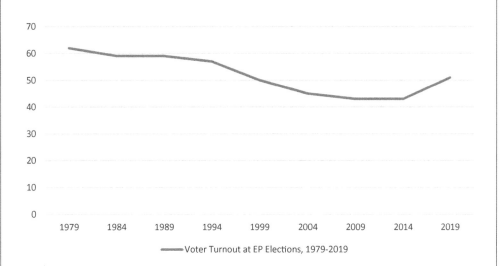

Voter Turnout at EP Elections, 1979-2019

FIGURE 7.2 Voter Turnout at European Parliament Elections, 1979–2019.

Source: European Parliament, at https://europarl.europa.eu/election-results-2019/en/turnout/ and Statista at www.statista.com/statistics/300427/eu-parlament-turnout-for-the-european-elections/.

around 43 percent in 2009 and 2014. Belgium, Luxembourg, and Malta have the highest turnout (70–90 percent), Italy and Greece hover in the range of 60–70 percent, but in almost all other countries fewer than half of all voters headed to the polls in EP elections before 2019. Results were particularly poor in 2004 among the new Eastern European members, which were taking part for the first time. Although large majorities turned out in Cyprus and Malta, less than 40 percent cast votes in most other countries, and just 21 percent in Poland, a trend that has mostly continued to this day in Eastern Europe.

The most compelling explanation for low voter turnout is the relative significance of "first-order" and "second-order" elections.[19] Since national elections determine who controls national executives and legislatures which make the decisions that are deemed most immediate and relevant in the lives of citizens, they are seen as the most important elections ("first order") by voters and parties alike. They attract more attention, are more hard fought, and garner more direct interest among voters in their outcome – hence turnout at national elections is greater. By contrast, European elections are considered less important ("second order") because there is less at stake, especially in choosing an executive/government (see Chapter 5 on this).

Yet over the last two EP election cycles some evidence has emerged that EP elections are no longer strictly second-order elections. In 2019, turnout increased to 50 percent – attributed by many observers to mobilization of both strong EU supporters and EU-skeptical/hostile voters (see Figure 7.2). Indeed, some have argued that the EU to some extent represents a new polarizing issue or "cleavage" within the Europe-wide party system, much as the owner/worker conflict arising in the nineteenth century produced socialist parties and the "postmaterialist/materialist" conflict of the 1970s spawned modern green parties.[20] While the 2014 elections brought a record number of EU-skeptical and EU-hostile MEPs to the EP, liberal and green parties (both strongly supportive of the EU) did especially well in 2019 while EU-hostile parties did worse than expected (although such parties still captured around 25 percent of the seats). Moreover, pro-EU parties (many of them, again, green parties) have made impressive gains in national elections over the last several years (in Germany, the Netherlands, Finland, and Sweden) while new pro-EU parties (in Spain and Poland) have emerged in a kind of anti-populist, pro-EU backlash.[21] In short, recent elections have demonstrated a growing fault line or cleavage over the future of Europe and the EU.

Despite the distinctive political group system in the EP, these groups are much less well known to national voters than their constituent parties. They have not yet developed a habit of campaigning on a cross-Europe platform, which means that voters are still presented on election day with a choice among national parties rather than among European party groups (which is part of the reason why European elections are run more on national than on European issues). At the same time, though, the political groups have become more cohesive in spite of the sheer number of their constituent parties, and the distinctions across the ideological spectrum are clear.[22]

Several rules govern the formation of political groups, the most basic being that a group must have at least twenty-five members, who must be elected from at least one-quarter of member states. No party group has ever had enough seats to form a majority, so multipartisanship has been the order of business: groups must work together in order to achieve a majority. Frequent changes in the number and makeup of party groups also impact the balance of power. Through all those changes, three groups have developed a particular consistency: the socialists (on the center left), the liberals (now called "Renew Europe," in the center), and the EPP (on the center right).

Moving from left to right on the ideological spectrum, the party groups in 2020 (see Figure 7.3) were as follows:

European United Left–Nordic Green Left (GUE–NGL). The European United Left (EUL) is the main product of the game of musical chairs played on the left of Parliament since the mid-1980s. A Communist Group was formed in 1973, but the collapse of the Soviet Union in 1989 encouraged the Italian and Spanish delegations to form their own EUL, while hardline communists from France, Greece, and Portugal formed Left Unity. By 1994 only the EUL remained, consisting mainly of the Spanish, French, and Italians. In 1995 the label Nordic Green Left was added to account for the arrival of new MEPs from Finland and Sweden. After 2014 the group included members from fourteen EU states, the biggest national blocs coming from Germany, France, and Spain. The GUE–NGL is now the smallest group in the EP, losing eleven seats in 2019. It is sharply critical of the EU but not anti-EU per se.

Progressive Alliance of Socialists and Democrats (S&D). The S&D is the main center-left group and was for many years the largest in Parliament, intensifying concerns of conservative Euroskeptics about the interventionist tendencies of the EU. However, the 1999 elections saw a rightward shift within the European electorate and a reaction in the UK against the Labour Party. As a result, the group found itself losing more than forty seats and relegated to second place in the EP where it has remained since. The S&D has shades of opinion ranging from former communists on the left to more moderate social democrats toward the center, but is strongly supportive of the EU and has generally more ideological consistency than its key competitor, the EPP (see below). Its members span almost every EU member state, with those from Spain, Italy, and Germany forming the biggest national blocs. In the 2019 election it lost thirty-one seats as part of an anti-establishment party backlash.

The Greens–European Free Alliance (Greens–EFA). Usually associated with environmental issues, the Greens in fact pursue a wider variety of interests related to social justice and refuse to be placed on the traditional ideological spectrum. Once part of the Rainbow

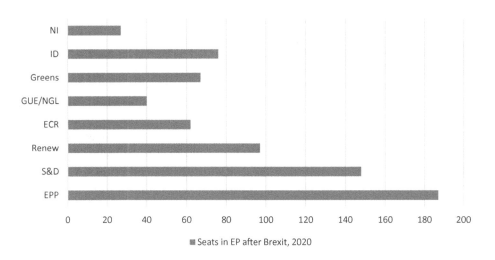

■ Seats in EP after Brexit, 2020

FIGURE 7.3 Political Groups Representation in the European Parliament after Brexit, 2020.

Source: European Parliament, *News*, January 31, 2020, at www.europarl.europa.eu/news/en/press-room/20200130IPR71407/redistribution-of-seats-in-the-european-parliament-after-brexit.

Group, the Greens formed their own group after doing well in the 1989 elections. In 1999 their numbers jumped from twenty-seven to thirty-eight, which – when added to the seven members of the European Free Alliance, a small cluster of regional parties – made the Greens a significant force and now the fourth biggest group in the EP. In 2019, the Greens–EFA (seen as a pro-EU alternative to the establishment EPP and S&D) were one of the big winners in EP elections, gaining twenty-two seats. Their biggest national blocs come from France and Germany. Critical of what they see as the too-cozy relationship between corporations and the EU, they nevertheless are strong supporters of the EU project and therefore one of the main enemies of right-wing populists.

Renew Europe. Formerly known as the Alliance of Liberals and Democrats for Europe, it contains members from all but nine member states. Since the inception of the EP it has consistently been the third largest group in the EP and along with the Greens was a big winner in 2019, gaining thirty-nine seats. Renew Europe is difficult to pinpoint in exact ideological terms, but most of its MEPs fall in or around the center and are ardent supporters of the EU. The largest delegation now comes from France, namely, Emmanuel Macron's *En Marche*.

European People's Party (EPP). The EPP is the major party group on the political center right and the biggest group in the EP. It began life as a grouping of Christian democratic parties from the six founding member states, and long stood for the mainstream Christian democratic principles of social justice, liberal democracy, a mixed economy, and European federalism. The group's policies changed, however, as it incorporated center-right parties from other member states that subscribed neither to Christian democracy nor to European federalism,[23] and in 1976 it changed its name to the European People's Party. Though the EPP remains the biggest party in the EP, it lost heavily in the 2019 European elections. The EPP's biggest national bloc comes from Germany but one of its member delegations – Hungary's Fidesz – has been suspended due to rule of law concerns and a controversial 2019 EP election campaign which targeted Commission president Juncker.

European Conservatives and Reformists Group (ECR). The ECR was created before the 2009 EP elections by the UK's David Cameron and Mirek Topolanek, the leader of the Czech Civic Democratic Party; it was later joined by the Polish Law and Justice Party. Fiercely Euroskeptic but not as hostile to the EU as ID (see below), the ECR's website declares "Cooperation, yes! Superstate, no!"[24] ECR's biggest national blocs now come from Eastern Europe, most especially Poland, and include the right-wing populist Swedish Democrats as well.

Identity and Democracy (ID). Openly EU-hostile political groups go back to the Europe of Nations party grouping of 1994, with ID (after merging with another anti-EU political group, Europe of Freedom and Direct Democracy, in 2019) being its latest incarnation. Identity and Democracy boasts seventy-three MEPs from nine member states, including Marine Le Pen's National Rally, Austria's FPÖ, Vlams Belang (Belgium), the Italian Lega and 5-Star parties, Alternative for Germany, Freedom and Direct Democracy (Czech Republic), the Finns Party, the Danish People's Party, and the Conservative People's Party of Estonia. As of this writing, however, it has failed in its attempt to woo Viktor Orbán's Fidesz, Poland's Law and Justice, and the Swedish Democrats (all of whom are EU-skeptical if not EU-hostile) to ID.

Non-Attached Members (NI). One could call these the "outliers" of the EP. Parliament has always had a number of MEPs who, for reasons of independence or failure to reach agreement with any established political group, operate outside the group structure of the EP. They have rarely numbered more than two to three dozen but until the UK left the EU included twenty-nine members of the UK's Brexit Party in addition to twenty-eight other non-attached MEPs.

HOW PARLIAMENT WORKS

Conventional democratic legislatures have a virtual monopoly on the introduction, amendment, and adoption of new laws (although final adoption is normally subject to signature by the executive or the head of state). However, such is not the case with the EP, which – thanks to efforts by member states to preserve their powers in the Council of Ministers – has been left with a mix of formal and informal powers, ranging from the modest to the significant. These powers fall broadly into three main groups: legislative, budgetary, and institutional supervision and oversight.

Powers over Legislation

Although the Commission has a monopoly on the development of proposals for new laws, the EP employs informal channels of influence open to it at this stage. For example, it can send representatives to the early development meetings held by the Commission, at which point it can encourage the Commission to address issues it prioritizes. It can also publish "own initiative" reports in which it draws attention to a problem, almost daring the Commission and the Council of Ministers to respond. The EP has been, for example, a legislative entrepreneur on a variety of environmental issues, sparking EU bans on imports of seal products from Canada, kangaroo products from Australia, old growth lumber from Canada, and the fur of animals caught using leghold traps in Russia and North America.[25] Generally, though, Parliament must wait until it receives a proposal from the Commission before it can really get down to work. At that point, it enters a process of give and take with the Council of Ministers that has swelled to complex proportions.

Initially, Parliament was limited mainly to the consultation procedure, under which it can either accept or reject a proposal from the Council of Ministers or ask for amendments. If amendments are needed, they are made by the Commission, and the new proposal is sent back to the Council of Ministers, which then decides whether to accept or reject the proposal, to which it can make additional changes if desired. No limit is placed on how long Parliament can take to give its opinion, and so it has the power of delay – a traditional practice of opposition parties in many national legislatures. This power attained new significance with the 1980 isoglucose case; Parliament was subsequently able to drag its feet as a means of getting the Council to take its opinion seriously.[26] The consultation procedure is now rarely used.

The SEA increased the powers of Parliament, introducing a cooperation procedure under which Parliament gained the right to a second reading for certain laws adopted by the Council of Ministers, notably those relating to regional policy, the environment, and the European Social Fund. Accordingly, Parliament was now involved more directly in the legislative process and no longer had a purely consultative role.[27] Maastricht extended the procedure to cover a variety of new policy areas, but then it was all but eliminated by the Amsterdam treaty.

Maastricht further strengthened the powers of Parliament by introducing the codecision procedure, renamed the "ordinary legislative procedure" by Lisbon (see Box 7.3), which is now the standard approach to lawmaking. Initially, codecision meant that Parliament possessed the right to a third reading on certain kinds of legislation, the list of which was then expanded to include laws relating to the single market, research and development, consumer protection, the environment, education, and culture, and then expanded again by Lisbon to include agriculture, fisheries, the structural funds, and transport. This effectively granted the EP equal powers with the Council of Ministers on decision making, making the two institutions into co-legislatures. At one time the Council of Ministers could still overrule the EP's rejection of a new proposal after a third reading, but this power was abruptly ended by the

Treaty of Amsterdam. Consequently, an EP–Council conciliation committee must now meet after the second reading to see if it can craft an agreeable joint text, which in most cases it does. The new text then goes to the EP and the Council for a third reading and a vote.

Finally, under the consent procedure, Parliament has veto powers over the Council on the following: allowing new member states to join the EU and giving other countries associate status; the conclusion of international agreements; penalties the Council may choose to impose on a member state for serious and persistent violations of fundamental rights; any efforts to introduce a uniform electoral system for European elections; and the powers and tasks of the European Central Bank. Maastricht also extended Parliament's powers over foreign policy issues by obliging the presidency of the European Council to consult with the EP on the development of the Common Foreign and Security Policy. During the 1990s the EP used the consent (then known as assent) procedure several times to delay agreements between the EU and third parties. For example, it held up an agreement with Russia in protest of Russian policy in Chechnya, with Kazakhstan in protest of that country's poor democratic record, and with Turkey in protest of human rights violations.[28]

Box 7.3 Congratulations, Bill – You're a Law! The Ordinary Legislative Procedure

The tension between intergovernmental and supranational pressures in the EU has resulted in constant change in the decision-making procedure of the EP, leading to the current preferred arrangement, known as the "ordinary legislative procedure." Debate between the EP and the Council of Ministers over the adoption of new laws in most areas involves the following steps:

1   The Commission sends a proposal for a new law to Parliament and the Council of Ministers.
2   The relevant parliamentary standing committee looks it over and draws up a report (which may be seen and commented upon by other committees with an interest in the issue, by individual MEPs, and by political groups). Parliament then votes on the report in a plenary session. This is the *first reading*.
3   If no changes are suggested, or if the Council agrees with the EP's suggested changes, then the proposal is adopted. But if the Council disagrees with the suggested changes, it modifies them in a common position.
4   The common position then goes to Parliament, which has three months to respond. If it approves the common position or fails to act by the deadline, the amended proposal is adopted. But the relevant parliamentary committee may reject the common position or propose amendments. Its recommendation is then discussed by Parliament in a *second reading*.
5   The changes are forwarded to the Commission, which gives its opinion. The proposal then goes to the Council, which can accept the changes – in which case the proposal is adopted – or reject them. In the latter case, the proposal is sent to a conciliation committee, which works to reconcile the differences.
6   If the committee cannot agree within six weeks, the proposal lapses. But in most cases, the committee reaches agreement and issues a joint text, which then goes to Parliament for approval. This is the *third reading*. If Parliament approves the joint text, the proposal is adopted, but if rejected, the proposal lapses.

The cumulative effect of all these changes has been to equalize the power between the Council of the EU and Parliament over the adoption of most new laws. In other words, the EU now has a bicameral legislature in all but name. The changes have also encouraged party groups in Parliament to cooperate more closely, and have made the EP a new target for lobbyists trying to influence the shape of new legislation (see Chapter 10).

In addition, the role of member state parliaments in the lawmaking process has increased along with the EP in recent years. The presidents or speakers of member states' parliaments meet with the EP every year and discuss broad areas of cooperation, and regular interparliamentary meetings take place to talk about draft law. More importantly, if enough national parliaments think that member states' fundamental powers are affected by EU legislation (under the principle of subsidiarity) they can issue a "yellow card" or "orange card," asking the EU to reconsider the proposal. However, none of these give national parliaments actual veto power. In 2018 the EP received 473 such submissions from parliaments in member states.[29]

Powers over the Budget

Parliament has joint powers with the Council of the EU over confirming the EU budget, so that the two institutions comprise the budgetary authority of the EU. Parliament meets with the Council biannually to consider a draft developed by the Commission and to discuss possible amendments. It can ask for changes to the budget, it can ask for new appropriations for areas not covered (but it cannot make decisions on how to raise money), and ultimately – with a two-thirds majority – it can completely reject the budget, which it has done only three times so far (in 1979, 1982, and 1984). The Commission normally introduces a draft budget in April each year and – following meetings between the Council and the Commission – adopts it in July, then sends it to the EP for two readings. Only when Parliament has adopted the budget (usually in December) and the budget has been signed by the president of the EP does it come into force.

Powers over Other EU Institutions

Parliament has several direct powers over other EU institutions, including the right to debate the annual legislative program of the Commission, a practice introduced by Jacques Delors during the mid-1980s that has since been used by the Commission to emphasize its accountability to Parliament.[30] It can also take the Commission or the Council of the EU to the Court of Justice over alleged infringements of the treaties and has had the power since 1994 to approve the appointment of the Commission president and all of the commissioners. Although it cannot vote on individual commissioners, concerns raised by the EP about individuals can block their appointment (see Chapter 5). The extension of the term of the College of Commissioners from four years to five (to coincide with the term of the EP) significantly altered the relationship between the two institutions.

The makeup of the College is not tied to the balance of party power in the EP (in the way that the membership of governments in parliamentary systems is a reflection of party numbers in the legislature). However, the EP's right to vote on the proposed membership of the College is a step closer to the day when there will be ideological and policy alignment between the two, and membership of the College of Commissioners will reflect the balance of party power in the EP.

The most potentially disruptive of Parliament's powers over the Commission is its ability – under certain conditions and with an absolute majority of MEPs and a two-thirds majority of votes cast – to force the resignation of the entire College of Commissioners through a motion of censure. Much like a nuclear weapon, though, this power is mainly a deterrent; censure motions have been proposed, but they have all been defeated or withdrawn. As noted in Chapter 5, the closest the EP has come to removing the College was during a vote in January 1999 over charges of fraud and corruption; 232 MEPs voted in favor of removing the College, but this was far less than the required two-thirds majority of 416. Nonetheless, the size of the negative vote shocked the Commission and triggered the creation of a committee of inquiry, whose report ultimately brought down the College. The event has gone down as a watershed in the relationship between the EP and the Commission.

The EP also has a critical relationship with the Council of Ministers. Apart from having equal powers with the Council over the adoption of most new laws, Parliament also closely monitors the work of the Council, regularly submitting oral and written questions on matters of policy. The two institutions work particularly closely together on policy issues such as the Common Foreign and Security Policy, judicial cooperation, asylum and immigration issues, and international crime. The president of the EP also gives an address at the opening of every meeting of the European Council, expressing the views of Parliament on its agenda.

These views hold particular weight these days as Parliament has taken the initiative through the years to win new powers over the work of EU institutions. For example, it introduced its own question time in 1973 (similar to Prime Minister's Question Time in the UK) and so can demand oral or written replies to questions from commissioners, helping to make them more accountable through the oversight process. It initiated the 1992 reconfiguration of the number of seats in Parliament, and it spearheaded the campaign for the creation of the Court of Auditors in 1993. It can generate public debate on EU policies and set up committees of inquiry, as it did during 1996 to look into the crisis set off by mad cow disease in the UK. All in all, the EP has flexed its newly acquired muscles to, if not set the EU's agenda, at least make that agenda more accountable, transparent, and democratically decided.

QUESTIONS TO CONSIDER

1   In terms of its power, how has the EP evolved over the years, and what difference have such changes made to its relationships with other EU institutions?
2   How is the EP similar to and different from other legislatures, such as the US Congress? Should the EP be given the same powers as the US Congress?
3   Why has the EP failed to capture the imagination of EU voters? What more could be done to address its lack of a strong psychological link with EU citizens?

NOTES

1   John Gillingham, *Coal, Steel, and the Rebirth of Europe, 1945–55*, 282 (New York: Cambridge University Press, 1991).
2   See discussion in Berthold Rittberger, *Building Europe's Parliament: Democratic Representation Beyond the Nation-State*, chapter 3 (Oxford: Oxford University Press, 2005).
3   Richard Corbett, Francis Jacobs, and Michael Shackleton, *The European Parliament*, 8th ed., 240. (London: John Harper, 2011).
4   Renaud Dehousse, *The European Court of Justice*, 98 (New York: St. Martin's, 1998).
5   "European Parliament Not Moving from Strasbourg, France Says," *Reuters*, December 17, 2017, at www.reuters.com/article/us-france-eu/european-parliament-not-moving-from-strasbourg-france-says-idUSKBN1DX0HS, accessed July 24, 2019.
6   Roy Perry, MEP, quoted in David Judge and David Earnshaw, *The European Parliament*, 163 (Basingstoke, UK: Palgrave Macmillan, 2003).

7 On recent challenges to the EP's Strasbourg location, see "Scrap Strasbourg Seat, Urges Italy's Di Maio," *Euractiv*, January 15, 2019, at www.euractiv.com/section/eu-elections-2019/news/scrap-strasbourg-seat-urges-italys-di-maio/, accessed January 16, 2019.

8 Andrew Gimson, *Boris: The Rise of Boris Johnson*, 108 (London: Simon and Schuster, 2006).

9 For more discussion on the multisite issue, see Judge and Earnshaw, *The European Parliament*, 158–163.

10 Corbett, Jacobs, and Shackleton, *The European Parliament*, 119.

11 In 2019, however, all the other political groups in the EP blocked members of the ID group from chairing any significant committees in an attempted *cordon sanitaire* of the right-wing populists. See "MEPs Shut Out Nationalists from Key Posts," *Euractiv*, July 11, 2019, at www.euractiv.com/section/politics/news/meps-shut-out-nationalists-from-key-posts/, accessed July 24, 2019.

12 "How Many MEPs?" *News of the European Parliament*, at www.europarl.europa.eu/news/en/faq/12/how-many-meps, accessed July 24, 2019.

13 European Parliament, "The Impact of the UK's Withdrawal on the Institutional Set-up and Political Dynamics Within the EU," Policy Department for Citizens' Rights and Constitutional Affairs, April 2019, at www.europarl.europa.eu/RegData/etudes/STUD/2019/621914/IPOL_STU(2019)621914_EN.pdf, accessed June 1, 2019.

14 Simon Hix and Christopher Lord, *Political Parties in the European Union*, 85–90 (New York: St. Martin's, 1997).

15 "European Parliament: Facts and Figures," *Briefing, European Parliament*, November 14, 2014, at www.europarl.europa.eu/EPRS/EPRS-Briefing-542150-European-Parliament-Facts-and-Figures-FINAL.pdf, accessed July 24, 2019.

16 "Women in National Parliaments," *Inter-Parliamentary Union*, 2019, at http://archive.ipu.org/wmn-e/classif.htm, accessed July 24, 2019. Figures are for 2019, for lower or single chambers of national legislatures.

17 This is especially true for anti-EU political groups. See Matteo Cavallaro, David Flacher, and Massimo Angelo Zanetti, "Radical Right Parties and European Economic Integration: Evidence from the Seventh Parliament," *European Union Politics* 19, no. 2 (2018): 321–343.

18 For a history of EU party groups, see Luciano Bardi, "Transnational Trends: The Evolution of the European Party System," in *The European Parliament: Moving Toward Democracy in the EU*, edited by Bernard Steunenberg and Jacques Thomassen (Lanham, MD: Rowman and Littlefield, 2002). For an overview of the groups, see Ariadna Ripoll Servent, *The European Parliament*, chapter 9 (London: Palgrave, 2017).

19 See K. Reiff and H. Schmitt, "Nine Second-Order National Elections: A Conceptual Framework for the Analysis of European Election Results," *European Journal of Political Research* 8, no. 1 (1980): 3–44; and Simon Hix and Bjørn Høyland, *The Political System of the European Union*, 3rd ed., 190–194 (Basingstoke, UK: Palgrave Macmillan, 2011).

20 See Lorenzo De Sio, Vincenzo Emanuele, and Nicola Maggini, "Conclusions," in *The European Parliament Elections of 2014*, edited by Lorenzo De Dio, Vincenzo Emanuele, and Nicola Maggini (Rome: Centro Italiano Studi Elettorali, 2014), at https://cise.luiss.it/cise/2014/07/29/the-european-parliament-elections-of-2014-the-e-book/, accessed November 6, 2014.

21 See "Who Loves You Baby: Europe's Anti-Nationalist Backlash," *The Economist*, May 11, 2017, at www.economist.com/europe/2017/05/11/europes-anti-nationalist-backlash, accessed May 18, 2017.

22 Simon Hix, Abdul G. Noury, and Gérard Roland, *Democratic Politics in the European Parliament* (New York: Cambridge University Press, 2007).

23 Judge and Earnshaw, *The European Parliament*, 133.

24 European Conservatives and Reformists Group at https://ecrgroup.eu/, accessed July 18, 2019.

25 Christopher Pienning, "The EP Since 1994: Making Its Mark on the World Stage," in *The 1999 Elections to the European Parliament*, edited by Juliet Lodge (Basingstoke, UK: Palgrave Macmillan, 2001).

26 Corbett, Jacobs, and Shackleton, *The European Parliament*, 200.

27 John Fitzmaurice, "An Analysis of the European Community's Cooperation Procedure," *Journal of Common Market Studies* 26, no. 4 (June 1988): 389–400.
28 Pienning, "The EP Since 1994."
29 European Parliament, "Relations with National Parliaments," *Annual Report 2018*, at www.europarl.europa.eu/relnatparl/en/home.html, accessed August 2, 2019.
30 Clive Archer and Fiona Butler, *The European Community: Structure and Process*, 2nd ed., 47 (London: Pinter, 1996).

BIBLIOGRAPHY

Archer, Clive and Fiona Butler, *The European Community: Structure and Process*, 2nd ed. (London: Pinter, 1996).
Bardi, Luciano, "Transnational Trends: The Evolution of the European Party System," in *The European Parliament: Moving Toward Democracy in the EU*, edited by Bernard Steunenberg and Jacques Thomassen (Lanham, MD: Rowman and Littlefield, 2002).
Cavallaro, Matteo, David Flacher, and Massimo Angelo Zanetti, "Radical Right Parties and European Economic Integration: Evidence from the Seventh Parliament," *European Union Politics* 19, no. 2 (2018): 321–343.
Corbett, Richard, Francis Jacobs, and Michael Shackleton, *The European Parliament*, 8th ed. (London: John Harper, 2011).
Daniel, William T., *Career Behaviour and the European Parliament: All Roads Lead Through Brussels?* Oxford: Oxford University Press, 2015.
De Sio, Lorenzo, Vincenzo Emanuele, and Nicola Maggini, "Conclusion." In *The European Parliament Elections of 2014*, edited by Lorenzo De Dio, Vincenzo Emanuele, and Nicola Maggini. Rome: Centro Italiano Studi Elettoralia. www.researchgate.net/publication/282979135_The_European_Parliament_Elections_of_2014, accessed 6 November 2014.
Dehousse, Renaud, *The European Court of Justice*. New York: St. Martin's, 1998.
Economist, The, "Who Loves You Baby: Europe's Anti-Nationalist Backlash," May 11, 2017, at www.economist.com/europe/2017/05/11/europes-anti-nationalist-backlash, accessed May 18, 2017.
Euractiv, "Scrap Strasbourg Seat, Urges Italy's Di Maio," January 15, 2019, at www.euractiv.com/section/eu-elections-2019/news/scrap-strasbourg-seat-urges-italys-di-maio/, accessed January 16, 2019.
Euractiv, "MEPs Shut Out Nationalists from Key Posts," July 11, 2019, at www.euractiv.com/section/politics/news/meps-shut-out-nationalists-from-key-posts/, accessed July 24, 2019.
European Parliament, "European Parliament: Facts and Figures," *Briefing*, November 14, 2014, at www.europarl.europa.eu/EPRS/EPRS-Briefing-542150-European-Parliament-Facts-and-Figures-FINAL.pdf, accessed July 24, 2019.
European Parliament, "Relations with National Parliaments," *Annual Report 2018*, at www.europarl.europa.eu/relnatparl/en/home.html, accessed August 2, 2019.
European Parliament, "How Many MEPs?" *News of the European Parliament*, at www.europarl.europa.eu/news/en/faq/12/how-many-meps, accessed July 24, 2019.
European Parliament, "The Impact of the UK's Withdrawal on the Institutional Set-up and Political Dynamics Within the EU," Policy Department for Citizens' Rights and Constitutional Affairs, April 2019, at www.europarl.europa.eu/RegData/etudes/STUD/2019/621914/IPOL_STU(2019)621914_EN.pdf, accessed June 1, 2019.
Fitzmaurice, John, "An Analysis of the European Community's Cooperation Procedure," *Journal of Common Market Studies* 26, no. 4 (June 1988): 389–400.
Gillingham, John, *Coal, Steel, and the Rebirth of Europe, 1945–55* (New York: Cambridge University Press, 1991).
Gimson, Andrew, *Boris: The Rise of Boris Johnson* (London: Simon and Schuster, 2006).
Hix, Simon and Bjørn Høyland, *The Political System of the European Union*, 3rd ed. Basingstoke, UK: Palgrave Macmillan, 2011.
Hix, Simon and Christopher Lord, *Political Parties in the European Union* (New York: St. Martin's, 1997).

Hix, Simon, Abdul G. Noury, and Gérard Roland, *Democratic Politics in the European Parliament* (New York: Cambridge University Press, 2007).

Inter-Parliamentary Union, "Women in National Parliaments," at http://archive.ipu.org/wmn-e/classif.htm, accessed July 24, 2019.

Judge, David, David Earnshaw, Neil Nugent, and William E. Paterson, *The European Parliament*, 2nd ed. (Basingstoke, UK: Palgrave Macmillan, 2008).

Pienning, Christopher, "The EP Since 1994: Making Its Mark on the World Stage," in *The 1999 Elections to the European Parliament*, edited by Juliet Lodge (Basingstoke, UK: Palgrave Macmillan, 2001).

Reiff, Karlheinz and Hermann Schmitt. "Nine Second-Order National Elections: A Conceptual Framework for the Analysis of European Election Results," *European Journal of Political Research* 8, no. 1 (1980): 3–44.

Reuters, "European Parliament Not Moving from Strasbourg, France Says," December 17, 2017, at www.reuters.com/article/us-france-eu/european-parliament-not-moving-from-strasbourg-france-says-idUSKBN1DX0HS, accessed July 24, 2019.

Rittberger, Berthhold, *Building Europe's Parliament: Democratic Representation Beyond the Nation-State* (Oxford: Oxford University Press, 2005).

Servent, Ariadna Ripoll, *The European Parliament* (London: Palgrave, 2017).

Shackleton, Michael and Richard Francis Jacobs, *The European Parliament*, 8th ed. (London: John Harper, 2011).

FURTHER READING

Michael Shackleton and Richard Francis Jacobs, *The European Parliament*, 8th ed. (London: John Harper, 2011).

A standard reference work on the EP, written by an MEP and two staff members and describing in some detail the powers and workings of Parliament.

Ariadna Ripoll Servent, *The European Parliament* (London: Palgrave, 2017); David Judge, David Earnshaw, Neil Nugent, and William E. Paterson, *The European Parliament*, 2nd ed. (Basingstoke, UK: Palgrave Macmillan, 2008).

Two surveys of the EP, including chapters on its history, its powers and organization, the party groups, and its role in EU decision making.

William T. Daniel, *Career Behaviour and the European Parliament: All Roads Lead Through Brussels?* (Oxford: Oxford University Press, 2015).

A study of the evolution of career behaviors of MEPs.

CHAPTER 8

The Court of Justice of the European Union

CHAPTER OVERVIEW

- The least well known of the EU institutions, the Court of Justice of the European Union is the judicial arm of the EU, responsible for interpreting the meaning of the treaties and for resolving disputes between the member states, EU institutions, and individuals affected by EU law.
- The Court consists of twenty-seven judges appointed for six-year renewable terms by common accord of the member states, headed by a president, assisted by eleven advocates general charged with reviewing cases as they come to the Court and delivering independent opinions. Below this body there is also the General Court, which serves as the first point of decision on less complicated cases and on cases involving disputes between EU institutions and their employees.
- The Court can be considered the unsung hero of European integration: well respected and relatively uncontroversial, the Court has created a body of law that is uniformly interpreted and applied throughout the EU and has issued judgments that, together, have greatly facilitated the integration process.

The Court of Justice of the European Union (officially simply the Court of Justice, or CJ) is the judicial arm of the EU. Its charge is to rule on the "constitutionality" of all EU law, to decide on conformity with the treaties of any international agreement considered by the EU, to give rulings to national courts in cases in which there are questions about EU law, and to rule in disputes involving EU institutions, member states, individuals, and corporations. Based in Luxembourg, the Court consists of twenty-seven judges appointed for six-year renewable terms of office. As the workload of the Court has increased, so subsidiary courts have been created: a Court of First Instance (now called the General Court) was set up in 1989 to deal with less complicated cases and to oversee disputes involving EU institutions and their staff.

The contribution of the Court to European integration has been critical, because without a body of law that can be uniformly interpreted and applied throughout the EU, the Union would have little authority, and its decisions and policies would be arbitrary and inconsistent. By working to build such a body of law, the CJ – perhaps the most purely supranational of the major EU institutions – has been a key player in promoting integration.

Unlike the US Supreme Court, which bases its rulings on judicial review of the Constitution, the CJ has so far had no constitution beyond the accumulated treaties and laws agreed to by the member states. Yet because the treaties have needed interpretation and clarification, and just as the US Supreme Court helped clarify its own powers with decisions such as

Marbury v. *Madison* (the 1803 decision establishing the power of judicial review), so has the CJ.[1] Its rulings have established that the Treaty of Rome is a constitutional instrument that imposes direct and common obligations on member states, established the primacy of EU law, and greatly simplified completion of the single market. Court decisions have carried weight on issues as varied as the free movement of people, money, goods, and services; the external relations of the EU; competition policy; human rights; gender equality; and external trade.

Despite its critical contributions to the process and goals of European integration, the work of the Court has attracted relatively little political attention or analysis. As public interest has focused on the Commission and the Council of the EU, the Court has quietly gone about the business of interpreting EU law, its members remaining the least well known of all the leading actors in the EU system. Unlike judgments of the US Supreme Court, which often dominate national headlines and generate public debate, rulings by the CJ garner substantially less notice.

EVOLUTION

The Court was established in 1952 as the Court of Justice of the European Coal and Steel Community (ECSC) and envisioned as a watchdog for the Treaty of Paris and to rule on the legality of decisions made by the ECSC High Authority in response to complaints submitted by either the member states or the national coal and steel industries; the Treaty of Paris was its primary source of authority. During its brief existence, it concluded 137 decisions, many of which are still relevant to EU law today.[2]

The Treaties of Rome created separate courts for the European Economic Community (EEC) and the European Atomic Energy Community (Euratom), but a subsidiary agreement gave jurisdiction over the treaties to a common seven-member Court of Justice of the European Communities. Consisting of members appointed by the Council of Ministers on the recommendation of the member states, it heard cases involving disputes between Community institutions and member states, and its verdicts were final. The Court's power, reach, and significance grew as the work of the Community expanded, as membership grew during the 1970s and 1980s, and as it issued more judgments against Community institutions and member states. Although decision making in the EU revolved around the axis of the Commission and the Council of Ministers, the Court made pivotal decisions with far-reaching consequences for the process of European integration. Three of its most famous cases illustrate its contribution.

First, the principle of direct effect (EU law is directly and uniformly applicable in all member states) is a consequence of the 1963 *Van Gend en Loos* decision, one of the landmark judgments handed down by the CJ. A Dutch transport company had brought an action against Dutch customs for increasing the duty it had to pay on a product imported from Germany. Its lawyers argued that this violated Article 12 of the EEC Treaty, which, in the interest of building the common market, prohibited new duties or increases in existing duties. The Dutch government argued that the Court had no power to decide whether the provisions of the EEC Treaty prevailed over Dutch law and that resolution fell exclusively within the jurisdiction of national courts. The CJ disagreed, ruling that the treaties were more than international agreements and that European Community (EC) law was "legally complete … and produces direct effects and creates individual rights which national courts must protect."[3] Direct effect was reaffirmed in 1976 in another seminal case, *Defrenne* v. *Sabena*, discussed in Chapter 4.

Second, in another ground-breaking case the principle of the supremacy of EU law (EU law trumps national law in policy areas where the EU has responsibility, comparable to the supremacy clause in Article VI, Section 2 of the US Constitution) was established with the 1964 decision *Flaminio Costa* v. *ENEL*. Costa was an Italian who had owned shares in Edison Volta, an electricity supply company. When the company was nationalized in 1962 and incorporated into the new National Electricity Board (ENEL), Costa refused to pay his electric bill (equivalent to about $1.50), claiming he had been hurt by nationalization, which he argued was contrary to the spirit of the Treaty of Rome. The local court in Milan asked the CJ for a preliminary ruling, even though both the Italian government and ENEL argued that there were no grounds for taking the case to the European Court. The government further argued that a national court could not take a dispute over domestic law to the European Court.

The Court countered that by creating:

> a Community of unlimited duration, having its own institutions, its own personality, its own legal capacity … and real powers stemming from limitation of sovereignty or a transfer of powers from the States to the Community … the Member States have limited their sovereign rights, albeit within limited fields, and have thus created a body of law which binds both their nationals and themselves.[4]

Third, in another landmark ruling the issue of the supremacy of European law was confirmed – and the jurisdiction of the Community extended – with a dispute that erupted in 1967 over the issue of human rights. The EEC Treaty had said nothing about this issue, a reflection once again of how little authority the member states were prepared to surrender to the EEC and how laser focused they had been on economic integration. In October 1967 the German Constitutional Court argued that the EEC had no democratic basis because it lacked protection for human rights and that the Community could not deprive German citizens of the rights they held under German law.[5] The CJ refuted this in *Nold* v. *Commission*, in which it established that "fundamental rights form an integral part of the general principles of law."[6] (See Box 8.1.)

Box 8.1 The EU Charter of Fundamental Rights: A Bill of Rights for the EU?

An example of the manner in which a Court ruling can have broader policy implications is showcased by the issue of human rights. The European Convention on Human Rights was adopted in 1950 by the Council of Europe in order to protect human rights and basic freedoms. Although all EC/EU member states signed the convention, support for the idea of the EC/EU developing its own charter of human rights simmered, the intent being not to change the list of rights so much as to sharpen their visibility to Europeans.[7]

New impetus emerged in 1996 when the CJ ruled that the treaties did not give the EU the power to accede to the convention. On German initiative, members agreed to the drawing up of the charter at the Cologne European Council in June 1999 establishing a sixty-two-member Convention. This body would consist of representatives of the member states, the European Parliament (EP), and national legislatures. It had its first meeting in December 1999 and produced a draft formally adopted in December 2000. Points raised in the charter include:

- Freedom of thought, conscience, religion, expression, and assembly
- The right of all citizens to education (including the possibility of free compulsory education), property and asylum, equality before the law, access to social security and health care, freedom of movement within the EU, and a fair and public trial
- The prohibition of the death penalty, torture, human cloning, slavery, and child labor
- The right of workers to collective bargaining and action, and protection from unjustified dismissal.

Signed by all EU member states, the charter was more a "solemn declaration" than a legally binding document. It would have been incorporated into the European constitution, in spite of concerns from some EU member states that it would have created new legal obligations sure to erode national sovereignty and that it was more appropriate to have some of the issues decided by elected political leaders rather than unelected judges.[8] However, it was not officially incorporated into the Lisbon treaty but rather "solemnly proclaimed," albeit given the "same legal value as the treaties" according to Article 6.

STRUCTURE

The CJ is based in a cluster of buildings in the Centre Européen, a network of EU institutions situated on the Kirchberg Plateau above the city of Luxembourg. The Luxembourg government purchased the land in 1961 as a site for the EC institutions, presumably in the hope that they would all eventually migrate there. Opening in 1973, the black steel and glass Palais de Justice has since been expanded four times in response to EU enlargement and the growing workload of the Court. It is now part of a modest but not insubstantial complex that includes the Secretariat of the European Parliament, buildings for the Commission and the Council of Ministers, the seat of the Court of Auditors, and the headquarters of the European Investment Bank.[9]

The Court has four main elements: the judges, the president of the Court, the advocates general, and the General Court, renamed from the Court of First Instance after Lisbon.

The Judges

The CJ has (after Brexit is complete) twenty-seven judges, each appointed for a six-year renewable term of office. About half come up for renewal every three years, resulting in staggered terms. Theoretically, the judges have always been appointed by common accord of the member state governments, so there is no national quota and there is no "Spanish seat" or "Slovenian seat" on the Court. Judges do not even have to be EU citizens; as Court president Lord McKenzie Stuart quipped in 1988, it could be made up "entirely of Russians."[10] In practice, however, because every member state has the right to make one appointment, all judges are national appointees. The persistence of this practice emphasizes the role that national interests still play in EU decision making. However, Lisbon added a new layer to the appointment process by stipulating that before being appointed by the member states, candidates must first be vetted by a seven-member panel consisting of former members of the CJ, members of national constitutional courts, and lawyers, of whom one is nominated by the EP. The panel gives its opinion, leaving the states free to decide how to act.

PHOTO 8.1 The Building of the Court of Justice of the EU in Luxembourg.

In addition to being acceptable to all of the other member states, judges must be scrupulously independent and must avoid promoting the national interests of their home states. They must also be qualified lawyers, or as the Treaty of Paris so thoughtfully put it, they must "possess the qualifications required for appointment to the highest judicial offices in their respective countries or … be jurisconsults of recognized competence." (In contrast, US Supreme Court justices do not have to be attorneys, although in practice they all have been.) Some European judges have come to the Court with experience as government ministers, some have held elective office, and others have had careers as lawyers and academics, but, since the Treaty of Rome, they have all been lawyers.[11]

Although most judges are renewed at least once, the Court has far more turnover than the US Supreme Court, where appointments are for life. Life appointments have the benefit of encouraging independence and exploiting experience, but they also contribute to the highly charged political nature of US Supreme Court appointments and reduce the injection of new thinking. Appointments to the European Court, by contrast, are both relatively frequent and nonpolitical. The average age of CJ judges in 2019 was fifty-nine (compared to sixty-seven for US justices) and two-thirds had served less than ten years on the Court; in contrast, US justices had held their posts for an average of fourteen years (skewed lower by two new appointments in the last two years). The 2004–2007 enlargement of the EU brought twelve new judges into the Court, along with a significant body of new thinking, perspectives, and priorities (see Table 8.1 for the court's current composition).

European judges enjoy immunity from having suits brought against them while they are on the Court, and even after they have left they cannot be sued for their decisions. They are not allowed to hold administrative or political office while on the Court. They can resign, but can be removed only by the other judges and the advocates general (not by member states or other EU institutions), and then only by unanimous agreement that they are no

TABLE 8.1 Judges of the European Court of Justice, 2020

Name	Member State	Year of Birth	Year of Appointment
Nuno José Cardoso da Silva Piçarra	Portugal	1957	2018
Niilo Jääskinen	Finland	1958	2019
Rosario Silva de Lapuerta	Spain	1954	2003
Koen Lenaerts	Belgium	1954	2003
Endre Juhász	Hungary	1944	2004
Constantinos Lycourgos	Cyprus	1964	2014
Peter Goerge Zuereb	Malta	1954	2018
Marko Ilešič	Slovenia	1947	2014
Jiří Malenovský	Czech Republic	1950	2004
Küllike Jürimäe	Estonia	1962	2013
Eugene Regan	Ireland	1952	2015
Nils Wahl	Sweden	1961	2019
Lars Bay Larsen	Denmark	1953	2006
Lucia Serena Rossi	Italy	1958	2018
Jean-Claude Bonichot	France	1955	2006
Thomas von Danwitz	Germany	1962	2006
Alexander Arabadjiev	Bulgaria	1949	2007
Camelia Toader	Romania	1963	2007
François Biltgen	Luxembourg	1958	2013
Marek Safjan	Poland	1949	2009
Daniel Šváby	Slovenia	1951	2009
Andreas Kumin	Austria	1965	2009
Alexandra Prechal	Netherlands	1959	2010
Irmantas Jarukaitis	Lithuania	1973	2018
Carl Gustav Fernlund	Sweden	1950	2011
Siniš Rodin	Croatia	1963	2013
Michail Vilaras	Greece	1950	2015

Source: Court of Justice of the European Union at https://curia.europa.eu/jcms/jcms/Jo2_7026/en/.

longer doing their job adequately.[12] Almost all the judges have been men. In 2020 there were just five women on the Court: Rosario Silva de Lapuerta from Spain, Camelia Toader from Romania, Küllike Jurimäe from Estonia, Lucia Rossi from Italy, and Alexandra Prechal from the Netherlands.

Though all judges can sit together as a full court, they do so only for the most important cases, while the rest are heard by chambers of three or five judges, or by a Grand Chamber of fifteen judges. Chambers at one time heard only cases that did not need to be brought before the full Court, such as staff cases. Due to an increased workload, any case can now be assigned to a chamber, including preliminary rulings and actions brought by or against member states (unless a member state or an institution specifically asks for a hearing before the full Court, or unless the case is particularly important or complex).

Unlike all of the other EU institutions, in which English is slowly becoming the working language, the Court mainly uses French, although a case can be heard in any of the official languages of the EU. When the defendant is a member state or a citizen of a member state, the case must be heard in the defendant's language – resulting in a large number of translators among its 1,500 staff members.

The President

While the chief justice in the US is nominated by the president and must be confirmed by the US Senate, the president of the European Court of Justice is elected by the judges from among their own number in a secret ballot by majority vote to serve a three-year renewable term. The president presides over meetings of the Court and is responsible for technical issues such as assigning cases to chambers, appointing judge-rapporteurs (see later in this chapter), and deciding the dates for hearings. Presidents also exert considerable influence over the political direction of the Court, like the chief justice of the US Supreme Court, but their exact role is subject to much less public and political scrutiny. Former president Vassilios Skouris (2003–2015) articulated well the role of the president and the court as a whole:

> The Commission … is a political body with the right of initiative. The Court of Justice has never been and could never be like that. We rule on the cases that are brought before us…. The importance of the role of the Court is a good subject for conferences and universities but at the end of the day it's a court of justice that carries out a normal task for any court: to rule on the cases, and nothing more.[13]

In 2015, the Court selected a new president, Koen Lenaerts (see Table 8.2). First appointed to the Court in 2003, Lenaerts earned law and other advanced degrees in Belgium and at Harvard and was later a visiting professor at both Harvard Law School and at the College of Europe in Bruges, Belgium.

The Advocates General

Because it is based on the French legal model, the Court has eleven advocates general who review each of the cases as they come in, study the arguments, and deliver preliminary opinions in court before the judges decide on what action to take and which EU laws apply. Although the judges are not obliged to agree with these opinions nor even to refer to them, they nonetheless provide the main point of reference from which to reach a decision. In theory the eleven advocates general are appointed (like judges) by common accord of the governments of the member states, but in practice one is appointed by each of the five

TABLE 8.2 Presidents of the European Court of Justice

Term	Name	Member State
1958–1961	A.M. Donner	Netherlands
1961–1964	A.M. Donner	Netherlands
1964–1967	Charles Hammes	Luxembourg
1967–1970	Robert Lecourt	France
1970–1973	Robert Lecourt	France
1973–1976	Robert Lecourt	France
1976–1979	Hans Kutscher	West Germany
1979–1980	Hans Kutscher	West Germany
1980–1984	J. Mertens de Wilmars	Belgium
1984–1988	Lord McKenzie Stuart	United Kingdom
1988–1991	Ole Dule	Denmark
1991–1994	Ole Dule	Denmark
1994–1997	Gil Carlos Rodríguez Iglesias	Spain
1997–2000	Gil Carlos Rodríguez Iglesias	Spain
2000–2003	Gil Carlos Rodríguez Iglesias	Spain
2003–2006	Vassilios Skouris	Greece
2006–2009	Vassilios Skouris	Greece
2009–2012	Vassilios Skouris	Greece
2012–2015	Vassilios Skouris	Greece
2015–	Koen Lenaerts	Belgium

biggest member states and others are chosen by the smaller states; one of the members is selected by his/her peers as First Advocate General on a one-year rotation. As with Court judges, most advocates general have been men; the only woman serving in 2020 was Juliane Kokott of Germany (Eleanor Sharpston from the UK having left after Brexit).

The General Court

As European integration deepened and widened, the CJ became busier: in the 1960s it was hearing about fifty cases per year and making fifteen to twenty judgments and the volume of work grew tremendously during the 1970s and 1980s. It was particularly busy after 1987, hearing cases and making preliminary rulings on issues relating to the single market in the lead-up to 1992. Consequently there were more delays, with the Court taking up to two years to reach a decision. To help clear the logjam, the Single European Act (SEA) created a subsidiary Court of First Instance, renamed the General Court by the Treaty of Lisbon.

While the CJ completed 760 cases in 2018 – ten times the number heard by the US Supreme Court – the General Court heard an additional 1,009.[14]

The General Court is the first point of decision on some of the less complicated cases involving aspects of competition, actions brought against the Commission under the Treaty of Paris, and disputes between EU institutions and their staff. The latter responsibility was handed off to a new EU Civil Service Tribunal in 2004, but the Tribunal was merged back into the General Court in 2016. If the cases are lost at this level, the parties involved have the right to appeal to the CJ, in much the same way as parties losing a case in a federal district court or circuit court of appeal in the US can appeal to the Supreme Court.

Structural reform of the General Court began soon after Lisbon with proposals to create other specialized courts to handle the increasingly heavy case load – as had once prompted the creation of the Court of First Instance/General Court itself. This effort met resistance from the member states, as did the suggestion to simply increase the number of General Court judges by six or nine members: the latter option held out the prospect of more judges coming from some member states than others. In the end, the solution was to simply double the size of the court to fifty-six members, phased in from 2015–2019.[15] Although the General Court has its own rules of procedures, it operates in much the same way as the CJ (although it has no advocates general). It can sit as a full court, as a Grand Chamber of fifteen judges, or in smaller chambers of five, three, or even single judges. Members are selected for six-year terms while a president elected by the judges serves a three-year renewable term. Judge Marc Jaeger of Luxembourg, a member of the court since 1996, has served as president since 2007.

SOURCES OF EU LAW

While the US federal and state constitutions provide the foundations of the American legal system, the EU has no constitution in the form of a single codified document that is the functional equivalent of the US Constitution. However, it does have treaties that have been regularly amended over time and collectively function as something like a constitution of the EU.[16] They include the Treaty of Paris (until it expired in July 2002), the Treaties of Rome, the Merger Treaty, treaties of accession signed by new members, the SEA, Maastricht, Amsterdam, Nice, Lisbon, various other key EU agreements, and all related annexes and amendments. Collectively, they form the primary source of European law.[17] There are also secondary sources of EU law, so described because they spring from the primary sources. These consist of all the individual binding laws adopted by the EU (regulations, directives, and decisions – see Box 5.3), relevant international law (most of which is weak and vague but which the Court still often uses to create precedent), and the Court's own interpretation. Judgments by the CJ have helped focus and fortify EU law, making up for the weaknesses that have often arisen out of the compromises made to reach agreement on various laws. The Court not only gives technical interpretations but often goes a step further, filling in gaps and clarifying confusion.

As the EU evolved, pressure grew for agreement on a constitution that would bring together all of the principles established by the treaties and case law. Federico Mancini, a former judge on the CJ, argued in 1991 that the direction in which EU case law had moved since 1957 coincided with "the making of a constitution for Europe." He noted that the EU was created by a treaty (unlike the US, which is founded on a constitution), that the EEC Treaty did not safeguard the fundamental rights of individuals or recognize a right to European citizenship, and that the main work of the Court had been to "constitutionalize" the

EEC Treaty and "to fashion a constitutional framework for a quasi-federal structure in Europe."[18] Against this background, the publication of the 2003 draft constitutional treaty was inevitable, and its collapse unfortunate.

HOW THE COURT WORKS

The CJ is the supreme legal body of the EU; its decisions are final, and it is the final court of appeal on all EU laws. As such, it has played a vital role in determining the character of the EU and in extending the reach of EU law. For example, when the Community slipped into a hiatus in the late 1970s and early 1980s, the Court kept alive the idea of the Community as something more than a customs union.[19] It has been particularly involved in cases relating to the single market, nowhere more so than in the *Cassis de Dijon* decision, establishing the principle of mutual recognition (see Box 8.2) that lay at the heart of the SEA.[20]

The core goal of the Court is to help build a body of common law for the EU that is equally, fairly, and uniformly applied throughout the member states. It ensures this aim by interpreting EU treaties and laws and in some cases taking responsibility for directly applying those laws. EU law takes precedence over the national laws of member states when the two come into conflict, but only in areas in which the EU is active (that is, has "competence") and the member states have ceded powers to the EU. The Court, for example, does not have jurisdiction over criminal and family law; it has made most of its decisions on the economic issues in which the EU has been most actively involved, and has been less involved with policy areas in which the EU has been less active, such as education and health.

Box 8.2 Booze and the Single Market

Of all the cases heard and rulings made by the Court regarding the single market, few were more fundamental than those establishing the principle of mutual recognition, under which a product made and sold legally in one member state cannot be barred from another member state.

The roots of the issue go back to a 1979 case arising out of West Germany's refusal to allow imports of a French blackcurrant liquor, Cassis de Dijon, because its alcohol content (15–20 percent) was below the German minimum for fruit liqueurs (25 percent). The importer charged that this amounted to a "quantitative restriction on imports," which was prohibited under the Treaty of Rome. The CJ concurred, ruling that alcoholic beverages lawfully produced and marketed in one member state could not be prohibited from sale in another on the grounds that they had a lower alcohol content.[21] In other words, a member state could not refuse a product from another member state just because it was produced differently. Although this decision established the principle of mutual recognition, it did not prevent challenges from occurring.

The issue reared its head again in the 1984 case *Commission* v. *Federal Republic of Germany* over the question of beer imports into West Germany. Thanks to the *Rein-heitsgebot* (a purity law passed in 1516 by the Duke of Bavaria), German beer is allowed to contain only malted barley, hops, yeast, and water. Germans are big beer drinkers – consuming an average of 38 gallons (173 liters) per person per year – and long refused to import foreign beer on the grounds that most such beer contained "additives" such as rice, maize, sorghum, flavoring, and coloring (much like a recent

Budweiser advertisement which lampooned its competitors for using corn syrup). The Commission sued Germany on the grounds that a 1952 German law effectively prevented any beer being imported or sold in Germany that did not meet the *Reinheitsgebot*, thereby infringing the Treaty of Rome.[22] Not to be outdone, Germany argued that since the average German male relies on beer for a quarter of his daily nutritional intake, allowing imports of "impure" foreign beer would pose a risk to public health!

But the Court disagreed: it ruled in 1987 that Germany could not use the public health argument to ban beer imports and had to accept foreign beer imports as long as brewers printed a list of ingredients on their labels. The Court decision simplified decisions on issues of trade between member states, setting a precedent for the import of food and drink. Booze could now flow freely across the EU.

Court proceedings usually begin with a written application, which is filed by a lawyer with the court registrar and published in its *Official Journal*. This document describes the dispute, explains the grounds for the application, and gives the defendant a month to respond. The president then assigns the case to a judge-rapporteur (a judge of the Court who is charged with drawing up a preliminary report on the case), while the first advocate general appoints an advocate general to the case. The advocate general and judge-rapporteur make their recommendations to the Court, and the case is assigned to a chamber. The case is then argued by the parties involved at a public hearing before the chamber, the larger chambers being reserved for only the most important cases. At the end of the oral phase, the advocate general delivers an opinion, and once the chamber has reached a decision, it delivers judgment in open court.

The entire process can take as long as two years for preliminary rulings, although the average has fallen recently as the workload has been shared among chambers and with the General Court. Though Court decisions are technically supposed to be unanimous, votes are usually taken on a simple majority, as in the US Supreme Court. Unlike the US Supreme Court, however, all the votes of the European Court are secret, so it is never publicly known who, if anyone, dissented. Like its US counterpart, the Court has no direct powers to enforce its judgments; implementation mainly falls to national courts or the governments of the member states, with the Commission keeping a close watch. Maastricht endowed the CJ with new powers by allowing it to impose fines, but the question of how the fines would be collected was left open.

Two main categories constitute the work of the Court: preliminary rulings and direct actions.

Preliminary Rulings

These rulings make up the most important part of the Court's work and account for the overwhelming percentage of the cases it considers (see Figure 8.1). Under the Treaty of Rome, a national court can (and sometimes must) ask the CJ for a ruling on the interpretation or validity of an EU law that arises in a national court case. The issue of validity is particularly critical, because chaos would reign if national courts could declare EU laws invalid.[23] Members of EU institutions can also ask for preliminary rulings, but most are made on behalf of a national court and are binding on the court in the case concerned. (The word *preliminary* is misleading: the rulings are usually requested and given *during* a case, not before it opens; the term *concurrent rulings* might be more appropriate.)

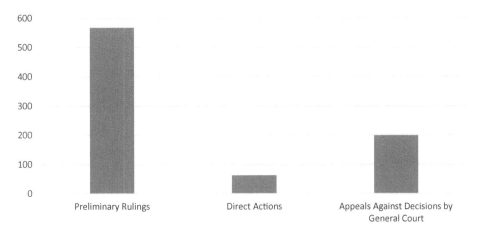

FIGURE 8.1 Types of Cases Heard by the Court of Justice, 2018.

Source: European Court of Justice, *Annual Report 2018: The Year in Review*, at https://curia.europa.eu/jcms/upload/docs/application/pdf/2019-04/ra_pan_2018_en.pdf.

The *Van Gend en Loos* and *Flaminio Costa* cases are classic examples of preliminary rulings, but two other rulings had crucial implications for individual rights as well. In *Cowan v. Le Tresor Public*, the Court ruled on a case involving a British citizen who in 1989 was mugged outside a subway station in Paris. Under French law, he could have claimed state compensation for damages, but the French courts held that he was not entitled to damages because he was neither a French national nor a resident. Cowan argued that this judgment amounted to discrimination. The CJ held that because Cowan was a tourist and was receiving a service, he could invoke Article 7 of the Treaty of Rome, which prohibits discrimination between nationals of member states on the grounds of nationality.[24] Individual rights prevailed again in *Tanja Kreil* v. *Bundesrepublik Deutschland*, in which the Court was asked for a preliminary ruling by a German administrative court on a case involving a lawsuit against the German military. At that time (2000) Germany banned women from serving in the armed forces. The Court determined that Germany's policy violated the equal treatment of women and men in employment, and in 2001 the German military allowed its first female volunteers to join.[25]

Direct Actions

These are cases in which an individual, corporation, member state, or EU institution brings proceedings directly before the CJ (rather than a national court), usually with an EU institution or a member state as the defendant. They can take several forms.

Actions for Failure to Fulfill an Obligation

In these cases a member state has failed to meet its obligations under EU law and either the Commission or a member state can file suit. The defending member state is given two months to make restitution, so most of these cases are settled before they go to the CJ. If a state fails to comply once proceedings have begun, the case goes to the Court, which investigates the problem and determines the measures to be taken; these can involve a fine or suspension of EU payments to the state (under the European Regional Development Fund, for example).

The Commission has regularly taken member states to the Court on the grounds that they have not met their obligations under the SEA (see Chapter 5). Although individuals cannot bring such cases, interest groups have been known to report a member state to the Commission for failing to enforce an EU law. The Commission then takes the member state to the Court. Private companies are also often key players, especially in issues involving competition and trade policy. Even companies based in the US, Japan, and other countries can take a case to the Court if they think a member state is discriminating against them or their products.

Actions for Annulment

These actions aim to ensure that EU laws (even nonbinding opinions and recommendations) conform to the treaties, and they are brought in an attempt to cancel those that do not conform. If a member state, an individual, or one of the main EU institutions believes that an EU law is illegal (in whole or in part), they may ask for an annulment. The effect is to give the Court the power to review the legality of the acts of the EU institutions. The defendant is almost always the Commission or the Council of the EU, because proceedings are usually brought against an act one or the other has adopted.[26] One exception was Luxembourg's inconclusive attempt in 1981 to challenge a EP resolution that all future plenary sessions of Parliament should be held in Strasbourg (Case 230/81).

Actions for Failure to Act

These actions target the failure of an EU institution to act in accordance with the terms of the treaties, and they can be brought by other institutions, member states, or individuals who are directly and personally involved. For example, the EP brought such an action against the Council of Ministers in 1983 (Case 13/83), charging that the Council had failed to agree to a Common Transport Policy as required under the EEC Treaty.[27] The Court ruled in 1985 that although there was an obligation, no timetable had been agreed to, so it was up to the member states to decide how to proceed.[28]

Actions for Damages

These cases involve damages claimed by third parties against EU institutions and their employees. A claim could be made that the institution was acting illegally, or an individual could claim his or her business was being hurt by a piece of EU law. Most of these cases are heard by the General Court.

Actions by Staff

The only cases in which a private individual can go directly to the Court, actions by staff involve litigation brought by staff members against EU institutions as their employers. For example, someone who works for the EP might ask the Court for a ruling on the application of a staff regulation, an instance of gender discrimination, a biased staff report, or a decision to hold a civil service exam on a religious holiday in their home country. Staff actions account for about one-third of the Court's overall workload.

Appeals

The CJ may hear appeals on points of law regarding judgments made by the General Court. There were 199 such cases in 2018.

Others

The Court also has the right of opinion in cases in which a decision is required on the compatibility of draft international agreements with the treaties. The Commission, the Council of Ministers, and member states can ask for a Court opinion, and if the Court rules unfavorably, the draft agreement must be revised accordingly before the EU can sign it. Finally, the Court can be called in to arbitrate both on contracts concluded by or on behalf of the EU (conditional proceedings) and in disputes between member states over issues relating to the treaties.

QUESTIONS TO CONSIDER

1 How does the US Supreme Court's power of judicial review compare to the authority of the CJ?
2 Compare the selection process for the Supreme Court with that of the CJ. Should judges for the CJ be elected? If not, should they be subject to the same kind of hearings given Supreme Court nominees? Should the judges have lifetime appointments?
3 Is the CJ a political body? If so, whose interests does it serve?

NOTES

1 For a comparison of US and EU law see R. Daniel Kelemen, *Eurolegalism: The Transformation of Law and Regulation in the European Union* (Cambridge, MA: Harvard University Press, 2011).
2 K.P.E. Lasok and D. Lasok, *Law and Institutions of the European Communities*, 7th ed., 15 (London: Butterworths, 2001).
3 *Van Gend en Loos* v. *Nederlandse Administratie Belastingen* (Case 26/62), in Court of Justice of the European Communities, *Reports of Cases Before the Court*, 1963.
4 *Flaminio Costa* v. *ENEL* (Case 6/64), in Court of Justice of the European Communities, *Reports of Cases Before the Court*, 1964.
5 G. Federico Mancini, "The Making of a Constitution for Europe," in *The New European Community: Decisionmaking and Institutional Change*, edited by Robert O. Keohane and Stanley Hoffmann, 187 (Boulder: Westview Press, 1991).
6 *Nold, Kohlen-und Baustoffgrosshandlung* v. *Commission* (Case 4/73), in Court of Justice of the European Communities, *Reports of Cases Before the Court*, 1974.
7 Jonas Bering Liisberg, "Does the EU Charter of Fundamental Rights Threaten the Supremacy of Community Law?" working paper (New York: Jean Monnet Center, New York University School of Law, 2001).
8 See Steve Peers and Angela Ward, eds., *The EU Charter of Fundamental Rights: Politics, Law and Policy* (Oxford: Hart, 2004).
9 The Court of Justice should not be confused with two other Europe-based international courts: the Strasbourg-based European Court of Human Rights (which comes under the jurisdiction of the Council of Europe and promotes human rights issues in Europe) and the International Court of Justice (which is part of the United Nations system, is based in The Hague, and arbitrates on issues relating to UN activities).
10 L. Neville Brown and Tom Kennedy, *The Court of Justice of the European Communities*, 5th ed., 45 (London: Sweet and Maxwell, 2000).
11 Renaud Dehousse, *The European Court of Justice: The Politics of Judicial Integration*, 8 (New York: St. Martin's, 1998).
12 K.P.E. Lasok, *European Court Practice and Procedure*, 3rd ed., 7–8 (Haywards Heath, UK: Tottel, 2007).
13 Vassilios Skouris, interview, *Financial Times* (London), June 30, 2004.

14 *Annual Report of the Court of Justice of the European Communities* (2019), at https://curia.europa. eu/jcms/upload/docs/application/pdf/2019-04/ra_pan_2018_en.pdf, accessed July 15, 2019.

15 Franklin Dehousse, *The Reform of the EU Courts (II). Abandoning the Management Approach by Doubling the General Court* (Brussels: Royal Institute for International Relations. 2016), at http://aei.pitt.edu/73725/1/ep83.pdf.pdf, accessed July 15, 2019.

16 See David Phinnemore and Clive H. Church, *Understanding the European Union's Constitution* (London: Routledge, 2005), and Jean-Claude Piris, *The Constitution for Europe: A Legal Analysis* (Cambridge: Cambridge University Press, 2006).

17 Lasok and Lasok, *Law and Institutions of the European Communities*, chapter 4.

18 Mancini, "The Making of a Constitution for Europe," 177–179.

19 Martin Shapiro, "The European Court of Justice," in *Euro-Politics: Institutions and Policymaking in the "New" European Community*, edited by Alberta Sbragia (Washington, DC: Brookings Institution, 1992).

20 Dehousse, *The European Court of Justice*, 84–88.

21 *Rewe-Zentral AG* v. *Bundesmonopolverwaltung fur Branntwein* (Case 120/78), Court of Justice of the European Communities, *Reports of Cases Before the Court*, 1979.

22 *Commission of the European Communities* v. *Federal Republic of Germany* (Case 178/84), Court of Justice of the European Communities, *Reports of Cases Before the Court*, 1987.

23 Brown and Kennedy, *The Court of Justice of the European Communities*, 173–176.

24 *Cowan* v. *Le Tresor Public* (Case 186/87), in Court of Justice of the European Communities, *Reports of Cases Before the Court*, 1989.

25 *Tanja Kreil* v. *Bundesrepublic Deutschland* (Case 285/98), in Court of Justice of the European Union, Judgment of the Court of 11 January 2000, at https://eur-lex.europa.eu/legal-content/ EN/TXT/HTML/?isOldUri=true&uri=CELEX:61998CJ0285, accessed July 16, 2019.

26 Lasok, *European Court Practice and Procedure*, 323.

27 For a discussion of the relationship between the EP and CJ, see Margaret McCown, "The European Parliament Before the Bench: ECJ Precedent and EP Litigation Strategies," *Journal of European Public Policy* 10, no. 6 (2003): 974–995.

28 *European Parliament* v. *Council* (Case 13/83), in Court of Justice of the European Communities, *Reports of Cases Before the Court*, 1985.

BIBLIOGRAPHY

Arnull, Anthony, *The European Union and Its Court of Justice*, 2nd ed. (Oxford: Oxford University Press, 2006).

Brown, L. Neville and Tom Kennedy, *The Court of Justice of the European Communities*, 5th ed. (London: Sweet and Maxwell, 2000).

Court of Justice of the European Union, *Van Gend en Loos* v. *Nederlandse Administratie Belastingen* (Case 26/62), in *Reports of Cases Before the Court*, 1963.

Court of Justice of the European Union, *Flaminio Costa* v. *ENEL* (Case 6/64), in *Reports of Cases Before the Court*, 1964.

Court of Justice of the European Union, *Nold, Kohlen-und Baustoffgrosshandlung* v. *Commission* (Case 4/73), in *Reports of Cases Before the Court*, 1974.

Court of Justice of the European Union, *Rewe-Zentral AG* v. *Bundesmonopolverwaltung fur Brannt-wein* (Case 120/78), in *Reports of Cases Before the Court*, 1979.

Court of Justice of the European Union, *European Parliament* v. *Council* (Case 13/83), in *Reports of Cases Before the Court*, 1985.

Court of Justice of the European Union, *Commission of the European Communities* v. *Federal Republic of Germany* (Case 178/84), in *Reports of Cases Before the Court*, 1987.

Court of Justice of the European Union, *Cowan* v. *Le Tresor Public* (Case 186/87), in *Reports of Cases Before the Court*, 1989.

Court of Justice of the European Union, *Tanja Kreil v Bundesrepublic Deutschland* (Case 285/98), Judgment of the Court of 11 January 2000, at https://eur-lex.europa.eu/legal-content/EN/TXT/ HTML/?isOldUri=true&uri=CELEX:61998CJ0285, accessed July 16, 2019.

Court of Justice of the European Union, *Annual Report of the Court of Justice of the European Communities* (2019), at https://curia.europa.eu/jcms/upload/docs/application/pdf/2019-04/ra_pan_2018_en.pdf, accessed July 15, 2019.

Dawson, Mark, Bruno DeWitte, and Elise Muir, eds., *Judicial Activism at the European Court of Justice* (Cheltenham, UK and Northampton, MA: Edward Elgar, 2013).

Dehousse, Franklin, *The Reform of the EU Courts (II). Abandoning the Management Approach by Doubling the General Court* (Brussels: Royal Institute for International Relations, 2016), at http://aei.pitt.edu/73725/1/ep83.pdf.pdf, accessed July 15, 2019.

Dehousse, Renaud, *The European Court of Justice: The Politics of Judicial Integration* (New York: St. Martin's, 1998).

Financial Times (London), Interview with Vassilios Skouris, June 30, 2004.

Horspool, Margot, Matthew Humphreys, and Michael Wells-Greco, *European Union Law*, 10th ed. (Oxford: Oxford University Press, 2018).

Kelemen, R. Daniel, *Eurolegalism: The Transformation of Law and Regulation in the European Union* (Cambridge, MA: Harvard University Press, 2011).

Lasok, K.P.E., *European Court Practice and Procedure*, 3rd ed. (Haywards Heath, UK: Tottel, 2007).

Lasok, K.P.E. and Dominik Lasok, *Law and Institutions of the European Communities*, 7th ed. (London: Butterworths, 2001).

Liisberg, Jonas Bering, "Does the EU Charter of Fundamental Rights Threaten the Supremacy of Community Law?" working paper (New York: Jean Monnet Center, New York University School of Law, 2001).

Mancini, G. Federico, "The Making of a Constitution for Europe," in *The New European Community: Decisionmaking and Institutional Change*, edited by Robert O. Keohane and Stanley Hoffmann, 177–195 (Boulder: Westview Press, 1991).

McCown, Margaret, "The European Parliament Before the Bench: ECJ Precedent and EP Litigation Strategies," *Journal of European Public Policy* 10, no. 6 (2003): 974–995.

Peers, Steve, and Angela Ward, eds., *The EU Charter of Fundamental Rights: Politics, Law and Policy* (Oxford: Hart, 2004).

Phinnemore, David and Clive H. Church, *Understanding the European Union's Constitution* (London: Routledge, 2005).

Piris, Jean-Claude, *The Constitution for Europe: A Legal Analysis* (Cambridge: Cambridge University Press, 2006).

Rosas, Allan, Egils Levits, and Yves Bot, eds., *The Court of Justice and the Construction of Europe: Analyses and Perspectives on 60 Years of Case Law* (The Hague: T.M.C. Asser, 2013).

Shapiro, Martin, "The European Court of Justice," in *Euro-Politics: Institutions and Policymaking in the "New" European Community*, edited by Alberta Sbragia (Washington, DC: Brookings Institution, 1992).

Weatherill, Stephen, *Cases and Materials on EU Law*, 11th ed. (Oxford: Oxford University Press, 2014).

FURTHER READING

Anthony Arnull, *The European Union and Its Court of Justice*, 2nd ed. (Oxford: Oxford University Press, 2006).
> This is still the best general study of the organization, jurisdiction, and procedure of the Court of Justice.

Mark Dawson, Bruno DeWitte, and Elise Muir, eds., *Judicial Activism at the European Court of Justice* (Cheltenham, UK and Northampton, MA: Edward Elgar, 2013).
> An edited volume exploring debates on the political role of the CJ and how activist it has been in pursuing integration.

Allan Rosas, Egils Levits, and Yves Bot, eds., *The Court of Justice and the Construction of Europe: Analyses and Perspectives on 60 Years of Case Law* (The Hague: T.M.C. Asser, 2013).

Published by the CJ to celebrate its sixtieth anniversary, this edited volume has contributions from legal experts throughout the EU on topics ranging from the structure and function of the CJ and the EU's legal basis to rights of EU citizens.

Stephen Weatherill, *Cases and Materials on EU Law*, 11th ed. (Oxford: Oxford University Press, 2014); Margot Horspool, Matthew Humphreys, and Michael Wells-Greco, *European Union Law*, 10th ed. (Oxford: Oxford University Press, 2018).

Just two of the many studies of EU law that have been published in recent years.

CHAPTER 9

The European Central Bank and other EU Bodies and Agencies

CHAPTER OVERVIEW

- Along with the major EU institutions, other EU bodies and specialized agencies emerged over the decades to deal with specific issue areas. Most prominent among these has been the European Central Bank (ECB), founded in 1998 to oversee monetary policy for countries in the eurozone. The ECB is composed of an executive board with a president, a Governing Council consisting of the nineteen central bank governors from each state in the eurozone and the ECB's executive board, and a General Council comprised of the central bank governors of all the EU member states.
- The ECB has become a powerful and important EU institution. Though previously it did not exercise many of the powers of the US Federal Reserve Board in managing an economy, it has now started to move in this direction in the wake of the financial and debt crisis.
- In addition to the ECB, one of the most important developing groups of actors in the EU's institutional framework are specialized EU agencies and advisory groups. These agencies and advisory groups – for example, the European Environmental Agency, the European Police Office (Europol), and the Committee of the Regions (CoR) – have grown significantly over the last twenty years, with the EU taking on the trappings of a federal administration for Europe.

Along with the major EU institutions surveyed in previous chapters, there is a growing family of other EU bodies and specialized agencies dealing with more focused interests of the EU. Chief among these is the ECB, which is responsible for managing the euro, guiding monetary policy, and setting interest rates for the eurozone. Modeled on the German Federal Bank (Bundesbank) and headquartered in Frankfurt, the ECB is led by a president, executive board, and a Governing Council which includes the executive board as well as the nineteen central bank governors from each state in the eurozone. Until recently, it had not had the global political and economic clout, nor played the more direct political role of the US Federal Reserve in managing the economy. Since the onset of the financial and debt crisis, however, its role and visibility have increased markedly.

As the reach of the EU has broadened and deepened, the work of specialized agencies and other EU institutions – as well as the pressure to create new ones, a process referred to as "agencification" – has also grown. Some agencies, of course, have been there since the early days, while others have been set up more recently in response to new needs. As their number and authority has risen, the EU has begun to look as if it has a federal administration. This administration includes agencies such as the EU Environmental agency, which provides information on the environment and helps the EU to implement and evaluate environmental policy, and Europol, a criminal intelligence organization that oversees information exchange on problems such as terrorism and drug trafficking. Meanwhile, other bodies such as the Economic and Social Committee provide employers, workers, and other sectional interests with a forum in which they can meet and formulate advice for the EU institutions, while the CoR does much the same for local and regional governments.

FINANCIAL INSTITUTIONS

Understandably, as the economy has always been the main focus of European integration, financial bodies are the most significant of other EU institutions beyond the five main ones. In addition to the powerful ECB, these include the European Investment Bank (EIB), the European Bank for Reconstruction and Development (EBRD), and the European Banking Authority (EBA).

European Central Bank (ECB)

Created in 1998, the ECB has become one of the most powerful and visible of other EU institutions. Its main job (the so-called "single mandate") is to ensure price stability by setting interest rates and managing foreign reserves for the countries participating in the euro, now used officially by well over 300 million consumers in nineteen countries, and unofficially by millions more in many other countries. As the euro has become more familiar to governments, business, and consumers, so the ECB has grown in stature. David Howarth and Peter Loedel may have been overstating the case when they once described it as a "leviathan" and "the most important institutional creation in Europe since the institutionalization of the nation state in the seventeenth century,"[1] but it is certainly symbolic of the extent to which national powers have been pooled at the European level. Historically it has not had the global political and economic clout, nor played the more direct political role of the US Federal Reserve, but its role has burgeoned in the wake of the eurozone crisis.

First proposed in 1988, the basic framework of the Bank was described in the Maastricht treaty, and its precursor – the European Monetary Institute (EMI) – was founded in 1994, charged with strengthening central bank cooperation and coordination of monetary policy in preparation for the creation of the euro. The ECB replaced the EMI and was formally established on June 1, 1998. Based in Frankfurt, Germany, the Bank works within two overlapping spheres: the European System of Central Banks, of which all national banks in the EU are members, and the Eurosystem, which comprises only the national banks of those member states that have adopted the euro.

The Bank has three main organizational units. First is the Governing Council, consisting of the nineteen central bank governors from each state in the eurozone and the Bank's Executive Board. This group meets twice-monthly to discuss monetary and economic developments in the eurozone and to make decisions on monetary policy. Despite discussion before the creation of the bank that there should be a weighted voting system, Germany rejected this proposal and instead Governing Council decisions require consensus or, if need be, a simple majority.[2] Second, there is the Executive Board, consisting of the president (currently, Christine Lagarde, see Box 9.1), the vice president, and four other members, all of them appointed by "common accord" of the member state governments to serve nonrenewable terms of eight years. The board manages the day-to-day business of the Bank and implements eurozone monetary policy in accordance with Governing Council decisions. Finally, the Bank has links to non-eurozone countries through the General Council, composed of the central bank governors of the EU member states. If and when all EU member states adopt the euro, the General Council will be dissolved.

The Bank got off to a shaky start, thanks to yet another of the farcical nationalistic squabbles that occasionally divert the work of EU institutions. Most governments were in favor of seeing Wim Duisenberg, the Dutch president of the EMI, confirmed as the first president of the ECB. The French government disagreed, preferring the governor of the Bank of France, Jean-Claude Trichet. After a twelve-hour debate at the May 1998 summit, convened to launch the euro, a messy compromise was reached whereby Duisenberg would serve half a term (1998–2002), then would "voluntarily" step down in favor of Trichet. As it turned out, Trichet's appointment was delayed because of a court case resulting from charges that he ignored financial mismanagement at the Credit Lyonnais bank while he was an official with the French Treasury. He was cleared in June 2003 and took over as ECB president for an eight-year term in November of that year. Mario Draghi, governor of the Bank of Italy, succeed Trichet in November 2011 and in that role served during a crucial period in the Bank's history before ending his term. In 2019 Christine Lagarde of France and former head of the International Monetary Fund (IMF) (although herself a lawyer, not an economist) took over as president.

Endowed with significant policy-making powers and considerable autonomy, the Bank plays a major role in the direction of European integration.[3] It was based on the model of the German Bundesbank, famous for both its competence and its independence. The Bundesbank, created in 1957, was based loosely on the model of the US Federal Reserve.[4] So important was the Bundesbank model that Chancellor Helmut Kohl's insistence that the Bank be headquartered in Frankfurt won out over French arguments that it should be based in France, which had a long history of political interference in monetary affairs.[5] The German role in both the design and the location of the Bank ensured that the German model of central banking and monetary policy was exported throughout the eurozone, although the ECB's direction under Draghi often ruffled feathers in Berlin (see discussion below).

Box 9.1 Madame President: Christine Lagarde

PHOTO 9.1 Christine Lagarde, President of the ECB.

Source: © European Union, 2019.

Christine Lagarde, recently selected as the president of the ECB, was something of a surprise choice. Although very well respected as the managing director of the IMF, she is neither an economist nor what could be called an EU insider. Lagarde was born in Paris in 1956, obtained a law degree at the University of Paris and a Master's degree at the Political Science Institute in Aix-en-Provence. After working at the law firm of Baker McKenzie, specializing in Labor, Antitrust, and Mergers and Acquisitions (later rising to become chairman of its Global Executive Committee), Lagarde joined the French government in 2005 as the Minister for Foreign Trade and later as Minister for Finance and Economy, the first woman to hold these posts among G-7 countries. In that capacity she also chaired Ecofin (see Chapter 6) and acted as chair for the G-20 when France took over the presidency in 2011.

Lagarde's selection as ECB president and the choice of Germany's Ursula von der Leyen to head the European Commission signal an important advance for women breaking into the "boys club" of EU top jobs, a precedent set with former High Representative for Foreign Affairs and Security Policy Federica Mogherini in 2014. Nevertheless, women in 2019 were overlooked for other top posts (such as the new European Council president and new High Representative, see Chapter 6). Indeed, there continues to be a significant gender disparity in most EU institutions, the EP excepted: of the twenty-seven leaders of EU states who sit in the European Council only four are women; there are only two women on the governing council of the ECB; and women continue to be a minority in the Commission (albeit, with a record twelve in the new Commission). Meanwhile, the underrepresentation of minorities also continues: while minority groups make up about ten percent of the population of EU member states, only five percent of MEPs are people of color. The EU still has major strides to make to close the gender and minority gap.

Since the onset of the eurozone crisis, the single mandate has been stretched considerably, and the ECB has arguably come to closely resemble the present US Federal Reserve, which in addition to price stability focuses on other issues, such as keeping borrowing costs low, battling unemployment, and in general helping to steer economic policy. While Mario Draghi consistently maintained during the crisis that the ECB must take joblessness and other economic concerns into account when trying to ensure its single mandate, others were not so sure that the ECB's actions constituted business as usual. As Catherine Mann, chief economist for the Organisation for Economic Cooperation and Development, pronounced at the time: "The single mandate is dead."[6] Most notably, the ECB's decision in the spring of 2015 to purchase government bonds was extremely controversial. The ECB's actions were prompted by events described in Chapter 4: with a number of eurozone countries' government bonds at or nearing "junk" status, the ECB sought to reassure investors (and thus lower highly indebted countries' borrowing costs) by buying those bonds itself. In this respect, the ECB's actions closely paralleled those traditionally pursued by the US Federal Reserve, which also buys government debt to both increase the money supply and to keep US government borrowing costs low. Draghi's actions met with considerable criticism, most notably from Germany and Jens Weidmann, head of the Bundesbank (and himself a member of the governing council of the ECB). For Weidmann, and others, the ECB's decision to buy government debt of eurozone countries was both a violation of the single mandate and a dangerous precedent which risked pushing inflation rates up. As the financial and debt crisis eased, the ECB under Draghi stopped adding to its stock of government and corporate bonds. However, the Bank indicated after disappointing economic numbers in the summer of 2019 that it was ready to resume the practice, as well as a program which allows commercial banks to borrow money from the ECB at zero interest on the condition that these banks lend money in turn to businesses or consumers.[7]

Not quite as controversial has been the creation of a Banking Union which puts the ECB in charge of supervising banks in the EU in order to ward off the kinds of problems that emerged in the financial and debt crisis. Consensus prevailed on the two fundamental pillars of the Banking Union at the June 2012 European Council meeting: it provided for a single, supervisory mechanism or regulator for all member state banks, and a single resolution mechanism to deal with bank failures. The Banking Union survived a challenge in Germany's constitutional court in 2019 – critics argued that it violated national sovereignty over banking – but in a backhanded way: usurping national powers over regulating banks would indeed be unconstitutional but the Banking Union is legal because, according to the court, it still left direct supervision of banks in national hands.[8] Still being studied is a Europe-wide deposit insurance system (similar to the Federal Deposit Insurance Corporation, or FDIC, in the US), although agreement on this proposal is still laboriously working its way through the EU institutions.[9]

European Investment Bank (EIB)

Based in Luxembourg, the EIB is an autonomous institution set up in 1958 under the terms of the Treaty of Rome to encourage "balanced and steady development" within the European Economic Community (EEC) by providing long-term finance for capital projects. It must give preference to projects that help the poorer regions of the EU and promote transport and communications networks, environmental protection, energy conservation, and the modernization and improved competitiveness of EU industry; it can also make loans to non-EU members. Its funds derive from borrowing on worldwide capital markets and from subscriptions by EU member states. Dealing only in large loans, it rarely lends more than half of the total investment cost of a project, and often cofinances projects with other banks. The EIB's single biggest project was the Eurotunnel between the UK and France, which opened in 1994 (and has operated at a loss ever since). It has also supported the Airbus project and France's high-speed train system (see Chapter 12), financed projects that were aimed at helping Eastern European countries prepare for EU membership, and funded development projects in poorer non-European countries such as Lesotho and Chad. Since the financial and debt crises it has dramatically escalated its annual levels of lending.

The EIB is managed by a board of governors consisting of the finance ministers of the member states, who appoint a decision-making board of directors (representatives from all the member states plus a representative from the European Commission) to five-year renewable terms, and a nine-person management committee to six-year renewable terms. Werner Hoyer was reelected as the head of the management committee in 2017.

European Bank for Reconstruction and Development (EBRD)

While not formally an EU institution, the work of the EBRD is significant for the economic policies of the EU. Much like the International Bank for Reconstruction and Development (the World Bank), the EBRD was founded to provide loans, encourage capital investment, and promote trade; yet its specific focus has been on assisting the countries of Eastern Europe make the transition to free-market economies. Suggested by French president François Mitterrand in 1989 and endorsed by the European Council, the EBRD began operations in March 1991 and quickly became the single largest investor in Eastern Europe and the former Soviet Union. While the World Bank lends mainly to governments, the EBRD (at the insistence of the US) makes 60 percent of its loans to the private sector.

Based in London, it is an independent bank owned and operated by its sixty-one shareholder countries, together with the EU and the EIB; the largest shares are held by the US, the UK, France, Germany, Italy, and Japan. It has a board of governors consisting of representatives from each shareholder country, typically the minister of finance. The board appoints a president who oversees the operations of the Bank; Sir Suma Chakrabarti of the UK was reelected as the president in 2016 to another four-year term.

European Banking Authority (EBA)

An independent EU agency, the EBA's function is to ensure effective bank regulation across the EU. As the EU seeks to create a single rulebook for financial institutions throughout the member states, the EBA plays a critical role. It assesses the risks and vulnerabilities of banks, chiefly through conducting stress tests (i.e., tests of the financial soundness of a bank) which can help identify weaknesses in a bank's capital reserves and lending practices. A successor to an older institution, the Committee of European Banking Supervisors, it was established in 2011 during the financial and debt crisis. A significant flaw of the old Committee of European Banking Supervisors was that it lacked the institutionalization and regulatory teeth to keep up with cross-border mergers and acquisitions as well as foundering on member states' unwillingness to give up their prerogatives on bank oversight. The EBA was relocated to Paris from London in the wake of the Brexit vote.

AGENCIES OF THE EU

As the EU scholar Merijn Chamon notes, the definition of "agency" has been quite muddled in EU official definitions over the years, with considerable confusion over terminology: agencies have been classified as "community" agencies, "executive" agencies, "regulatory" agencies, "decentralized" agencies, and "permanent" agencies.[10] More as a matter of now-established practice than an attempt at a precise legal definition, official EU websites today have settled on the following umbrella definition for all EU agencies: "EU agencies are distinct bodies from the EU institutions – separate legal entities set up to perform specific tasks under EU law."[11] The first agencies were created in the 1970s, mostly to assist the EU in carrying out its activities and to reduce the workload of the Commission. An explosion of agencies in the 1990s erupted under the pressure to complete the internal market: the EU needed technical, scientific, and legal expertise in harmonizing standards across the member states (for example, the Community Plant Variety Office). A final wave of agency creation surged over the last decade and a half in a variety of areas, many of these having to do with perceived weaknesses in the regulatory framework or in order to avert potential crises (e.g., the European Union Agency for Cybersecurity).

Agencies come in two broad varieties. "Executive agencies" are set up for a fixed period, and include such bodies as the Consumers, Health, Agriculture and Food Executive Agency; the Innovation and Networks Executive Agency; and the Education, Audiovisual and Culture Executive Agency. Less numerous and important for the overall work of the EU, they are "executive" insofar as they are created and their staff is controlled by the Commission, and they are "centralized" inasmuch as most are located in Brussels. Meanwhile, "decentralized agencies" are defined by the EU as statutory bodies – that is, are established by law and have their own legal personality – nominally autonomous from the main EU institutions. Decentralized agencies are thus permanent institutional actors of the EU, set up for an indefinite period, and located across the member states.[12] These agencies are empowered to gather information, coordinate national agencies across the member states, provide technical advice, issue reports, and in some cases implement EU policies on a host of specific concerns – food safety, medicine, gender equality, workplace safety, disease prevention and control, transportation safety, and many others (see Box 9.2).

Box 9.2 A Bureaucracy of Our Own: Agencies of the EU

In addition to the institutions discussed in the body of the text, the EU has created numerous agencies to deal with specific aspects of its work. Listed in order of their year of creation, they include the following:

* *European Centre for the Development of Vocational Training* (CEDEFOP; Thessaloniki, Greece, 1975).
* *European Foundation for the Improvement of Living and Working Conditions* (EUROFOUND; Dublin, 1975).
* *European Satellite Centre* (Madrid, 1992). Analyzes satellite information in support of EU foreign and security policy.
* *European Monitoring Centre for Drugs and Drug Addiction* (Lisbon, 1993). Provides information on drugs and drug addiction that can be used in anti-drug campaigns.
* *Translation Centre* (Luxembourg, 1994). A self-financing office that helps most of these specialized agencies with their translation needs.
* *European Agency for Safety and Health at Work* (EU-OSHA; Bilbao, Spain, 1994). Provides information in support of improvements in occupational safety and health.
* *European Medicines Agency* (EMCDDA; Lisbon, Portugal, 1995). Supplies all of the EU with an overview of drug use in Europe in order to support the work of member states.
* *Community Plant Variety Office* (Angers, France, 1995). An independent agency that is responsible for implementing EU plant variety rights.
* *European Food Safety Authority* (Parma, Italy, 2002). Provides independent scientific advice on issues relating to food safety.
* *European Aviation Safety Agency* (Cologne, Germany, 2002). Promotes civil aviation safety in the EU.
* *European Maritime Safety Agency* (Lisbon, 2002). Promotes maritime safety and pollution prevention.
* *European Railway Agency* (Valenciennes/Lille, France, 2004). Promotes an integrated and competitive European rail network.
* *European Centre for Disease Prevention and Control* (Stockholm, 2005). Works to strengthen Europe's defenses against infectious disease.
* *European Union Agency for Cybersecurity* (Heraklion, Greece, 2005). Now known as the European Union Agency for Cybersecurity (but still using the acronym ENISA from its previous name), ENISA helps member states coordinate cybersecurity efforts through improving their capabilities.
* *European Securities and Markets Authority* (ESMA; Paris, 2011). Replacing the older Committee of European Securities Regulators, ESMA gained strength after the financial and debt crisis. It is the EU's financial markets watchdog.
* *European Asylum Support Office* (Valletta, Malta, 2011). Responsible for fortifying the cooperation of EU member states on asylum and charged with helping to implement a Common European Asylum system.
* *Frontex* (Warsaw, 2016). Known formerly as the European Border and Coast Guard Agency and a successor to a previous organization, Frontex was strengthened in 2016 in the wake of the migration crisis with the objective of transforming it into a border and coast guard agency. See discussion in Chapter 13.

Three important decentralized agencies are Europol, Eurojust, and the European Environmental Agency (EEA).

Europol

With the Single European Act opening up the borders between member states, some direction had to be given to the development of police cooperation; hence the creation of Europol. Based in The Hague, the European Police Office is not a law enforcement body in the pattern of the FBI in the US but a criminal intelligence organization more like Interpol, the international police organization founded in 1923 and headquartered in Lyon, France. Its job is to oversee an EU-wide system of information exchange targeted at combating terrorism, drug trafficking, vehicle smuggling, clandestine immigration networks, illegal nuclear material trafficking, money forging and laundering, and other serious forms of international crime. It coordinates operations among the national police forces of the EU, playing a supporting role to them. Some scholars see it as the forerunner of a European police force, but since there is no common penal code or police law in the EU, such a force is unlikely to emerge any time soon.[13]

Set up in 1994 as the Europol Drugs Unit, it operated in limbo thanks to a refusal by the UK government to agree on questions about Europol's job duties as interpreted by the European Court of Justice. The UK acquiesced when it received an opt-out on Court rulings. The Europol Convention was signed at the European Council in Florence in June 1996, and Europol became fully operational in July 1999. It is overseen by a management board with one representative from each of the member states, and it is run by a directorate made up of a director appointed for four years (and who can be renewed for another term), and three deputies appointed for four-year terms, renewable once. The appointments are made by the Council of Ministers for Justice and Home Affairs who, along with the EP, also approves Europol's budget.

Eurojust

Based also in The Hague, Eurojust was formally established in 2002 and works with member states to coordinate efforts in fighting crime – requesting an investigation or a prosecution be initiated in a state or helping to coordinate prosecutorial or police efforts between different states, such as setting up a joint task force or investigation. It is composed of a college of national members – overwhelmingly police officers, prosecutors, and judges – from each EU member state. Led by a president and two vice presidents (chosen by the college), Eurojust focuses on particular grave criminal threats to EU citizens, such as terrorism, drug trafficking, human trafficking, fraud, corruption, and money laundering. It works closely with Europol and complements the work of another organization, the European Judicial Network, which encourages judicial cooperation among the member states in civil and commercial matters.

European Environmental Agency (EEA)

Based in Copenhagen, the EEA's chief task is to provide independent information on environmental conditions across the EU, as well as in Iceland, Norway, Switzerland, and Turkey. The EEA works closely with member states to sharpen the effectiveness of EU and national environmental policies. With a staff of 200, the EEA's main contribution is information gathering and monitoring of environmental conditions in Europe.

OTHER EU BODIES

A number of other EU bodies play prominent roles in the EU, some as a part of the EU administrative machine, others nominally distinct and which act in an advisory or support capacity. Three especially important ones are the *Court of Auditors, European Economic and Social Committee (EESC)*, and *Committee of the Regions (CoR)*.

The Court of Auditors

The Court of Auditors is the EU's financial watchdog, based in Luxembourg and founded in 1977 to replace the separate auditing bodies for the EEC/Euratom and for the European Coal and Steel Community. The Court likes to call itself the "financial conscience" of the EU. It carries out annual audits of the accounts of all EU institutions to ensure that revenue has been raised and expenditure incurred in a lawful and regular manner and to monitor the Union's financial management. Its most important job relates to the EU budget, which it audits on the basis of both accounts supplied by the Commission by June each year and its own independent research. The Court reports back to the Commission, the Council of Ministers, and Parliament by the end of November each year. Though Parliament is supposed to approve the Court's report by the following April, it can use the report to force changes in the Commission's spending and accounting habits.

The Court has issued often scathing criticisms of waste, mismanagement, and fraud in the EU's financial affairs, decrying everything from excessive expense claims by European commissioners to massive fraud in funds made available under the Common Agricultural Policy. It has been particularly critical in recent years of the inadequacy of steps taken by the Commission to keep an eye on how structural funds are used and managed. Although the nature of its work would seem to make it unpopular with the Commission, in fact the two bodies have a close working relationship. The Court also has a symbiotic relationship with Parliament; each has helped promote the powers and the profile of the other.

One auditor is appointed from each of the member states of the EU for a six-year renewable term. Nominations come from the national governments and must be approved unanimously by the Council of Ministers following nonbinding approval by Parliament (which the EP would like to upgrade to binding approval). The auditors then elect one of their number to serve as president for three-year renewable terms. The members of the Court must belong to an external audit body in their own country or have other appropriate qualifications, but they are expected to act in the interests of the EU and to be completely independent. Much like the Court of Justice, the members can sit in chambers of a few members each.

European Economic and Social Committee (EESC)

The EESC is based in Brussels. It is an advisory body set up under the Treaty of Rome to give employers, workers, and other sectional interests a forum in which they could meet, talk, and issue opinions to the Commission, the Council of Ministers, and the EP. Modeled on parallel bodies that existed in five of the six founding members of the EEC (Germany being the exception), it originated in part because of fears that the EP would not represent sectional interests; the fears proved unfounded. In 2020, the EESC had 326 members drawn from the member states roughly in proportion to population size, with a staff of 700 and a secretary general (see Table 9.1). Proposed by national governments and appointed by the Council of Ministers for renewable four-year terms, members are constituted in three groups:

- Group I comes from industry, services, small businesses, chambers of commerce, banking, insurance, and similar areas.
- Group II is made up of representatives from labor unions.
- Group III ("Diversity Europe") represents more varied interests, such as agriculture, consumer and environmental groups, and the professions.

Every two and a half years the EESC elects a bureau with a president and two vice presidents (chosen from each of the three groups in rotation), who preside over two-day meetings of the Committee in Brussels nine times each year. Six sections (agriculture, economic and monetary union, employment and social affairs, external relations, the single market, and transport, energy and infrastructure) are further subdivided into subcommittees and study groups. Although questions have long been raised about its value, consultation of the EESC by the Commission is mandatory in several areas, including agriculture, the movement of workers, social policy, regional policy, and the environment.

The fundamental weakness of the EESC is that, although the Commission is obliged to consult it in certain cases laid out by the Treaty of Lisbon, neither the Commission nor the Council of Ministers is obliged to act on its opinions or views. "Consultation" is an ambiguous concept, and although the Commission can "take note" of an EESC opinion and the Council of Ministers can recognize a "useful" opinion, this recognition amounts to little. The influence of the EESC is further minimized by the fact that its members are unpaid part-time appointees (they can claim expenses for attending meetings) and are not officially recognized as representatives of the bodies to which they belong. Also, EU proposals are often sent to the EESC only after they have reached an advanced stage of agreement by the

TABLE 9.1 Membership of the EESC and the CoR, 2020

France	24	Sweden	12
Germany	24	Croatia	9
Italy	24	Denmark	9
Spain	21	Finland	9
Poland	21	Ireland	9
Romania	15	Lithuania	9
Austria	12	Slovakia	9
Belgium	12	Latvia	7
Bulgaria	12	Slovenia	7
Czech Republic	12	Estonia	6
Greece	12	Cyprus	5
Hungary	12	Luxembourg	5
Netherlands	12	Malta	5
Portugal	12	**Total**	326

Source: European Economic and Social Committee, at www.eesc.europa.eu/en/members-groups.

Council of Ministers and Parliament. The best that can be said of the EESC is that it is another forum for the representation of sectional interests.

Committee of the Regions (CoR)

The CoR is also based in Brussels and arose to address disparities in wealth and income across Europe which have always posed a handicap to the process of integration; there can never be balanced free trade, a true single market, or even meaningful economic and political union so long as some parts of the EU are richer or poorer than others. The problem was addressed by the creation of three entities: the European Regional Development Fund in 1975, the ad hoc Assembly of European Regions in 1985, and the Consultative Council of Regional and Local Authorities in 1988. The need for a stronger response led to the formation under the terms of Maastricht of the CoR.

The CoR met for the first time in January 1994. It has a similar membership structure as the EESC: 350 members chosen by the member states and appointed by the Council of Ministers for four-year renewable terms, grouped according to political affiliation (EPP, S&D, Greens, etc.). Although Maastricht did not specify what qualifications Committee members should possess (beyond saying they should be "representatives of regional and local bodies"), most are elected local government officials, including mayors and members of state, regional, district, provincial, and county councils. Because there is a significant gender disparity in member states' regional and local bodies, this disparity prevails in the CoR as well. In order to correct this inequity, the leadership Bureau of the CoR recently made recommendations on gender-balanced participation, namely, urging member states to include at least fifty percent women on their nomination lists.[14] The CoR meets in plenary session five times per year and has the same advisory role as the EESC. It must be consulted by the Commission and the Council of Ministers on issues relating to economic and social cohesion, trans-European networks (see Chapter 12), public health, education, and culture, and provides the EU with a local and regional perspective on policy. However, it suffers from the same structural problems as the EESC.

QUESTIONS TO CONSIDER

1 How does the ECB now compare to that of the US Federal Reserve? What are the advantages and disadvantages of it becoming even more like the Fed?
2 What has the EU done since 2010 to strengthen oversight of the financial sector? Given the central role that banks played in the European financial and debt crisis has it done enough?
3 How does the EU's use of specialized agencies compare to that of the US? Has the development of "agencification" gone too far or not far enough?

NOTES

1 David Howarth and Peter Loedel, *The European Central Bank: The New European Leviathan?* 2nd ed., xi (Basingstoke, UK: Palgrave Macmillan, 2005).
2 Madeleine Hosli, *The Euro. A Concise Introduction to European Monetary Integration*, 48 (Boulder/London: Lynne Rienner, 2005).
3 Jakob de Haan and Helge Berger, eds. *The European Central Bank at Ten* (Berlin/Heidelberg: Springer Verlag, 2010).

4 Karl Kaltenthaler, *Policy-Making in the European Central Bank: The Masters of Europe's Money*, 165, 168–169 (Lanham, MD: Rowman and Littlefield, 2006).
5 Howarth and Loedel, *The European Central Bank*, 44.
6 Jack Ewing, "European Central Bank Expands Mandate as It Struggles to Keep Zone Intact," *New York Times*, May 24, 2015, at www.nytimes.com/2015/05/25/business/international/european-central-bank-expands-mandate-as-it-struggles-to-keep-zone-intact.html, accessed May 25, 2015.
7 See Jack Ewing, "ECB Revives a Stimulus Measure, a Sign of Worry," *New York Times*, March 7, 2019, at www.newsstandhub.com/en-us/the-new-york-times/ecb-revives-a-stimulus-measure-a-sign-of-worry, accessed March 7, 2019; Jack Ewing, "As Recession Fears Grow in Europe, Central Bank Signals Stimulus Increase," MSNBC, June 19, 2019, at www.msn.com/en-us/money/markets/as-recession-fears-grow-in-europe-central-bank-signals-stimulus-increase/ar-AAD4CKy, accessed July 30, 2019.
8 Karin Matussek, "German Judges Reopen Old Wounds Over Scope of ECB Powers," Bloomberg, July 30, 2019, at www.bloomberg.com/news/articles/2019-07-30/german-top-court-rejects-suits-challenging-eu-s-banking-union-jypk5po2, accessed July 30, 2019.
9 "Banking Union," Fact Sheets on the European Union, at www.europarl.europa.eu/factsheets/en/sheet/88/banking-union, accessed July 30, 2019.
10 Merijn Chamon, *EU Agencies. Legal and Political Limits to the Transformation of the EU Administration* (Oxford: Oxford University Press, 2016).
11 European Union, "Agencies and Other EU Bodies," at https://europa.eu/european-union/about-eu/agencies_en, accessed July 31, 2019.
12 The term "decentralized" is very imprecise, since other sub-types of agencies are also decentralized (i.e., not located in Brussels). Moreover, the permanence or transitory nature of agencies is itself muddled. In the absence of an acceptable alternative, I have simply followed official EU websites in distinguishing between the different sub-types of agency.
13 For a detailed study of Europol, see John D. Occhipinti, *The Politics of EU Police Cooperation: Toward a European FBI?* (Boulder: Lynne Rienner, 2003).
14 European Committee of the Regions, "Strategy for a Gender Balance in Members' Participation in the COR," April 9, 2019, at https://cor.europa.eu/en/members, accessed August 1, 2019.

BIBLIOGRAPHY

Chamon, Merijn, *EU Agencies. Legal and Political Limits to the Transformation of the EU Administration* (Oxford: Oxford University Press, 2016).
de Haan, Jakob, and Helge Berger, eds., *The European Central Bank at Ten* (Heidelberg: Springer, 2010).
European Committee of the Regions, "Strategy for a Gender Balance in Members' Participation in the COR," April 9, 2019, at https://cor.europa.eu/en/members, accessed August 1, 2019.
European Parliament, "Banking Union," Fact Sheets on the European Union, at www.europarl.europa.eu/factsheets/en/sheet/88/banking-union, accessed July 30, 2019.
European Union, "Agencies and Other EU Bodies," at https://europa.eu/european-union/about-eu/agencies_en, accessed July 31, 2019.
Ewing, Jack, "European Central Bank Expands Mandate as It Struggles to Keep Zone Intact," *New York Times*, May 24, 2015, at www.nytimes.com/2015/05/25/business/international/european-central-bank-expands-mandate-as-it-struggles-to-keep-zone-intact.html, accessed May 25, 2015.
Ewing, Jack, "ECB Revives a Stimulus Measure, a Sign of Worry," *New York Times*, March 7, 2019, at www.newsstandhub.com/en-us/the-new-york-times/ecb-revives-a-stimulus-measure-a-sign-of-worry, accessed March 7, 2019.
Ewing, Jack, "As Recession Fears Grow in Europe, Central Bank Signals Stimulus Increase," MSNBC, June 19, 2019, at www.msn.com/en-us/money/markets/as-recession-fears-grow-in-europe-central-bank-signals-stimulus-increase/ar-AAD4CKy, accessed July 30, 2019.
Groenleer, Martijn, *The Autonomy of European Union Agencies: A Comparative Study of Institutional Development* (Delft, Netherlands: Eburon Academic, 2011).

Hosli, Madeline, *The Euro. A Concise Introduction to European Monetary Integration* (Boulder/London: Lynne Rienner, 2005).

Howarth, David, and Peter Loedel, *The European Central Bank: The New European Leviathan?* 2nd ed. (Basingstoke, UK: Palgrave Macmillan, 2005).

Kaltenthaler, Karl, *Policy-Making in the European Central Bank: The Masters of Europe's Money* (Lanham, MD: Rowman and Littlefield, 2006).

Matussek, Karin, "German Judges Reopen Old Wounds Over Scope of ECB Powers," Bloomberg, July 30, 2019, at www.bloomberg.com/news/articles/2019-07-30/german-top-court-rejects-suits-challenging-eu-s-banking-union-jypk5po2, accessed July 30, 2019.

Ngin, Cedric, and Cedric Langing, *The European Central Bank and the Federal Reserve System – a General Comparison* (Cologne: GRIN Verlag, 2013).

Occhipinti, John D., *The Politics of EU Police Cooperation: Toward a European FBI?* (Boulder: Lynne Rienner, 2003).

FURTHER READING

David Howarth and Peter Loedel, *The European Central Bank: The New European Leviathan?* 2nd ed. (Basingstoke, UK: Palgrave Macmillan, 2005); Jakob de Haan and Helge Berger, eds. *The European Central Bank at Ten* (Heidelberg: Springer, 2010).

    Two of the increasing number of studies that are being written on this emerging and critical actor in European politics and economics.

Cedric Ngin and Cedric Langing, *The European Central Bank and the Federal Reserve System – a General Comparison* (Cologne: GRIN Verlag, 2013).

    A comparison of the organization, tasks, and objectives of the ECB and the Fed, with a chapter discussing how each dealt with the 2008 global economic crisis.

Martijn Groenleer, *The Autonomy of European Union Agencies: A Comparative Study of Institutional Development* (Delft, Netherlands: Eburon Academic, 2011); Merijn Chamon, *EU Agencies. Legal and Political Limits to the Transformation of the EU Administration* (Oxford: Oxford University Press, 2016).

    The first is a detailed study of six EU agencies, comparing how they operate and their power of autonomous decision making; the second surveys the full range of EU agencies and explores the expansion of decentralized bodies of the EU or "agencification."

CHAPTER 10

Representing Public Opinion in the EU

CHAPTER OVERVIEW

- Europeans have more complex attitudes about the EU than the labels "pro-EU" or "anti-EU" would suggest. As reflected in public polling, most Europeans are generally supportive of the EU, even while expressing some skepticism about particular policies and the way democracy works in the EU. A significant minority feel that their voices are not heard and fear a loss of national sovereignty and identity. Finally, others still have ambivalent attitudes, conscious of the benefits offered by the EU but not fully grasping its role in bringing these about, nor how the EU actually works.
- Besides elections to the European Parliament (EP) and public opinion polls conducted by the Commission, referendums act as important vehicles for EU citizens to voice their opinions on the EU. However, the use of referendums has had several distinct disadvantages, especially in their capacity to make integration more difficult.
- In recent years, interest groups have directed more of their attention to Brussels as EU policy has increasingly impacted the lives of Europeans. The work of interest groups is another avenue for citizens to make their voice heard.

As the powers and reach of the EU have grown, and as it has taken on more of the conventional features of a political system, so more Europeans have become interested in trying to influence its work. Even as late as the 1980s, European affairs attracted relatively little public attention, but – particularly since Maastricht, the failed attempt in 2004–2005 to agree on a constitution for the EU, Greece and problems in the eurozone, the refugee crisis, and Brexit – more people have come to realize that the EU affects their lives and have shown an increased interest in EU politics. As captured in public opinion polls, for some this interest has been positive, driven by a belief that the EU has an indispensable role to play in their lives or the lives of their countries. For others, it is a negative interest, driven by perceptions that the EU institutions are undemocratic, too intrusive, and too powerful. Many Europeans, however, still do not fully understand the EU's many functions and how it works.

While each of the individual member states of the EU has a well-developed civil society, the same cannot yet be said of the EU. Its institutions have long had a reputation among Europeans for being elitist and bureaucratic, and there is still a troubling distance between the EU and many of its citizens. Nevertheless, a European civil society is slowly emerging, thanks mainly to three developments. The first of these is the psychological effect of elections to the EP, examined in Chapter 7. National elections are considered more important by voters and political leaders, and European elections are often fought on national issues and approached by voters as opportunities to comment on the performance of their national governments.

Second, referendums (used irregularly by different member states) offer voters the opportunity to express themselves on European matters and to periodically home in on some of the big questions that face Europe. Some are votes on national policy (for example, joining the EU has been subject to confirmation in several countries, and in one country – Norway – majorities have twice voted against membership). Other referendums have had Europe-wide significance; for example, the ratification of the Maastricht and Nice treaties was delayed by negative votes in Denmark and Ireland, respectively, and the European constitution was derailed by negative votes in France and the Netherlands. The *absence* of referendums in some countries has also been critical, heightening criticisms of the manner in which some of the most important decisions on Europe are made.

Finally, as EU policy has had greater impact on the lives of Europeans, so interest groups have directed more of their attention to Brussels. Interest groups are invited to participate in the early planning stages of new legislative proposals, have developed often strong links with the Commission, are used by the Commission as a source of expertise and to report on the implementation of EU law by member states, and are generally seen as an increasingly effective channel for changing EU policy. Their work has helped buttress the legitimacy and responsiveness of the EU decision-making system.

WE THE PEOPLE: PUBLIC OPINION IN THE EU

Attitudes among Europeans toward the EU could be described as divided and complex. Generally, it can be said that a majority of Europeans are supportive and believe that the member states – and individual Europeans – have greatly benefitted from its creation and development, even if they are critical of certain EU policies or the way in which these are enacted. For example, a recent Pew Research Center poll found a significant majority of EU citizens had a favorable opinion of the EU, with strong support in Western European countries such as Sweden (72 percent), Germany (69 percent), and Spain (66 percent) as well as in the newer members of the bloc such as Poland (84 percent), Lithuania (83 percent) and even quarrelsome Hungary (67 percent).[1] Nevertheless, a significant minority of EU citizens view it unfavorably, despite supporting some key EU achievements. These Euroskeptics lament both the lack of transparency in the EU and the shift of sovereignty away from the member states.[2] In between these poles, many Europeans have more ambivalent feelings and/or do not fully understand how the EU works or fully grasp what impact it has had on their lives. In that sense, the EU is much like a national political system: the balance in the US between those who are politically knowledgeable, engaged, and supportive; those who are not supportive or engaged and may or may not be politically knowledgeable; and a host of others who fall in between is not completely different.

In order to sort out the complexity of attitudes among Europeans, political scientists have attempted to classify EU attitudes into a specific set of ideal types. For example, Taggart and Szczerbiak draw a distinction between "hard" and "soft" Euroskepticism, with the former wanting to withdraw from the EU or fundamentally alter the relationship between their country and the EU whereas the latter simply oppose further steps toward integration, treaty changes, or substantial revisions to EU policies.[3] Bulpitt has outlined four positions on the EU – pro-European, Euro-pragmatist, Euroskeptic, and anti-European.[4] While anti-Europeans are hostile to the entire EU project, Euroskeptics tend to be critical of each successive step toward closer integration, even if finally relenting. In a similar vein, Kopecký and Mudde use a four-fold classification system with "Euroenthusiasts," "Europragmatists" (who support the EU but are critical on many aspects of further integration), "Euroskeptics," and "Eurorejects" (the latter completely opposing the existence of the EU).[5]

Polls conducted by the Commission through its public opinion institution, Eurobarometer, reflect these different categories and the complexity and nuance of EU public opinion. For example, Europeans are divided on whether they think their voice counts in EU decision making, with 42 percent agreeing and much lower levels of agreement in a significant number of member states.[6] Skepticism about the EU is reflected in EU citizens' level of trust, with only 37 percent expressing trust in the EU in the spring of 2019, with the lowest levels in Greece and the Czech Republic (27 percent), France, Spain, and Italy (all hovering around 31 percent), and – unsurprisingly – the UK (26 percent).[7] Meanwhile, differences of opinion are to be found concerning the level of democracy in the EU. While nearly half (47 percent) of EU citizens are satisfied with the way democracy works in the EU, almost as many (43 percent) say they are not satisfied, with majorities dissatisfied in Greece, France, Spain, Italy, Slovakia, and Cyprus (see Figure 10.1).[8] Drilling down a little on this question, some fairly sharp divides emerge based on age and socioeconomic status. For example, those who classify themselves as in the upper or middle class are much more likely to be satisfied with democracy in the EU, as are the more well educated, and those in white-collar professions. Moreover, an age gap is apparent here: 15–24 year olds are far more likely to be satisfied with democracy in the EU (57 percent) than those aged fifty-five and over (41 percent).

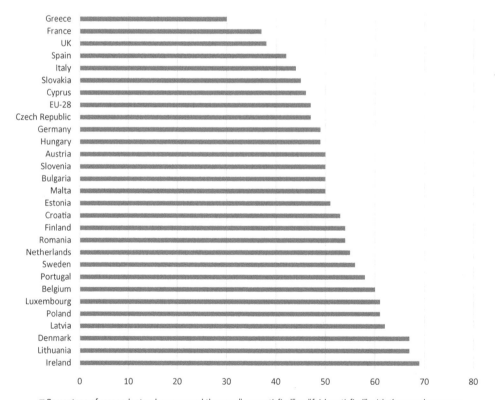

■ Percentage of respondents who answered they are "very satisfied" or "fairly satisfied" with the way democracy works in the EU

FIGURE 10.1 Satisfaction with Democracy in the EU.

Source: European Commission, Special Eurobarometer 486, Spring 2019, at https://ec.europa.eu/commfrontoffice/publicopinion/index.cfm/survey/getsurveydetail/instruments/special/surveyky/2225

These chasms between young and old, educated and less educated, white-collar versus blue-collar are reminiscent of the US today, as well as in the UK's Brexit vote. And it may indicate a growing divide between those who see the merits of globalization or internationalism (of which the EU is a symbol) and those who do not. When asked whether globalization threatens their country's identity, 45 percent of EU citizens agreed, with particularly high percentages in Greece (67 percent), Italy (58 percent), and Latvia, Estonia, and Cyprus (57 percent). However, differences based on age, income, education, and occupation stand out: across the EU the unemployed, blue-collar workers, the less educated, and older persons are far more likely than white-collar workers and younger people to hold this view. How the EU should interact with the member states may further highlight this split between those fearful of globalization and those who are not: while a little more than half of EU citizens think that more decisions today should be made at the EU level (54 percent), nearly four in ten disagree.

In contrast, there is much more unanimity on the concrete achievements of the EU. Eighty-one percent support the free movement of citizens to work, study, or to do business anywhere in the EU (see Figure 10.2), 73 percent support a common defense and security policy, and 65 percent are in favor of a common EU policy on migration. Indeed, EU citizens rank the free

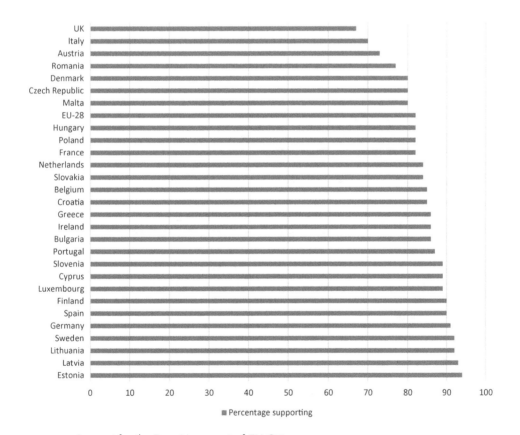

FIGURE 10.2 Support for the Free Movement of EU Citizens.

Source: European Commission, Special Eurobarometer 486, Spring 2019, at https://ec.europa.eu/commfrontoffice/publicopinion/index.cfm/survey/getsurveydetail/instruments/special/surveyky/2225

Note
Percentage of respondents who support the free movement of EU citizens who can live, work, study and do business anywhere in the EU.

movement of people, goods, and service as the most important achievement of the EU[9] with "peace among the member states" firmly in second place. The euro meanwhile enjoys support from more than six in ten respondents (66 percent), albeit with significantly higher levels of support among EU citizens already in the eurozone than in some member states – many in Eastern Europe – who are not (yet) members of the eurozone (see Figure 10.3).

How is it that solid majorities can support key achievements of the EU such as the free movement of people or the euro and yet still be sharply divided on whether the EU is democratic or whether their voice is heard? One answer is that this split might reflect a "knowledge gap" within the EU, a divide between citizens who are politically knowledgeable about what the EU has achieved and what it does in practice, and others who do not understand the EU – or misunderstand what it does and has achieved. Reminiscent of the famous Monty Python sketch in the film "Life of Brian," some citizens miss "what the EU has done for us," failing to realize, for

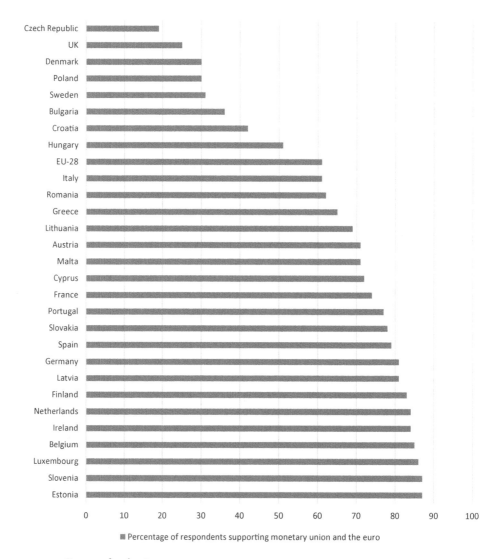

■ Percentage of respondents supporting monetary union and the euro

FIGURE 10.3 Support for the Euro.

Source: European Commission, Special Eurobarometer 486, Spring 2019, at https://ec.europa.eu/commfrontoffice/publicopinion/index.cfm/survey/getsurveydetail/instruments/special/surveyky/2225

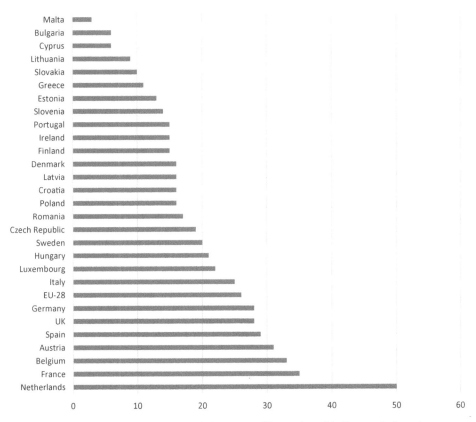

■ Percentage of respondents disagreeing with the statement "The members of the European Parliament are directly elected by the citizens of each member state."

FIGURE 10.4 Lack of Knowledge about How the EU Works.

Source: European Commission, Special Eurobarometer 486, Spring 2019, at https://ec.europa.eu/commfrontoffice/publicopinion/index.cfm/survey/getsurveydetail/instruments/special/surveyky/2225

example, how much trade in their country (and thus their economic prosperity) is dependent upon the EU's internal market or how the EU has helped to raise environmental or workplace safety standards.[10] In addition, a number of myths about what the EU actually does do are legendary.[11] Indeed, the Commission maintains a website listing hundreds of "Euromyths" with an A–Z index. These range from the classic "bendy bananas" (a popular myth in the UK for more than twenty years that the EU regulates the curvature of bananas) to pizza (the myth that the EU sets the size of pizza slices) to the amount of cleavage barmaids are allowed to display (a distortion of an EU directive on studying skin cancer). More concerning, just under four in ten Europeans say they do not understand how the EU works, ranging from a high of 52 percent in France to a low of 18 percent in Sweden. Indeed, a sobering percentage of EU citizens (26 percent) do not even know that members of the EP are directly elected (Figure 10.4).

CIVIL SOCIETY AND AN EU IDENTITY

One of the prerequisites for a successful political system is a strong civil society, consisting of all the voluntary and spontaneous forms of political association that evolve within a state and are not formally part of the state system, but show that citizens can operate independently of the state.[12] The EU is not a state, but it contains institutions responsible for making decisions that affect the lives of the people who live within its borders. As such, in order for it to succeed, Europeans must have some emotional identification (or a sense of belonging) with the EU, believe that the EU takes into account their concerns, and feel that they can engage with its work. However, as the discussion above and accounts of a "democratic deficit" suggest (see Box 10.1), the EU has fallen somewhat short in convincing its citizens on just those points.

Box 10.1 Is There Really a Democratic Deficit in the EU?

Critics have long charged that the EU suffers from what has been described as a "democratic deficit." This is the belief that EU decision making is not democratically accountable or transparent to the average citizen. Indeed, the lack of institutional openness and accountability has been a recurring theme in studies of the EU. The EP is the only directly elected EU body, but significant power lies with both the Commission and the Council of Ministers, neither of which has much direct public accountability. As one Member of the European Parliament (MEP) once quipped, if the European Community were a state and applied for Community membership, it would be turned down on the grounds that it was not a democracy.[13] Several problems contribute to the deficit:

- Meetings of the European Council, the Council of Ministers, the Committee of Permanent Representatives (Coreper), and the College of Commissioners are typically closed to the public, despite the fact that they make crucial decisions on law and policy.
- The citizens of Europe have no direct input into the process by which the president of the Commission or members of the College of Commissioners are chosen, and Parliament lacks the power of confirmation over individual commissioners or over judges in the Court of Justice.
- The governments of the member states often make key decisions (such as changes to the treaties) without a national vote.

But does the deficit really exist? Some have argued that the EU does not need the same democratic processes as national democracies because – if it is a confederation – it is a system in which governments interact, not people and governments. The governments of the member states are legitimized by the democratic processes in which their citizens participate (i.e., national elections) and are in turn given a mandate to negotiate on behalf of those citizens. The political scientist Andrew Moravcsik, for one, has challenged the idea that the EU lacks democratic legitimacy. He argues that the EU is a weak and dependent state structure, that EU institutions are under direct or indirect democratic control, that the Council of Ministers is democratically accountable, and that commissioners and judges on the Court of Justice are named by directly elected national governments.[14] Moreover, national governments have zealously guarded their rights to legislate on issues most important to their citizens (e.g., taxes, health care, pensions). As *The Economist* has colorfully put it, "The much-maligned distance between the EU and its voters is a feature, not a bug."[15]

The failure to completely inculcate an EU identity and draw it closer to its citizens has not been for lack of effort. Beyond the increased powers over the decades given to the most democratic of EU institutions, the EP, suggestions that the EU could do more to personally connect its work with average Europeans arose as early as 1975 in a report drawn up at the request of the European Council by Leo Tindemans, prime minister of Belgium. Little was done on this initiative until 1984, when attention turned briefly to the idea of a "people's Europe." Pietro Adonnino, a former Italian MEP, was appointed to chair a committee to make suggestions on closing the gap between the Community and its citizens. Its recommendations fell into three main parts:

1   It endorsed plans for a European passport and a European flag. All national passports – which came in different designs and colors – were replaced from 1986 onward by a burgundy-colored "European" passport bearing the words *European Union* in the appropriate national language, and the name and coat of arms of the holder's home state. These passports do not make their holders European citizens per se, but they do ensure that Europeans receive equal treatment by the customs and immigration authorities of other countries. Also, citizens of an EU member state finding themselves in need in a non-EU country where their home state has no diplomatic representation can receive protection from the embassy or consulate of any EU state that has a local office. Meanwhile, the Community adopted the flag that had been used by the Council of Europe since 1955, a circle of twelve gold stars on a blue background, which can now be seen flying on buildings throughout the EU.
2   Several Adonnino recommendations were adopted under the Single European Act (SEA), notably the easing of restrictions on the free movement of people and plans for the mutual recognition of professional qualifications. Despite the understanding that an open labor market would be essential to the single market, restrictions (albeit limited) still remain on the free movement of people within the EU (see Chapter 12).
3   The EU developed its own concept of European citizenship, although it is not quite the same as the citizenship we associate with conventional states or countries. According to the Treaty of Lisbon, "Every person holding the nationality of a Member State shall be a citizen of the Union," but it also states that "citizenship of the Union shall be additional to and not replace national citizenship" (Article 20). In other words, EU citizenship is mostly a symbolic notion, and distinctions among Europeans derive from their national citizenship, distinctions which continue to have political consequences. Thus while all EU citizens can now vote in and stand for local and EP elections in whichever country they are living (subject to residency requirements), they remain citizens of their own states, identify with those states, and carry important exclusive prerogatives of that state – for example, EU "citizens" cannot vote in each other's national elections.

Despite limitations, the changes that resulted from the Adonnino committee shifted the psychological relationship between Europeans and the EU institutions and helped make the EU more real to Europeans. Icons are an important element of belonging, and the European flag, for example, has played a vital role in giving the EU a personality that transcends the work of its bureaucrats. The same can be said of the euro: Europeans can now use it wherever they go in the eurozone, and the foreignness that came with different currencies – and reminded Europeans of their differences – has now, for the most part, vanished.

Yet there is still more to remind Europeans of what divides them than what unites them. Different parts of Europe have quite different histories, with which most other Europeans are not familiar. They have varied social policies born from a myriad of political attitudes and political culture, such as differences in the recognition of same-sex unions.[16] There are also strikingly contrasting attitudes toward economic policy and toward immigration and multiculturalism, both of which have been on display in the eurozone debt crisis/attitudes toward Greece as well as the refugee crisis. At a deeper psychological level, the work of the EU is compromised by the competing sense of affiliation that Europeans hold toward their home states versus the EU; most Europeans still feel closer to their own states, owe them their primary allegiance, and often view member states as competing with one another rather than being involved in a joint endeavor.

The as-yet-unfulfilled goal of the EU to inculcate a complete sense of belonging or attachment to an EU identity is borne out by opinion polls. Though almost 70 percent of EU citizens agree with the statement "You feel you are a citizen of the EU," significant differences prevail among the member states, with the lowest levels found in the Czech Republic and Italy (both at 56 percent), Greece (50 percent), and Bulgaria (47 percent). Meanwhile, although 51 percent of Europeans believe that "people in the European Union have a lot of things in common" more than four in ten (42 percent) disagree. As with questions on trust or democracy in the EU there is an age and socioeconomic gap here, with 15–39 year olds more likely to agree with this (56 percent) than those fifty-five or older (46 percent), and managers (60 percent) much more likely than the unemployed (44 percent) to agree.

Finally, a weak sense of shared culture in the member states deepens this estrangement from the EU. The lack of a shared culture is a problem that the EU has tried to address, driven by the commitment under Maastricht that it should "contribute to the flowering of the culture of the Member States" with a view to promoting and protecting the European cultural heritage. Toward that end, it has subsidized architectural restoration, encouraged the translation of works by European authors, and supported cultural activities such as the European Youth Orchestra, the declaration of European Capitals of Culture (including Florence, Dublin, Lisbon, Stockholm, and Liverpool), and the establishment of a European Cultural Month in cities in nonmember states (such as Krakow, Basel, and St. Petersburg).

While the sentiments behind such projects are laudable, the full development of a European identity can work only if it comes from Europeans themselves, which in turn demands that Europeans must see themselves as distinctive, as united by common interests and values, and as engaged in a shared endeavor. A closer bond between citizens and the EU will not be truly forged until (1) Europeans can see more clearly the positive impact that decisions made at the level of the EU have on their lives, (2) they have additional meaningful channels through which they can shape those decisions, and (3) the freedom and wealth that the EU has undoubtedly created are more meaningfully translated into the lives of average citizens. Some channels for shaping decisions by citizens do exist, and their significance has been growing, but the stakes have not always been high enough to inspire a higher level of participation. For now, the most significant links between the people and the EU lie in three main arenas: election to the EP (discussed in Chapter 7), referendums, and the work of interest groups.

REFERENDUMS

In addition to elections and opinion polls, citizens in the member states have expressed their opinions on European issues through national referendums. Not every member state offers them, they have only been used for selected issues, and the results of most have been unexceptional, but some have had conspicuous political effects with EU-wide implications and have occasionally halted the process of integration in its tracks. Most referendums have fallen into one of two major categories:

Whether or not to join the EU. These referendums have been held only by newer members of the EU, beginning with the votes held in Denmark, Ireland, and Norway in 1972. A majority of Danes and Irish approved, but a majority of Norwegians disapproved, saying no in a second referendum in 1994. The UK held a referendum in 1975 on continued membership in the Community following renegotiation of the terms, but its real purpose was to settle a division of opinion within its own government. All three countries that joined the EU in 1995 held referendums, as did nine of the twelve countries that joined in 2004. Croatia also followed suit, holding a referendum on EU membership in January 2012, which cleared its way to joining the Union. In contrast, when Bulgaria and Romania joined in 2007, neither used a referendum.

Whether or not to accept a new treaty. These have been used most often by Denmark, France, and Ireland, with sometimes surprising results. Denmark held a vote on the SEA in 1986, mainly to outmaneuver the Danish Parliament, which had voted against ratification. A majority of Danes said yes on that occasion, but a majority turned down Maastricht in 1992, and a majority of Irish voters turned down the Treaty of Nice in 2001. The negative votes resulted in changes to the treaties and also drew attention to the elitist nature of EU decision making, obliging European leaders to stop taking public opinion for granted. Referendums held in 1998 in Denmark and Ireland on the terms of the Amsterdam treaty were both positive. Most famously, referendums took place in France, Luxembourg, the Netherlands, and Spain in 2005 on the constitutional treaty, which French and Dutch voters rejected. Six other member states that had planned referendums put them on hold.

Ireland in particular has had headline-grabbing results with its referendums: constitutionally required to have a vote on a treaty whenever national sovereignty is at stake, Irish voters snubbed the Treaty of Lisbon in 2009. A new referendum on Lisbon was held later that year, only after the Irish government negotiated written assurances from the EU on treaty provisions, and was passed successfully. More recently, a new fiscal compact negotiated by EU leaders during the debt crisis also was put to a vote in Ireland in May 2012. This time a second referendum was a moot point, as some 60 percent of Irish voters approved the new pact.

Although an argument can be, and has been, made that the use of referendums allows citizens more direct input into decision making, they have several distinct disadvantages. Because voters are almost always asked to vote up or down on a particular referendum question, the wording of the question can play a significant role in the outcome. The complexities and subtleties of treaties are, not surprisingly, largely lost in this process. Additionally, referendums often function as "second-order" elections, that is, voters' decisions are guided less by the issue at hand than by their judgment of national incumbent governments (see Chapter 7). Of course, holding repeated referendums on a single issue (as Ireland has a number of times) can get around these difficulties, but this has some public relations cost as it appears member states will repeat the process until they "get it right."

INTEREST GROUPS

As vibrant democracies, every member state of the EU has a diverse and active community of interest groups that works to influence government on a plethora of issues, using multiple methods. Interest groups can be understood as more or less well-defined groups who attempt to influence the results of politics without actually being part of the formal political process. When policy was formulated primarily at the national or local level, these groups devoted most of their attention to trying to influence national and local governments. But as a growing number of decisions occurred at the European level, more groups focused their efforts on European-level policy making, particularly in the European Commission and the EP.[17] Consistent with the EU's origins in economic integration, business interests have been active lobbyists since the creation of the European Economic Community in 1958 (for example, the Association of European Chambers of Commerce) and agricultural lobbies since the introduction of the Common Agricultural Policy. Other commercial and economic interest groups (e.g., the European Round Table of Industrialists, composed of executives of big European firms) became active around the time of the SEA, while the interests of labor (chiefly through the European Trade Union Confederation) have risen in prominence since the 1970s. In addition, individual corporations and businesses are represented directly or by lobbying firms. Interest groups opened offices in growing numbers in Brussels or became part of Brussels-based umbrella organizations in the 1980s and 1990s and by 2006 there were estimated to be more than 850 EU-level interest groups (or Eurogroups), representing business interests, labor, public interests, and the professions.[18]

Because they have often cut across national frontiers to promote the shared sectional interests of groups of people in multiple member states, interest groups have provided an important counterbalance to the nationalist and intergovernmental inclinations of EU policy making, The representation of interests at the European level has grown more diversified and specialized, and these interest groups are becoming protagonists – they now try to shape policy rather than simply monitor events, using increasingly sophisticated means to attract allegiance.[19] A kind of symbiotic relationship has developed between the Commission and interest groups, with the former actively supporting the work of many groups and giving them access to its advisory committee meetings, and the latter doing what they can to influence the content and development of policy and legislative proposals as they work their way through the Commission.

Naturally, as the EU has become increasingly active in a broader variety of policy areas, so the number of special interest groups based in Brussels has increased, dealing with issues as diverse as the environment, consumer protection, transport, trade, and social policy. While overall more than three-quarters of EU interests groups could be classified as employers' interest associations, non-economic interest groups representing issues of general public interest have also sprung up in recent years, such as the European Citizens Action Service, the European Consumer Organization, the European Environment Bureau, Amnesty International, the European Anti-Poverty Network, the European Network Against Racism, and the European Women's Lobby (see Box 10.2). These associations use methods similar to those employed by groups at the national or local level, such as promoting public awareness in support of their cause, building membership numbers in order to increase their influence and credibility, representing the views of their members, and forming networks with other interest groups. Relative to business groups, however, many of these non-economic interest groups have critical handicaps:

- They tend to be relatively small and have neither the resources nor the professional expertise to compete with business federations.
- Their technical expertise does not always measure up to that of business groups, and they often lack the ability to discuss the costs and benefits of policy options in real terms. Much of the problem stems from their relative lack of resources; while the business lobby can often draw on the combined and substantial resources of some of the world's richest corporations, special interest groups can often do little more than utilize outside experts as occasional consultants. They also often lack the grasp of technical issues needed to debate the business lobby.

Box 10.2 Making Their Voices Heard: The European Women's Lobby

Created in 1990, the European Women's Lobby (EWL) is the largest European umbrella network of women's associations in the EU. With member organizations in all of the member states as well as in many of the candidate countries, its chief aim is to promote women's rights and equality between men and women in the EU as well as the mainstreaming of gender-equality perspectives in all EU policies. As its website states, the EWL's vision is of "a society in which women's contribution to all aspects of life is recognized, rewarded and celebrated – in leadership, in care and in production; all women have freedom of choice, self-confidence, and freedom from exploitation; and no woman has been left behind."[20]

The EWL originated in a conference in 1987 which brought together a number of organizations in the member states and called for an EU-wide structure that would be able to exert influence on European and national institutions to better represent women's interests. In 1990 the Commission granted its support for the foundation of the EWL with a secretariat based in Brussels. During the mid-1990s it fought for a new gender-equality clause in revisions to the Maastricht treaty, and in the later part of the decade the EWL created a "Wise Women's Group." This initiative was directly in response to the EU's decision to assemble a group of experts – the so-called "Wise Men" – to consult on the Treaty of Amsterdam. The EWL was able to deliver position papers to the EU and to present its views in hearings in the EP. Directly as a result of its work, gender equality ascended to a fundamental right within the EU, while Article 3 of the treaty incorporated the principle of gender mainstreaming into all policies of the union.

- Brussels-based umbrella organizations are dependent for much of their support on their member organizations, most of which still focus more on trying to influence policy at the national rather than the European level. There is relatively little cross-national cooperation among special interest groups.
- The compartmentalized nature of policy making within the Commission requires that groups be able to monitor and respond to policy developments in multiple directorates-general (DGs). Though they need to go beyond the DG that deals most obviously with their policy area and work with other DGs as well, they often lack the staff to be able to do so.

At the same time, groups have several important cards that they can play, and they have become better over time at exploiting their strengths, which include the following:

- The ability to influence the political agenda in Brussels by building pan-European coalitions and mustering the forces of the thousands of regional, national, and local groups active in the EU. Unlike business (which is often limited by narrow agendas and conflicts of interest), special interest groups are capable of viewing their long-term interests through a coordinated pan-European lens, providing a balance to the narrower views of the Commission.
- The ability to be of service by providing information. Often overworked and under-staffed, DGs must rely on outside sources for expert technical information, and lack the resources adequately to monitor compliance with EU law. National interest groups in particular can exert influence by actively assisting the Commission with the provision of technical information and by acting as watchdogs over compliance.[21]

Overall, the activities of interest groups have helped alleviate the problem of the democratic deficit by offering Europeans channels outside the formal structure of EU institutions through which they can influence EU policy. They have also helped to focus the attention of interest group members on how the EU influences the policies that affect their lives, have helped to draw people more actively into the process by which the EU makes its decisions, and have encouraged them to bypass their national governments and to focus their attention on European responses to shared and common problems.

QUESTIONS TO CONSIDER

1 What are the major obstacles to developing a primary European identity, and can Europe be more like the US, where an overarching American identity trumps regional identities?
2 Should more states in the EU make use of referendums for questions concerning the EU as a way of improving the EU's democratic record, or are referendums harmful to the EU project?
3 For proponents of a more integrated Europe, what are the benefits of interest groups to the EU?

NOTES

1 Kat Devlin, "Attitudes toward EU Are Largely Positive, both within Europe and outside It," Pew Research Center, October 21, 2019, at www.pewresearch.org/fact-tank/2019/10/21/attitudes-toward-eu-are-largely-positive-both-within-europe-and-outside-it/, accessed October 23, 2019.
2 For a review of Euroskepticism, see Benjamin Leruth, Nicholas Startis, and Simon Usherwood, eds., *The Routledge Handbook of Euroscepticism* (London: Routledge, 2017).
3 Paul Taggart and Aleks Szczerbiak, "Conclusions: Opposing Europe? Three Patterns of Party Competition over Europe," in *Opposing Europe: The Comparative Party Politics of Euroscepticism*, edited by Paul Taggart and Aleks Szczerbiak (Oxford: Oxford University Press, 2008, 2 volumes).
4 Jim Bulpitt, "Conservative Leaders and the Euro Ratchet: Five Doses of Scepticism," *The Political Quarterly* 63, no. 3: 258–275.
5 Petr Kopecký and Cas Mudde, "The Two Sides of Euroscepticism: Party Positions on European Integration in East Central Europe," *European Union Politics*, 3, no. 3 (2002): 297–326.
6 European Commission, Standard Eurobarometer, spring 2015, at https://ec.europa.eu/commission/presscorner/detail/en/IP_15_5451.
7 Still, this low level of trust might not simply reflect on the EU but rather express a generalized lack of trust in all levels of government. Eurobarometer polls have consistently shown that EU citizens' trust in their national parliaments and governments is even lower (ranging from the mid-twenties in 2012 to the low thirties in 2019). And this issue of trust is not just a European phenomenon: Americans' trust in their government continues to remain near historic lows, with only about 24 percent saying they trust the federal government always or most of the time. See "Public Trust in Government: 1958–2014," Pew Research Center, at www.people-press.org/2014/11/13/public-trust-in-government/.
8 Unless otherwise noted, all figures cited here come from the European Commission, *Special Eurobarometer 486* (Spring 2019), at https://ec.europa.eu/commfrontoffice/publicopinion/index.cfm/survey/getsurveydetail/instruments/special/surveyky/2225.
9 Another 26 percent specifically mention the ability to study in another member state through the Erasmus program, discussed in Chapter 14.

10 For an EU-themed adaptation of the Monty Python Sketch ("What Has the EU Ever Done for Us?") see www.youtube.com/watch?v=q5D0t6ejcGE.

11 See David Charter, *What Has the EU Ever Done for Us? How the European Union Changed Britain – What to Keep and What to Scrap* (London: Bitback Publishing, 2017).

12 Michael Edwards, *Civil Society* (Cambridge: Polity, 2005).

13 David Martin, quoted in Vernon Bogdanor and Geoffrey Woodcock, "The European Community and Sovereignty," *Parliamentary Affairs* 44, no. 4 (October 1991): 481–492.

14 Andrew Moravcsik, "Democracy and Constitutionalism in the European Union," *ECSA Review* 13, no. 2 (spring 2000): 2–7.

15 "How the EU is Trying to Find Out What on Earth Europeans Want," *The Economist*, May 10, 2018, at www.economist.com/europe/2018/05/10/how-the-eu-is-trying-to-find-out-what-on-earth-europeans-want, accessed May 17, 2018.

16 Paul Geitner, "On Gay Marriage, Europe Strains to Square 27 Interests," *New York Times*, July 26, 2012, A3.

17 Sonia Mazey and Jeremy Richardson, "Interest Groups and the Brussels Bureaucracy," in *Governing Europe*, edited by Jack Hayward and Anand Menon (Oxford: Oxford University Press, 2003); Justin Greenwood, *Interest Representation in the European Union*, 4th ed. (London: Red Globe/Macmillan, 2017).

18 Richard Balme and Didier Chabanet, *European Governance and Democracy: Power and Protest in the EU* (Lanham, MD: Rowman and Littlefield, 2008).

19 Mark Aspinwall and Justin Greenwood, "Conceptualising Collective Action in the European Union: An Introduction," in *Collective Action in the European Union*, edited by Justin Greenwood and Mark Aspinwall (New York: Routledge, 1998).

20 European Women's Lobby, "Mission, Vision and Values," at www.womenlobby.org/Mission-vision-and-values-588?lang=en, accessed August 7, 2019.

21 For more details, see John McCormick, *Environmental Policy in the European Union*, 111–122 (Basingstoke, UK: Palgrave Macmillan, 2001).

BIBLIOGRAPHY

Aspinwall, Mark, and Justin Greenwood, "Conceptualising Collective Action in the European Union: An Introduction," in *Collective Action in the European Union*, edited by Justin Greenwood and Mark Aspinwall (New York: Routledge, 1998).

Balme, Richard, and Didier Chabanet, *European Governance and Democracy: Power and Protest in the EU* (Lanham, MD: Rowman and Littlefield, 2008).

Bitonti, Alberto, and Phil Harris, eds., *Lobbying in Europe: Public Affairs and the Lobbying Industry in 28 EU Countries* (London: Palgrave Macmillan, 2017).

Bogdanor, Vernon, and Geoffrey Woodcock, "The European Community and Sovereignty," *Parliamentary Affairs* 44, no. 4 (October 1991): 481–492.

Bulpitt, Jim, "Conservative Leaders and the Euro Ratchet: Five Doses of Scepticism," *The Political Quarterly* 63, no. 3 (1992): 258–275.

Charter, David, *What Has the EU Ever Done for Us? How the European Union Changed Britain – What to Keep and What to Scrap* (London: Bitback Publishing, 2017).

Devlin, Kat, "Attitudes toward EU are Largely Positive, both within Europe and outside It," Pew Research Center, October 21, 2019, at www.pewresearch.org/fact-tank/2019/10/21/attitudes-toward-eu-are-largely-positive-both-within-europe-and-outside-it/, accessed October 23, 2019.

Edwards, Michael, *Civil Society* (Cambridge: Polity, 2005).

Economist, The, "How the EU Is Trying to Find Out What on Earth Europeans Want," May 10, 2018, at www.economist.com/europe/2018/05/10/how-the-eu-is-trying-to-find-out-what-on-earth-europeans-want, accessed May 17, 2018.

European Commission, *Standard Eurobarometer*, Spring 2015, at https://ec.europa.eu/commission/presscorner/detail/en/IP_15_5451.

European Commission, *Special Eurobarometer 486* (Spring 2019), at https://ec.europa.eu/commfrontoffice/publicopinion/index.cfm/survey/getsurveydetail/instruments/special/surveyky/2225.

European Women's Lobby, "Mission, Vision and Values," at www.womenlobby.org/Mission-vision-and-values-588?lang=en, accessed August 7, 2019.

Geitner, Paul, "On Gay Marriage, Europe Strains to Square 27 Interests," *New York Times*, July 26, 2012, A3.

Greenwood, Justin, *Interest Representation in the European Union*, 3rd revised ed. (Basingstoke, UK: Palgrave Macmillan, 2011).

Kopecký, Petr, and Cas Mudde, "The Two Sides of Euroscepticism: Party Positions on European Integration in East Central Europe," *European Union Politics*, 3, no. 3 (2002): 297–326.

Mendez, Fernando, Mario Mendez, and Vasiliki Triga, *Referendums in the European Union: A Comparative Inquiry* (Cambridge: Cambridge University Press, 2016).

Leruth, Benjamin, Nicholas Startis, and Simon Usherwood, eds., *The Routledge Handbook of Euroscepticism* (London: Routledge, 2017).

Mazey, Sonia and Jeremy Richardson, "Interest Groups and the Brussels Bureaucracy," in *Governing Europe*, edited by Jack Hayward and Anand Menon (Oxford: Oxford University Press, 2003).

McCormick, John, *Environmental Policy in the European Union* (Basingstoke, UK: Palgrave Macmillan, 2001).

Moravcsik, Andrew, "Democracy and Constitutionalism in the European Union," *ECSA Review* 13, no. 2 (spring 2000): 2–7.

Pew Research Center, *Public Trust in Government: 1958–2014*, at www.people-press.org/2014/11/13/public-trust-in-government/.

FURTHER READING

Fernando Mendez, Mario Mendez, and Vasiliki Triga, *Referendums in the European Union: A Comparative Inquiry* (Cambridge: Cambridge University Press, 2016).

>One of the best scholarly analyses of referendums in the EU.

Alberto Bitonti and Phil Harris, eds., *Lobbying in Europe: Public Affairs and the Lobbying Industry in 28 EU Countries* (London: Palgrave Macmillan, 2017).

>A series of case studies on lobbying of the EU member states, with contributions from both political scientists and lobbyists.

Justin Greenwood, *Interest Representation in the European Union*, 3rd revised ed. (Basingstoke, UK: Palgrave Macmillan, 2011).

>A survey of the work of interest groups at the national and European levels, with chapters on business, professional, labor, and public interest groups.

PART III

Policies

CHAPTER 11

Public Policy and the Budget of the EU

CHAPTER OVERVIEW

- Most public policy within the EU continues to be made at the member state level. However, in a growing number of areas – including various economic, foreign, and social policies – decisions are made at the EU level.
- The classical elements of the public policy cycle are agenda setting, formulation, legitimation, implementation, and evaluation. For a variety of reasons, all of these stages of the policy cycle are more complex within the EU than they are for normal states.
- The EU has its own budget, although it is far smaller than most national budgets and must be balanced each year. Contributions from its member states form the major source of revenue for the EU; its major expenditures include development funds for poorer regions of the EU and agricultural support for EU farmers. The impact of Brexit on the budget of the EU will probably necessitate a small increase in member states' contributions and selected cuts in some expenditures, or a combination of both.

Public policies are the courses of action that governments deliberately pursue (or avoid) when faced with the problems and needs of the societies they govern. When parties or candidates run for office, they publish a list of ideas and proposals for dealing with society's needs. Once elected, they supposedly set out to govern on the basis of those ideas and try to put the proposals into effect. Promises sometimes get lost in the mix, and governments change direction when faced with new problems, yet their actions (or lack of action) collectively define their policies. Discussions of policy often include words such as *goals*, *programs*, *platforms*, *objectives*, *values*, and *needs*, and policies are usually expressed as laws, orders, regulations, and public statements. Put another way, if elections and public opinion are the inputs of politics in a democracy, then public policies are the outputs.

Debates have long raged about how policy is made and implemented at the national level in democracies, even though most have relatively stable, predictable, and institutionalized systems of government. Applied to the EU, those debates are more complicated. Not only is its administrative structure quite different from those found in conventional states, but there is no agreement on how to characterize the EU, which is in a constant state of evolution: its rules change, its membership changes, its policy agenda changes, and its priorities are frequently redefined. Today's EU traces its origins back to the early 1950s, but its ultimate destination is still unclear, and it may never reach a state of stable equilibrium.[1] And because of its uniqueness, much of the standard political science vocabulary – which is geared toward policy at the national level – does not help us understand how it works. The different policy areas in which the EU has been active have been studied in much depth, but our understanding of the overall EU policy process is still patchy.

In spite of all the questions about the sources and limits of EU power, there is no doubt that its authority has deepened and broadened. Where once European integration focused on coal and steel policy, the member states have transferred (or pooled) so much authority that the EU now has an impact on most aspects of European economic, foreign, and social policy, with national policies and governing structures being changed and aligned by EU laws and policies. And yet the powers of the EU are often misunderstood and exaggerated; much of the authority for decision making still rests in the hands of the governments of the member states. And despite concerns about loss of sovereignty and complaints about the mythical powers of "Brussels," the EU still wields few direct powers of enforcement and implementation, and it has only a small budget (about €165 billion in 2019, equivalent to less than one-twentieth of the US federal budget). Against that background, this chapter examines how EU policy is made and implemented, and discusses some of the principles of the EU policy process. It ends with an analysis of the structure and policy implications of the budget.

THE POLICY CYCLE

Different approaches to the study of public policy abound but the most common method is to describe it in terms of a cycle. The problem with this approach is that it suggests that policy making is more logical and ordered than it really is – certainly more so than it is in the complex and often arcane world of European policy making.[2] But the approach has the advantage of imposing some order on a complex process. In the case of the EU, that cycle has six key steps: agenda setting, formulation, legitimation, adoption, implementation, and evaluation.

Agenda Setting

Before a policy choice can be made, the existence of a problem must be acknowledged, and the problem must be accepted as a legitimate concern of government and placed on the public agenda. The definition of the public agenda is shaped by prevailing economic, social, and ideological values; by the nature and extent of government authority; and by changing levels of public and political interest. Some issues almost perpetually appear on the agenda, some never make it to the agenda at all, some appear for a brief period of time then disappear, and still others come and go. The broad or perpetual issues are those that tend to affect most people most of the time, such as economic questions, social issues, foreign policy, and the environment. Issues that rarely make it onto the EU agenda are those that are still mainly the responsibility of the member states, including welfare, health care, taxation, education, public safety, and crime.

It is important to appreciate that there is no single agenda in the EU, but rather a plethora:

- The institutional agendas of the Commission, Parliament, and the Council of Ministers
- The sub-institutional agendas of directorates-general within the Commission
- Regional agendas pursued by groups of member states (poorer states will have different needs from richer states, agricultural states will have different needs from industrial states, and so on)

- National agendas pursued by individual member states
- Cross-national agendas pursued by like-minded groups in multiple states, such as the environmental lobby, farmers, or multinational corporations
- Social agendas pursued by groups or movements dealing with issues such as individual rights, transparency in government, education, and health care.

One key difference between agenda setting at the national and European levels lies in the relative roles of public accountability. Elected leaders at the national level often push issues onto the policy agenda in response to public opinion, ostensibly because they want to represent the public will but also because they want to be reelected. In that sense, agenda setting is voter driven. In the EU, however, most authority for agenda setting rests with the European Council and the Commission, neither of which is elected or directly accountable to an EU-wide constituency and thus is less subject to national voter influence. But mixed public opinion about European integration has combined with negative votes on key European initiatives (the Danish rejection of Maastricht in 1992, the Irish rejection of Nice in 2001, the Dutch and French rejection of the constitutional treaty in 2005) and, more recently, EP elections to encourage both bodies to pay more attention to public opinion.

A second difference lies in the level of ease in identifying solutions. At the national or subnational level, it is easier (but by no means easy) to identify problems and their causes and so to push the issue onto the policy agenda and formulate a response. At the EU level, the sheer complexity and variety of the needs, values, and priorities of the member states make it more difficult to ascertain the existence or the causes of problems or the potential effects of policy alternatives. Unemployment, for example, can have different root causes from one member state to another, tied to macroeconomic policies and varying policies on education, job training, and unemployment benefits. This inconsistency causes difficulty when making the case for placing an issue on the agenda.

While the European Council and the Commission are the primary agenda setters, they are subject to a wide range of pressures and influences:

- Treaty obligations
- Pressures to harmonize national laws and policies so as to avoid economic or social variation among the member states, and to remove obstacles to free trade
- Policy evolution, in which policy responses are redefined as better understanding emerges about the causes and effects of problems
- Legislative pressures, which trigger new proposals for legislation
- Pressures from EU institutions, including judgments by the Court of Justice, or pressure on the Commission from the European Parliament (EP) or the Council of Ministers to develop new laws or policies
- Initiatives by individual national leaders or groups of leaders
- Public opinion
- Internal pressures, such as ongoing concerns about unemployment or the need to monitor the movement of criminals around the EU
- External pressures, such as trade wars with the US, the fallout with the US over Iraq, or heightening tensions between the EU and Russia over Ukraine
- The requirements of international law – many EU laws and policies have sprung from the requirements of international treaties that the EU has signed
- Emergencies or crises, such as the crisis in the eurozone, the refugee crisis, and Brexit.

Overall then, agenda setting in the EU represents a combination of (1) the extent to which national governments are prepared to allow the EU to have authority in different fields, (2) the extent to which economic, political, or technical pressures demand an EU response, and (3) the compromises reached in the process of resolving the often conflicting demands and needs of the member states. Various models have been developed to understand how EU agenda setting works (see Box 11.1), but the sheer size and complexity of the EU make it impossible to reach agreement on which offers the best explanation.

Formulation

Once a problem or a need has been recognized, a response must be formulated. This step will typically involve the development of a plan or program, which may include agreeing on new laws and new spending, issuing instructions to bureaucrats, making a series of public statements designed to draw attention to a problem, or encouraging changes in patterns of

---

Box 11.1 Who Sets the European Agenda?

Most studies of public policy argue that agenda setting is determined in one of three ways, all of which are reflected in the EU:

- The *pluralist approach* argues that policy making is divided into separate arenas influenced by different groups and that government is ultimately the sum of all competing interests in a society. The most important of these groups in the EU system are the member states themselves, but pluralists usually think in terms of more specific interests. Thus, farmers exert influence through their defense of the Common Agricultural Policy, and environmental interest groups have successfully lobbied the Commission and Parliament and have occasionally used the EU to bypass their own national governments.
- The *elitist approach* contends that decision making is dominated by a power elite consisting of those with the means to exert influence, whether it be money, status, charisma, or some other commodity. The EU is elitist in that leaders of the member states, the Council of Ministers, the Committee of Permanent Representative (Coreper), and the unelected and only indirectly accountable European commissioners make important decisions. The EU's "democratic deficit" comes largely from the fact that so few individuals in the EU power structure are elected and that so many of their meetings take place out of public view. However, the rise of interest group lobbying and the growing strength of the EP have made the policy process more open and democratic.
- The *statecentric approach* argues that the major source of policies is the environment in which policy makers find themselves, and that the government itself, rather than external social interests, is the locus of agenda setting. The EU is state-centric in that the setting of the EU agenda has been determined in large part by the nature of integration. EU leaders made a conscious decision to sign the Single European Act, for example, which meant the EU had to become involved in a wide variety of new policy areas and to deepen its authority in policy areas in which it was already engaged.

behavior. On the other hand, policy makers might decide to ignore a problem or to deliberately take no action, perhaps because the problem is too complex, or because there is doubt about its causes and about the best response, or simply because it is politically expedient to push it aside. A deliberate lack of action is just as much a part of public policy as a decision to act.

In an ideal world, some kind of methodical and rational policy analysis should be conducted in which the causes and dimensions of a problem are studied and all possible options and their relative costs and benefits considered before taking action. But this approach rarely happens; policy is often the byproduct of incrementalism, intuition, opportunism, or responses to emergencies or changes in public opinion. One famous study by the American scholar Charles Lindblom argues that policy making is often simply a matter of "muddling through."[3] Several obstacles interfere with its orderly formulation:

- As in all aspects of life – and especially government – people disagree over problems, their causes, and their urgency. What may seem logical, moral, or reasonable to one person may seem illogical, immoral, or unreasonable to another.
- Policy makers may not always have enough information to glean a clear understanding of a problem or its causes, and even when they do, they may not always agree on its interpretation. What, for example, causes poverty? Are people poor because they lack the will or ambition to improve their lives, because of their social environment, or because political and economic barriers make it impossible for them to improve their lives?
- Responses to problems reflect personal, social, and ideological biases. A conservative Czech prime minister will see policy issues in a different light than his or her Spanish socialist or Swedish social democrat counterpart because of different ideological values, divergent worldviews, and the unique needs of their constituencies.
- It is frequently difficult or impossible to be sure about the outcomes of a policy or how that policy will work in practice. Even with the best intentions and the finest research and planning, policies can have unintended or unanticipated consequences.
- The distribution of power in any system of government is often ambiguous, partly because constitutions are subject to different interpretations and partly because the process of government is determined by *implied* powers, by the values and personalities of officeholders, and by the varied ways in which officeholders use the powers of the same office. For example, the role of the European Commission in the policy process has depended less on the terms of the president's job than on the president's personality and his or her institutional resources.

The major focus of policy formulation in the EU is the Commission, which has the sole power to initiate new legislation, is responsible for protecting the treaties and ensuring that their spirit is expressed in specific laws and policies, and is charged with overseeing the EU budget. However, the Commission does not work in a vacuum: it listens to national governments, public opinion, interest groups, corporations, and policy think tanks, and is often influenced by the ideological, social, or national biases that its own staff bring to their analysis of a problem. The European Council will often also have an impact on policy formulation, since it decides not just *what to do* but sometimes *how to do it*. Furthermore, as a result of lobbying and discussion by the Council of Ministers and the EP, Commission proposals often change course.

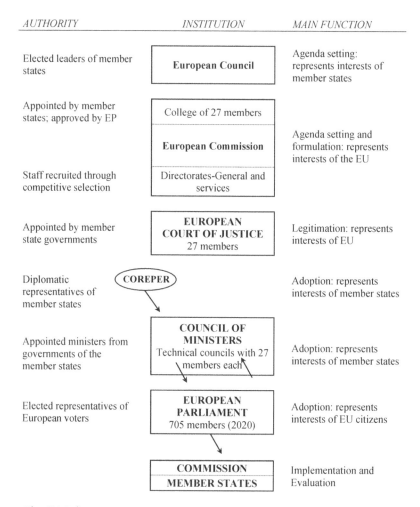

AUTHORITY	INSTITUTION	MAIN FUNCTION
Elected leaders of member states	**European Council**	Agenda setting: represents interests of member states
Appointed by member states; approved by EP	College of 27 members	Agenda setting and formulation: represents interests of the EU
	European Commission	
Staff recruited through competitive selection	Directorates-General and services	
Appointed by member state governments	**EUROPEAN COURT OF JUSTICE** 27 members	Legitimation: represents interests of EU
Diplomatic representatives of member states	COREPER	Adoption: represents interests of member states
Appointed ministers from governments of the member states	**COUNCIL OF MINISTERS** Technical councils with 27 members each	Adoption: represents interests of member states
Elected representatives of European voters	**EUROPEAN PARLIAMENT** 705 members (2020)	Adoption: represents interests of EU citizens
	COMMISSION MEMBER STATES	Implementation and Evaluation

FIGURE 11.1 The EU Policy Process.

Legitimation

In a democratic system, few policies are likely to be able to succeed unless, at a minimum, they are founded on legal authority and win public recognition. *Legitimacy* is a concept that describes the extent of the belief of citizens that the government under which they live has the authority to govern and make laws, and also describes the extent to which the actions of government are regarded as proper and acceptable. *Legitimation* is the process by which a government gives legitimacy to its actions; in other words, its policies must be converted into generally acceptable means for achieving its objectives. Legitimation in the EU derives from one of four main channels: the treaties, legislation, decisions by the European Court of Justice, and public opinion.

Leon Lindberg has argued that "the essence of a political community … is the existence of a legitimate system for the resolution of conflict, for the making of authoritative decisions for the group as a whole."[4] The less legitimacy such a community enjoys, the less it will be able to achieve by democratic means. In political systems founded on the rule of law (government based on a mutually agreed set of rules and laws, to which all residents are equally subject), there are usually few questions regarding the authority of government to make and implement policies. With the EU, however, the authority and powers of EU institutions have long been bones of contention.

Among the EU's fundamental handicaps is the authority gap – the difference between what EU institutions would *like* to be able to do and what EU citizens and governments *allow* them to do. That gap is wide, but it has slowly been narrowing, aided by direct elections to the EP: despite its weaknesses and historically low voter turnout, Parliament is still the only institution in the EU system that is directly accountable to the citizens. Voting in fair, regular, and competitive elections is one of the foundations of political legitimacy, and direct elections to Parliament have helped to significantly augment the credibility and legitimacy of the EU (and this despite the anti-establishment results of the last two EP elections!). Its legitimacy has also grown simply with the passage of time: EU citizens are learning to live with the effects of integration, and the EU is becoming more real, more permanent, and more acceptable.

Adoption

Once a new law or policy has been formulated, it must be adopted. Responsibility for this outcome is shared between the Council of Ministers (particularly Coreper) and the EP. Adoption has become more complex and time consuming as the EP has won new powers relative to the Council, and particularly since the introduction of the codecision procedure (now the ordinary legislative procedure). The EP has become more forceful in offering amendments to proposals from the Commission, to some extent making up for the relatively limited role that it has in the formulation phase.

Driving the adoption of a new proposal are the negotiating styles of the representatives of each member state, which will be influenced by tradition, by the attitude of the home government toward European integration, and by the extent to which a member state depends on EU law. For example, UK civil servants long were widely regarded as among the most efficient and effective at the EU level, and the UK has had a reputation for taking its obligations under EU law seriously, certainly ironic given its historical relationship with the EU and Brexit. Italy and Greece have taken their obligations less seriously, and they have frequently been taken to the Court of Justice for failure to meet their obligations.

Implementation

Policies are merely words or ideas until they are implemented and enforced. In the case of the EU this means monitoring the application of new laws and regulations, arguably the most difficult step in the policy cycle. To assume that once the EU has made a decision it will automatically be enforced is delusory; policies can be reinterpreted and redefined even at this stage.[5] Many different obstacles can arise:

- A lack of political agreement or political will
- The inefficiency of the institutions responsible for implementation
- A lack of cooperation from the subjects of policy (people, corporations, public agencies, and governments); inadequate funding
- A lack of workable or realistic goals
- A redefinition of priorities as a result of changed circumstances or new data
- A lack of agreement on underlying goals and the best methods of implementation
- Conflicting interpretations

- A lack of public support; inefficiency, stagnation, or conflicting interests within bureaucracies
- Unanticipated structural problems or side effects.

Responsibility for overseeing implementation lies with the Commission, although it must work through the bureaucracies of member states to ensure that governments turn EU laws and policies into practical change on the ground. The Commission also relies on individuals and interest groups to review the progress of implementation, and on the Court of Justice to ensure that laws are uniformly interpreted and applied and that disputes are resolved. Implementation has also been made easier by the creation of specialized agencies such as Europol and the European Central Bank, with responsibilities in focused policy areas.

Evaluation

The final stage in the policy cycle is determining whether a law or policy has worked. This process is difficult unless specific goals were set from the beginning and unless member states can be trusted to report accurately to the Commission on the results of policies. In many cases it is almost impossible to know which actions resulted in which consequences, particularly in the more complex areas of policy, such as economic management. Assuming, however, that the outcomes of policies can be identified and measured (in whole or in part), policies can be continued, adjusted, or abandoned. Evaluation in the EU is a joint effort carried out by a combination of the Commission, the Council of Ministers, the European Council, the EP, and reports from member states, interest groups, and individuals.

FEATURES OF THE POLICY PROCESS

To better understand the EU's policy process, the US model offers a helpful comparison. Writing about the policy process in the US, Guy Peters argues that "American government has a number of structures but no real organization." He notes the lack of effective coordination and control, which he argues was intentional, given the concern of the framers of the US Constitution about the potential for tyranny by a powerful central executive.[6] In many respects, the same can be said about policy making in the EU. No real organization exists, in large part owing to ubiquitous concerns about loss of sovereignty. The result has been a policy process driven not just by the usual pressures of compromise and opportunism, but also by some features that are unique to the European experience.

Compromise and Bargaining

Except in dictatorships, all politics is a matter of compromise (a reality that many lawmakers in the US Congress seem lately to have forgotten!). Individuals cannot always have it their own way, because there are always others who will disagree with their analyses of problems, their suggested prescriptions, and their priorities. The fewest compromises are needed in unitary systems of government with a history of majoritarian political parties (such as, until recently, Spain), where the focus of political power rests with a national government usually made up of a single political party. More compromises are needed in federal systems such as Belgium and Germany, where there is a division of powers between national and subnational government, or in member states governed by coalitions (e.g., Austria, Denmark, or Portugal).

Political Games

Struggles for power and influence drive politics, with one person or group trying to press its views on others. In the EU the extent to which member states and institutions compete with each other can magnify these struggles. Peters has described three sets of interconnected games in the EU: a national game among member states, which are trying to extract as much as possible from the EU while giving up as little as possible; a game played out among EU institutions, which are trying to win more power relative to one another; and a bureaucratic game in which the directorates-general in the Commission are developing their own organizational cultures and competing for policy space.[7] Peters argues that policy making has become fragmented as institutional and policy goals have parted company and discrete policy communities have emerged.[8]

Incrementalism

Owing to concerns about the loss of national sovereignty, the absence of a consensus on the wisdom of European integration, and the need for constant compromise, EU policy making is generally slow and cautious. The EU occasionally has agreed on relatively dramatic policy initiatives (such as the Single European Act, Maastricht, the launch of the euro, and eastern enlargement), but most EU policy making is based on gradual and incremental change. Due to its array of counterweights and counterbalances in the policy process, member states and EU institutions can rarely take the initiative without conferring first with other member states or EU institutions. The process has sometimes slowed to the point where critics of integration have complained about inertia, but the achievements have been substantial. None, however, sprang from the ether; all emerged incrementally from a combination of opportunity and need.

Multispeed Integration

In the US – even though individual states have different policies with regard to capital punishment, speed limits, voting procedures, and rates of taxation, for example – the country is generally moving at the same pace in most key policy areas. In other words, different states do not opt in or out of different federal policy areas according to local political preferences. In the EU, by contrast, not all member states have adopted exactly the same sets of common policies, and so they are moving at different speeds. As an example, despite the universal adoption of laws and policies on the single market and agricultural policy, only nineteen of the twenty-seven member states have adopted the euro.

Subsidiarity

One of the key principles of European integration has been the requirement that, except in those policy areas that fall exclusively within the competence of the EU (such as competition, customs, trade, and fiscal policy in the eurozone), the EU should take action only in those areas or on those problems in which it makes more sense to take joint action than to leave it to the member states. In other words, the EU should do only what it does best, and the member states should do everything else. There are no hard rules regarding the best division of responsibilities, which are shared in almost every field of policy. But it has come to be understood that certain issues are best addressed jointly (such as the single market and external trade negotiations), and there is political resistance to the EU becoming involved in policy areas still viewed as falling under the purview of member states, such as education, health care, policing, criminal justice, and taxation. One result has been a variation from one policy area to another in the precise procedures for making policy.

Europeanization

In thinking about the way the European Community (EC) would make decisions, Jean Monnet envisioned that European policies would simply replace national policies. Otherwise known as the Community method,[9] this was the earliest, simplest, and purest of the different models of European policy making, but it was also the most difficult to achieve because it assumed wholesale agreement on switching authority from the member states to the EU. What has instead happened, according to many who study the EU, has been a process of Europeanization, in which laws and policies in the member states have been brought into alignment with EU law and policy through a process of harmonization, or perhaps even of homogenization,[10] although opinion is divided on the extent of its reach and usefulness in understanding the EU policy process.[11] It is also unclear to what extent the pressures driving policy change have been clearly European, as opposed to coming from the member states or driven by international pressures such as globalization.

Spillover

Critics of the EU (like critics of the US federal government) have often charged that it has over-reached in too many policy areas, but often it has had little choice: the launch of a new initiative can reveal or create new problems that in turn trigger a demand for additional supporting initiatives. As Aaron Wildavsky put it, policy can become its own cause.[12] Spillover (discussed in Chapter 1) has been an ongoing feature of policy making in the EU, the prime example coming from efforts to complete the single market. The task of removing barriers to the free movement of people, money, and goods and services could be achieved neither easily nor quickly, and involved making many adjustments – anticipated or not – that opened up the European market. This almost by necessity signaled a move into new areas of policy that were never anticipated by the founding treaties, including social issues, working conditions, and the environment.

THE BUDGET

Arguably the biggest influence on policy at any level of government is the budget. The amount of money a government has available – and how and where it decides to raise and spend that money – shapes both its policy choices and the true effectiveness of policy implementation. It is often less a question of *how much* is raised and spent than of *how* and *where* that money is raised and spent. Controversies swirl in the US over budget deficits, the national debt, wasted spending, and the billions spent on defense instead of on education, health care, and infrastructure. The EU budget, too, is controversial, but less for how EU funds are spent than for how they are raised. The depth of the debate is surprising given the small amount involved: around €165 billion ($183 billion) in 2019 – less than the US federal government spent to service interest on the national debt.

The EU budget has three notable features:

- The EU has a long-term budget (five years), the Multiannual Financial Framework (MFF), which is proposed by the Commission and then negotiated with the Council of

Ministers and the EP. The MFF sets limits for EU spending as a whole and for different policy areas, and the annual budget for the EU must be confined to the limits set by the MFF. Consequently, the annual budget usually falls under the MFF target so as to allow the bloc to react to unforeseen developments.

- Unlike almost any national budget, the EU budget must be balanced. This means that there is no EU debt, sparing the EU the headaches which normally accompany debts (such as interest payments). In this regard the EU stands in stark contrast to the US, which has had an annual budget surplus in only eleven years since 1945. Meanwhile, the annual budget deficit in the US is expected to be about $1 trillion by 2020.
- The sources and the quantity of EU revenues lay at the heart of the conflicts that have emerged during the evolution of the EU. The biggest battles have been waged over the balance between national contributions (which give member states leverage over the EU) and the EU's own sources of revenue. The greater the latter, the greater independence the EU would have, and the greater the concerns about loss of national sovereignty by the member states.[13]

Revenues

While the European Coal and Steel Community generated its own income, raised by a levy on producers, the European Economic Community (EEC) and Euratom, as with most international organizations, were originally funded by national contributions. The contributions to the EEC were calculated roughly on the basis of size; thus France, Germany, and Italy each contributed 28 percent, Belgium and the Netherlands 7.9 percent, and Luxembourg 0.2 percent. In an attempt to win more independence, the Commission in 1965 proposed that the revenue from tariffs placed on imports from outside the EC should go directly to the Community, thereby providing the EC with its own resources. At the same time, Parliament began pushing for more control over the budget as a means of gaining more influence over policy. However, Charles de Gaulle thought the Commission had too much power already, and it was these proposals (combined with France's opposition to reform of the Common Agricultural Policy) that led to the 1965 empty chair crisis.

Pressure for budgetary reform persisted regardless, and changes between 1970 and 1975 led gradually to an increase in the proportion of revenues derived from the EC's own resources: customs duties, levies on agricultural imports, and a proportion (no more than 1 percent) of value-added tax (VAT). Two problems with this formula emerged. First, it took no account of the relative size of member state economies. This became a particular problem for states such as the UK, which paid much more into the EU coffers than it received. Second, the amounts involved were insufficient to meet the needs of the Community, which was not allowed to run a deficit or to borrow to meet shortfall. Further reducing the EC's freedom of action was the fact that two-thirds of spending went to agricultural price supports, which grew as European farmers produced more crops. At the same time, revenue from customs duties dropped because the Community's external tariffs were reduced, revenue from agricultural levies plunged as the EC's self-sufficiency in food production grew, and income from VAT failed to grow quickly enough because consumption was falling as a percentage of the Community's gross domestic product (GDP).[14] The problem was compounded by the unwillingness of some member states to raise the limit on the EC's own resources.

By the early 1980s the Community stood on the brink of insolvency, and it was obvious that either revenues had to be increased or expenditures had to be restructured or cut. Margaret Thatcher's insistence on a recalculation of the UK's contribution brought to a head the issue of budget reform; at her first European Council appearance in 1979 she bluntly told her Community partners, "I want my money back." A complex deal was eventually struck in 1984 by which the UK (and other countries, such as Germany) was given a rebate and its contribution was cut, and the Community's own resources were increased with the setting of a new ceiling of 1.4 percent from VAT. More reforms agreed to at an extra-ordinary meeting of the European Council in Brussels in February 1988 resulted in the current structure of revenue raising:

- The budget cannot be greater than 1.2 percent of the combined GNI (gross national income) of the member states.

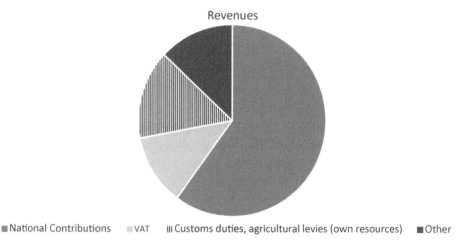

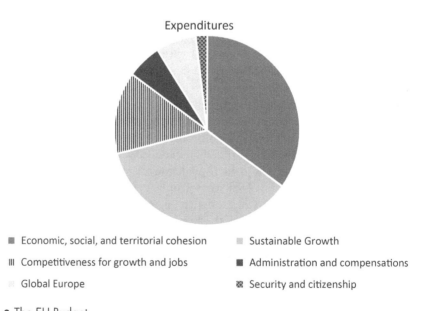

FIGURE 11.2 The EU Budget.

Source: European Commission, at https://ec.europa.eu/info/strategy/eu-budget/documents/annual-budget/2019_en, www.consilium.europa.eu/en/policies/eu-budgetary-system/eu-annual-budget/2019-budget/, and https://europa.eu/rapid/press-release_IP-18-6381_en.htm.

Note
Figures are for 2019.

- About 60 percent of revenues in 2019 came from national contributions based on national GNI levels (up from 40.5 percent of revenues in 2000). Each member state pays a set amount in proportion to its GNI.
- Revenues from VAT accounted for about 12 percent of revenues in 2019, down from 38 percent in 2000.
- Around 15 percent of revenues in 2019 came from customs duties on imports from non-member states and from agricultural levies.
- Just under 13 percent of revenue came from other sources (e.g., interest on late payments and fines and contributions from non-EU countries to particular programs).

Obviously, this formula produces a system in which the richer states make the biggest net contributions, while the poorer states have the biggest net receipts. This does not mean richer states always accept this system happily, however. For example, as part of negotiations for the new 2021–2027 MFF, Germany recently demanded that the EU budget not exceed 1 percent of the EU's total GDP, a move that would signal Germany is not prepared to increase its contribution despite worries about the hole Brexit might blow in the EU budget.[15] Moreover, for the 2021–2027 MFF and in light of Brexit, the Commission has proposed phasing out all country rebates.[16]

Expenditures

As with almost any budget, EU expenses consist of a combination of mandatory payments that leave little room for maneuver (such as agricultural price supports) and discretionary payments (such as spending on regional or energy policy) where there is more flexibility. However, unlike the US budget, which is subject to extensive horse-trading and often seems geared mainly to short-term "wins" for the party controlling Congress, EU budgeting and policy making is much more data-driven (with hordes of experts and specialists chiming in) and focused on long-range goals as articulated in the MFF. EU spending in 2019 was committed as follows:

- Thirty-five percent of spending (about €58 billion) went to economic, social, and territorial cohesion, the largest share of which is the cohesion funds, but also including support for projects and activities on entrepreneurship, innovation, information, technical assistance, and youth employment initiatives, the development of transportation networks, and the European Satellite Navigation Systems (Galileo).
- Thirty-six percent (about €60 billion) went to sustainable growth/natural resources, including rural development funds and agricultural subsidies and supports to fisheries. Funding for the Common Agricultural Policy still soaks up a very large share of the EU budget. However, because of reforms in agricultural policy (see Chapter 13), the proportion of EU spending that goes to agriculture has plunged from its peak during the 1970s, when it accounted for nearly 75 percent of the budget. For the 2021–2027 MFF, the Commission has proposed that agriculture will account for only 30 percent of the EU budget.
- Fourteen percent (about €23 billion) went to competitiveness for growth and jobs, which included areas such as innovation and technological development, education and job retraining, and the improvement of energy and digital networks.
- A small percentage (2 percent) was budgeted for security and citizenship, including border protection and other administrative costs associated with asylum and immigration issues.

- Another 7 percent of the budget (about €11 billion) was earmarked for the EU to use as a global player, including pre-accession funds (for prospective EU states), humanitarian aid, and development cooperation and other funds tied to the Common Foreign and Security Policy.
- Finally, only about 6 percent (about €10 billion) went to administrative costs for the EU institutions. As an indication of how much misunderstanding there is about those institutions – particularly the Commission – public opinion polls have routinely found that most Europeans perceive administration as one of the major costs of the EU.

Given the GDP of the UK and its subsequent national contribution, what impact will Brexit have on the EU budget? Estimates vary here, depending on the terms of the departure – no deal or an arrangement whereby the UK continues to contribute in some way to the EU – and the EU is planning for a variety of possible scenarios. A no-deal Brexit would mean no revenues would flow in from the UK; at the same time, the EU would benefit from customs duties now imposed at "non-members" levels and EU expenditures would go down as a result of the withdrawal of EU financial commitments toward the UK. A deal of some sort would preserve a (reduced) contribution from the UK to EU coffers as well as some reduced expenditures geared toward the UK. Overall, it can be said that Brexit will probably necessitate an increase in member states' contributions, selected cuts in some expenditures, or a combination of both. Figuring out how to plug the Brexit hole will undoubtedly keep EU accountants busy for many months.

QUESTIONS TO CONSIDER

1 What distinctive features of public policy making in the EU make this more challenging than in conventional states?
2 How does the EU compare with the US federal government in terms of its taxing authority? Should the EU have greater independence in this, say by having its own income tax?
3 What do the various categories of expenditures from the EU budget say about policy priorities within the EU?

NOTES

1 See the discussion in Brigid Laffan, Rory O'Donnell, and Michael Smith, *Europe's Experimental Union: Rethinking Integration* (London: Routledge, 2000), and Sonia Mazey, "European Integration: Unfinished Journey or Journey Without End?" in *European Union: Power and Policy-Making*, 2nd ed., edited by Jeremy Richardson (New York: Routledge, 2001).
2 For a portrait of the complexity, see Jeremy Richardson, "Policy-Making in the EU: Interests, Ideas and Garbage Cans of Primeval Soup," in *European Union: Power and Policy-Making*, 2nd ed., edited by Jeremy Richardson (New York: Routledge, 2001); see also Sebastiaan Princen, *Agenda-Setting in the European Union* (New York: Palgrave Macmillan, 2009).
3 Charles Lindblom, "The Science of 'Muddling Through,'" *Public Administration Review* 19, no. 2 (1959): 79–88.
4 Leon N. Lindberg, *The Political Dynamics of European Economic Integration*, vii (Stanford: Stanford University Press, 1963).
5 See Simona Milio, *From Policy to Implementation in the European Union: The Challenge of a Multi-Level Governance System* (London: Tauris Academic, 2010), and Christoph Knill, "Implementation," in *European Union*, edited by Richardson.

6 B. Guy Peters, *American Public Policy: Promise and Performance*, 9th ed., 25 (Washington, DC: CQ Press, 2012).
7 B. Guy Peters, "Bureaucratic Politics and the Institutions of the European Community," in *Euro-Politics: Institutions and Policymaking in the "New" European Community*, edited by Alberta Sbragia, 106–107 (Washington, DC: Brookings Institution, 1992).
8 Peters, "Bureaucratic Politics and the Institutions of the European Community," 115–121.
9 See Leon N. Lindberg and Stuart A. Scheingold, *Europe's Would-Be Polity: Patterns of Change in the European Community* (Englewood Cliffs, NJ: Prentice Hall, 1970).
10 Edward C. Page, "Europeanization and the Persistence of Administrative Systems," in *Governing Europe*, edited by Jack Hayward and Anand Menon (Oxford: Oxford University Press, 2003).
11 See Page, "Europeanization and the Persistence of Administrative Systems," and Paolo Graziano and Maarten P. Vink, eds., *Europeanization: New Research Agendas* (Basingstoke, UK: Palgrave Macmillan, 2007).
12 Aaron Wildavsky, ed., *Speaking Truth to Power: The Art and Craft of Policy Analysis*, 62–85 (Boston: Little, Brown, 1979).
13 For a brief survey of EU budgetary battles, see Brigid Laffan and Johannes Lindner, "The Budget: Who Gets What, When and How?" in *Policy-Making in the European Union*, 6th ed., edited by Helen Wallace, Mark A. Pollack, and Alasdair R. Young (Oxford: Oxford University Press, 2010).
14 Michael Shackleton, *Financing the European Community*, 10–11 (New York: Council on Foreign Relations Press, 1990).
15 See Peter Müller and Christian Reiermann, "Germany Seeks to Limit EU Budget Contribution," *Der Spiegel*, September 20, 2019, at www.spiegel.de/international/europe/germany-seeks-to-cap-eu-budget-at-1-percent-of-gdp-a-1287817.html, accessed September 21, 2019.
16 See European Commission, *Communication from the Commission to the European Parliament, The European Council, The Council, The European Economic and Social Committee and the Committee of the Regions. A Modern Budget for A Union that Protects, Empowers, and Defends. The Multiannual Financial Framework for 2021–2027*, at https://eur-lex.europa.eu/legal-content/EN/TXT/?uri=COM%3A2018%3A321%3AFIN, accessed October 16, 2019. Also see European Council and Council of the European Union, "Own Resources for 2021–2027," at www.consilium.europa.eu/en/policies/eu-budgetary-system/eu-revenue-own-resources/2021-2027/, accessed October 16, 2019.

BIBLIOGRAPHY

Cipriani, Gabriele, *Financing the EU Budget: Moving Forward or Backwards?* (Brussels: Centre for European Policy Studies, 2014).
European Commission, *Communication from the Commission to the European Parliament, The European Council, The Council, The European Economic and Social Committee and the Committee of the Regions. A Modern Budget for A Union that Protects, Empowers, and Defends. The Multiannual Financial Framework for 2021–2027*, at https://eur-lex.europa.eu/legal-content/EN/TXT/?uri=COM%3A2018%3A321%3AFIN, accessed October 16, 2019.
European Council and Council of the European Union, "Own Resources for 2021–2027," at www.consilium.europa.eu/en/policies/eu-budgetary-system/eu-revenue-own-resources/2021-2027/, accessed October 16, 2019.
Graziano, Paolo, and Maarten P. Vink, eds., *Europeanization: New Research Agendas* (Basingstoke, UK: Palgrave Macmillan, 2007).
Knill, Christoph, "Implementation," in *European Union: Power and Policy-Making*, 2nd ed., edited by Jeremy Richardson (New York: Routledge, 2001).
Laffan, Brigid, and Johannes Lindner, "The Budget: Who Gets What, When and How?" in *Policy-Making in the European Union*, 6th ed., edited by Helen Wallace, Mark A. Pollack, and Alasdair R. Young (Oxford: Oxford University Press, 2010).
Laffan, Brigid, Rory O'Donnell, and Michael Smith, *Europe's Experimental Union: Rethinking Integration* (London: Routledge, 2000).

Lindberg, Leon N., *The Political Dynamics of European Economic Integration* (Stanford: Stanford University Press, 1963).

Lindberg, Leon N. and Stuart A. Scheingold, *Europe's Would-Be Polity: Patterns of Change in the European Community* (Englewood Cliffs, NJ: Prentice Hall, 1970).

Lindblom, Charles, "The Science of 'Muddling Through,'" *Public Administration Review* 19, no. 2 (1959): 79–88.

Mazey, Sonia, "European Integration: Unfinished Journey or Journey Without End?" in *European Union: Power and Policy-Making*, 2nd ed., edited by Jeremy Richardson (New York: Routledge, 2001).

Milio, Simona, *From Policy to Implementation in the European Union: The Challenge of a Multi-Level Governance System* (London: Tauris Academic, 2010).

Müller, Peter and Christian Reiermann, "Germany Seeks to Limit EU Budget Contribution," *Der Spiegel*, September 20, 2019, at www.spiegel.de/international/europe/germany-seeks-to-cap-eu-budget-at-1-percent-of-gdp-a-1287817.html, accessed September 21, 2019.

Page, Edward C., "Europeanization and the Persistence of Administrative Systems," in *Governing Europe*, edited by Jack Hayward and Anand Menon (Oxford: Oxford University Press, 2003).

Peters, B. Guy, "Bureaucratic Politics and the Institutions of the European Community," in *Euro-Politics: Institutions and Policymaking in the "New" European Community*, edited by Alberta Sbragia, 106–107 (Washington, DC: Brookings Institution, 1992).

Peters, B. Guy, *American Public Policy: Promise and Performance*, 9th ed. (Washington, DC: CQ Press, 2012).

Princen, Sebastiaan, *Agenda-Setting in the European Union* (New York: Palgrave Macmillan, 2009).

Richardson, Jeremy, "Policy-Making in the EU: Interests, Ideas and Garbage Cans of Primeval Soup," in *European Union: Power and Policy-Making*, 2nd ed., edited by Jeremy Richardson (New York: Routledge, 2001).

Shackleton, Michael, *Financing the European Community* (New York: Council on Foreign Relations Press, 1990).

Wallace, Helen, Mark Pollack, and Alasdair Young, eds., *Policy-Making in the European Union*, 7th ed. (Oxford: Oxford University Press, 2014).

Wildavsky, Aaron, ed., *Speaking Truth to Power: The Art and Craft of Policy Analysis*, 62–85 (Boston: Little, Brown, 1979).

FURTHER READING

Sebastiaan Princen, *Agenda-Setting in the European Union* (New York: Palgrave Macmillan, 2009).
    A study of what policy areas get put on the EU agenda, with comparative case studies in environmental and health policy in the US and the EU.

Helen Wallace, Mark Pollack, and Alasdair Young, eds., *Policy-Making in the European Union*, 7th ed. (Oxford: Oxford University Press, 2014).
    An edited collection focusing on specific policy areas, including agriculture, the single market, competition, and social policy.

Simona Milio, *From Policy to Implementation in the European Union: The Challenge of a Multi-Level Governance System* (London: Tauris Academic, 2010).
    An examination of the deficiencies of EU policy implementation at the member-state level, with Italy, Spain, and Poland as case studies.

Gabriele Cipriani, *Financing the EU Budget: Moving Forward or Backwards?* (Brussels: Center for European Policy Studies, 2014).
    A highly readable study of the budget-making process in the EU.

CHAPTER 12

The Single Market, Monetary Union, and Regional Development Policy

CHAPTER OVERVIEW

- European integration has always been a function of economic integration. Intended to promote peace and prosperity in the early years of the EU, in the last two decades significant progress has been made in breaking down the remaining physical, fiscal, and technical barriers to integration and the completion of a single market for the EU.
- One of the most visible emblems of economic integration has been the euro, now used by nineteen countries. Created in 1999 as the linchpin of plans for a monetary union already given shape at Maastricht, the euro has been a singular achievement and a boon for consumers and business. But the rules and mechanisms governing the euro have been found wanting, and were at the heart of a eurozone debt crisis that shook the EU.
- "Cohesion" is the name encompassing a number of EU policies and funds aimed at EU regions and designed to offset some of the distortions and inequalities of the single market. Cohesion policy thus attempts to provide more balanced economic and social development within the bloc.

What we now know as the EU began life as the European Economic Community, and therein lies a fundamental clue to how the process of European integration has evolved: it was launched as a limited experiment in economic cooperation, was broadened during the 1960s to become a customs union, wrestled during the 1970s with attempts to build common economic policies and exchange rate stability, launched a new initiative in the late 1980s to complete the single market, and then agreed on the steps that led in 1999 to the creation of a monetary union and adoption of a single currency, the euro, across the countries of the eurozone. The changes wrought have not just affected the lives of Europeans but have been felt on a global scale: the EU is one of the world's wealthiest marketplaces, has one of the world's leading international currencies, and – with just 7 percent of the world's population – it is one of the three largest global players in international trade, along with the US and China.

The EU has advanced in other policy areas too (such as agriculture, the environment, regional development, and foreign policy), but the engine of integration has ultimately been the economy. Economic integration was intended to promote peace and prosperity by generating the wealth and opportunity that would allow Europe to recover from the ravages of war. By no means was the process smooth sailing, and while most of Western Europe prospered during the 1950s, by the early 1980s the EU confronted numerous problems, including energy crises, exchange rate instability, high unemployment, low growth in productivity, and economic stagnation. Since then much has changed. The near completion of the single market has helped boost productivity and wealth, European corporations have become bigger and more competitive, and trade and foreign investment have grown. Despite worries about sustained economic growth in the wake of the eurozone crisis, the evolution of the single market and economic integration over the last several decades has been truly remarkable.

At the same time, member states are well aware that economic integration and the growth of the single market have not equally benefitted all areas of the EU. Balanced economic and social development – or "cohesion" in EU jargon – remains rocky as long as large differences exist in levels of wealth, income, and opportunity. Most economists agree that the free market unavoidably contains or promotes social and economic inequalities that have so far defied attempts to remove them, and that equality is more an ideal than an achievable objective. The Treaty of Rome noted the need for an improved standard of living in Europe, but economic expansion and profit lay at the heart of the single market program, and less attention centered on the quality of life. By the early 1970s, however, focus shifted to encouraging an equitable distribution of the benefits of integration. The 1973 enlargement, and especially the 2004–2007 entrance into the EU by Eastern European states, accelerated the process by widening the gap between the richest and poorest parts of the Community and drawing new attention to the importance of removing social differences. Issues such as employment, working conditions, social security, labor relations, education, training, housing, and health all climbed up the agenda at this time. Today, cohesion policy (or "economic, social, and territorial cohesion") is the second biggest item on the EU budget at about 35 percent in 2019.

THE SINGLE MARKET AND EUROPE 2020

Whatever has been said and done regarding the many different facets of European integration, the fundamental goal of the Treaty of Rome – and of much that was later done in its name – was the completion of a single European market in which there would be free movement of people, money, and goods and services. Early progress was uneven, leading eventually to the idea of "relaunching" Europe, which was to be the foundation of the Single European Act. Its core objective was to finally remove the remaining barriers to the single market, which took three main forms:

- *Physical barriers*. Internal customs and border checks persisted because national governments sought to control the movement of people (especially illegal immigrants), collect taxes and excise duties on traded goods, and enforce different health standards. The checks were removed in stages during the late 1980s and early 1990s, member states agreeing at the same time to work toward police cooperation (to which end they created Europol in 1999) and toward common measures on visas, immigration, extradition, and political asylum.
- *Fiscal barriers*. Indirect taxation caused distortions of competition and artificial price differences among the member states and thus formed a barrier to the single market. Posing a particular problem were different rates of value-added tax (VAT, a consumption tax assessed on the value that is added to goods and services) and excise duties on items such as tobacco and alcohol. Agreement was reached first on a minimum rate of 15 percent VAT, then on minimum rates for excise duties, and then on an EU-wide VAT system under which tax is collected only in the country of origin.

- *Technical barriers.* Different technical regulations and standards persisted, most based on concerns about safety, health, and environmental and consumer protection. The Community had tried to develop EC-wide standards, but this time-consuming task did little to discourage the common image of interfering Eurocrats. Three breakthroughs helped simplify the process: the 1979 *Cassis de Dijon* decision (see Chapter 8, Box 8.2) confirmed the principle of mutual recognition, a 1983 law required member states to tell the Commission and other member states if they planned new domestic technical regulations, and the *Cockfield White Paper* included a new approach to technical regulation. Consequently, instead of having the Commission work out agreements on every rule and regulation, the Council of Ministers would agree on laws that had general objectives, and detailed specifications could then be drawn up by private standards institutes.

Despite much progress along the way during this time, there was also less progress than champions of the single market would have liked, as well as calls in the late 1990s – led by UK prime minister Tony Blair and Spanish prime minister José María Aznar – for a new focus on modernizing the European economy. Accordingly, the European Council meeting in Lisbon in March 2000 set the goal of making the changes needed to finally complete the single market and lift the EU up to the levels of competitiveness and dynamism that are features of the US economy. The Lisbon Strategy called on EU governments to make a wide range of changes, including integration and liberalization of the telecommunications market, liberalization of the natural gas and electricity markets, liberalization of services, rationalized road tax and air traffic control systems, lowering of unemployment, movement toward harmonization of EU corporate tax, and more progress toward making the EU a digital, knowledge-based economy.[1] However, it was already clear by 2004 that the Lisbon Strategy was sputtering because too few EU governments had been prepared to make the necessary reforms. Consequently, the strategy was reformulated as Europe 2020 with a new emphasis on innovation, education, social inclusion, climate and energy policy, poverty reduction, and job creation, all to be completed by 2020. As a way of monitoring progress of member states toward achieving the goals of Europe 2020, the EU created the "European Semester" (a six-month period at the beginning of each year), in which member states align their budgetary and economic policies with agreed-upon EU objectives.

With many, although not all, of the obstacles removed, the single market has made accelerated progress. Important exceptions exist of course, especially in the area of services (such as financial, transport, or construction services), which have encountered fierce resistance.[2] Yet the restrictions of even a generation ago have mostly evaporated and the member states of the EU are now better understood as one large multinational marketplace rather than as a cluster of individual national marketplaces. The effects of this near completion of the single market are illustrated by progress in four areas of policy: rights of residence; the development of European transport, telecommunication, and energy networks; corporate mergers and acquisitions; and competition policy.

Rights of Residence

All citizens or legal residents of an EU member state now have the right to enter and live in any other EU member state, although restrictions can be imposed for security or public health reasons. Indeed, within the Schengen area almost no restrictions and no identification checks exist at internal borders (although this has changed somewhat in the last several years, see Box 12.1); border posts have been removed, and the only indication that a road traveler is moving from one country to another is a sign announcing that they are entering a different country.

Box 12.1 No Passport Needed? The Schengen Agreement

Frustrated by the lack of progress on opening borders, representatives from France, Germany, and the Benelux states met in June 1985 near the Luxembourg town of Schengen and signed an agreement allowing for free movement of people among signatory states. A second agreement was signed in 1990, and borders were opened in 1995. Twenty-six European countries are now fully participating members of the agreement: all EU member states except Bulgaria, Cyprus, Ireland, and Romania, along with Iceland, Liechtenstein, Norway, and Switzerland. The UK claimed concerns about the difficulty that an island state faces in controlling illegal immigration (one of the key issues in Brexit) while Ireland has stayed out until now mainly because of its passport union with the UK. Travel between the UK and Ireland, on the one hand, and the UK and the rest of "Schengenland" on the other, has been complicated by Brexit and it is unclear what future form this will take. Croatia is set to join Schengen in 2020.

The agreement resulted not only in passport-free travel for EU citizens (and the requirement of only a single visa for noncitizens), but also the end of all but security checks at airports for flights among signatory states, the drawing up of rules for asylum seekers, cross-border rights of surveillance and hot pursuit for police forces, the strengthening of legal cooperation, and the creation of the Schengen Information System, which provides police and customs officials with a database of undesirables whose entry into Schengenland they want to control. Schengen countries are, however, allowed to reimpose border patrols for short periods in cases of particular need, as Portugal did during the 2004 European Football Championship and as France did in the wake of the terrorist attacks in Paris in November 2015.

More concerning for the future of Schengen was the reimposition of border checks/passport controls in Denmark and in several other EU states, such as Sweden and Slovenia, in the wake of the refugee crisis and terrorist attacks, checks intended to be temporary but which have yet to be lifted. With the COVID-19 pandemic, border checks – indeed border closings – have been reestablished throughout the EU, and whether this will become the new norm after the crisis passes is an open question. Indeed, as will be discussed in Chapter 14 on the role and function of Justice and Home Affairs, the goal of open internal borders that Schengen represents has met head on with disputes over how to handle the flow of migrants into the EU. France, meanwhile, has argued for a revision of Schengen so that known threats to all of Europe can be addressed at EU border states. Schengen most certainly will undergo some substantial changes in the near future.

Nationals of one member state are entitled to health care in all other member states if needed, and can buy almost any goods or services for personal use and take them home. They have the right to work, study, settle, or retire in any other member state, and to be enrolled at an educational institution, subject only to the proviso that they have sufficient resources to sustain themselves. Migrants can take all their personal possessions with them without paying duties or taxes, but road vehicles moved from one country to another must be registered and taxed in the new country; EU driver's licenses are valid throughout the EU. Migrant workers can also move all their financial assets with them and receive the same social security, welfare, and health-care benefits as local workers, as long as they make contributions. Once they retire, they are allowed to stay in the country in which they were working, with the same access to retirement benefits as local nationals. Meanwhile, they can vote or run for office in local elections (without losing the right to vote in equivalent elections at home) and can also vote or run in European Parliament elections (but in one country at a time).

Transport, Telecommunication, and Energy Networks

Markets are only as close as the ties that bind them, and one of the priorities of economic policy in the EU has been to build a system of trans-European networks (TENs) aimed at integrating the transport, energy supply, and telecommunications systems of the member states, thereby pulling the EU together and promoting mobility. The TENs policy gained a legal base with Maastricht, and since then a list of priority projects has been developed and work is underway on many of them. A Europe-wide rail network has been in the works, including thirty "priority axes" such as the Paris–Brussels–Cologne–Amsterdam–London high-speed rail system and high-speed rail links through southwest and eastern Europe. A European highway system, meanwhile, has aimed at connecting the existing motorways of the UK, autobahns of Austria and Germany, auto routes of Belgium and France, *autopistas* of Spain, *autostrada* of Italy, and filling in critical gaps in the poorer peripheral regions of the EU.

Europeans have long hoped to develop independence from American technology by working on a European navigation satellite system known as Galileo, designed to be not so much an alternative, but a complement to the US-operated Global Positioning System (GPS). GPS was developed by the US Department of Defense mainly for military purposes, and because the US reserves the right to limit its signal strength, or to close public GPS access completely during times of conflict, there are clear incentives for the EU to develop its own system. Several non-EU countries have joined the project, including China and India, and there has been talk of several others joining in the future, including Australia, Brazil, Canada, Japan, Mexico, and Russia. Developmental problems delayed the launch of Galileo, and when it finally began a pilot phase in 2016 it continued to be plagued by serious mishaps.[3] For the 2021 to 2027 Multiannual Financial Framework, the Commission wants to allocate another sixteen billion euros for a space program that would include Galileo.

As early as the 1990s the EU recognized that a common energy policy was vital to the further development of the internal market. The focus of a common energy policy now centers on further liberalization of the energy market as well as energy efficiency. The 2020 Energy Strategy therefore has five goals – developing energy efficiency (in buildings, products, transport), the development of a pan-European energy market (with all the necessary infrastructure of pipelines, transmission lines, etc.), consumer choice in energy supplies and consistent energy market standards, the development of cutting-edge and environmentally friendly technology, and the cultivation of good relations of the EU's external suppliers of energy.[4] Given that about a quarter of the EU's natural gas needs come from Russia (via pipelines running through Ukraine), tensions with Russia make this goal extremely tricky. The construction of other pipelines via the Black Sea, Baltic Sea (the "Nord Stream" pipelines), and Balkans are equally controversial, with critics charging that it keeps the EU hostage to Russia.[5]

Corporate Mergers and Acquisitions

Before World War II many of the world's biggest corporations were European. More global in scope than their American counterparts, they benefitted from the preferential markets created by colonialism. But after World War II European companies steadily lost markets at home and abroad to competition, first from the US and then from Japan. US and Japanese corporations were more dynamic, invested more in research and development, and had access to large home markets. European business, meanwhile, was handicapped in its attempts to move across borders into neighboring states, facing merger and capital gains taxes, double taxation on company profits, different legal systems, differences in regulations and standards, and limits on the movement of goods and services. Although the growth of the European single market changed the rules and increased the opportunities for Europe-wide corporate operations and larger-scale production, progress was snail-like.

Consequently, the Commission became immersed in trying to overcome market fragmentation and the emphasis placed by national governments on promoting the interests of often state-owned "national champions." Changes in company laws and regulations removed barriers to cross-border mergers, and the single market increased both the pressures and the opportunities for the development of pan-European corporations, as well as the number of consumers they could reach. The result has been an unprecedented surge of takeovers and mergers involving European companies since the mid-1980s: in 1984–1985 there were 208 mergers and acquisitions in the European Community (EC); in 1989–1990 there were 622, and – for the first time – the number of intra-EC mergers overtook the number of national mergers.[6] In 1996 the value of cross-border mergers soared to a record of more than $250 billion, and the European mergers and acquisitions market now surpasses that in the US. Notable recent examples include:

- The aggressive program of takeovers pursued by the British cell phone company Vodafone, which merged in 1999 with the US company AirTouch, then with Bell Atlantic, and in 2000 took over the much bigger German company Mannesmann
- The 2000 mergers of British company Shire Pharmaceuticals and the Canadian company BioChem Pharma, and of British companies Glaxo Wellcome and SmithKline Beecham (itself the result of the 1989 merger of SmithKline of the US and the UK's Beecham Group) to become GlaxoSmithKline, one of the biggest pharmaceutical companies in the world
- The rise of ING, a Dutch company, to become the biggest commercial and savings bank in the world by 2014.

Competition Policy

While corporate mergers and acquisitions can further the functioning of the single market, they can also lead to market distortions. Although there can never be a perfectly free and open market, distortions resulting from monopolies and cartels (or even government subsidies to business) give unfair advantages to one competitor in the market over another. Consequently, the EU – and the institution charged specifically with overseeing this area, the Commission – has long been engaged in identifying and addressing such market distortions through a competition policy aimed at promoting liberalization of the market by preventing abuses (such as price fixing), monitoring state subsidies to corporations, and guarding against abuses of dominant position by bigger companies.[7] An EU regulation adopted in 1989 allows the European Commission to scrutinize all large mergers. So, for example, it revised the terms of a 2006 merger between French oil companies TotalFina and Elf Aquitaine and blocked the proposed takeover in 2007 by low-cost airline Ryanair of the Irish national airline Aer Lingus. The Commission can even try to block mergers involving companies based outside the EU, as it did unsuccessfully in the case of Boeing and McDonnell Douglas in 1997, and successfully in the case of the planned takeover of Honeywell by General Electric in 2001. The latter would have been the biggest merger in history and was approved by the US government, but the Commission argued that it would have created dominant positions in the markets for the supply of avionics and non-avionics equipment, particularly jet engines. An angry response from US politicians and media ensued, but the takeover was shelved nonetheless.[8]

More recently, in July 2019 the Commission announced a new round of antitrust charges against Google (the third since 2015), complaining that the internet giant's advertising products severely crippled consumer choice. Previously the Commission had charged Google in 2015 with abusing its market dominance, claiming that the company's Android smartphone software and search engine forced phone makers to favor the company's own services and applications in internet searches, while in 2018 it argued that Google had diverted traffic from competitors in order to favor its own comparison-shopping site. The Commission's actions have been cheered by a broad array of European businesses (such as Springer, a major German company and publisher of the huge German tabloid *Bild*) while critics contend that Google is being unfairly singled out.[9]

MONETARY UNION

Even if most Americans do not know much about the EU, none of those who have traveled to the EU can ignore one of the most visible effects: the euro. And the recent crisis in the eurozone has drawn even more American attention to the story of European integration. A total of nineteen EU member states now use the single currency, which was created in 1999 as the linchpin of a monetary union and finally replaced national currencies in the eurozone in early 2002. Its introduction was a momentous event: never before in history had a group of sovereign nations voluntarily given up their national currencies and adopted a common currency. Although primarily an economic achievement, in that it represented the final realization of the goal of European economic and monetary union, it was also a political achievement, in that its creation involved the surrender of significant national sovereignty by eurozone governments. It also had global economic implications, offering Europe a world-class currency that would sit alongside the US dollar and the Japanese yen and that posed the first serious threat to the global leadership of the US dollar since the latter had replaced the British pound in the 1950s.

Stable exchange rates had been considered by European leaders to be central to the building of a single market, but the postwar system of fixed exchange rates alleviated most of their concerns. It was only when this system crumbled with the US decision in 1971 to break the link between gold and the US dollar that European leaders paid more attention to the idea of monetary union. The earliest steps were derailed by international currency turbulence in the wake of the energy crises of the 1970s (see Chapter 3). The European Monetary System (EMS) followed in 1979 with the goals of creating a zone of exchange rate stability and keeping inflation under control. Although several member states struggled to meet its terms, the EMS contributed to exchange rate stability and to the longest period of sustained economic expansion since World War II.

Monetary union received new attention with the Delors Plan in 1989, the basic principles of which were affirmed by Maastricht. It was agreed that EU member states wanting to take part in the single currency had to meet four "convergence criteria":

- A national budget deficit of 3 percent or less of gross domestic product (GDP) (the average deficit in the member states fell from 6.1 percent of GDP in 1993 to 2.4 percent in 1997)

- A public debt of less than 60 percent of GDP
- A consumer inflation rate within 1.5 percent of the average in the 3 countries with the lowest rates
- A long-term interest rate within 2 percent of the average in the 3 countries with the lowest rates.

EU leaders decided in 1995 to call the new currency the "euro" and to introduce it in three stages. The first of those came in May 1998 with a decision on which countries were ready. All member states had met the budget deficit goal, but Greece failed to reduce its interest rates sufficiently; Germany and Ireland missed the inflation reduction target; and only seven member states had achieved the debt target.[10] However, Maastricht allowed

MAP 12.1 The Eurozone.

countries to qualify if their debt to GDP ratio was "sufficiently diminishing and approaching the reference value at a satisfactory pace," so all but the UK, Denmark, Greece, and Sweden were given the green light. This raised questions in the minds of Euroskeptics about how seriously the convergence criteria were being treated.

The second stage began on January 1, 1999, when (1) the euro became available as an electronic currency, (2) participating countries fixed the exchange rates of their national currencies against one another and against the euro, and (3) the new European Central Bank (ECB) began overseeing the single monetary policy. All the Bank's dealings with commercial banks and all its foreign exchange activities were transacted in euros, which was quoted against the yen and the US dollar. But opinion polls showing public opinion in many EU countries hostile to the euro sowed more doubts: a majority of Swedes were opposed, opposition in the UK ran three to one, and in a national referendum in September 2000 Danes voted against adopting the euro. Even the Germans were skeptical; they saw little advantage in monetary union and signed on only because they saw a need to reaffirm their commitment to Europe in the wake of German reunification.[11]

The final stage began in January 2002 when euro coins and notes began to replace national currencies in all the EU-15 member states except the UK, Denmark, and Sweden. Europeans were initially allotted six months to make the transition, but it went so smoothly that it was over by the end of February. In January 2007, Slovenia became the first new country to adopt the euro, followed by Cyprus and Malta in January 2008, Slovakia in 2009, Estonia in 2011, Latvia in 2014, and Lithuania in 2015.

The most immediate advantage of the new single currency to consumers, of course, was that they no longer needed to exchange currencies when moving from one eurozone country to another (a task not as urgent in our current era of electronic transactions) or pay fees charged by banks and bureaux de change. There is also greater transparency in that consumers can immediately see how much goods and services cost without having to convert prices back into their home currency. One of the other effects has been to allow consumers to compare the costs of living in different countries more easily. The euro also helps businesses, whose transactions are now easier to undertake and who do not have to be concerned about fluctuations in exchange rates.

As discussed in Chapters 3 and 4, for some critics of the euro, the biggest concern with its introduction was loss of sovereignty. Where national governments were once able to make largely independent decisions on interest rates, those decisions are now made on behalf of the nineteen eurozone countries by the ECB. Different countries have different economic cycles, economic structures, and levels of wealth and poverty, and having separate currencies allowed them to devalue, borrow, and adjust interest rates in response to changed economic circumstances. Now they must, in theory at least, try to move in concert with all their neighbors – particular economic circumstances be damned. The costs of this became almost immediately evident with the effects of the Stability and Growth Pact (SGP), signed in 1997 among the eurozone states at the insistence of Germany, setting targets for permissible levels of budget deficit and public debt along the lines of the convergence criteria. These concerns resurfaced as the European debt crisis deepened.[12]

For other critics the central problem of the euro has been the lack of the EU's power to effectively manage fiscal policy. Thus, while eurozone members all use the same currency, share the same monetary policy, and – until the global economic crisis – were all able to borrow at reasonable interest rates in capital markets, they have always had very different economies and thus have continued to set their own fiscal policies. This has led in the worst cases (Greece) to overspending and a subsequent debt trap whereby states cannot manage their deficits and loss of competitiveness by devaluing their currencies (in effect cutting wages and prices through devaluation). Meanwhile the SGP has also been criticized on the one hand as too lenient (allowing some fudging of the rules of the SGP) and on the other as too inflexible in that it made no distinctions among countries with different economic bases and different economic cycles. Indeed, Commission president Romano Prodi was even moved in October 2002 to abandon the usual language of diplomacy and to describe attempts to enforce the pact without taking heed of changing circumstances as "stupid."[13]

By the second half of 2003 the ECB was warning that most eurozone countries were in danger of failing to meet the target on budget deficits, thereby damaging prospects for economic growth. In November 2003 the two biggest eurozone economies – France and Germany – both exceeded the limits and prevented other EU finance ministers from imposing large fines on the two countries. Its ministers, along with their UK counterpart, argued that the rules of the pact were too rigid and needed to be applied more flexibly if they were to succeed. By December the pact had all but collapsed, and in 2005 the rules were relaxed in order to make it more achievable and enforceable. However, the world economic crisis that broke in 2007 made budget deficit limits much more difficult for members to achieve, and Greece soon became emblematic of the challenges of using the SGP to coordinate fiscal policy.

Although the global financial crisis affected all EU member states to one degree or another, it was the problems in Greece that precipitated a larger crisis in the eurozone. The EU's response to the situation in Greece and to the sovereign debt crisis was to substantially reform the SGP through a new series of agreements:

- The "fiscal compact," "six-pack," and "two-pack" agreements (see Box 12.2) which enshrine the rules of the SGP in national law and tighten budgetary enforcement and sanctions
- A plan to recapitalize troubled banks directly through the EU and attach this to a permanent bailout mechanism (the European Stability Mechanism, a kind of "European" International Monetary Fund)
- A root and branch reform of banking within the EU as part of a future EU banking union.

In December 2012 the EU agreed on the basic framework of EU banking regulation: it established the ECB as the single supervisor responsible for bank oversight for around 200 banks throughout the EU, including at least three banks from each member state and any bank having assets greater than €30 billion ($39 billion). However, another proposal to provide an EU deposit guarantee (similar to the Federal Deposit Insurance Corporation in the US) has not yet come to fruition, while an idea floated by several EU states to address the eurozone crisis – the issuing of "Eurobonds" (EU-wide treasury bonds) by the ECB – has been staunchly resisted by Germany and several other states. They argue that this would create a "moral hazard" – the incentivizing of high borrowing or high-risk economic behavior by member states who know that they are cushioned from negative consequences by a joint EU bond guaranteed by economically prudent EU member states.

The fiscal compact and other related SGP reforms thus tightened up the language and understanding of public debt and budget deficits, and the financial sanctions for those countries found not to be in compliance grew more stringent. Through these reforms of the SGP, the EU hopes to have constructed an early warning system for serious economic problems of any member state, as well as new corrective instruments it can use before economic difficulties develop into a full-blown crisis. However, only time will tell whether the EU has done enough to make the euro survive the next economic crisis.

Box 12.2 Firehoses for the Eurozone Crisis: The Six-Pack, Two-Pack, and Fiscal Compact

Enacted in 1997, the SGP attempts to coordinate national fiscal policies within the eurozone. It includes a preventive arm (setting out the acceptable limits for public debt and budget deficits) and a corrective arm (setting out the actions member states need to undertake if they do not meet these limits, as well as the steps the Commission can enact against countries which fail to take action).

Although the SGP was amended in 2005 to meet objections that its rules needed to be more flexible for member states in different stages of an economic cycle, the crisis in the eurozone exposed some serious weaknesses in both the preventive and corrective arms. More specifically, how the SGP's public debt and budget deficits were defined and operationalized, how member states' compliance to SGP rules were monitored, and how sanctions in the corrective arm were carried out proved to be woefully inadequate to the scope of the crisis. Consequently, the SGP was reformed in 2011 with the "six-pack," which includes five regulations and one directive covering all EU member states; a "two-pack" covering only the countries in the eurozone; and the Treaty on Stability, Coordination and Governance in the Economic and Monetary Union, informally known as the "fiscal compact" (for the fiscal policy provisions of the treaty). The fiscal compact was signed in 2012 by all member states of the EU except the Czech Republic and the UK, both of which objected to more EU interference in national fiscal policies.

Provisions in the six-pack, two-pack, and fiscal compact compel member states to enshrine the rules of the SGP into national law (preferably through a constitutional amendment); allow the European Court of Justice to impose financial sanctions upon states that do not do this; establish a more frequent and detailed reporting of states' economic and fiscal situation to the EU, including submitting draft budgets to the Commission and Eurogroup (a move critics see as empowering the EU to force budget cuts in member states); and scheduling additional EU summits to discuss economic cooperation and coordination. All member states (as part of the six-pack) are also required to participate in the European Semester, discussed earlier.

COHESION POLICY: BUILDING A LEVEL PLAYING FIELD

The EU may be one of the wealthiest regions in the world, but – as in the US – levels of wealth and opportunity are unequal. Not only are there significant economic and social disparities within most of its member states, but there are also disparities from one state to another. The scale of the problem ballooned with eastern enlargement, which brought into the EU new member states suffering the effects of decades of underinvestment and state economic control. The differences are glaring: using the comparative measure of per capita GDP (EU = 100), differences at the end of 2018 within the EU-28 ranged from 261 in Luxembourg to 51 in Bulgaria (see Figure 12.1).

Generally speaking, the wealthiest parts of the EU are in the north central area, particularly in and around the "golden triangle" between London, Dortmund, and Milan, while the poorest parts are the eastern, southern, and western peripheries, from the Baltic states down

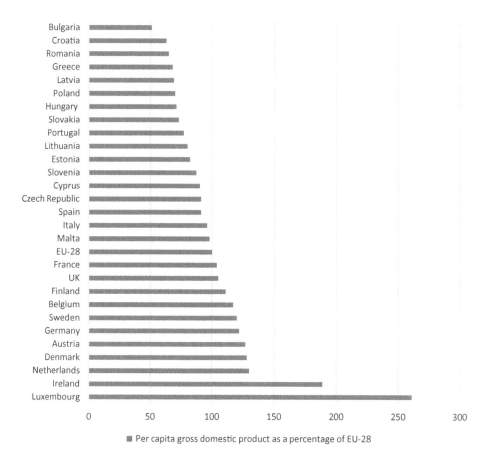

FIGURE 12.1 Differences in Economic Wealth.

Source: Eurostat, at https://ec.europa.eu/eurostat/statistics-explained/index.php/GDP_per_capita,_consumption_per_capita_and_price_level_indices, accessed December 19, 2019.

Note
Figures are for 2018.

to Cyprus and Greece, and across southern Italy to Spain, Portugal, and up to western Ireland and western Scotland. The EU's marginal areas are relatively poor for different reasons: some are depressed agricultural areas with little industry and high unemployment; some are declining industrial areas with outdated plants; others are geographically isolated from the prosperity and opportunity offered by bigger markets; and most suffer relatively low levels of education and health care and have underdeveloped infrastructure, especially roads and utilities.

Cohesion policy, as defined in the Single European Act, is aimed at "reducing disparities between the various regions and the backwardness of the least-favoured regions."[14] One of the core goals of this policy therefore has been to bring the poorer member states closer to the level of their wealthier partners for the purpose of a smoother functioning single market. In addition to this obvious economic benefit from spreading the largesse, there is an important psychological element to this effort: investments made by the EU in the poorer parts of the member states can help the citizens of those states more clearly see some of the benefits of EU membership, as well as capitalizing on the opportunities provided to wealthier states by building new markets.[15] Five main financial instruments, which together comprise the European Structural and Investment Funds, serve cohesion policy:

- The European Regional Development Fund, which directs funds to the poorest parts of the EU, invests in support for underdeveloped areas and inner cities, financing infrastructure, job creation, and aid for small firms.
- The European Social Fund, designed to promote employment and worker mobility, combats long-term unemployment and helps workers adapt to technological changes.
- The Cohesion Fund, set up in 1992 under the terms of Maastricht to compensate poorer states (in practice, Greece, Ireland, Portugal, and Spain) for the costs of tightening environmental regulations and to provide financial assistance for transport projects. Cyprus, Malta, and the Eastern European members have been added to the list of eligible countries, while Spain is being phased out.
- The European Agricultural Fund for Rural Development, created in 2006, was established to help modernize farming, diversify rural economies and develop rural areas, foster a higher level of food quality, and help to offset the costs of EU policies in the agricultural sector.
- The European Maritime and Fisheries Fund fosters sustainable development of coastal fishing areas and helps fishermen affected by EU policies designed to control overfishing.

The EU also has several other funds that are more specifically focused on particular problems or market areas, including:

- The European Union Solidarity Fund, created in 2002 in response to serious floods in Austria, the Czech Republic, France, and Germany, supports the EU in its efforts to respond quickly to natural disasters by helping with the costs of restoring infrastructure, providing temporary shelter, funding rescue services, and protecting the EU's cultural heritage.
- The European Globalisation Adjustment Fund, created in 2007, is designed to provide support for workers in the competitive global job market and to aid businesses affected by globalization in restructuring and rebuilding their competitiveness. The fund has been particularly targeted at those in the automobile, mobile phone, furniture, and textile and clothing industries.

Economies, of course, are complex entities that even economists do not fully understand, so the long-range effects of these kinds of investments are not always certain, and reducing the differentials is as much a function of sensible economic policies, changes in the wider economic environment, and the attitudes of individuals toward the creation and accumulation of wealth as it is of the redistribution of wealth. Furthermore, it is often impossible to ascertain which actions have resulted in particular effects. For example, the story of Ireland's remarkable economic transformation (the "Celtic Tiger") prior to the eurozone crisis was often touted as evidence of the possibilities of EU cohesion policy, but EU investments were only part of the formula. The prospects of similar investments bringing change to Greece were undermined there by the failure of the government to reduce its stake in major utilities, by inefficient bureaucratic procedures that discouraged the creation of new business, and by job protection policies that handicapped women and younger workers, something that became even more apparent as Greece slid into its debt crisis.[16] If Eastern Europe is to benefit fully from EU regional policy, then a change in domestic political and economic attitudes is just as important as investment from the wealthier EU states.

The spending priorities of these funds – who gets what and how much – were once based on dividing the regions of the EU into three categories known as Objectives 1, 2, and 3. These now have different names, even if the goals are largely the same.

- The Convergence Objective (formerly Objective 1) targets member states and regions with a per capita GDP of 75 percent or less of the EU average that are suffering from low levels of investment, higher than average unemployment rates, a lack of services for businesses and individuals, and poor basic infrastructure. Before eastern enlargement, they were mainly on the margins of the EU-15: Greece, southern Italy, Sardinia and Corsica, Spain, Portugal, Ireland, western Scotland, northern Finland, and eastern Germany. Yet except for a few sparsely populated areas in Scandinavia, the Convergence Objective has now moved east, with the region accounting for about 80 percent of spending for all of the funds. In addition to these criteria, this fund also highlights innovation and adaptability to economic and social change.
- The Regional Competitiveness and Employment Objective (formerly Objective 2) focuses on areas suffering from high unemployment, job losses, and industrial decline – mainly in older industrial regions undergoing economic change, rural areas facing a decline in traditional activities, and coastal areas with falling income from fisheries. This objective targets economically and socially troubled regions and tries to strengthen the attractiveness of these areas to investment (and thus employment).
- The Territorial Cooperation Objective (formerly Objective 3) attempts to encourage cooperation between European regions and the finding of common solutions to common development issues. This objective accounts for only a fraction of the total structural funds spent by the EU.

Whether the structural funds make much of a difference in reducing regional disparities is an open question. An independent report commissioned by the Prodi Commission and published in 2003 concluded that there was little hard evidence that the structural funds had made a significant impact in closing the wealth and competitiveness gap.[17] Although the Commission itself disagreed, the focus of regional policy was shifted to the current structure of funds and objectives. On the other hand, some have argued that although there has clearly been some waste and duplication of EU resources, the structural funds have helped reduce the income gap between rich and poor states.[18]

QUESTIONS TO CONSIDER

1 The North American Free Trade Association – and now the US–Mexico–Canada agreement (discussed briefly in Chapter 1) – and the EU remain very different entities. What kinds of physical, fiscal, and technical barriers would need to be overcome to achieve something like a single market made up of the US, Canada, and Mexico? Would this be desirable?

2 Why do some Eastern European countries remain enthusiastic about membership in the eurozone while others are more skeptical? What are the advantages or disadvantages it might bring them?

3 What is the purpose of having a cohesion policy? Does it make economic or political sense or would the EU be better off using its resources for other purposes?

NOTES

1 Anthony Wallace, "Completing the Single Market: The Lisbon Strategy," in *Developments in the European Union 2*, 2nd ed., edited by Maria Green Cowles and Desmond Dinan (New York: Palgrave Macmillan, 2004).

2 A proposed 2004 services directive (popularly known as the "Bolkestein Directive" after the commissioner who issued it, Fritz Bolkestein) sparked vehement pushback for its attempt to apply the country-of-origin principle to the service sector. Critics charged that it would allow service workers from low-regulation, low-wage member states to undercut the service sectors of more developed EU states. Crystallized in the image of the "Polish Plumber" – the symbol of the predatory low-wage worker – the directive was ultimately significantly weakened.

3 See Andrew Higgins, "Europe's Plan for GPS Limps to Crossroads," *New York Times*, February 6, 2013, at www.nytimes.com/2013/02/07/world/europe/europes-galileo-gps-plan-limps-to-crossroads.html, accessed March 1, 2013, and Palko Karasz, "Europe Billed Galileo as Its Answer to GPS. It's Been Mostly Down for Days," *New York Times*, July 16, 2019, at www.nytimes.com/2019/07/16/world/europe/galileo-outage.html, accessed October 17, 2019.

4 The European Commission, "2020 Energy Strategy," at https://ec.europa.eu/energy/en/topics/energy-strategy-and-energy-union/2020-energy-strategy, accessed October 18, 2019.

5 Steven Erlanger, "Pipelines from Russia Cross Political Lines," *New York Times*, October 7, 2019, at www.nytimes.com/2019/10/07/business/energy-environment/gas-nord-stream-pipeline.html, accessed October 15, 2019.

6 European Commission figures quoted in Loukas Tsoukalis, *The New European Economy Revisited: The Politics and Economics of Integration*, 3rd ed., 110 (Oxford: Oxford University Press, 1997).

7 Michelle Cini and Lee McGowan, *Competition Policy in the European Union* (London: Macmillan Press, 1998); Stephen Wilks, "Competition Policy: Towards an Economic Constitution," in *Policy-Making in the European Union*, 6th ed., edited by Helen Wallace, Mark A. Pollack, and Alasdair R. Young), 133–156 (New York: Oxford University Press, 2010).

8 See T.R. Reid, *The United States of Europe: The New Superpower and the End of American Supremacy*, 88–91, 94–105 (New York: Penguin, 2004).

9 See Mark Scoot and James Kanter, "Google Faces New Round of Antitrust Charges in Europe," *New York Times*, July 14, 2016, at www.nytimes.com/2016/07/15/technology/google-european-union-antitrust-charges.html, accessed August 1, 2016; and Mark Scott, "Google Fined Record $2.7 Billion in EU Antitrust Ruling," *New York Times*, June 27, 2017, at www.nytimes.com/2017/06/27/technology/eu-google-fine.html, accessed July 10, 2017.

10 *Economist, The*, "An Awfully Big Adventure," April 11, 1998.

11 Loukas Tsoukalis, "Monetary Policy and the Euro," in *Governing Europe*, edited by Jack Hayward and Anand Menon, 334–335 (Oxford: Oxford University Press, 2003).

12 For a discussion about the implications of the stability and growth pact, see Madeleine O. Hosli, *The Euro: A Concise Introduction to European Monetary Integration*, 67–69 (Boulder: Lynne Rienner, 2005).

13 "Prodi Disowns 'Stupid' Stability Pact," *Guardian*, October 18, 2002, at www.theguardian.com/business/2002/oct/18/theeuro.europeanunion, accessed October 15, 2019.

14 European Commission, "Cohesion Policy," at https://ec.europa.eu/regional_policy/archive/faq/q1/index_en.cfm, accessed October 16, 2019.

15 For a detailed review of the structure and effects of cohesion policy in the early 2000s, see European Commission, *Growing Regions, Growing Europe: Fourth Report on Economic and Social Cohesion* (Luxembourg: Office for Official Publications of the European Communities, 2007).

16 OECD, *Economic Survey of Greece 2005: The Fiscal Challenge*, July 7, 2005, at www.oecd.org/greece/economicsurveyofgreece2005thefiscalchallenge.htm, accessed July 10, 2005.

17 André Sapir et al., *An Agenda for a Growing Europe: Making the EU Economic System Deliver* (Oxford: Oxford University Press, 2004).

18 Robert A. Pastor, *Toward a North American Community*, 59–62 (Washington, DC: Institute for International Economics, 2001).

BIBLIOGRAPHY

Bachtler, John, Joaquim Oliveira Martins, Peter Wostner, and Piotr Zuber, *Towards Cohesion Policy 4.0: Structural Transformation and Inclusive Growth* (London: Routledge, 2019).

Baldwin, Richard E. and Charles Wyplosz, *The Economics of European Integration*, 5th ed. (New York: McGraw Hill, 2015).

Cini, Michell and Lee McGowan, *Competition Policy in the European Union* (London: Macmillan Press, 1998).

Economist, The, "An Awfully Big Adventure," April 11, 1998.

European Commission, "Cohesion Policy," at https://ec.europa.eu/regional_policy/archive/faq/q1/index_en.cfm, accessed October 16, 2019.

European Commission, *Growing Regions, Growing Europe: Fourth Report on Economic and Social Cohesion* (Luxembourg: Office for Official Publications of the European Communities, 2007).

European Commission, *2020 Energy Strategy*, at https://ec.europa.eu/energy/en/topics/energy-strategy-and-energy-union/2020-energy-strategy, accessed October 18, 2019.

Erlanger, Steven, "Pipelines from Russia Cross Political Lines," *New York Times*, October 7, 2019, at www.nytimes.com/2019/10/07/business/energy-environment/gas-nord-stream-pipeline.html, accessed October 15, 2019.

Guardian, "Prodi Disowns 'Stupid' Stability Pact," October 18, 2002, at www.theguardian.com/business/2002/oct/18/theeuro.europeanunion, accessed October 15, 2019.

Higgins, Andrew, "Europe's Plan for GPS Limps to Crossroads," *New York Times*, February 6, 2013, at www.nytimes.com/2013/02/07/world/europe/europes-galileo-gps-plan-limps-to-crossroads.html, accessed March 1, 2013.

Hosli, Madeline O., *The Euro: A Concise Introduction to European Monetary Integration* (Boulder: Lynne Rienner, 2005).

Karasz, Palka, "Europe Billed Galileo as Its Answer to GPS. It's Been Mostly Down for Days," *New York Times*, July 16, 2019, at www.nytimes.com/2019/07/16/world/europe/galileo-outage.html, accessed October 17, 2019.

Marsh, David, *The Euro: The Politics of the New Global Currency* (New Haven, CT: Yale University Press, 2010).

Matthijs, Matthias and Mark Blyth, eds., *The Future of the Euro* (Oxford: Oxford University Press, 2015).

OECD, *Economic Survey of Greece 2005: The Fiscal Challenge*, July 7, 2005, at www.oecd.org/greece/economicsurveyofgreece2005thefiscalchallenge.htm, accessed July 10, 2005.

Pastor, Robert A., *Toward a North American Community* (Washington, DC: Institute for International Economics, 2001).

Reid, T.R., *The United States of Europe: The New Superpower and the End of American Supremacy* (New York: Penguin, 2004).

Sapir, André, Aghion Giuseppe Bertola, Martin Hellwig, Jean Pisani-Ferry, Dariusz Rosati, José Viñals, Helen Wallace, Marco Buti, Mario Nava, and Peter M. Smith, *An Agenda for a Growing Europe: Making the EU Economic System Deliver* (Oxford: Oxford University Press, 2004).

Scott, Mark, and James Kanter, "Google Faces New Round of Antitrust Charges in Europe," *New York Times*, July 14, 2016, at www.nytimes.com/2016/07/15/technology/google-european-union-antitrust-charges.html, accessed August 1, 2016.

Scott, Mark, "Google Fined Record $2.7 Billion in EU Antitrust Ruling," *New York Times*, June 27, 2017, at www.nytimes.com/2017/06/27/technology/eu-google-fine.html, accessed July 10, 2017.

Stiglitz, Joseph E., *The Euro. How a Common Currency Threatens the Future of Europe* (New York/London: W.W. Norton & Company, 2016).

Tsoukalis, Loukas, *The New European Economy Revisited: The Politics and Economics of Integration*, 3rd ed. (Oxford: Oxford University Press, 1997).

Tsoukalis, Loukas, "Monetary Policy and the Euro," in *Governing Europe*, edited by Jack Hayward and Anand Menon, 334–335 (Oxford: Oxford University Press, 2003).

Wallace, Anthony, "Completing the Single Market: The Lisbon Strategy," in *Developments in the European Union*, 2nd ed., edited by Maria Green Cowles and Desmond Dinan, 100–125 (New York: Palgrave Macmillan, 2004).

Wilks, Stephen, "Competition Policy: Towards an Economic Constitution," in *Policy-Making in the European Union*, 6th ed., edited by Helen Wallace, Mark A. Pollack, and Alasdair R. Young, 133–156 (New York: Oxford University Press, 2010).

FURTHER READING

Richard E. Baldwin and Charles Wyplosz, *The Economics of European Integration*, 5th ed. (New York: McGraw Hill, 2015).

> A student-friendly introduction to EU economic integration, with separate chapters on the Common Agricultural Policy, trade policy, competition policy, monetary union, fiscal policy, and the eurozone crisis.

John Bachtler, Joaquim Oliveira Martins, Peter Wostner, and Piotr Zuber, *Towards Cohesion Policy 4.0: Structural Transformation and Inclusive Growth* (London: Routledge, 2019).

> An examination of the history of successes and failures of regional policy and an argument for policy changes necessary for the future Cohesion Policy.

David Marsh, *The Euro: The Politics of the New Global Currency* (New Haven, CT: Yale University Press, 2010); Matthias Matthijs and Mark Blyth, eds., *The Future of the Euro* (Oxford: Oxford University Press, 2015); Joseph E. Stiglitz, *The Euro. How a Common Currency Threatens the Future of Europe* (New York/London: W.W. Norton & Company, 2016).

> Three studies of the euro and its problems, with Stiglitz being particularly harsh in his criticisms.

CHAPTER 13

Agricultural and Environmental Policy

CHAPTER OVERVIEW

- The EU is one of the world's export powerhouses when it comes to agricultural products despite having only a small proportion of its population engaged in farming. The EU's approach to agriculture is defined by its Common Agricultural Policy, or CAP.
- For decades CAP was essentially a system of expensive, wasteful, protectionist, and controversial subsidies to farmers. Since the late 1990s, CAP has been fundamentally reformed, the results being significantly fewer EU funds spent on agriculture overall and the establishment of more attention given within agricultural policy to environmentally friendly and sustainable farming practices. However, some fundamental problems still plague CAP, particularly in the form of crony capitalism in several new member states.
- EU environmental policy has not only been widely welcomed and supported by the public, but has also assumed a much more prominent position within the EU. Indeed, the EU has become a world leader in the abatement of waste, the regulation of chemicals, and the reduction of greenhouse gases.

Except for those dealing with developing countries, textbooks on national politics rarely make much mention of agriculture. While important, to be sure (because we all need nutrition), in most liberal democracies agriculture plays only a small part in economic activity and is rarely a lead story, if only because so few people are employed in farming. But the situation was for many years quite different in the EU. Agriculture used to be a prominent issue – arguably the most important issue – in the EU. Indeed, after the Treaty of Rome the EU's CAP became one of the signature – albeit controversial – achievements in the expansion of the EU's scope and power. CAP's goals were to create a single market for agricultural products and to assure European Economic Community (EEC) farmers guaranteed prices for their produce. The logic of developing a single agricultural market had implications for functional spillover (see Chapter 1) as the EU saw the need to harmonize standards, be responsive to consumer safety issues, and take account of growing environmental concerns.

For decades agriculture topped the EU budget (it still swallowed about $64 billion/€59 billion in spending in 2018). It was also controversial: instead of operating on the principles of competition and free trade, it was protectionist, interventionist, and anti-market. This approach drew criticism not only from the member states but also from the EU's major trading partners, such as the US. *The Economist* was once moved to describe EU agricultural policy as "the single most idiotic system of economic mismanagement" ever devised by rich Western countries.[1] In the last decade much has changed in the EU. Although CAP still soaks up a healthy chunk of the EU budget, enlargement, global trade agreements, rising costs, and growing environmental concerns have spurred a series of fundamental reforms in the way in which CAP operates. However, some fundamental problems still plague CAP, chief among them corruption in the way in which CAP distributes its subsidies.

In contrast to agriculture, the environment represents one of the newest areas of EU policy making. Although EU initiatives on environmental policy have been relatively small in budget terms, since the 1980s environmental policy has assumed a more prominent position on the EU agenda and is a policy area that most Europeans agree is best addressed at the EU rather than the national level. The Treaty of Rome made ambiguous reference to promoting "harmonious development" and to raising living standards, but national governments in the 1950s were barely aware of the need to include environmental planning in their calculations. Later, concerns over the extent to which different environmental standards distorted competition and complicated progress on the building of a common market were the initial driver of environmental policy.

Since those narrow-sighted days, environmental issues have climbed up the EU agenda and the EU today is recognized as a world leader in this area. A series of environmental action programs in the 1970s and 1980s provided more consistency and direction, and the Single European Act gave the environment legal status within the Community. Maastricht, Amsterdam, and Lisbon placed further emphasis on sustainable development and environmental protection as part of "harmonious and balanced" economic growth, and institutional changes elevated the voice of public opinion (through the European Parliament) in designing environmental policy and introduced qualified majority voting on most environmental law and policy. The centrality of sustainability has been especially prominent in agricultural policy, where significant reforms over the last decade have placed environmentally sensitive practices at the heart of the EU's approach. Most recently, new public concerns about climate change have magnified the urgency of effective environmental policies.

AGRICULTURAL POLICY

At the time the Treaties of Rome were being negotiated, agriculture sat high on the domestic policy agendas of Western European governments. Not only were the disruptions of war and the memories of postwar food shortages and rationing still fresh in their minds, but agriculture still accounted for about 12 percent of the gross national product (GNP) of the Six (the founding member states) and for the employment of about 20 percent of the workforce.[2] Five factors account for agriculture's special perch.

First, agriculture was a key element in the tradeoff between France and Germany when the EEC was first discussed.[3] France was concerned that the single market would benefit German industry while providing the French economy with relatively few advantages, a possibility that was reflected in the statistics: agriculture accounted for 12 percent of GNP in France (compared with 8 percent in West Germany) and employed nearly 25 percent of the workforce (compared with 15 percent in West Germany).[4] Concerns that the single market would fall short on benefits to its farmers encouraged the French government to insist on a protectionist system.

Second, agricultural prices tend to fluctuate more than prices for most other goods, and since Europeans spend about one-quarter of their incomes on food, those fluctuations can reverberate throughout the economy. Price increases can contribute to inflation, while price decreases can force farmers to go deeper into debt, potentially leading to bankruptcies and unemployment. Exacerbating the problem of maintaining minimum incomes, mechanization has reduced the number of Europeans working in farming. Accordingly, it was argued in the

1950s that subsidies would help encourage people to stay in the rural areas and discourage them from moving to towns and cities and perhaps adding to unemployment problems.

Third, self-sufficiency in food has been a primary factor in determining the direction of agricultural policy. World War II opened Europeans' eyes to how much they depended on imported food and how prone those imports were to disruption in the event of war and other crises. Before the war, for example, the UK imported about 70 percent of its food, including wheat from the US and Canada, beef from Argentina, and sugarcane from the Caribbean. Thanks in part to a massive program of agricultural intensification launched after the war, the UK now imports less than one-third of its food. The pattern has been echoed across the EU, which has experienced a large decline in agricultural imports from outside the EU and a growth in trade among the member states.

Fourth, the EU is an agricultural export powerhouse, with exports in 2018 worth €138 billion.[5] With so much wealth and profit at stake, it is no brainer that European farmers are anxious to continue to protect their opportunities.

Fifth, although the farm vote in the EU is generally much smaller than it was during the mid-1960s, it is not insubstantial, and its balance initially changed with the 2004 enlargement. In the old EU-15, the number of people employed in agriculture has plummeted from about 25 percent of the population in 1950 to less than 5 percent today, but there are variations across countries: from 9 to 11 percent in Greece and Portugal, to around 4 percent in Austria and Finland, to less than 2 percent in the UK and Belgium. For many of the newer members of the EU, meanwhile, the percentage of the population engaged in agriculture is higher than in Western Europe but has plunged in recent years (with the exception of Romania, where it remains at a high level, about 23 percent).[6]

Farmers form an essential part of the rural fabric of most EU states and support a substantial number of people and services in small towns, villages, and rural areas. These populations add up to a sizable proportion of the vote, which no political party can afford to ignore, especially because there is little organized resistance to the agricultural or rural lobbies at either the national or the EU level. Farmers in the richer EU states have also traditionally had strong unions working for them; in addition to national unions, more than 150 EU-wide agricultural organizations have emerged, many of which directly lobby the EU.

France is a textbook case for the centrality of farming in a number of member states. The farming population there fell between 1950 and 2000 from 31 percent of the total population to just 1.8 percent,[7] yet farmers have long had strong influence over the French government, which has lobbied on their behalf in the halls and corridors of Brussels. French farmers have been keen on European agricultural subsidies and have developed a reputation for taking to the streets when they feel that their interests are threatened. To that point, they have used tactics such as letting cattle loose in local government buildings, blocking main highways with tractors, dumping farm waste on Parisian avenues, blocking the Eurotunnel to the UK (as part of a protest in 2000 against rising fuel prices), and even ransacking a McDonald's restaurant in protest against US duties on French cheeses (imposed after the EU banned imports of American hormone-treated beef).

The influence of the farm lobby in French domestic politics lies in the fact that just under 20 percent of agricultural production in the EU comes from France.[8] The role of the farm lobby must also be seen in the context of the French national psyche. Even though three of every four French citizens live in towns or cities, the rural ideal still has a nostalgic hold on the sentiments of many, as does the idea that France is still a great power. Even urban voters are prepared to defend the rural ideal, to which any attempts to reform European agricultural policy are seen as a threat. Recent developments suggest that the influence of farmers on domestic politics – and on EU agricultural policy – is declining. Many small farmers are living in poverty, thousands leave the land every year to look for other work, and the farm lobby has been unable to halt reforms to EU agricultural policy.

The core of the EU's approach toward agriculture is the CAP. Until recently, CAP was essentially a system of agricultural subsidies, with the following goals outlined in the Treaty of Rome: increased agricultural productivity, a "fair standard of living" for the farming community, stable markets, regular supplies, and "reasonable" prices for consumers. A landmark conference convened in Stresa, Italy, in July 1958, agreed on how these goals would be achieved: a single market in agricultural produce, "Community preference" (a polite term for protectionism aimed at giving EU produce priority over imported produce), and joint financing (the costs of CAP would be met by the Community rather than by individual member states). In practice, CAP guaranteed farmers throughout the EU the same minimum price for their produce, regardless of volume and prevailing levels of supply and demand, and all member states shared the financial burden of this subsidization.

Box 13.1 A New Focus on Sustainability? Reforming the Common Fisheries Policy

In addition to CAP, the EU also has a Common Fisheries Policy (CFP), the main goal of which has been to help support and keep viable the fishing industry in the member states by preventing overfishing, fostering sustainable fishing practices, and ensuring a sufficient quality and quantity for European consumers. Reforms over the years have promoted sustainability and attempted to minimize the impact of fishing on marine ecosystems by setting national quotas for catches and establishing rules on the type of fishing equipment used.

Fisheries policy was never quite as controversial nor as headline grabbing as agriculture, and the fishing industry employs only about 400,000 people.[9] However, the health of the fishing industry is a key part of life in coastal communities all around the EU; not only does the EU have the world's largest maritime territory, but coastal areas are home to 60 percent of its population, and they account for more than 40 percent of EU gross domestic product. Hence the issue has important economic implications for some of Europe's poorer regions.

Disputes over fishing grounds in European waters have occasionally led to bitter confrontations among Europe's neighbors. A prime example is the infamous cod wars of the 1960s between the UK and Iceland over access to fisheries in the North Atlantic. Similarly, in 1984 French patrol boats fired on Spanish trawlers operating inside the Community's 200-mile limit, and more than two dozen Spanish trawlers were intercepted off the coast of Ireland. Spain's fishing fleet dwarfed that of the entire European Community (EC) fleet at the time, and fishing rights dominated Spain's negotiations to join the EC. Spanish fishing boats became an issue in domestic UK politics in 1994 when Euroskeptics in the governing Conservative Party used the Spanish presence in traditional UK waters to complain about the detrimental effects of UK membership in the EU.

Efforts to resolve competing claims to fishing grounds and develop an equitable management plan for Community fisheries resulted in agreement on the CFP in 1983, which has since been modified several times. Among other measures, the CFP has attempted to regulate fisheries by imposing national quotas (Total Allowable Catches) on the take of Atlantic and North Sea fish and by regulating fishing areas and equipment. Problems with the enforcement of the CFP spurred the creation in

2005 of the Fisheries Control Agency, set up to pool EU and national fisheries control systems and resources.

However, serious problems plagued the CFP's quota system. For one thing, it has led to particularly distasteful and wasteful practices such as "discards," whereby (dead) fish are thrown back into the sea to avoid exceeding the quota, with some estimates suggesting that the discard in some EU fisheries approaches 70 percent of the total recorded catch![10] The CFP's shortcomings prompted then Maritime and Fisheries Commissioner Maria Damanaki in 2011 to declare CFP a "failure."[11] As a result, the CFP for the period 2014–2020 introduced several reforms, including a phase-in of a discard ban (for different species of fish), the creation of a maximum sustainable yield policy, and a new structural fund to support these reforms, the European Maritime and Fisheries Fund.

Costs have been borne by two funds, the most important of which is the European Agricultural Guarantee Fund (EAGF), created in 1962 and until recently the single biggest item in the EU budget; reforms to CAP brought the proportion of agricultural spending in the EC/EU budget down from about 75 percent in 1970 to its present figure. The EAGF protects markets and prices by buying and storing surplus produce and encouraging agricultural exports. Most of the money goes to producers of dairy products (the EU accounts for 60 percent of global dairy production) and to producers of cereals, oils and fats, beef, veal, and sugar. The other main fund associated with CAP, The European Agricultural Fund for Rural Development (EAFRD, the so-called "Second Pillar of CAP") finances the EU's contribution toward rural development programs.

In terms of increasing productivity, stabilizing markets, securing supplies, and protecting European farmers from the fluctuations in market prices, CAP has been a success. Encouraged by guaranteed prices, and helped by intensification and the increased use of fertilizers (EU farmers use nearly 2.5 times as much fertilizer per acre of land as US farmers), European agriculture has grown in leaps and bounds:

- European farmers have produced as much as possible from their land, with the result that production has shot up in virtually every area.
- The EU is self-sufficient in almost every product it can grow or produce in its climate (including wheat, barley, wine, meat, vegetables, and dairy products) and produces far more butter, cereals, beef, and sugar than it needs. The EU has become the world's largest exporter of sugar, eggs, poultry, and dairy products, accounting for nearly 12 percent of world food exports.
- Duplication has been reduced as member states have specialized in different products. Thus, the southern states encompass most of the permanent cropland while the northern states raise the most livestock.
- CAP has helped make farmers wealthier and their livelihoods more predictable and stable; farm incomes have grown at roughly the same rate as those in other economic sectors.

However, CAP became increasingly expensive as technological developments helped European farmers produce more food from less land, exceeding consumer demand for commodities such as butter, cereals, beef, and sugar. The EU tried to discourage production by subsidizing exports and by paying farmers not to produce food.

There were four specific problems emerged over the decades:

- EU farmers produced much more than the market could bear, so that excess production once had to be stockpiled in warehouses across the Community (the so-called butter mountains and wine lakes); much of the excess was sold cheaply to developing countries, undercutting farmers there and distorting the international marketplace.
- Stories of fraud and the abuse of CAP funds were rife, with rules encouraging farmers and suppliers to inflate production figures and even to claim subsidies for nonexistent stocks of food.[12]
- The income gap between rich and poor farmers in the EU was not reduced, and bigger, richer farms or agribusiness seemed to benefit the most.
- As CAP set artificially high prices for agricultural products, it upset consumers forced to pay inflated prices for the overproduction of food, which led in turn to greater skepticism about European integration. Meanwhile, environmentalists were unhappy about the way CAP encouraged the increased the use of chemical fertilizers and herbicides and encouraged farmers in wasteful practices.

Under the circumstances, the case for reform was glaring, but most suggestions came up against the resistance of farming lobbies and the governments over which they had the most influence.[13] Early efforts at reforming CAP included the Mansholt Plan of 1968, named for the incumbent European agriculture commissioner. Its main suggestion was that small farmers be encouraged to leave the land and farms be amalgamated into bigger and more efficient units, notions that were both vehemently opposed by small farmers in France and Germany. UK prime minister Margaret Thatcher brought new pressures for change during the early 1980s (although in truth she was concerned less with reforming CAP than with renegotiating UK contributions to the Community budget!). Her campaign to win a UK rebate drew new attention to the problem of agricultural overproduction, and by the late 1980s there was a general agreement on the need for reform.

Pressure for reform was increased by the international criticism leveled at CAP as the Community negotiated tariff reductions under the General Agreement on Tariffs and Trade (now the World Trade Organization, or WTO) and by the trade embargo imposed by the EC on Iraq during 1990–1991 (which caused a drop in export prices). In 1991 Agriculture Commissioner Ray MacSharry warned of the rising volume of stored agricultural produce and proposed replacing guaranteed prices with a system of direct payments to farmers if prices fell below a certain level while encouraging farmers to take land out of production (the "set-aside" system, whereby farmers would be compensated for subsidy reductions only if they took 15 percent of their land out of production).[14] In spite of the opposition of many farmers and their unions, the proposals were approved in 1992.

Pressures for change continued, however, fueled by continued pressure from major trading partners (particularly the US) but most especially by the prospect of increased CAP spending in new Eastern European member states. In the late 1990s, for example, it was estimated that while nearly one in five Poles worked in agriculture, half of them produced only enough to feed their families and contributed nothing to the broader market.[15] For the new members to receive immediate and unlimited access to CAP funding would likely have bankrupted the EU. At the same time, special efforts needed to be made to ensure that Eastern European governments and their farmers did not feel that they were being treated as second-class citizens. The compromise ultimately agreed on – and not met with great enthusiasm – was to allow Eastern European farmers a small but growing proportion of agricultural payments. Coming on top of the €22 billion ($31 billion) spent in 2000–2006 under a program called SAPARD (the Special

Accession Program for Agriculture and Rural Development, designed to help applicant countries prepare for CAP), a package worth €5.1 billion ($7.2 billion) was made available for 2004–2006, also ensuring that direct aid would be phased in over ten years, starting at 25 percent in 2004 and moving up in annual increments of 5 percent. In addition, a new fund – the EAFRD – was created in 2006 to help modernize farming (see Chapter 12 for more details).

In 1998, Agriculture Commissioner Franz Fischler introduced a sea change in CAP: his proposals shifted away from compensating farmers when prices dipped below a certain level toward instead subsidizing them for certain kinds of production. Fischler proposed price cuts on beef, cereals, and milk, the end of set-aside schemes, more environmental management conditions to be attached to payments to farmers, and more investment in rural development generally. The core idea behind these reforms was "decoupling," or breaking the link between subsidies and production, with the goal of encouraging farmers to produce for the market rather than for EU subsidies. A follow-up set of reforms agreed to in 2003 further advanced these goals. According to Fischler, the reforms left CAP "virtually unrecognizable from the days of old."[16]

Indeed, since 2005, the link between subsidies to farmers and the amount they produce has been broken, and farmers instead receive a single payment. Intervention prices on milk powder, butter, and other products have been reduced and direct payments for bigger farms cut. In 2008, the EU undertook a review of agricultural policy (the so-called health check) and made additional changes (such as abolishing milk quotas) as well as simplifying the new CAP system and decoupling CAP even more from compensation for production. More significantly, after a three-year review period of the entire CAP program in 2013 the EU proposed a new series of steps taken toward sustainable farming practices and environmental concerns as well as toward the modernization of farms in the newer EU member states. At that time, more flexibility was also introduced into CAP: the removal of production restraints for sugar, dairy, and wine so that farmers could respond to market changes, more room for member states to decide on how to spend CAP funds (big farms v. small, young farmers v. established ones, etc.), the phase-out of milk quotas, and the establishment of a new crisis reserve fund to respond to external threats to the agricultural sector.[17]

Overall, CAP reforms over the last decade and a half have reduced costs, severed the tie between production and income, and evolved to more environmentally sustainable agricultural practices,[18] such as spending a healthy percentage of direct payment for the specific purpose of improved use of natural resources. However, some critics have charged that these reforms have still not addressed some fundamental problems with CAP, pointing to several issues. First, recent reforms have primarily focused on how farmers receive payments, not the issue of subsidization itself, and a surprisingly high percentage of direct payments from CAP go to non-farming landowners or agri-business rather than to small farmers. This problem is particularly pronounced in some Eastern European member states where it is coupled with issues of corruption. For example, a *New York Times* investigation in the fall of 2019 found that widespread corruption existed in Hungary, the Czech Republic, Bulgaria, and Slovakia.[19] In Hungary, cronies of Prime Minister Viktor Orbán have squeezed small farmers, benefitting from the selling off of former state-owned farms through sweetheart deals from the government and forcing many small farmers out of business; in the Czech Republic, Prime Minister Andrej Babis changed rules that make it easier for large farming businesses – which Babis largely owns – rather than small farms to collect EU subsidies; in Bulgaria and Slovakia, the agricultural sector is dominated by a small number of large businesses, some of which are connected to organized crime. Since the distribution of EU agricultural subsidies within a member state have been at the discretion of that member state, the EU has been unable (critics would say unwilling) to tackle these problems, although this may change with the new Commission.[20]

PHOTO 13.1 Former Commissioner of Agriculture and Rural Development, Dacian Cioloş.
Source: © European Union, 2013, EC – Audiovisual Service.

Critics have also noted that although the EU had earlier floated the idea of eliminating export subsidies as well as a reduction in import duties for such goods in the international trade talks, this has been pushed into the future.[21] The EU's championing of free trade stands in stark contrast to its continued trade-distorting practices in the agricultural sector. Finally, it should be underscored that CAP still has a high price tag: it spends around $65 billion a year subsidizing agriculture, with many Eastern European states benefitting enormously.[22] On the revenue side of the ledger, after Brexit EU coffers will undoubtedly take a hit, with unforeseen implications for the budget – and therefore for the total cost balance of CAP. The process of reforming EU agricultural policy is far from over.[23]

ENVIRONMENTAL POLICY

Despite no specific mention of the environment in the Treaty of Rome, the ambiguous goal of "an accelerated raising of the standard of living" could be interpreted as opening the door to the environmental initiatives that came later. The Community agreed on several pieces of environmental law during the late 1950s and 1960s, dealing with issues such as the protection of workers from radiation and the management of dangerous chemicals. But these laws were prompted by the drive to build a single market and were incidental to the Community's overriding economic goals. As Delreux and Happaerts have noted, the early years of the Community's environmental policies "served economic purposes, especially the creation of the common market."[24] It was only during the 1970s that the EEC began to think about a broader environmental policy, encouraged by new public and political interest in the environment, arising in turn out of a combination of improved scientific understanding, several headline-making environmental disasters, new affluence among Western middle classes, and growing concern about quality-of-life issues.[25]

Changes in public and political opinion culminated in the landmark 1972 United Nations Conference on the Human Environment in Stockholm, which drew broader political and public attention to the problems of the environment for the first time, prompting the creation of national environmental agencies and a growth in the volume of national environmental law. In October 1972, just three months after Stockholm, the EEC heads of government meeting in Paris agreed to the need for an environmental policy, as a result of which the Commission adopted its first Environmental Action Programme (EAP) in late 1973. Subsequent EAPs came into force in 1977, 1982, 1987, 1993, and 2002, the most recent (the seventh) running until 2020.

The first two EAPs were based on taking preventive action and guarding against allowing different national policies to become barriers to building a common market. The Court of Justice made an important contribution in 1980 when – in response to a refusal by Italy to meet the deadline set by a directive on the biodegradability of detergents, on the grounds that the environment was not part of the policy competence of the Community – it argued that competition could be "appreciably distorted" without harmonization of environmental regulations.[26] States with weaker pollution laws, for example, had less of a financial and regulatory burden than those with stronger laws and might attract corporations wanting to build new factories with a minimum of built-in environmental safeguards.

The third EAP signaled a significant step forward in EU environmental policy, with a switch to a focus on environmental management as the basis of economic and social development. For the first time, environmental considerations were consciously factored in to other policy areas – notably agriculture, industry, energy, and transport – and were no longer subordinate to the goal of building a common market.[27] But these changes took place without amendments to the Treaty of Rome, so Community environmental policy lacked a clear legal basis and was technically unauthorized by the member states.[28] Additional complications arrived with enlargement to Greece, Portugal, and Spain, whose industries were relatively underdeveloped and whose environmental standards were relatively weak.

The accumulating problems finally received overdue attention via the Single European Act, which gave a legal basis to Community environmental policy and mandated environmental protection as a component of all EC policies. Maastricht provided further clarification by making "sustainable and non-inflationary growth respecting the environment" a fundamental goal of the EU, introducing qualified majority voting in the Council of Ministers on most environmental issues, and making environmental laws subject to codecisions by the European Parliament. The fifth EAP marked a sea change in the nature of EAPs, the first program with a substantive title ("Towards Sustainability") and incorporating a broader range of instruments in environmental policy. Amsterdam followed this precedent by listing sustainable development (discussed below) as one of the general goals of European integration. Finally, Lisbon specifically articulated within the treaty the core principles of European environmental policy.[29]

EU environmental policy has not covered the full range of issues usually dealt with by national-level policy (for example, it is barely active in land use management or forestry), but the number of environmental regulations and directions has increased dramatically over time (see Figure 13.1).

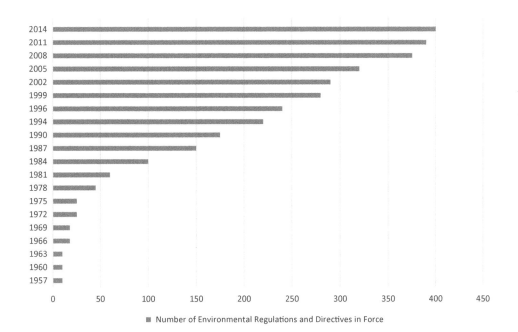

FIGURE 13.1 The Growth of Environmental Legislation in the EU.

Source: Eurex, adapted from Delreux and Happaerts, 2019.

In particular, it has been active on the following:

- *Water quality.* EU policy initially focused on public health and setting water quality standards for drinking and bathing water. Concerns about the aquatic environment hopped on the list with controls on the discharge of dangerous substances into inland and coastal waters. More recently there has been a strategic approach to water management, combining the different uses for which water needs to be protected.
- *Waste control.* Waste production from agriculture, mining, industry, and domestic households has prompted the EU to strive to reduce the amount produced, to encourage recycling and reuse, to improve controls on waste disposal, and to control the transport of wastes across national borders.
- *Air quality.* Air pollution was a latecomer to the agenda, with most key EU laws dating only from the late 1980s and based on setting uniform air quality standards or on controlling emissions from vehicles or industrial plants. EU laws now deal with controls on sulfur dioxide, lead, fine particles, nitrogen dioxide, benzene, carbon monoxide, and heavy metals.
- *Chemicals.* The control of dangerous chemicals and other substances has been at the heart of the single biggest body of EU environmental law, focusing on the handling of new chemicals, accidents at chemical plants, pesticides, and trade in dangerous chemicals.
- *Nature Protection and Biodiversity.* EU policy on the protection of wildlife and natural habitats has come mainly in response to the terms of international treaties, particularly those dealing with trade in endangered species and the protection of migratory species.
- *Noise pollution.* It is debatable whether or not noise is really an environmental issue, but this has not discouraged the EU from developing a large body of law aimed at making Europe a quieter place, and limiting noise from road vehicles, aircraft, compressors, tower cranes, welding generators, power generators, and concrete breakers.

- *Genetically modified organisms.* European consumers have been far more concerned than Americans about the genetic modification of plant-based food, an issue that has sparked conflict with the US. Genetic modification is widely used in this country (creating what critics like to call "Frankenfood"), and their potential export to the EU has become an issue in transatlantic trade discussions.

The central institutional body within the EU dealing with the environment is the European Environmental Agency (EEA). As discussed in Chapter 9, the EEA does not have regulatory power – indeed, there is no overall regulatory agency for the EU like the Environmental Protection Agency in the US – but is instead an information-gathering agency which assists the Commission in making proposals. In order to achieve its goal, the EEA receives data provided by the member states and aggregates this data through a trans-European network known as EIONET (European Environmental Information and Observation Network). Through EIONET, the EEA has been able to standardize environmental methodologies throughout the EU, thus sharpening the effectiveness of EU and national environmental policies.

Public opinion has driven EU action: Eurobarometer polls have consistently found that more than two-thirds of Europeans believe that decisions on the environment should be taken at the EU level rather than at the national level and that pollution is an urgent and immediate problem. Public interest in the environment has also been reflected in the election of members of Green political parties to the national legislatures of most member states, including Austria, Belgium, Finland, Germany, Greece, Ireland, Italy, Luxembourg, Portugal, and Sweden. Greens have also become members of coalition governments in several countries, including Belgium, Finland, France, Germany, and Italy, and have been elected to the European Parliament from more than a dozen EU states.

Much has been achieved by the EU, and policy in the EU is now driven more by the needs and effects of regional integration than by the priorities of the individual member states. But the results remain patchy, with continued concerns over issues such as air quality in the cities (particularly in Eastern Europe), mostly from heavy and growing concentrations of road traffic; the effects of intensive agriculture on natural habitats; the pollution of freshwater sources by sewage, pesticides, and industrial waste; and the lack of significant progress in the development of waste disposal policies.

Nevertheless, over the decades the EU has quietly built an impressive body of policies and laws on the environment. While this achievement has drawn relatively little public or political attention, the explosion of international interest being paid to a single issue, climate change, has magnified the importance of environmental issues for Europeans and hence for the EU (see Box 13.2). Scientists outlined the mechanics of the problem in the 1980s and, together with environmental interest groups, tried to draw the attention of political leaders. But it was only in the early years of the twenty-first century that it became a headline issue.

Climate change has been described as the ultimate global environmental issue, and the ability of environmental problems to cross national frontiers is well known, leading since the mid-1970s to a new emphasis on international responses to such problems as air pollution and the management of shared rivers. However, national governments have often been reluctant to take unilateral action for fear of losing comparative economic advantage, and unwilling to give significant powers to international organizations, such as the United Nations Environment Program, and to commit to ambitious goals under the terms of international environmental treaties. Regional integration – of which the EU is a textbook case – offers something of a solution to both dilemmas. As states become more dependent on trade and foreign investment and more inclined to reduce the barriers to trade, so the logic goes, they will be more inclined to eliminate any differences in environmental standards that may cause trade distortions, particularly if they know that their neighbors are moving in the same direction.

Box 13.2 The EU as an International Climate Change Leader

Although in the 1970s and early 1980s the US, not the EU, was the unquestioned international leader in environmental issues, over the last several decades the EU has increasingly taken over that role. Attempts to address climate change is the most outstanding example here. The EU has been at the forefront of international action to reduce emissions of greenhouse gases such as carbon dioxide (CO_2), to which end it championed the signature of the 1992 UN Framework Convention on Climate Change as well as a protocol to the convention, signed in Kyoto, Japan, in 1997, designed to give the convention some substance. In 2000 the Commission launched the European Climate Change Program, which identified measures that could be taken to reduce emissions, and in 2002 the EU ratified the Kyoto Protocol, committing it to cutting CO_2 emissions by 8 percent on 1990 levels by 2008–2012. At the heart of EU efforts was an emissions trading scheme, launched in 2005, under which member states set a national cap on CO_2 emissions from industries (based on emission allowances). Those that use less than their allotted number of allowances can sell them to companies having trouble meeting the limits.

The results have been mixed. By 2004 the EU had reduced its CO_2 emissions by 7.3 percent, compared to a rise in US emissions of 15.8 percent.[30] But seven member states – Austria, Belgium, Denmark, Ireland, Italy, Portugal, and Spain – projected that they would exceed their emission limits. In March 2007, the EU announced a long-term strategy aimed at making sure that by 2020 (1) at least 20 percent of its energy comes from renewable sources, (2) at least 10 percent of the fuels used in transport will be biofuels (fuel made from plant matter such as corn and sugarcane), and (3) CO_2 emissions will be cut by 20 percent below 1990 levels – or 30 percent if the US (which until this time had refused to take much decisive action), China, India, and Russia followed the EU lead. The agreement included all member states and was intended to be a bargaining position as preparations were made for a replacement to the Kyoto Protocol, which expired in 2012. A follow-up meeting to the March 2007 agreement was held in December 2009 with signatories to Kyoto meeting in Copenhagen to try to strengthen the Kyoto agreement. Despite EU ambitions, however, it ended in failure with no agreed-to binding targets.

Consequently, a greater sense of urgency surrounded new climate change talks in Paris in December 2015. Despite a dampened mood created by terrorist attacks in Paris two weeks earlier, negotiators secured a historic accord: though some critics faulted the Paris Accord for not having a robust enforcement mechanism, 100 nations nevertheless agreed to hold global temperature increases to 1.5°C or "well below two degrees," and wealthy countries pledged hundreds of millions of dollars to help developing nations with cleaner energy technologies to help achieve this. Just as encouragingly, rising economic powers (but heavy polluters) China and India both softened their negotiating position from the Copenhagen round of talks and signed on. While the Obama administration (unlike earlier US administrations) backed up its words of concern about global climate change with actual deeds and real pledges in signing on to Paris, the new Trump administration pulled out of the agreement – a deep disappointment to its allies. Despite this setback, the EU remains committed on its part to honoring the Paris Accord, even if its member states have sometimes been reluctant to take the difficult steps to ensure that this happens.[31]

Partly because of the need to address climate change, the EU approach to environmental policy is based on the concept of sustainable development; its role in EU environmental planning has grown tremendously over the years.[32] Sustainable development can be defined as development that "meets the needs of the present without compromising the ability of future generations to meet their own needs."[33] The Single European Act outlined one of the Community's environmental objectives as the "prudent and rational utilization of natural resources"; Maastricht called explicitly for "sustainable and non-inflationary growth respecting the environment"; and the Treaty of Amsterdam spoke of the need for "balanced and sustainable development of economic activities." Indeed, Amsterdam made sustainable development one of the core objectives of the EU, so that it now applies to everything the EU does (e.g., agricultural policy). The seventh EAP (now in effect) highlights this core objective by identifying three priority areas for the EU: sustaining "natural capital" (natural resources) and halting biodiversity loss, continuing to transform the EU into a low-carbon economy and trying to achieve an ambitious target of capping greenhouse gas emissions, and improving air and water quality that are a threat to human health.[34] It includes a strategy for reaching the EU's long-term objectives by 2050.

In giving the principle of sustainability so much emphasis, the EU stands in contrast to the US. For US policy makers, "conservation" (which means much the same as sustainable development) was at the heart of early approaches to the management of land, waterways, and forests, and the management of public land has been guided since 1960 by the Multiple-Use Sustained-Yield Act, which requires that it be used for different purposes and in a sustainable manner. But sustainable development has yet to be adopted as part of a generalized policy on the environment in the US, and consumption has long been at the heart of American consumer approaches to natural resources, encouraged by the sense that the US is so big and so well endowed that limits are unlikely to be reached. The differences are revealed in the statistics: per capita, Americans use roughly four times as much water as Europeans, more than twice as much energy, and generate one and a half times as much municipal waste.[35] In significant ways, the US – arguably the home of modern environmental consciousness – appears to be falling well behind the EU in recognizing and acting upon what is among the most important policy areas of the present and future.

QUESTIONS TO CONSIDER

1 Why has agriculture historically been of particular importance to the EU?
2 What were the essential elements of the CAP before 2000? What caused it to change and in what ways?
3 Why did it take so long for environmental policy to assume a prominent place in the EU? What can be considered the successes of EU environmental policy? Failures?

NOTES

1 Thomas Fuller, "The Next Europe/An Expanding Union: the EU Pays the Price for Farm Subsidies," *New York Times*, June 27, 2002, at www.nytimes.com/2002/06/27/news/the-next-europe-an-expanding-union-eu-pays-the-price-for-farm-subsidies.html, accessed June 1, 2008.
2 European Commission, *The Agricultural Situation in the Community*, 1993 Report, Table 3.5.1.3 (Luxembourg: Office for Official Publications, 1994).
3 Wyn Grant, *The Common Agricultural Policy*, 71–72 (New York: St. Martin's, 1997).

4 H. von der Groeben, *The European Community, the Formative Years: The Struggle to Establish the Common Market and the Political Union (1958–1966)*, 71–72 (Brussels: European Commission, 1987).

5 European Commission, *EU Trade in Agricultural Goods*, at https://ec.europa.eu/eurostat/web/products-eurostat-news/-/DDN-20190423-1. See also European Commission, "EU Leading in Global Agri-Food Trade," Press Release, September 4, 2019, at https://ec.europa.eu/commission/presscorner/detail/en/IP_19_5527.

6 European Commission, "Farmer and the Agricultural Labour Force – Statistics," *Eurostat*, at https://ec.europa.eu/eurostat/statistics-explained/index.php/Farmers_and_the_agricultural_labour_force_-_statistics.

7 Christilla Roederer-Rynning, "Agricultural Policy: The Fortress Challenged," in *Policy-Making in the European Union*, 6th ed., edited by Helen Wallace, Mark A. Pollack, and Alasdair R. Young, 163 (Oxford, UK: Oxford University Press, 2010).

8 European Commission, "Statistical Factsheet," June 2019, at https://ec.europa.eu/info/sites/info/files/food-farming-fisheries/farming/documents/agri-statistical-factsheet-eu_en.pdf.

9 Christian Lequesne, "Fisheries Policy: Letting the Little Ones Go?" in *Policy-Making in the European Union*, edited by Wallace, Pollack, and Young.

10 Annalisa Barbieri, "Discard This Common Fisheries Policy and Stop the Waste," *Guardian*, March 2, 2011, at www.theguardian.com/commentisfree/2011/mar/02/discard-common-fisheries-policy-waste-eu, accessed March 10, 2011.

11 "EU Revamps Fishing Policy to Save Depleted Stocks," BBC News Europe, July 13, 2011, at www.bbc.com/news/science-environment-14133913, accessed July 14, 2011.

12 Brigid Laffan, *The Finances of the European Union*, 207–210 (New York: St. Martin's, 1997).

13 See Desmond Dinan and Marios Camhis, "The Common Agricultural Policy and Cohesion," in *Developments in the European Union 2*, 2nd ed., edited by Maria Green Cowles and Desmond Dinan (Basingstoke, UK: Palgrave Macmillan, 2004).

14 David P. Lewis, *The Road to Europe: History, Institutions and Prospects of European Integration 1945–1993*, 337 (New York: Peter Lang, 1993).

15 James Arnold, "Down on the Farm," BBC News Online, December 3, 2002, at http://news.bbc.co.uk/2/hi/business/2514705.stm.

16 Franz Fischler, speech before the First European Parliamentary Symposium on Agriculture, Brussels, October 16, 2003.

17 European Commission, "Overview of CAP Reform 2014–2020," at https://ec.europa.eu/info/sites/info/files/food-farming-fisheries/farming/documents/agri-policy-perspectives-brief-05_en.pdf, accessed December 31, 2013.

18 For an assessment of efforts at "greening" agriculture in the EU, see Ivana Ilić, Bojan Krstić, and Sonja Jovanović, "Environmental Performances of Agriculture in the European Union Countries," *Economics of Agriculture* 1, no. 64 (2017): 41–55.

19 Salm Gebrekidan, Matt Apuzzo, and Benjamin Novak, "The Money Farmers: How Oligarchs and Populists Milk the EU for Millions," *New York Times*, November 3, 2019, at www.nytimes.com/2019/11/03/world/europe/eu-farm-subsidy-hungary.html, accessed November 4, 2019.

20 See Matt Apuzzo, "EU Farm Chief Pledges to Tackle Corruption in Subsidy Program," *New York Times*, January 23, 2020, at www.nytimes.com/2020/01/23/world/europe/farm-subsidies-corruption.html?smid=nytcore-ios-share, accessed January 26, 2020.

21 European Union, "Agriculture: Not Just Farming," 2012, at http://europa.eu/pol/agr/index_en.htm; Stefan Tangermann, "The EU CAP Reforms: Implications for Doha Negotiations," at www.ictsd.org/sites/default/files/downloads/2014/07/part2-8.pdf.

22 *The Economist*, citing a paper from the Centre for Global Development, has found that farm income in some member states (e.g., Latvia, Estonia, and Greece) comes disproportionately from EU support, not from agricultural profitability. See "Some Farmers Are Especially Good at Milking European Taxpayers," *The Economist*, November 21, 2019, at www.economist.com/europe/2019/11/21/some-farmers-are-especially-good-at-milking-european-taxpayers, accessed November 23, 2019.

23 See Christilla Roederer-Rynning and Alan Matthews, "What Common Agricultural Policy after Brexit?" *Politics and Governance* 7, no. 3 (2019): 40–50.

24 Tom Delreux and Sander Happaerts, *Environmental Policy and Politics in the European Union*, 15 (London: Palgrave, 2019). On the history of the EU's environmental policies up until Maastricht, see Philipp M. Hildebrand, "The European Community's Environmental Policy, 1957 to 1992: From Incidental Measures to an International Regime?" in *A Green Dimension for the European Community: Political Issues and Processes*, edited by David Judge (London: Frank Cass, 1993).

25 See chapter 3 in John McCormick, *The Global Environmental Movement*, 2nd ed. (London: John Wiley, 1995).

26 *Commission* v. *Italy* (Case 91/79), Court of Justice of the European Communities, *Reports of Cases Before the Court*, 1980.

27 Hildebrand, "The European Community's Environmental Policy, 1957 to 1992."

28 Eckard Rehbinder and Richard Steward, eds., *Environmental Protection Policy, vol. 2: Integration through Law: Europe and the American Federal Experience*, 19 (Florence: European University Institute, 1985).

29 For a detailed discussion of EU environmental principles, see Delreux and Happaerts, *Environmental Policy and Politics in the European Union*.

30 United Nations Framework Convention on Climate Change, 2007, at https://unfccc.int/resource/docs/publications/handbook.pdf, accessed April 7, 2007.

31 A recent "Climate Pact" discussed by the Merkel government provides an example here: while critics accused the government of doing too little, one of the government's coalition partners, the Bavarian CSU, is balking at what it sees as too ambitious and costly concrete measures. See "CSU blockiert Beschluss zu Klimaprogramm," *Der Spiegel*, October 2, 2019, at www.spiegel.de/politik/deutschland/klimaprogramm-kabinett-verschiebt-klimadebatte-a-1289668.html, accessed October 2, 2019.

32 See Susan Baker and John McCormick, "Sustainable Development: Comparative Understandings and Responses," in *Green Giants: Environmental Policy of the United States and the European Union*, edited by Norman J. Vig and Michael G. Faure (Cambridge, MA: MIT, 2004).

33 World Commission on Environment and Development, *Our Common Future*, 8 (Oxford: Oxford University Press, 1987).

34 European Commission, "Living Well, within the Limits of Our Planet. 7th EAP – the New General Union Environment Action Programme to 2020," at https://ec.europa.eu/environment/action-programme/index.htm, accessed January 26, 2020.

35 Figures are from 2012; OECD, oecd.org and from World Bank, worldbank.org.

BIBLIOGRAPHY

Apuzzo, Matt, "EU Farm Chief Pledges to Tackle Corruption in Subsidy Program," *New York Times*, January 23, 2020, at www.nytimes.com/2020/01/23/world/europe/farm-subsidies-corruption.html?smid=nytcore-ios-share, accessed January 26, 2020.

Arnold, James, "Down on the Farm," BBC News Online, December 3, 2002, at http://news.bbc.co.uk/2/hi/business/2514705.stm.

Baker, Susan and John McCormick, "Sustainable Development: Comparative Understandings and Responses," in *Green Giants: Environmental Policy of the United States and the European Union*, edited by Norman J. Vig and Michael G. Faure (Cambridge, MA: MIT, 2004).

Barbieri, Annalisa, "Discard This Common Fisheries Policy and Stop the Waste," *Guardian*, March 2, 2011, at www.theguardian.com/commentisfree/2011/mar/02/discard-common-fisheries-policy-waste-eu, accessed March 10, 2011.

BBC News Europe, "EU Revamps Fishing Policy to Save Depleted Stocks," July 13, 2011, at www.bbc.com/news/science-environment-14133913, accessed July 14, 2011.

Court of Justice of the European Communities, "*Commission* v. *Italy* (Case 91/79)," *Reports of Cases Before the Court*, 1980.

Delreux, Tom, and Sander Happaerts, *Environmental Policy and Politics in the European Union* (London: Palgrave, 2016).

Dinan, Desmond and Marios Camhis, "The Common Agricultural Policy and Cohesion," in *Developments in the European Union*, 2nd ed., edited by Maria Green Cowles and Desmond Dinan (Basingstoke, UK: Palgrave Macmillan).

Economist, The, September 29, 1990.

Economist, The, "Some Farmers are Especially Good at Milking European Taxpayers," November 21, 2019, at www.economist.com/europe/2019/11/21/some-farmers-are-especially-good-at-milking-european-taxpayers, accessed November 23, 2019.

European Commission, *The Agricultural Situation in the Community*, 1993 Report (Luxembourg: Office for Official Publications, 1994).

European Commission, *EU Trade in Agricultural Goods*, at https://ec.europa.eu/eurostat/web/products-eurostat-news/-/DDN-20190423-1.

European Commission, "Overview of CAP Reform 2014–2020," at https://ec.europa.eu/info/sites/info/files/food-farming-fisheries/farming/documents/agri-policy-perspectives-brief-05_en.pdf, accessed December 31, 2013.

European Commission, "Farmer and the Agricultural Labour Force – Statistics," *Eurostat*, November 2018, at https://ec.europa.eu/eurostat/statistics-explained/index.php?title=Farmers_and_the_agricultural_labour_force_-_statistics.

European Commission, "Statistical Factsheet," June 2019, at https://ec.europa.eu/info/sites/info/files/food-farming-fisheries/farming/documents/agri-statistical-factsheet-eu_en.pdf.

European Commission, "EU Leading in Global Agri-Food Trade," Press Release, September 4, 2019, at https://ec.europa.eu/commission/presscorner/detail/en/IP_19_5527.

European Commission, "Living Well, within the Limits of Our Planet. 7th EAP – The New General Union Environment Action Programme to 2020," at https://ec.europa.eu/environment/action-programme/index.htm, accessed January 26, 2020.

European Union, "Agriculture: Not Just Farming," 2012, at https://europa.eu/european-union/topics/agriculture_en.

Fischler, Franz, Speech before the First European Parliamentary Symposium on Agriculture, Brussels, October 16, 2003, at http://aei.pitt.edu/85887/1/2003.10.21.pdf.

Fuller, Thomas, "The Next Europe/An Expanding Union: the EU Pays the Price for Farm Subsidies," *New York Times*, June 27, 2002, at www.nytimes.com/2002/06/27/news/the-next-europe-an-expanding-union-eu-pays-the-price-for-farm-subsidies.html, accessed June 1, 2008.

Gebrekidan, Salm, Matt Apuzzo, and Benjamin Novak, "The Money Farmers: How Oligarchs and Populists Milk the EU for Millions," *New York Times*, November 3, 2019, at www.nytimes.com/2019/11/03/world/europe/eu-farm-subsidy-hungary.html, accessed November 4, 2019.

Grant, Wyn, *The Common Agricultural Policy* (New York: St. Martin's, 1997).

Haas, Dieter, *Agricultural Policies in the EU and US: A Comparison of Policy Objectives and their Realization* (Frankfurt: AV Akademikerverlag, 2012).

Hildebrand, Philipp M., "The European Community's Environmental Policy, 1957 to 1992: From Incidental Measures to an International Regime?" in *A Green Dimension for the European Community: Political Issues and Processes*, edited by David Judge (London: Frank Cass, 1993).

Hill, Berkeley and Sophia Davidova, *Understanding the Common Agricultural Policy* (New York: Routledge, 2012).

Ilić, Ivana, Bojan Krstić, and Sonja Jovanović, "Environmental Performances of Agriculture in the European Union Countries," *Economics of Agriculture* 1, no. 64 (2017): 41–55.

Laffan, Brigid, *The Finances of the European Union* (New York: St. Martin's, 1997).

Lequesne, Christian, "Fisheries Policy: Letting the Little Ones Go?" in *Policy-Making in the European Union*, 6th ed., edited by Helen Wallace, Mark A. Pollack, and Alasdair R. Young (Oxford, UK: Oxford University Press, 2010).

Lewis, David P., *The Road to Europe: History, Institutions and Prospects of European Integration 1945–1993* (New York: Peter Lang, 1993).

McCormick, John, *The Global Environmental Movement*, 2nd ed. (London: John Wiley, 1995).

Rehbinder, Eckhard and Richard Steward, eds., *Environmental Protection Policy, vol. 2: Integration through Law: Europe and the American Federal Experience* (Florence: European University Institute, 1985).

Roederer-Rynning, Christilla, "Agricultural Policy: The Fortress Challenged," in *Policy-Making in the European Union*, 6th ed., edited by Helen Wallace, Mark A. Pollack, and Alasdair R. Young (Oxford, UK: Oxford University Press, 2010).

Roederer-Rynning, Christilla, and Alan Matthews, "What Common Agricultural Policy after Brexit?" *Politics and Governance* 7, no. 3 (2019): 40–50.

Selin, Henrik and Stacy D. VanDeveer, *European Union and Environmental Governance* (New York: Routledge, 2015).

Der Spiegel, "CSU blockiert Beschluss zu Klimaprogramm," October 2, 2019, at www.spiegel.de/politik/deutschland/klimaprogramm-kabinett-verschiebt-klimadebatte-a-1289668.html, accessed October 2, 2019.

Swinnen, Johann, *The Perfect Storm: The Political Economy of the Fischler Reforms of the Common Agricultural Policy* (Brussels: Centre for European Policy Studies, 2009).

Tangermann, Stefan, "The EU CAP Reforms: Implications for Doha Negotiations," at www.ictsd. org/sites/default/files/downloads/2014/07/part2-8.pdf.

United Nations, *United Nations Framework Convention on Climate Change*, 2007, at https://unfccc.int/resource/docs/publications/handbook.pdf, accessed April 7, 2007.

von der Groeben, Hans, *The European Community, the Formative Years: The Struggle to Establish the Common Market and the Political Union (1958–1966)* (Brussels: European Commission, 1987).

FURTHER READING

Berkeley Hill and Sophia Davidova, *Understanding the Common Agricultural Policy* (New York: Routledge, 2012); Johann Swinnen, *The Perfect Storm: The Political Economy of the Fischler Reforms of the Common Agricultural Policy* (Brussels: Centre for European Policy Studies, 2009).
> Two excellent studies of CAP, the former focusing on the policy process and the latter on the effects of the reforms in the 2000s.

Tom Delreux and Sander Happaerts, *Environmental Policy and Politics in the European Union* (London: Palgrave, 2016).
> One of the best and most comprehensive overviews of EU environmental policy and policy making.

Henrik Selin and Stacy D. VanDeveer, *European Union and Environmental Governance* (New York: Routledge, 2015).
> An evaluation of the achievements and shortcomings of EU environmental policy, written with advanced undergraduates in mind.

Dieter Haas, *Agricultural Policies in the EU and US: A Comparison of Policy Objectives and their Realization* (Frankfurt: AV Akademikerverlag, 2012).
> A comparison of EU and US environmental policy, examining whether the two systems are growing more similar.

CHAPTER 14

Social Policy, Justice and Home Affairs, and other Policies

CHAPTER OVERVIEW

- More controversial among some member states, EU social policy aims toward providing one avenue to balanced development and reducing structural inequalities by setting standards for the improvement of working and living conditions, workers' rights, and gender equality, among other issues.
- EU education policies can also be seen as tools for balanced development and reducing structural inequalities throughout the union by increasing the portability of educational opportunities and qualifications.
- Justice and home affairs (JHA), aimed at securing an "Area of Freedom, Justice, and Security" for the EU, has moved over the course of the last two decades from being a peripheral area of loose intergovernmental cooperation to an issue area requiring more robust integration of policies, laws, and approaches. The migration crisis has led to a tighter focus on securing EU borders. Consequently, much of JHA today straddles the line between an EU internal and an EU external policy area.

As we have seen in previous chapters, there is strong support among Europeans for public programs aimed at redistributing wealth and providing safety nets for those who find themselves at a disadvantage. Under regional/cohesion policy, national programs have been buttressed by a series of Europe-wide efforts to address the regional disparities which exist within and between member states. Meanwhile, EU social policy also addresses disparities, specifically problems relating to employment, including job creation, the free movement of labor, improved living and working conditions, discrimination and gender equality, and protecting the rights and benefits of workers. These issues were mostly ignored until the 1970s, when a series of social action programs provided new focus, to be followed in 1989 by the controversial Social Charter, which pushed the EU further toward protecting the rights of workers. The linchpin of EU social policy today is the European Employment Strategy, part of Europe 2020 and implemented through the European semester, a process of close policy coordination among EU member states. The European Employment Strategy is aimed at addressing the worryingly high and curiously persistent unemployment rates in parts of the EU, while the European Social Agenda is a program of activities geared toward providing jobs, fighting poverty, reforming pensions and health care, and addressing inequality and discrimination.

Since regional disparities in economic opportunity are in part a function of different levels of attainment and quality of education, education policy is another area in which the logic of the single market has demanded some Europe-wide approaches. EU education policy attempts to address regional disparities through educational programs aimed at maximizing the portability of educational qualifications; it can therefore be seen as an attempt not only to ameliorate disparities but to create greater economic opportunities for those in the poorer states and regions of the EU. The challenges for the EU in this area can be fully appreciated through a comparison with the US. In the US labor market, the education system is highly standardized (despite some differences between the states), qualifications are fully portable, and there is a common language. Consequently, few technical barriers impede the free movement of people: if Americans want to move to a different part of the country in search of better jobs or a different lifestyle, or if they are transferred by their employer from one office to another, their educational qualifications are recognized, and most people speak the same language. But the same has not been true in the EU. Apart from the obvious problem of almost every state speaking a different language, the educational systems of almost every state have historically diverged, and deciding the equivalency of qualifications has been difficult. As a result, member states have made concerted efforts – particularly since Maastricht – to encourage educational exchanges and to ease the portability of educational qualifications.

Similarly reflecting the logic of the single market, as the EU has moved from being overwhelmingly an association promoting narrow economic integration before the 1980s to one in which political and social integration have now assumed more prominent positions, cooperation in the area of border control, judicial cooperation, and law enforcement have also grown – including standardizing asylum policies, managing legal immigration while battling illegal immigration, and monitoring and controlling terrorism, drugs, human trafficking, and organized crime. JHA was made one of the three pillars in the Maastricht treaty, and was intergovernmental in its decision-making structure. After the abolition of the pillar system by Lisbon, JHA was brought under the community method, although substantial work remains to be done to achieve a truly integrated approach to cross-national crime fighting and – most especially – confront migration and asylum challenges. JHA and its goal of securing an Area of Freedom, Justice, and Security (AFJS) has both an external and internal dimension. As one analyst has succinctly put it, "EU policy is to establish common standards with regard to border management at the Union's external borders to enable … an area of freedom, security, and justice without control at internal borders."[1] JHA/AFJS, thus, in an important sense, straddles the line between an EU internal and an EU external policy area.

SOCIAL POLICY

Cohesion in the EU has meant investments not only in agriculture, industry, and services but also in social matters such as the rights of workers and women, and improved working and living conditions. Social policies are a logical outcome of the long histories of welfare promotion in individual Western European states and an important part of the drive toward building a single market by ensuring equal opportunities and working conditions. At the same time, they have been controversial and have led to some of the most bruising ideological battles the EU has witnessed since its foundation. Generally speaking, social policies win favor from national labor unions, the Commission, and Parliament (at least when it was dominated by social democratic parties) and opposition from business interests and conservative political parties, which argue that social policy threatens to make European companies less competitive in the global market.[2]

Even though worker mobility and the expansion of a skilled labor force were important parts of the idea of building a common market, the Treaty of Rome ultimately rested on the naive assumption that the benefits of the single market would improve life for all European workers. This conceit was true to the extent that it helped increase wages and improved the quality of life for many farmers, but market forces failed to deal with gender and age discrimination, disparities in wage levels, different levels of unemployment, and safety and health in the workplace. Although the treaty made it the Community's business to address working conditions, equal pay for both sexes, and social security for migrant workers, and to set the goal of creating the European Social Fund (ESF) to help promote worker mobility, social questions dropped down the Community agenda as it concentrated on completing the single market and resolving battles over agricultural policy; the movement of workers was meanwhile heavily restricted.

The widened economic gap brought on by enlargement in 1973 pushed social issues back up the agenda, and the first in a series of four-year Social Action Programmes was launched in 1974, aimed at developing a plan of action to achieve full employment, improved living and working conditions, and gender equality. A combination of recession and ideological resistance from several European leaders ensured that the words failed to be translated into deeds, although spending increased under the ESF, aimed at helping to combat long-term unemployment and creating jobs and training schemes for young people. ESF spending since the mid-1980s has accounted for 7–10 percent of the annual EU budget. In the upcoming budget cycle (2021–2027) the ESF budget has been set at €101 billion. The ESF is targeted at, among other things, fostering quality employment and increased labor mobility, promoting social inclusion and combatting discrimination, and investing in education and vocational retraining.[3]

The Single European Act (SEA) underlined the importance of social policy by raising questions about the mobility of workers and bringing up concerns about "social dumping" (money, services, and businesses moving to those parts of the EU with the lowest wages and social security costs). It codified the principle of "minimum harmonization" – a threshold which national legislation had to meet – for workers' health and safety. The Commission began promoting social policy more actively, trying to focus the attention of national governments on the "social dimension" of the single market. However, economic recession ensured that the SEA initially lacked bite to its social dimension, which encouraged Commission president Jacques Delors, a moderate socialist, to launch an attempt in 1988 to draw more attention to the social consequences of the single market.

The idea of a charter of basic social rights had been introduced by the Belgian presidency of the Council of Ministers in 1987, modeled on Belgium's new national charter. The concept was taken up by Delors in 1989 and was escalated by the determination of the socialist government of François Mitterrand in France to promote social policy during its presidency of the European Community. Germany was also in favor – despite being led by the moderate conservative government of Helmut Kohl – as were states with socialist governments, such as Greece and Spain. By contrast, the conservative Margaret Thatcher was enthusiastically opposed; she considered it "quite inappropriate" for laws on working regulations and welfare benefits to be set at the Community level and saw the Charter of the Fundamental Social Rights of Workers (the Social Charter) as "a socialist charter – devised by socialists in the Commission and favored predominantly by socialist member states."[4] In the event, the Social Charter was adopted at the 1989 Strasbourg summit by eleven of the twelve member states – all but the UK.

The Social Charter consolidated all of the social policy goals that had been mentioned throughout the life of the Community, including freedom of movement, improved living and working conditions, vocational training, gender equality, and protection for children, the elderly, and people with disabilities, but it was heavy on general goals and light on specifics. An action program listed forty-seven measures that needed to be taken, but the challenge of reaching unanimity in the Council of Ministers produced little progress. The UK was regularly painted as the major opponent of the Social Charter, but heated debate swirled around several other member states over working hours, maternity leave, and employment benefits for part-time workers.

Plans to incorporate the Social Charter into Maastricht collapsed when the government of John Major in the UK again refused to go along, so a compromise was reached whereby the Charter was attached to Maastricht as a protocol and the UK was excluded from voting in the Council on social issues while the other member states formed their own ad hoc social community. Everything changed in 1997, when the incoming government of Tony Blair committed the UK to the goals of the social protocol, and it was incorporated into the treaties by the Treaty of Amsterdam.

Despite all the rhetoric about social matters, the focus of most attention since 1991 has been on just one problem: the failure of the EU to ease unemployment, the persistence of which was once described as equivalent to the persistence of poverty in the US.[5] The single market has been unable to generate enough jobs for Europeans, so that while unemployment in late 1997 hovered around 5 percent in the US and 4 percent in Japan, it ranged between 4–6 percent in the Netherlands, the UK, and Sweden, 10 percent in Germany, 13 percent in France, Ireland, and Italy, and a high of nearly 19 percent in Spain.[6] By 2007 the figures had improved but were still not impressive: Poland and Belgium reached double digits, France and Germany were at 8–9 percent, and the eurozone was running at 7.1 percent, compared to a healthy 4.5 percent in the US.

The reasons for such high unemployment rates even before the global economic and European debt crisis (and now with the impact of the COVID-19 crisis) are debatable, but are at least in part attributable to the role of unions and a less flexible labor market than in the US. Another factor is the size of the black market, which is all but institutionalized in southern Italy, where it overlaps with the destructive power of organized crime. Also, while millions of new jobs were created in the EU prior to the global economic crisis, nearly half were temporary or part-time jobs, and many were in the service sector. Because men and women new to the job market were filling many of these jobs, their creation did little to help ease long-term unemployment. The EU launched a host of retraining programs and shifted resources to the poorer parts of the EU through various regional and social programs, but with mixed results. In the words of two analysts, EU employment policy had "high visibility but little focus" while the search for solutions was hampered by a lack of support among member states, which have traditionally been responsible for employment policy.[7]

The Amsterdam treaty introduced a new employment chapter that – while leaving competence for employment policy in the hands of member states – called on them to work toward a coordinated strategy for employment. Amsterdam also maintained the commitment to a high level of employment, emphasized that employment was a matter of "common concern" to member states, contained the principle of "mainstreaming" employment policy (account should be taken of the employment impact of all EU policies), and set up a system for sharing information on the employment policies of the member states. It also obliged the EU and member states to work toward a coordinated strategy on employment; to promote a skilled, trained, and adaptable workforce; and to encourage labor markets that were responsive to economic change. In November 1997 the European Council met in Luxembourg with employment as the sole item on its agenda and launched the European Employment Strategy, agreeing to common guidelines on employment policy, including fresh starts for the young and the long-term unemployed and simplified rules for small and medium-sized enterprises. The long-term goal of the Strategy was to raise the overall EU employment rate to 70 percent by 2010 and the employment rate among women to 60 percent. Indeed, a focus on gender was incorporated into the "pillars" of equal opportunity employment.[8]

However, the global financial and eurozone crises put an end to these plans, at least over the short term. Then came the Greek debt crisis, the bursting of the housing bubbles in Ireland and Spain, and the long-term effects of anemic economic growth in Italy, which combined to spur a significant surge of unemployment in some EU member states (although initially not in others, such as Austria, Belgium, and Germany, where the rates actually declined). Spain and Greece were by 2012 suffering the worst at around 25 percent and 22 percent unemployment respectively. Over the course of a sixteen-month period from the spring of 2011 to the fall of 2012, unemployment increased by some two million persons across the EU, with the unemployment rate rising a percentage point, to 11 percent, and female unemployment also rising. Unemployment was even more pronounced in the euro-zone than in the non-eurozone countries. Perhaps most dramatically, youth unemployment in the EU shot to almost 23 percent, with the biggest rises in Greece and Spain, but also in countries less dramatically affected by the eurozone crisis, such as the UK. By 2019 the situation had markedly improved: unemployment in the EU was averaging just over 6 percent, ranging from a high of about 17 percent in Greece to around 3 percent in Germany and a little over 2 percent in the Czech Republic (Figure 14.1). Of course, what the employment landscape will look like after the COVID-19 pandemic is anyone's guess.

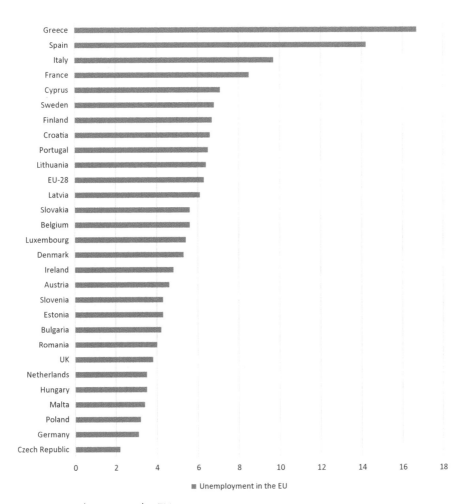

FIGURE 14.1 Unemployment in the EU.

Source: Eurostat, at https://ec.europa.eu/eurostat/statistics-explained/index.php/Unemployment_statistics, accessed December 19, 2019.

Note
Figures are for October 2019.

Along with the overall unemployment numbers, the EU has been particularly concerned about youth unemployment – which still remains unacceptably high throughout the bloc, but especially in Greece (40 percent), Spain (33 percent), and Italy (30 percent) – and about employment opportunities for women. In the EU, a significant gap still exists between male (77 percent) and female employment (65 percent). Many factors contribute to this disparity: parenthood impacts women's participation in the job market significantly more than men's; part-time employment is dominated by women; the availability of affordable child care and family leave policies are uneven across the member states; and many economic disincentives and barriers impede women's full participation.[9] Although reconciliation of work and family life is a significant objective for the EU, labor market, taxation, and social security systems based on male breadwinner models are still largely the province of member states, not the EU.[10] Meanwhile, for over a decade the EU has set goals for both dramatic increases in women's paid employment and an increase in the number of women in corporate boardrooms. Yet the success of the EU's long-term overall unemployment strategy remains an open question, as do its initiatives aimed at youth and female unemployment.

EDUCATION AND LANGUAGES

It had been understood as early as the signing of the Treaty of Rome that an open labor market was an essential part of the creation of a true single market, and although every citizen of the Community was given the right to "move and reside freely" within the territory of the member states, this was subject "to limitations justified on grounds of public policy, public security or public health." The movement of workers was initially seen mainly in economic terms, so the emphasis was placed on removing the barriers for those EU citizens who were economically active. Migration was limited, at first because governments wanted to discourage skilled workers from leaving for other countries and subsequently because of the lack of opportunities in the target states.[11]

Today, as noted in Chapter 12, there is virtually unlimited movement for all legal EU citizens in most of the member states (excluding Ireland, Bulgaria, Croatia, Cyprus, and Romania). There is no question that Europeans have become more mobile in the last generation, and the numbers of nonnationals living in member states have multiplied. Although immigration initially flowed from the south to the north and consisted largely of workers from Mediterranean states seeking employment and then bringing their families with them, immigration flows in recent years have become much more complex, and there has been an increase in the movement of professionals and managers. As a result, member states have made concerted efforts – particularly since Maastricht – to encourage educational exchanges and to ease the portability of educational qualifications. At the core of these efforts is Erasmus Plus, created in January 2014 and bringing together all of the EU's previous programs for education, training, youth, and sport. The most important of the programs under the Erasmus Plus umbrella are:

- Comenius, aimed at preschool through secondary education and supporting school partnerships, the training of staff, and the building of networks. Recent projects have included intercultural education aimed at combating violence, racism, and xenophobia; the creation of a network to examine the meaning of European citizenship; and the promotion of environmental education.
- Erasmus, aimed at higher education and encouraging student and faculty exchanges among colleges and universities and greater cooperation among institutions of higher

education within the EU, as well as facilitating educational exchanges between the EU and non-EU countries, many of them in the developing world (Erasmus Mundus). As many as four million students will have participated in Erasmus (launched in 1987) by 2020 and something of an "Erasmus generation" (see Box 14.1) has emerged.

- Leonardo da Vinci, aimed at vocational education. (Grundtvig, below, is aimed at the world of adult education; both have similar goals of promoting mobility and cooperation.)
- Grundtvig (named for a nineteenth-century Danish theologian), an adult education/retraining program which promotes cross-border mobility and cooperation.

The direction of EU education policy has been shaped profoundly by the Lisbon Strategy (see Chapter 4) and Europe 2020 (see Chapter 12), which have provided encouragement for greater mobility and retraining, with their focus on EU competitiveness in a global marketplace. Meanwhile, the portability of qualifications has been a particular priority, fostered since 1999 by what is known as the Bologna Process, aimed at establishing a European higher education area within which university education is compatible, comparable, and transferable, and making European higher education more attractive and internationally competitive. In 2010 Bologna Process members expanded, creating the European Higher Education Area and now including forty-eight member states inside and outside of the EU. The logic of Bologna is fairly simple: instead of students being restricted to attending college or university in their home state, they are now able to consider options in different member states and transfer credits from one country to another in much the same way as American students can transfer credits across US states.

Box 14.1 Gen-E? Erasmus and Post-National Identities

The idea that international education is critical to future success has gained wide currency among Europe's younger generation. Since the launch of Erasmus, the number of students studying and gaining degrees outside of their country of origin has exploded. And as the SEA, the Maastricht treaty, and the Schengen agreement have enabled people to move freely across borders within the EU, the number of younger people who have stayed on to work in their new home or who have sought career opportunities throughout the EU has also increased. This generation – the cosmopolitan young who study and work outside their country of origin, are highly mobile, multilingual, make friends across borders, and sometimes marry citizens of other member states – has been dubbed the "Erasmus Generation." The name denotes, of course, a loose sociological category, not a fixed institution. Nevertheless, the Erasmus Generation does have its own organizations, such as the Erasmus Student Network,[12] (an interdisciplinary student association which works to improve the accessibility of student mobility in higher education and has chapters in thirty-five countries) and garagErasmus[13] (the first foundation focused on the Erasmus generation, attempting to promote professional mobility and contacts through commercial partnerships with public and private institutions).

Although it would be too much to suggest that this is a generation completely without borders, it is nevertheless true that younger, educated Europeans are almost equally at home in their adopted countries as they are in their home country. And they appear to share something of a common culture. As the journalist T.R. Reid has noted, the Erasmus generation tends to "read the same books, wear the same clothes, watch the same shows ... and drink the same cocktails."[14] More importantly, the Erasmus

Generation has a much stronger sense of a common European identity, premised on support for democracy, environmental concerns, and the use of soft power more than hard power (see Chapters 15 and 16) in foreign policy. As discussed in Chapter 10, Eurobarometer polls have shown that a solid majority of people under twenty-five feel at least as much European as they do their own national identity.[15] Significantly too, an overwhelming majority of younger, and more educated UK voters voted remain in the Brexit referendum – only to be deeply disappointed at the ultimate result. Could these trends in Europe portend the creation of a truly European identity? Although this seems far less likely today in the current climate of ascendant nationalism and populism, if a common European identity takes root it could blunt the claws of national wrangling in the EU seen heretofore.

Under Bologna, a European Credit Transfer and Accumulation System (ECTS) allows for study at any university in the EU to be translated into a common credit system, with one academic year of study equal to sixty ECTS credits. A bachelor's degree or its equivalent requires 180 to 240 ECTS credits, and a master's degree or equivalent requires ninety to 120 ECTS credits. Degrees can still retain their different names, but most EU member states have switched to a common bachelor's degree system: so, for example, Italy has converted its four- to six-year *laurea* into a three-year undergraduate *laurea triennale* and a two-year postgraduate *laurea magistrale*, and Austria's *Magister* and *Diplom* have been replaced with a *Bakkalaureus*. All EU member states have signed on to the process, along with Turkey, Russia, and almost every other European country. The US is also affected, thanks to the transatlantic flow of students looking to transfer their educational achievements when they enroll in American universities.

Language training is another key facet of worker mobility: the inability to speak more than one language not only discourages migration but can also pose a handicap to multinational businesses by making it more difficult to build exports. There is also an important psychological effect: the inability to speak more than one language reminds Europeans of their differences and makes it more difficult to gain insight into the way other European societies think and work. Unlike the US, which has a common language (but is increasingly having to plan for the growth in the number of Spanish-speaking immigrants), the EU is home to many different languages. In addition to twenty-four official languages (Bulgarian, Croatian, Czech, Danish, Dutch, English, Estonian, Finnish, French, Gaelic, German, Greek, Hungarian, Italian, Latvian, Lithuanian, Maltese, Polish, Portuguese, Romanian, Slovak, Slovenian, Spanish, and Swedish), there are many local languages (including Basque, Catalan, Occitan, Corsican, and Welsh), dozens of dialects, and other languages spoken by non-EU European countries.

Learning a second language is compulsory in lower secondary education in every EU member state, although requirements tail off in upper secondary education. English is by far the preferred language of study, being the preference of students in every EU member state for which there are data (except Ireland, of course). German is a popular second choice (eight countries), followed by French (six countries). In spite of the historic place of the Franco-German relationship at the center of Europe, only 13 percent of German adults in a Commission study in 2012 claimed to have a knowledge of French (compared to 56 percent who are familiar with English) and only 9 percent of French adults know German (compared to 44 percent who claim to know English).[16] Not surprisingly perhaps, younger people, white-collar professionals, and those who were employed have higher levels of foreign-language knowledge and skills.[17]

The issue of language cuts to the core of cultural pride and particularly upsets the French, who have done everything they can to stop the perfidious spread of "franglais" – the common use of English words in French, such as *le jumbo jet* (officially *le gros porteur*) and *le fast food* (officially *pret-à-manger*). Despite the number of EU employees who work as translators, the publication of every key EU document in all official languages, and the attempts by France to stave off the inroads made by English and Anglo-American culture, almost all EU business today is conducted in English or French. Germany has been eager to ensure that its native language is not forgotten, and one of the consequences of the 2004 enlargement was an increase in the number of Europeans who spoke German, thus altering the linguistic balance of power. But it is inevitable that English – powered by its use as the global language of commerce and entertainment – will continue its trend toward becoming the common language of Europe, presenting the French with, so to speak, a *fait accompli*.

JUSTICE AND HOME AFFAIRS

Although by the mid-1970s member states had begun to exchange information and undertake limited cooperation in response to increased concerns about growing migration, asylum, and transnational crime challenges, there was no reference to JHA in the Treaty of Rome and hence no institutionalization of JHA concerns. As the idea of completion of the single market was pushed forward by SEA, by Schengen (see Chapter 12), and by Maastricht, it was clear that a more focused, structured, and integrated approach to JHA by the EU was also needed.

Maastricht made police and judicial cooperation one of the three pillars of the EU (the Common Foreign and Security Policy and the European Economic Community being the other two), and established a new European Police Office (Europol, see Chapter 9) to help coordinate cross-border police actions. However, since the kinds of security issues addressed by JHA are central to many issues deeply entrenched in national political and judicial systems, all of which relate strongly to national sovereignty,[18] differences of opinion quickly emerged as to how JHA issues were to be tackled. Consequently, as part of the pillar system of Maastricht, JHA issues were reserved for intergovernmentalism (that is, unanimity), hindering a truly integrated European approach.

The Treaty of Amsterdam – reflecting general dissatisfaction with intergovernmentalism – gave JHA added importance by creating an "area of freedom, security and justice" (AFSJ) within the EU. The goal of AFJS was to reduce the barriers to movement across borders while safeguarding the safety and security of EU citizens. As a result of Amsterdam and a follow-up European Council summit in Tampere (Finland) in October 1999, Schengen countries were brought into the common *acquis* (excepting the UK, Denmark, and Ireland, which received opt-outs), and asylum, immigration, and judicial cooperation were made EU responsibilities. EU member states moved toward developing a Common European Asylum System which attempted to harmonize standards for reviewing asylum applications as well as rules for the recognition of refugees. JHA/AFJS moved even closer to the top of the EU agenda following the 1999 conflict in Kosovo which saw 800,000 ethnic Albanians flee their homes, and the 2001 terrorist attacks in the US.[19] Consequently, in 2004 the European Council adopted the Hague Programme, which aimed to create a comprehensive asylum and refugee policy by 2010. As a result, Frontex – an EU agency which coordinates border management for frontline EU states and whose budget has grown significantly since the beginning of the migration crisis – was created, along with an EU "Blue Card" (a work and residence permit for skilled migrant labor, modeled on the US Green Card). Finally, the

Hague Programme also developed a provision of crime "threat assessments" and strengthened information gathering and sharing within the Schengen area to combat terrorism.

The Treaty of Lisbon underscored the evolution of JHA/AFJS by abolishing the pillar system and moving JHA/AFJS into the mainstream of EU decision making (rather than leaving it as a stand-alone, intergovernmental area, as continues to be the case for the Common Foreign and Security Policy). Special opt-outs for the non-Schengen states (Denmark, Ireland, and, until Brexit made this a moot point, the UK) continue, of course; some issues will continue to be decided by unanimity; and community action is complicated by the involvement of non-EU members Iceland, Liechtenstein, Norway, and Switzerland in Schengenland. However, justice and home affairs has evolved from a rather loose cooperative arrangement to one more closely resembling other policy fields within the EU, and the normal procedure of qualified majority voting will now operate within many areas of JHA/AFJS.

One of the notable areas of successful cooperation has been the European Arrest Warrant (EAW). Proposed in 2001 by the European Council and adopted by all member states in 2005, it requires any EU state to arrest and transfer a criminal suspect or those convicted of a serious crime back to the issuing state within ninety days. The EAW is intended to accelerate the speed and ease of extradition: before the EAW was introduced, extradition took an average of one year, but that has now been cut to an average of forty-eight days. It prevents a member state from refusing to surrender its own nationals (as many states had done either outright or under certain conditions spelled out in national law) and thus extends the principle of mutual recognition to the area of judicial and police cooperation. The use of the EAW has increased steadily since 2004, with around 15,000 being issued annually within the EU today. Among the notable cases of the EAW have been the arrest of a failed London bomber caught in Italy in 2004; a German serial killer tracked down in Spain; and a gang of armed robbers sought by Italy whose members were arrested in six different EU countries.

On the other hand, asylum and migration policy in the EU, which first made headlines in 2015 amidst the beginning of a dramatic refugee crisis, underscores serious deficits in this area of JHA/AFJS. Since its inception, Frontex has developed "rapid border intervention teams" or RABITs, which send patrol boats, helicopters, and aircraft to perceived security threats to EU borders. In February 2011 "Operation Hermes" began to conduct surveillance of the eastern Mediterranean in the aftermath of violence in Libya and the overthrow of the Gaddafi regime. With the further deterioration of the situation in Libya as well as the steady increase in refugees (from Syria and Iraq in the wake of ongoing civil wars and from Asian and African refugees fleeing conflicts and poverty) a similar operation, "Operation Triton," was launched in 2014. However, Italy – which up until 2014 conducted its own independent operation patrolling the Mediterranean ("Mare Nostrum") before it was forced to shut it down under pressure from other EU states – criticized Operation Triton as vastly underfunded. This proved prophetic when huge numbers of refugees, aided by human smugglers, boarded boats in the spring of 2015 with catastrophic results. After an estimated 1,500 migrants died off the Libyan coast in early 2014 – some 900 alone dying in one weekend in April – EU leaders met in an emergency meeting and pledged to send additional ships and to increase funding for Operational Triton.

Asylum policy significantly shifted in 1990 with the Dublin Convention and various revisions in 2003, 2008, and 2013 (now known simply as the Dublin Regulation or Dublin III). Dublin established a procedure for asylum seekers whereby they must generally lodge their claim in the first country in the EU which they enter in order to prevent "asylum shopping" for the highest social benefits; those frontline states then become responsible for registering the asylum seeker and taking fingerprints. Angela Merkel's decision to suspend Dublin in light of the overwhelming number of refugees seeking asylum in the EU (primarily in Germany and

PHOTO 14.1 Refugees Wait to Enter Macedonia from Greece, 2016.
Source: © iStock Editorial/Getty Images Plus.

Scandinavia) was hugely controversial (see Chapter 4) but intended only as an emergency measure. Nevertheless, asylum policy remained largely deadlocked over both the procedure for accepting refugees (with countries such as France, Italy, and especially Germany having much higher acceptance rates than countries such as Greece or many eastern European states) and the question of how asylum seekers would be distributed across member states – a sensitive issue to many member states whose publics remain skeptical if not hostile to immigrants. Moreover, frontline states such as Italy have proposed ending the link between the point of arrival and the responsibility for processing an asylum claim. As of this writing, an agreement toward a common EU approach to refugees and asylum remains deadlocked.

Critics have pointed to the inherent contradictions contained within the JHA/AFJS and the gradual "securitizing" of asylum and migration, i.e., the domination of JHA/AFJS by security concerns. The single biggest contradiction is among the lack of a burden-sharing mechanism for asylum, almost completely open Schengen borders which guarantee freedom of movement within the EU, and the inequality inherent in the Dublin Regulation, which places undue burdens on frontline states and incentivizes them to simply keep people out of their states (but not necessarily out of the EU). This contradiction was massively exposed during the migration crisis. As Rainer Bauböck has written, "This combination of open internal borders with external borders that states lacked incentives to control, produced the massive migration of refugees via the Balkan route to their desired destinations in summer 2015."[20] The contradiction between open internal borders and rigid (in theory) external borders was latent in Schengen from its very inception. As Tony Judt once put it, "In opening the internal frontiers between some EC member states … the agreement resolutely reinforced the external borders separating them from outsiders. Civilized Europeans could indeed transcend boundaries – but the 'barbarians' would be kept resolutely beyond them."[21] Unless the EU devotes ever larger shares of its resources to simply patrolling EU borders and keeping out asylum seekers while further eroding Schengen as a fail-safe, it will of necessity have to solve this contradiction.

QUESTIONS TO CONSIDER

1 Why has EU social policy been controversial and what might Brexit mean for its future development?
2 What might the effects of the Erasmus generation be on European integration and a European identity, especially in light of calls for overhauling the Schengen agreement?
3 How has the European refugee crisis exposed the limitations of JHA/AFJS?

NOTES

1 Thierry Balzacq, "The External Dimension of EU Justice and Home Affairs: Tools, Processes, Outcomes," CEPS Working Document #303, Centre for European Policy Studies, September 2008, 4.
2 Robert Geyer and Beverly Springer, "EU Social Policy after Maastricht: The Works Directive and the British Opt-Out," in *The State of the European Union, vol. 4: Deepening and Widening*, edited by Pierre-Henri Laurent and Marc Maresceau, 208 (Boulder: Lynne Rienner, 1998).
3 European Commission, "European Social Fund," at https://ec.europa.eu/esf/main.jsp?catId=62&langId=en, accessed December 19, 2019; European Parliament, "Fact Sheets on the European Union: European Social Fund," 2015, at www.europarl.europa.eu/aboutparliament/en/displayFtu.html?ftuId=FTU_5.10.2.html. For an analysis of the impact of the ESF, see Jacqueline Brine, *The European Social Fund and the EU: Flexibility, Growth, Stability* (London: Continuum, 2002).
4 Margaret Thatcher, *The Downing Street Years*, 149 (New York: HarperCollins, 1993).
5 Ralf Dahrendorf, *The Modern Social Conflict*, 149 (London: Weidenfeld and Nicholson, 1988).
6 Richard Jackman, "European Unemployment: Why Is It So High and What Should be Done about It?" Reserve Bank of Australia, 1998 Conference, at www.rba.gov.au/publications/confs/1998/jackman.html, accessed April 28, 2020.
7 Geyer and Springer, "EU Social Policy after Maastricht," 208.
8 See Agnès Hubert, "Gendering Employment Policy: From Equal Pay to Work-Life Balance," in *Gendering the European Union. New Approaches to Old Democratic Deficits*, edited by Gabriele Abels and Joyce Marie Mushaben, 146–168 (Basingstoke: Palgrave Macmillan, 2012).
9 European Commission, "Women in the Labour Market," European Semester Thematic Factsheet, 2017, at https://ec.europa.eu/info/sites/info/files/european-semester_thematic-factsheet_labour-force-participation-women_en_0.pdf, accessed December 20, 2019.
10 See Maria Stratigaki, "Gendering the Social Inclusion Agenda: Anti-Discrimination, Social Inclusion and Social Protection," in *Gendering the European Union. New Approaches to Old Democratic Deficits*, edited by Abels and Mushaben, 169–186.
11 Ian Barnes and Pamela M. Barnes, *The Enlarged European Union*, 108 (London: Longman, 1995).
12 See the Erasmus Student Network website, https://esn.org/, for more information.
13 See the garagErasmus website, www.garagerasmus.org/, for more information.
14 T.R. Reid, *The United States of Europe. The New Superpower and the End of American Supremacy*, 200 (New York: Penguin Books, 2004).
15 In one poll from 2012, the figures for young people under 25 was 67 percent. See European Commission, *European Citizenship: Report*, 2012, at https://ec.europa.eu/commfrontoffice/publicopinion/archives/eb/eb77/eb77_citizen_en.pdf, accessed December 18, 2019.
16 European Commission, *Europeans and Their Languages*, at https://ec.europa.eu/commfrontoffice/publicopinion/archives/ebs/ebs_386_en.pdf, accessed December 18, 2019.
17 Eurostat, "Foreign Language Skills Statistics," 2019, at https://ec.europa.eu/eurostat/statistics-explained/index.php/Foreign_language_skills_statistics, accessed December 18, 2019.
18 Sandra Lavenex, "Justice and Home Affairs: Communitarization with Hesitation," in *Policy-Making in the European Union*, edited by Wallace, Pollack, and Young, 457–480.

19 John D. Occhipinti, *The Politics of EU Police Cooperation: Toward a European FBI?* (Boulder, CO: Lynne Rienner, 2003).
20 Rainer Bauböck, "Refugee Protection and Burden-Sharing in the European Union," *Journal of Common Market Studies* 56, no. 1 (2018): 141–156.
21 Tony Judt, *Postwar: A History of Europe Since 1945*, 534 (New York: Penguin, 2005).

BIBLIOGRAPHY

Anderson, Karen, *Social Policy in the European Union* (New York and London: Palgrave Macmillan, 2015).

Balzacq, Thierry, "The External Dimension of EU Justice and Home Affairs: Tools, Processes, Outcomes," CEPS Working Document #303, Centre for European Policy Studies, September 2008.

Barnes, Ian and Pamela M. Barnes, *The Enlarged European Union* (London: Longman, 1995).

Bauböck, Rainer, "Refugee Protection and Burden-Sharing in the European Union," *Journal of Common Market Studies*, 56, no. 1 (2018): 141–156.

Brine, Jacqueline, *The European Social Fund and the EU: Flexibility, Growth, Stability* (London: Continuum, 2002).

Dahrendorf, Ralf, *The Modern Social Conflict* (London: Weidenfeld and Nicholson, 1988).

European Commission, *European Citizenship: Report*, 2012, at https://ec.europa.eu/commfront office/publicopinion/archives/eb/eb77/eb77_citizen_en.pdf, accessed December 18, 2019.

European Commission, "Women in the Labour Market," European Semester Thematic Factsheet, 2017, at https://ec.europa.eu/info/sites/info/files/european-semester_thematic-factsheet_labour-force-participation-women_en_0.pdf, accessed December 20, 2019.

European Commission, *Europeans and Their Languages*, at https://ec.europa.eu/commfrontoffice/ publicopinion/archives/ebs/ebs_386_en.pdf, accessed December 18, 2019.

European Commission, "European Social Fund," at https://ec.europa.eu/esf/main.jsp?catId=62& langId=en, accessed December 19, 2019.

European Parliament, "Fact Sheets on the European Union: European Social Fund," 2015, at www.europarl.europa.eu/aboutparliament/en/displayFtu.html?ftuId=FTU_5.10.2.html.

Eurostat, "Foreign Language Skills Statistics," 2019, at https://ec.europa.eu/eurostat/statistics-explained/index.php/Foreign_language_skills_statistics, accessed December 18, 2019.

Geyer, Robert and Beverly Springer, "EU Social Policy after Maastricht: The Works Directive and the British Opt-Out," in *The State of the European Union, vol. 4: Deepening and Widening*, edited by Pierre-Henri Laurent and Marc Maresceau (Boulder: Lynne Rienner, 1998).

Hubert, Agnès, "Gendering Employment Policy: From Equal Pay to Work-Life Balance," in *Gendering the European Union. New Approaches to Old Democratic Deficits*, edited by Gabriele Abels and Joyce Marie Mushaben, 146–168 (Basingstoke: Palgrave Macmillan, 2012).

Jackman, Richard, "European Unemployment: Why Is It So High and What Should be Done about It?" Reserve Bank of Australia, 1998 Conference, at www.rba.gov.au/publications/ confs/1998/jackman.html, accessed April 28, 2020.

Judt, Tony, *Postwar: A History of Europe Since 1945* (New York: Penguin, 2005).

Lavenex, Sandra, "Justice and Home Affairs: Communitarization with Hesitation," in *Policy-Making in the European Union*, 7th ed., edited by Helen Wallace, Mark Pollack, and Alasdair Young, 457–480 (Oxford: Oxford University Press, 2014).

Occhipinti John D., *The Politics of EU Police Cooperation: Toward a European FBI?* (Boulder, CO: Lynne Rienner, 2003).

Reid, T.R., *The United States of Europe. The New Superpower and the End of American Supremacy* (New York: Penguin Books, 2004).

Rifkin, Jeremy, *The European Dream: How Europe's Vision of the Future Is Quietly Eclipsing the American Dream* (New York: Tarcher, 2004).

Russell, James W., *Double Standard: Social Policy in Europe and the United States*, 4th ed. (Lanham, MD: Rowman and Littlefield, 2018).

Stratigaki, Maria, "Gendering the Social Inclusion Agenda: Anti-Discrimination, Social Inclusion and Social Protection," in *Gendering the European Union. New Approaches to Old Democratic*

Deficits, edited by Gabriele Abels and Joyce Marie Mushaben, 169–186 (Basingstoke: Palgrave Macmillan, 2012).

Thatcher, Margaret, *The Downing Street Years* (New York: HarperCollins, 1993).

Vermeulen, Gert and Wendy De Bondt, *EU Justice and Home Affairs: Institutional and Policy Development* (Antwerp, Belgium: Maklu Publishers, 2014).

FURTHER READING

Karen Anderson, *Social Policy in the European Union* (New York and London: Palgrave Macmillan, 2015).

> A survey of the evolution of social policy in the EU – its increasing importance and effects on member states.

James W. Russell, *Double Standard: Social Policy in Europe and the United States*, 4th ed. (Lanham, MD: Rowman and Littlefield, 2018).

> Compares the comprehensive Western European welfare model with the minimalist American model, assessing their responses to a variety of social problems.

Jeremy Rifkin, *The European Dream: How Europe's Vision of the Future Is Quietly Eclipsing the American Dream* (New York: Tarcher, 2004).

> A controversial assessment by an American economist and writer of the contrasting European and American social models.

Gert Vermeulen and Wendy De Bondt, *EU Justice and Home Affairs: Institutional and Policy Development* (Antwerp, Belgium: Maklu Publishers, 2014).

> A survey of the historical and institutional development of JHA, covering the main topical areas of policy making.

CHAPTER 15

Security and Global Power

CHAPTER OVERVIEW

- Launched by the Maastricht treaty and since that time modified and strengthened, the Common Foreign and Security Policy (CFSP) is at the heart of EU foreign policy. Despite the CFSP making it easier for the EU to speak with one voice in foreign policy matters, there remains a gap between the potential influence of the EU and its actual performance. Combined, the EU has one of the largest militaries in the world in terms of both personnel and military equipment, yet the EU has not been able to project a unified front in security matters and therefore act decisively in military matters on the world stage.
- The compound effects of the financial crisis, the rise of populism and authoritarianism throughout the world, the weakening of postwar rules-based regimes for international cooperation, and Brexit have required new thinking on the part of the EU. Consequently, the EU has initiated the EU Global Strategy (EGS), which includes several initiatives intended to respond more quickly and robustly to the EU's foreign policy challenges.
- Compared to its relatively undersized role in security and lack of hard power, the EU's soft power in the global arena is beyond doubt: among other things, the EU is one of the world's largest trading powers and the biggest source of foreign investment in the world. What effects Brexit will have on the EU's economic clout and soft power advantage is hard to calculate, but it is almost certain to do some damage.

For those who question the merits and achievements of European integration, one of the clearest examples of the gap between promise and achievement lies in the field of foreign policy. The EU is clearly an economic and trading powerhouse, and yet most observers argue that it is punching below its weight when it comes to turning its wealth into global political influence. Attempts to explain the contradiction have been many and varied, but at the heart of the issue lie three problems.

First, military power dominates most analyses of international influence. The claim, for example, that the US is the world's last remaining superpower rests mainly on the size, reach, and technological prowess of the US military. The fact that the EU has not built a common military or sufficiently developed a common security policy is seen by most critics as undermining Europe's claims to global power. Second, the EU has not yet been able to always project a united front on the most troubling international problems, or to make its voice heard. It has been slowly, if haltingly, building a common foreign and security policy, and it has developed common positions and strategies on a wide range of issues, yet it has also been left with much egg on its face by disagreements over how to respond to problems in the Balkans, in the Arab world (such as Libya and Syria), and in Ukraine and Russia.

Third, more public attention has been drawn to the EU's short-term policy failures than to its longer-term successes. Much of what the EU has achieved in foreign policy has been a result of steady investments of time, diplomacy, and encouragement, little of which attracts headlines in the same way, for example, as its public failure to agree over whether or not to support the US-led invasion of Iraq or its inability to project a common position toward Russia.

Paradoxically, most of the criticism of the EU stems from the fact that more is now *expected* of it as an international actor. It is not that the EU has failed to provide leadership, but rather that its failures are at odds with expectations for an economic superpower. The lessons have not been lost on European leaders, for whom the divisions over the 1990–1991 Gulf War and the 1991–1995 crises in the Balkans were wake-up calls and the divisions over Iraq reminders of how much more work needed to be done. Not only were Europe's leaders in disagreement with each other over Iraq, but also those in favor of the invasion were at odds with their own publics: polls found that large majorities in every EU country – even prospective Eastern European member states – were opposed to the war, and several governments that supported the war (notably in Spain, Italy, and the UK) paid the price through loss of public support.

Hopes for a more assertive international role for the EU after the Lisbon treaty have been diminished in the wake of the eurozone crisis, the rise of authoritarianism throughout the world (especially a more aggressive Russia), challenges to the rules-based international order (for example, though various trade wars), and – more recently – Brexit and its impact. As a result, EU foreign policy ambitions have been scaled down and reconceptualized, most notably through a new EGS and the PESCO framework (Permanent Structured Cooperation) which while attempting to enhance the EU's military capability and cooperative ability to respond to crises nevertheless acknowledge the limits of EU power. At the same time, the EU's real strengths have always lain not in its military credentials but in its impact as a new kind of civilian superpower. It has been more adept at employing soft power (incentives and influence through economic and cultural power) rather than hard power (threats, coercion, and force tied to military power) to achieve change (see Box 15.1), a quality that often places it at an advantage in a world where globalization, economic investment, and international cooperation are still important norms, even if these norms have weakened over the last half decade.

Box 15.1 Europe's Soft Power Advantage

Since the end of the Cold War and the breakup of the Soviet Union, majority opinion holds that we have moved into a new unipolar international era in which there is only one remaining superpower: the US. Samuel Huntington wrote in 1999 of the US as the "lonely superpower," existing in a world in which there were no significant other powers and it could resolve important international issues alone, with no combination of other states having the power to prevent it.[1] John Ikenberry later argued that the preeminence of American power was unprecedented in modern history: "We live in a one-superpower world, and there is no serious competitor in sight."[2] Former French foreign minister Hubert Védrine went further, claiming that the US was a hyperpower, enjoying a level of global influence unprecedented in history.[3] Most of these claims about US power are based on its military dominance, and certainly the statistics are impressive: the US has the world's biggest and most technologically advanced military, and a defense budget that is almost bigger than that of the rest of the world combined.[4] But military might is not always what it seems. The examples of Vietnam and Iraq show that there are limits to what military force can achieve, and some argue that military power may make the world less secure by encouraging hostility from states that feel threatened by US power.[5]

It is here that a useful distinction can be made between hard power and soft power.[6] All great powers have hard and soft power tools available to them, but there has been a tendency in recent years to associate hard power with the US and soft power with the EU. The US has a long history of using diplomacy, political support, and economic investment effectively to bring change, but critics of US foreign policy point to US actions in the Middle East as examples of its tendency to rely heavily on its military power to achieve its objectives. Those same critics argue that hard power can be counterproductive, as it rarely brings about permanent positive change and can actually heighten tensions by making the US appear to be a threat to world peace. Rather than being a leader for change, the US from this perspective often acts like a "rogue nation,"[7] losing much of its ability to persuade.

Meanwhile, claims of European global power are dismissed by cynics mainly on the basis that the EU does not have a large, combined military or much desire to use what it has, except for peacekeeping. But there is evidence to suggest that the EU's preference for soft power may actually be its trump card. The idea of encouraging a change in behavior through incentives rather than threats, through opportunities and negotiation rather than through violence and intimidation, carries considerable weight in the era of globalization. A growing number of analysts argue that rather than shirking on defense, the EU is instead expanding the set of tools it applies to post–Cold War security and defense problems, relying less on defense than on economics, diplomacy, and engagement by negotiation.[8]

If the definition of power is expanded to include its political, economic, moral, and cultural aspects, then the idea of the US as the world's only superpower loses some of its luster. Rather than an international system based on military unipolarity, we may actually be living in a multipolar world of hard and soft power in which the US and the EU share influence and resources with a growing network of emerging regional powers in Asia and Latin America, such as Brazil, China, and India. All of these (most especially, of course, China) have the potential to become superpowers, raising the prospects of a new international order, but for now the two most important poles in the international system might well be the US and the EU, and they offer two contrasting notions of how power might be used.

TOWARD A COMMON FOREIGN POLICY

Foreign policy was a latecomer to the agenda of European integration. It was not mentioned in the Treaty of Rome, and the Community focused most of its attention during the 1950s and 1960s on internal economic matters. Modest progress began to be made with the agreement in 1970 of European Political Cooperation (EPC), a loose and voluntary foreign policy process that revolved around regular meetings of the Community foreign ministers. EPC helped European leaders learn to negotiate shared positions, a habit formally recognized when it was agreed under the Single European Act that member states would "endeavor jointly to formulate and implement a European foreign policy." But the problems of a "mixed system" remained: instead of developing a common overall policy – or even a set of common targeted policies – the Community was driven by a combination of national and common policies.[9]

The resulting difficulties were exposed by events in the 1990s. First came the Gulf War of 1990–1991, when the US responded quickly to the August 1990 Iraqi invasion of Kuwait, orchestrated a multinational air war against Iraq, and launched a four-day ground war in February 1991. The UK provided strong support and placed a large military contingent under US operational command; France also made a large military commitment but placed more emphasis on a diplomatic resolution in order to maintain good relations with Arab oil producers and protect its weapons markets; and Germany was constrained by a postwar tradition of pacifism and constitutional limits on the deployment of German troops outside the NATO area. An abashed Luxembourg foreign minister, Jacques Poos, admitted that the Community's response illustrated "the political insignificance of Europe." For Belgian foreign minister Mark Eyskens, it showed that the EC was "an economic giant, a political dwarf, and a military worm."[10]

The Community's shortcomings were revealed again in the Balkans, where the end of the Cold War released the ethnic, religious, and nationalist tensions that had been kept in check by the Tito regime (1944–1980). When Croatia and Slovenia unilaterally declared independence in June 1991, the Yugoslav federal army responded with force, throwing down a challenge for the Community to intervene. There was early promise in an EU-brokered peace conference, and a buoyant Jacques Poos declared, "This is the hour of Europe, not of the United States."[11] But when the Community recognized Croatia and Slovenia in January 1992, it lost its credibility as a neutral arbiter, and it was left eventually to the US to broker the 1995 Dayton Peace Accords. Then, when ethnic Albanians in Kosovo tried to break away from Yugoslavia in 1997–1998, it was left to NATO – again under US leadership – to organize the bombing campaign against Serbia in March–June 1999. This was to be the catalyst that finally encouraged the EU to take action on building a military capability.[12]

Progress was made with Maastricht, by which the EU agreed on the CFSP, which represented a stronger commitment to a common foreign policy: joint action could be initiated and implemented by qualified majority voting (QMV) in the Council (although unanimity was still the norm on the biggest questions), security issues were fully included, and the CFSP was part of the institutional structure of the EU.[13] The CFSP brought a convergence of positions among the member states on key international issues, helped by improved links among the foreign ministers and by the EU's development of joint actions and of common strategies and positions.

The Treaty of Amsterdam introduced a few important changes, creating the post of High Representative (see Box 15.2) and introducing the notions of general guidelines and "common strategies" for CFSP which were to be decided unanimously (although the precise implementation of such strategies would be decided through QMV). The Treaty of Lisbon clarified some of the initial confusion on institutional roles within the CFSP remaining after Amsterdam, yet difficulties remain, mostly stemming from the fact that member states' foreign policy is not subsumed under EU foreign policy but exists alongside it (even if, as articulated in Lisbon, these two should not be in conflict). And even though there is no longer a separate "pillar" for CFSP as under Maastricht, it remains intergovernmental. Furthermore, the Commission and European Parliament have limited roles in the CFSP: the former has no right of initiation for CFSP policies, while the latter has only consultative powers. Commission policy differences among the governments of the member states also hobble CFSP – some have national agendas that they want to pursue. France, for example, has special interests in its former colonies, while Austria, Finland, Ireland, and Sweden want to maintain their neutrality.

There has also been historically a more fundamental strategic division in foreign policy: Atlanticists (the Netherlands, Portugal, and several Eastern European states along with, of course, the now departing UK) favor a close foreign policy association with the US, while Europeanists (chief among them, France) prefer greater European independence. When the European Security and Defence Identity was launched in 1994 in an attempt to underpin the CFSP by developing a separate European initiative on security matters, Atlanticists felt that it should be tied closely to NATO, while Europeanists saw it as an opportunity to develop some real independence from the US. Meanwhile, the US is content to see the Europeans taking responsibility for those tasks from which NATO should best keep its distance, but it insists that there should be no overlap or rivalry in the event of the creation of a separate European institution. A new element was added to the debate in 2004, when seven Eastern European states – whose governments mainly hold Atlanticist views – joined both NATO and the EU.

Box 15.2 Who Speaks for Europe?

One of the persistent problems with the development of a European foreign policy has been a lack of focus and leadership. This is not an issue in the US, where the president and the secretary of state between them clearly represent national policy. But in the EU, the presidency of the Council of Ministers changes every six months, and for many years there was no one figure in the EU institutions who could act as an authoritative focal point for discussions with other countries. This presented a problem for any non-EU governments that wanted to negotiate or do business with the EU, summed up nicely in the (sadly apocryphal) question credited to former US secretary of state Henry Kissinger, "When I want to speak to Europe, whom do I call?"[14]

The division of external relations portfolios in the Commission ended with the creation in 1999 of a single external relations portfolio, but the waters were muddied when a second position was created at Amsterdam in the form of the High Representative for the CFSP, who was intended to be the spokesperson on foreign affairs. The first officeholder was Javier Solana, former secretary general of NATO, who was appointed in 1999 for an initial five-year term, renewed in 2004.

The Treaty of Lisbon brought significant change as well as some clarity, combining the post of external relations commissioner with the High Representative in the new position of the High Representative for CFSP and External Relations. The High Representative is charged under Lisbon with "conducting" the CFSP, chairing the Foreign Affairs Council in the Council of Ministers, and serving as a vice president in the Commission, giving the EU's external policies more consistency among its various institutions. At the same time, the president of the European Council (created by Lisbon) as well as the president of the Commission still "speak for Europe" in their own capacities. Still, although Kissinger's question cannot quite be said to have been definitively answered, Lisbon has brought a little more clarity to how the EU handles its external relations – and who is ultimately responsible for it.

TOWARD A COMMON SECURITY POLICY

Security issues have been the most troubling element of attempts to build a common European foreign policy, having been repeatedly sidetracked by debates over the place of NATO (see membership of NATO in Table 15.1). Although Western European forces have always

TABLE 15.1 Membership of NATO		
Albania (2009)	Greece (1952)	**Norway**
Belgium	Hungary (1999)	Poland (1999)
Bulgaria (2004)	**Iceland**	Portugal
Canada	Italy	Romania (2004)
Croatia (2009)	Lithuania (2004)	Slovenia (2004)
Czech Republic (1999)	Lithuania (2004)	Slovenia (2004)
Denmark	Luxembourg	Spain (1982)
Estonia (2004)	**Montenegro** (2017)	**Turkey** (1952)
France	Netherlands	**United Kingdom**
Germany (1955)	**North Macedonia** (2020; expected)	**United States**

Note
Founding members unless otherwise indicated by year of membership. EU member states that are not members of NATO are Austria, Cyprus, Finland, Ireland, Malta, and Sweden. Boldface = non-EU member states.

made up the bulk of NATO's military capability in Europe, NATO has always been politically dominated by the US, and most Europeans (France excepted) have been content with the security blanket provided by the Americans. But since the end of the Cold War, there has been pressure to redefine the mission of NATO, the key question being the tripartite relationship between the US, the EU, and NATO. The Trump administration's mixed messages on NATO – harshly criticizing fellow NATO members and suggesting that the alliance might no longer be needed but criticizing France's Macron for calling NATO "brain dead" and reaffirming the US commitment to NATO – have added even more uncertainty. Beyond this, general cooperation among EU member states on military matters has historically been slow in coming.

For a while, one way out of the dilemma was offered by the Western European Union (WEU), an organization founded in 1954 in the wake of the collapse of the European Defence Community, which committed its members to much stronger joint defense obligations than NATO. But it was never elevated to the same status as NATO and found itself stretched beyond its limits by the 1990–1991 Gulf War. Following a 1992 meeting of WEU foreign and defense ministers at Petersberg, near Bonn, a declaration was issued that limited the WEU to the Petersberg tasks: humanitarian, rescue, peacekeeping, and other crisis management operations, including peacemaking. Meanwhile, an attempt had been made outside formal Community structures to address the lack of a joint military force with the creation in 1991 of an experimental Franco-German brigade. In May 1992 this was converted into Eurocorps, a joint military force that has been operational since November 1995, consisting of up to 60,000 troops from Belgium, France, Germany, Luxembourg, and Spain. It has sent missions to Bosnia (1998), Kosovo (2000), and Afghanistan (2004 to the present).

In 1997 the Amsterdam treaty resulted in a closer association between the WEU and the EU, and the Petersberg tasks were incorporated into the EU treaties. That same year, Tony Blair became UK prime minister and signaled his willingness to see the UK play a more central role in EU defense matters. He and French president Jacques Chirac began to more fully explore the potential of the Anglo-French axis in European security matters, and – after a December 1998 meeting in St. Malo, France – the two leaders declared that the EU should be in a position to play a full role in international affairs and "must have the capacity for autonomous action, backed up by credible military forces, the means to decide to use them, and the readiness to do so." They suggested the creation of a European Rapid Reaction Force (RRF), which was later endorsed by German chancellor Gerhard Schröder.[15]

In 1999 the EU launched the European Security and Defence Policy (ESDP). An integral part of the CFSP, this was to consist of two key components: the Petersberg tasks and a 60,000-member RRF that could be deployed at sixty days' notice, be sustained for at least one year, and carry out these tasks. The plan was to have it ready by the end of 2003, but while it was declared partly operational in December 2002 and launched its first mission – a peacekeeping operation in Macedonia – in March 2003, it took longer to finalize than initially estimated. ESDP was renamed the Common Security and Defence Policy (CSDP) by the Lisbon treaty. Although CSDP continues to operate under the principle of unanimity, Lisbon provided the possibility for "enhanced cooperation," whereby member states with more robust military capabilities are allowed, with the EU's blessing, to create a limited but more structured cooperative arrangement for peacekeeping, disarmament, and other military operations.

In December 2003, the European Council adopted the European Security Strategy, the first ever declaration by EU member states of their strategic goals. The Strategy declared that the EU was "inevitably a global player" and "should be ready to share in the responsibility for global security." It listed the key threats facing the EU as terrorism, weapons of mass destruction, regional conflicts, failing states, and organized crime. Indeed, fighting terrorism has been particularly important since that time (particularly in light of the November 2015 terrorist attacks in Paris, which led France to invoke the mutual assistance clause of the Lisbon treaty) and the EU has pursued cooperation agreements with countries around the world in joint counter-terrorism programs. More conventionally, in May 2004, EU defense ministers agreed on the formation of several battle groups that could be deployed more quickly and for shorter periods than the RRF, be used in support of UN operations, and be capable of anything up to full-scale combat situations. The groups would consist of 1,500 troops each, could be committed within fifteen days, and could be sustainable for between thirty and 120 days.

A decade and a half since that time, the combined effects of the financial crisis, the rise of populism and authoritarianism throughout the world, and the challenge to the neo-liberal global economic order with its rules-based regimes for international cooperation have required new thinking on the part of the EU. As one analyst has suggested, "rather than being the vanguard of a new liberal order, the EU now appears to be a besieged 'postmodern' island in a world ruled by realpolitik."[16] Moreover, the departure of the UK from the EU will deal EU foreign policy ambitions a further blow, given that the UK has been, along with France, the major military power within the bloc as well as the world's fifth-largest economy.[17] In addition, with Brexit the EU will lose one of the two permanent seats it holds (by virtue of two of its member states, France and the UK) on the UN's Security Council. Consequently, in 2016 then High Representative Mogherini issued the EGS. While calling for strengthening EU military capabilities, enhancing its capacity to respond more quickly to crises, and developing a deeper level of defense cooperation among member states, the EGS acknowledges the changed global circumstances in which EU the now lives. Rather than an idealistic vision of how the EU can actively shape an ever more democratizing, peaceful, and orderly world, the document strikes a modest tone, with its most frequent phrases being "principled pragmatism," "practical" approaches to global challenges, and supporting the "resilience" of fragile states through new security and defense initiatives.[18]

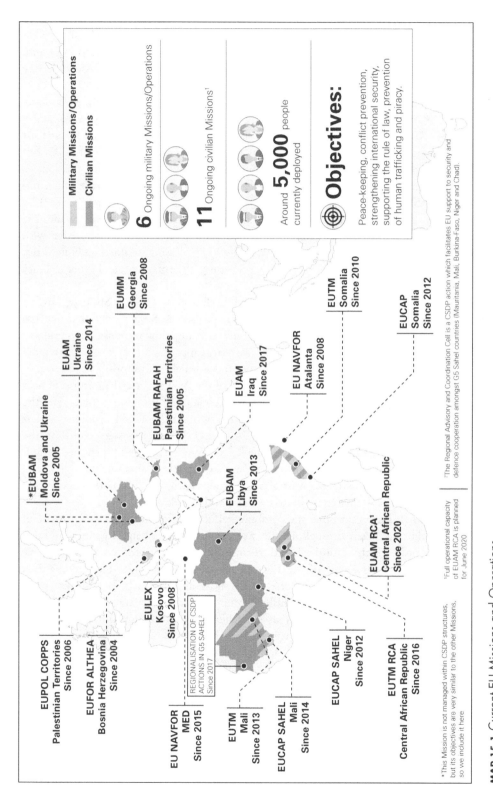

MAP 15.1 Current EU Missions and Operations.

Source: © European Union, 1995–2020, European Union External Action.

Two of the most important initiatives were begun in 2017 with the establishment of an office of Military Planning and Conduct Capability (or MPCC, a sort of military head-quarters of the EU, long resisted by the UK) and a framework for joint military action known as "Permanent Structured Cooperation" (PESCO). While the MPCC is responsible for the operational planning and conduct of the EU's military training missions abroad, PESCO is both a framework and process to enhance defense cooperation among the twenty-five member states who participate in it. Denmark and Malta have opted out, as has the UK as it leaves the EU, although there is some discussion that third-party states such as the UK and Norway could be included in a revised PESCO. PESCO is designed as a way to invest, plan, develop, and operate security cooperation between the member states but not all states have to take part in all of its projects, only the ones in which they wish to (and have the military capabilities to do so). Thus far, PESCO projects include or will include operations such as a joint EU intelligence school, deployable military disaster relief, an unmanned anti-submarine system and attack helicopters, and a cyber rapid response team.

Important differences on particular aspects of the CFSP still exist, however, with a recent example – Emmanuel Macron's insistence on creating the European Intervention Initiative (a group of fourteen countries which will jointly plan for future crises, sharply resisted by Germany) – illustrating the political disagreements still plaguing member state cooperation.[19] However, it is important to note that in spite of all these disagreements, the EU has achieved more on security cooperation than most people think, driven by a desire to decrease its reliance on the US.[20] It has, for example, taken part in many military actions over the last decade and a half.[21] In 2003, it deployed peacekeeping troops in Macedonia (Operation Concordia) and the Democratic Republic of Congo (Operation Artemis), and in December 2004 it launched its biggest peacekeeping mission when 7,000 troops (many coming from outside the EU, it is true) took over from NATO in Bosnia. By 2006, the EU was contributing 50 percent of the peacekeeping forces in Bosnia (where the Office of High Representative in charge of implementation of the Dayton Peace Accords has always been held by an EU national), and 70 percent of the forces in Kosovo.

In addition to military missions, the EU also has police and other missions in Somalia (maritime security), Libya (above all, in fighting smuggling networks), Kosovo (rule of law and police reform), Iraq (security sector reform), and a longstanding presence in the Palestinian Territories (see Map 15.1). National military interventions have also continued, including the UK's operation in Sierra Leone in 2001 (establishing order after a UN force had failed), France's operations in Côte d'Ivoire in 2002 and in Mali in 2013.

TRADE POLICY AND SOFT POWER

Whatever the doubts and questions about the EU's military power discussed above, the EU's massive economic presence – and thus its considerable soft power – is uncontested:

- After the US, it is the wealthiest capitalist marketplace in the world, about the same size as the BRIC countries (Brazil, Russia, India, and China) combined, accounting for almost a quarter of global economic output although only representing seven percent of the world's population (see Figure 15.1).
- It is one of the world's biggest trading powers, accounting for just under 16 percent of world exports in goods and 15 percent of imports, and about a quarter of trade in services (see Figure 15.2). The EU is the top trading partner for eighty countries.

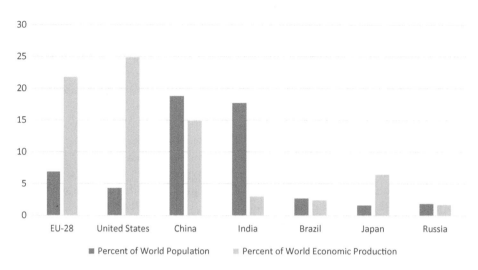

FIGURE 15.1 The EU in the Global Economy.

Source: Economic figures 2016 from Eurostat at https://ec.europa.eu/eurostat/statistics-explained/index.php?title=The_ EU_in_the_world_-_economy_and_finance and theGlobalEconomy.com at www.theglobaleconomy.com/compare-countries/; Population figures 2018 from Eurostat at https://ec.europa.eu/eurostat/statistics-explained/index.php/The_ EU_in_the_world_-_population#Population_change and Worldometers at www.worldometers.info/world-population/population-by-country/.

- Its currency, the euro, is the second most important currency in the world, behind the US dollar (see Figure 15.3).
- It is the biggest source of foreign direct investment in the world, accounting for over a third of the world's inward flow of foreign direct investment and about 50 percent of all outward flow.[22]
- It is the biggest market in the world for mergers and acquisitions; European multinationals have grown rapidly in strength and reach, reclaiming some of the dominant positions they held before the rise of competition from the US and Japan.

These developments have made the EU an economic superpower, willing and able to exert its economic influence on a global scale. In perhaps no other area has the impact of European integration been more substantial than in the field of trade, where – in contrast to its difficulties in agreeing on a common foreign and security policy – the EU has built common positions and wielded them to great effect. The basis of its success is the Common Commercial Policy (CCP), contained in the Treaty of Rome.

As discussed in Chapter 1, the Bretton Woods conference in 1944 reached understanding on an Anglo-American proposal to promote free trade, nondiscrimination, and stable rates of exchange. Bretton Woods was in effect an agreement on procedures to regulate the postwar international monetary system – rules-based regimes for international cooperation which have defined the postwar international order. This system was to be buttressed by the creation of new international organizations: the General Agreement on Tariffs and Trade (later to become the World Trade Organization or WTO in 1995), the International Monetary Fund, and the World Bank and International Bank for Reconstruction and Development, the latter two intended as sources of capital and financial assistance for developing states. The Treaty of Rome removed tariffs between the EU member states – thus leading to the formation of a customs union – and created the CCP, which designated a single representative for external trade negotiations (trade in services and intellectual products were initially excluded

Merchandise Trade, 2018

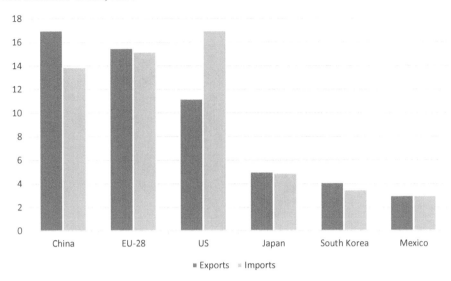

Commercial Services Trade, 2018

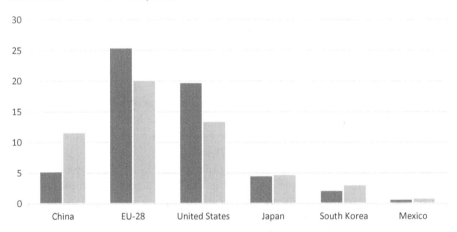

FIGURE 15.2 The EU Share of World Trade.

Source: Eurostat, "International Trade in Goods," at https://ec.europa.eu/eurostat/statistics-explained/index.php/International_trade_in_goods, accessed January 29, 2020; Eurostat, "World Trade in Services," https://ec.europa.eu/eurostat/statistics-explained/index.php/World_trade_in_services#International_trade_in_services_.E2.80.94_overview, accessed January 30, 2020.

but Lisbon changed this). In other words, since the Treaty of Rome and the creation of the CCP, all trade disputes between, for example, Germany and the US or France and the US are negotiated between the EU and the US, not between the US and Germany or France. Different member states, of course, have different trade interests (and different trade philosophies, some being more in favor of free trade and some more protectionist). A common position is hammered out between the member states and the Commission, and negotiations at the WTO are conducted through the EU commissioner for trade.

Aimed officially at contributing "to the harmonious development of world trade, the progressive abolition of restrictions on international trade, and the lowering of customs barriers,"

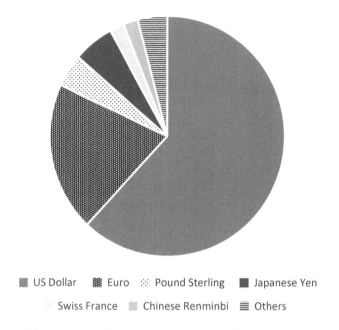

US Dollar   Euro   Pound Sterling   Japanese Yen

Swiss France   Chinese Renminbi   Others

FIGURE 15.3 Shares of Currencies in Global Foreign Exchange Reserves.

Source: International Monetary Fund, "Currency Composition of Official Foreign Exchange Reserves," at http://data. imf.org/?sk=E6A5F467-C14B-4AA8-9F6D-5A09EC4E62A4, accessed January 30, 2020.

the CCP was designed to protect the EU's trading interests. It was not fully put in place until the completion of the single market, but along the way it helped establish strong EU positions on global trade negotiations and protected the EU's balance of trade; after running surpluses for the previous five years, in 2018 the EU had a small trade deficit of $27.5 billion – compared to a US trade deficit in 2018 of $621 billion.[23]

The growing confidence of the EU on trade matters is reflected in the number of times it has been involved in cases brought before the WTO. If a country adopts a trade policy measure or takes an action that is considered to be a breach of a WTO agreement, the dispute can be taken to the WTO, which investigates and issues a judgment that is binding upon member states. Not surprisingly – given that they are two of the world's biggest trading powers – the EU and the US have brought more cases before the WTO than anyone else, and in many instances the disputes have been between the EU and the US (see Chapter 16).

The EU has not always been able to have its way on trade negotiations, and at least one analysis finds a mismatch between the institutional unity of the EU on trade issues and its external bargaining power.[24] But the statistics make a compelling case, and whatever doubts may be cast on the internal economic policies of the EU – regarding low economic growth, high unemployment, and an aging population (see previous chapters) – the global economic presence of the EU is clear.

To be sure, military power is still needed to deal with the most serious security problems, but in a world of globalization, new technology, and greater market freedom, economic power has many advantages over the power of violence, and – on this front at least – the EU is in a commanding position. The EU's economic clout is thus its chief asset in asserting soft power. This is true both in terms of its ability to stand toe to toe with rival powers, such as the US or China, but also in its ability to exercise influence in its regional neighborhood and in farther-flung regions of the world. In particular, the EU's financial carrots and sticks hold considerable influence – most especially through development aid – in shaping political behavior all over the globe, as we shall see in the next chapter.

What effects Brexit will have on the EU's economic clout and thus its soft power advantage are hard to calculate, but it is certain that there will be some impact. As one observer has argued, "Any room the EU walks into, it will carry less weight than when the UK was a member."[25] While it will continue to have a powerful position in the world and substantial leverage in any trade negotiations, the loss of the world's fifth-largest economy and the EU's hub for financial services cannot help but do damage.

QUESTIONS TO CONSIDER

1   What have been the chief obstacles preventing the EU from projecting a more robust military capability? What effect will Brexit have on the EU's ambitions? Is hard power still important in today's world?
2   To what degree has the global environment surrounding the EU's foreign policy ambitions changed in the last decade and a half? What has been the EU's response?
3   In which concrete ways does the EU's global economic power translate into political influence around the world? What effects may Brexit have on the EU's soft power advantage?

NOTES

1   Samuel Huntington, "The Lonely Superpower," *Foreign Affairs* 78, no. 2 (March–April 1999).
2   G. John Ikenberry, "Introduction," in *America Unrivaled: The Future of the Balance of Power*, edited by G. John Ikenberry, 1 (Ithaca: Cornell University Press, 2002).
3   Hubert Védrine with Dominique Moïsi, *France in an Age of Globalization*, 2 (Washington, DC: Brookings Institution, 2001).
4   See International Institute for Strategic Studies, *The Military Balance 2011* (London: Routledge, 2011).
5   See discussion in Chalmers Johnson, *Blowback: The Costs and Consequences of American Empire* (New York: Metropolitan, 2000).
6   See Klaus Knorr, *Power and Wealth: The Political Economy of International Power*, 3–4 (New York: Basic Books, 1973). Joseph S. Nye, *Bound to Lead: The Changing Nature of American Power* (New York: Basic Books, 1991), and *Soft Power: The Means to Success in World Politics* (New York: PublicAffairs, 2004).
7   For further discussion, see Clyde Prestowitz, *Rogue Nation: American Unilateralism and the Failure of Good Intentions* (New York: Basic Books, 2003).
8   See Janet Adamski, Mary Troy Johnson, and Christina M. Schweiss, eds., *Old Europe, New Security: Evolution for a Complex World* (Aldershot: Ashgate, 2006).
9   Jean Groux and Philippe Manin, *The European Communities in the International Order* (Brussels: Commission of the European Communities, 1985).
10 Craig R. Whitney, "War in the Gulf: Europe; Gulf Fighting Shatters Europeans' Fragile Unity," *New York Times*, January 25, 1991, Section A, 11.
11 Quoted in Alan Riding, "Conflict in Yugoslavia: Europeans Send High-Level Team," *New York Times*, June 29, 1991, Section 1, 4.
12 J. Bryan Collester, "How Defense 'Spilled Over' into the CFSP: Western European Union (WEU) and the European Security and Defense Identity (ESDI)," in *The State of the European Union: Risks, Reform, Resistance, and Revival*, edited by Maria Green Cowles and Michael Smith (Oxford: Oxford University Press, 2000).

13 Michael Smith, "What's Wrong with the CFSP? The Politics of Institutional Reform," in *The State of the European Union, vol. 4: Deepening and Widening*, edited by Pierre-Henri Laurent and Marc Maresceau (Boulder: Lynne Rienner, 1998).

14 William Echikson, "Europe Shows Muscle in this Trade War," Bloomberg, May 4, 1997, at www.bloomberg.com/news/articles/1997-05-04/europe-shows-muscle-in-this-trade-tussle-intl-edition, accessed April 28, 2020.

15 For more details, see Collester, "How Defense 'Spilled Over' into the CFSP."

16 Stefan Lehne, "Is there Hope for EU Foreign Policy?" Carnegie Europe, December 5, 2017, at https://carnegieeurope.eu/2017/12/05/is-there-hope-for-eu-foreign-policy-pub-74909, accessed January 5, 2020.

17 On the implications of Brexit for EU security and defense policy, see Michael Smith, "The European Union and the Global Arena: In Search of Post-Brexit Roles," *Politics and Governance* 7, no. 3 (September 2019): 83–92.

18 *Shared Vision, Common Action: A Stronger Europe. A Global Strategy for the European Union's Foreign and Security Policy*, European External Action Service, June 28, 2016, at https://op.europa.eu/en/publication-detail/-/publication/3eaae2cf-9ac5-11e6-868c-01aa75ed71a1, accessed January 5, 2020.

19 "Europe Needs to Defend Itself Better, but Cannot Do without America," *The Economist*, November 21, 2019, at www.economist.com/europe/2019/11/21/europe-needs-to-defend-itself-better-but-cannot-do-without-america, accessed December 1, 2019.

20 Seth Jones, *The Rise of European Security Cooperation* (Cambridge, UK: Cambridge University Press, 2007).

21 Bastian Giegerich and William Wallace, "Not Such a Soft Power: The External Deployment of European Forces," *Survival* 46, no. 2 (January 2004): 163–182.

22 European Parliament, "Fact Sheets on the European Union," at www.europarl.europa.eu/factsheets/en/sheet/160/the-european-union-and-its-trade-partners, accessed January 29, 2020.

23 Eurostat, "International Trade in Goods," at https://ec.europa.eu/eurostat/statistics-explained/index.php/International_trade_in_goods, accessed January 29, 2020.

24 Sophie Meunier, *Trading Voices: The European Union in International Commercial Negotiations* (Princeton, NJ: Princeton University Press, 2005).

25 Paul Taylor, senior fellow at Friends of Europe, cited in Steven Erlanger, "Brexit Is Here, and It's a Texas-Size Defeat for the EU," *New York Times*, January 29, 2020, at www.nytimes.com/2020/01/29/world/europe/brexit-brussels-eu.html?smid=nytcore-ios-share, accessed January 29, 2020.

BIBLIOGRAPHY

Adamski, Janet, Mary Troy Johnson, and Christina M. Schweiss, eds., *Old Europe, New Security: Evolution for a Complex World* (London: Routledge, 2017).

Bindi, Federiga, ed., *The Foreign Policy of the European Union. Assessing Europe's Role in the World* (Washington, DC: Brookings Institution Press, 2010).

Chelotti, Nicola, *The Formulation of EU Foreign Policy: Socialization, Negotiations, and Disaggregation of the State* (London and New York: Routledge, 2016).

Collester, J. Bryan, "How Defense 'Spilled Over' into the CFSP: Western European Union (WEU) and the European Security and Defense Identity (ESDI)," in *The State of the European Union: Risks, Reform, Resistance, and Revival*, edited by Maria Green Cowles and Michael Smith (Oxford: Oxford University Press, 2000).

Echikson, William, "Europe Shows Muscle in this Trade War," Bloomberg, May 4, 1997, at www.bloomberg.com/news/articles/1997-05-04/europe-shows-muscle-in-this-trade-tussle-intl-edition, accessed April 28, 2020.

Erlanger, Steven, "Brexit Is Here, and It's a Texas-Size Defeat for the EU," *New York Times*, January 29, 2020, at www.nytimes.com/2020/01/29/world/europe/brexit-brussels-eu.html?smid=nytcore-ios-share, accessed January 29, 2020.

Economist, The, "Europe Needs to Defend Itself Better, but Cannot Do without America," November 21, 2019, at www.economist.com/europe/2019/11/21/europe-needs-to-defend-itself-better-but-cannot-do-without-america, accessed December 1, 2019.

European External Action Service, *Shared Vision, Common Action: A Stronger Europe. A Global Strategy for the European Union's Foreign and Security Policy*, June 28, 2016, at https://op.europa.eu/en/publication-detail/-/publication/3eaae2cf-9ac5-11e6-868c-01aa75ed71a1, accessed January 5, 2020.

European Parliament, "Fact Sheets on the European Union," at www.europarl.europa.eu/factsheets/en/sheet/160/the-european-union-and-its-trade-partners, accessed January 29, 2020.

Eurostat, "International Trade in Goods," at https://ec.europa.eu/eurostat/statistics-explained/index.php/International_trade_in_goods, accessed January 29, 2020.

Giegerich, Bastian and William Wallace, "Not Such a Soft Power: The External Deployment of European Forces," *Survival* 46, no. 2 (January 2004): 163–182.

Groux, Jean and Philippe Manin, *The European Communities in the International Order* (Brussels: Commission of the European Communities, 1985).

Hill, Christopher and Michael Smith, eds., *International Relations and the European Union*, 3rd ed. (Oxford: Oxford University Press, 2017).

Howorth, Jolyon, *Security and Defence Policy in the European Union*, 2nd ed. (Basingstoke: Palgrave Macmillan, 2014).

Huntington, Samuel, "The Lonely Superpower," *Foreign Affairs* 78, no. 2 (March–April 1999).

Ikenberry, G. John, ed., *America Unrivaled: The Future of the Balance of Power* (Ithaca: Cornell University Press, 2002).

International Institute for Strategic Studies, *The Military Balance 2011* (London: Routledge, 2011).

Johnson, Chalmers, *Blowback: The Costs and Consequences of American Empire* (New York: Metropolitan, 2000).

Jones, Seth, *The Rise of European Security Cooperation* (Cambridge, UK: Cambridge University Press, 2007).

Keukeleire, Stephan and Tom Delreaux, *The Foreign Policy of the European Union*, 2nd ed. (Basingstoke: Palgrave Macmillan, 2014).

Knorr, Klaus, *Power and Wealth: The Political Economy of International Power* (New York: Basic Books, 1973).

Meunier, Sophie, *Trading Voices: The European Union in International Commercial Negotiations* (Princeton, NJ: Princeton University Press, 2005).

Nye, Joseph S., *Bound to Lead: The Changing Nature of American Power* (New York: Basic Books, 1991).

Nye, Joseph S., *Soft Power: The Means to Success in World Politics* (New York: PublicAffairs, 2004).

Prestowitz, Clyde, *Rogue Nation: American Unilateralism and the Failure of Good Intentions* (New York: Basic Books, 2003).

Riding, Alan, "Conflict in Yugoslavia: Europeans Send High-Level Team," *New York Times*, June 29, 1991, Section 1, 4.

Smith, Michael, "What's Wrong with the CFSP? The Politics of Institutional Reform," in *The State of the European Union, vol. 4: Deepening and Widening*, edited by Pierre-Henri Laurent and Marc Maresceau (Boulder: Lynne Rienner, 1998).

Smith, Michael, "The European Union and the Global Arena: In Search of Post-Brexit Roles," *Politics and Governance* 7, no. 3 (September 2019): 83–92.

Whitney, Craig R., "War in the Gulf: Europe; Gulf Fighting Shatters Europeans' Fragile Unity," *New York Times*, January 25, 1991, Section A, 11.

Védrine, Hubert with Dominique Moïsi, *France in an Age of Globalization* (Washington, DC: Brookings Institution, 2001).

FURTHER READING

Strangely enough for an area in which critics charge that the EU has not lived up to expectations, there are numerous published studies on different aspects of the EU's foreign and security policy. The following is just a small selection.

Nicola Chelotti, *The Formulation of EU Foreign Policy: Socialization, Negotiations, and Disaggregation of the State* (London and New York: Routledge, 2016).

> An analysis of how foreign policy is made in the EU, using a database of questionnaires and interviews with national diplomats and members of working parties and committees of the Council of Ministers.

Christopher Hill and Michael Smith, eds., *International Relations and the European Union*, 3rd ed. (Oxford: Oxford University Press, 2017).

> An edited collection with chapters on goals, institutions, processes, and specific activities and impacts.

Janet Adamski, Mary Troy Johnson, and Christina M. Schweiss, eds. *Old Europe, New Security: Evolution for a Complex World* (London: Routledge, 2017).

> Presents a sharp critique of the idea that the EU is not pulling its weight by arguing that – instead of relying on military means – it is developing a variety of economic and diplomatic tools to respond to security problems.

Federiga Bindi, ed., *The Foreign Policy of the European Union. Assessing Europe's Role in the World* (Washington, DC: Brookings Institution Press, 2010); Stephan Keukeleire and Tom Delreaux, *The Foreign Policy of the European Union*, 2nd ed. (Basingstoke: Palgrave Macmillan, 2014); Jolyon Howorth, *Security and Defence Policy in the European Union*, 2nd ed. (Basingstoke: Palgrave Macmillan, 2014).

> Three excellent studies of the foreign policies of the EU.

CHAPTER 16

The EU and the World

CHAPTER OVERVIEW

- The EU's relationship with the US is by far its most important one. However, it has not always been easy: they were wary of each other before World War II, but the Cold War forged a relationship of both common democratic values and mutual security needs, even if occasional tensions arose. Since the end of the Cold War, however, differences have become both sharper and clearer. With the arrival of the Trump administration the relationship between the EU and the US has grown even more challenging.
- Beyond its relationship with the US, the EU has important, productive, and yet fraught relationships with Russia and Turkey. It has also been developing important relationships with rising world and regional powers such as Brazil, India, and most especially China.
- In addition, the EU has significant relationships with its regional neighbors – many of whom are potential future members of the EU – as well as with countries in the global south, mostly former colonies in Africa, the Caribbean, and Asia. In these relationships, the EU's use of soft power is clearly on display. It is a benefactor (through development assistance) as well as an economic competitor to many countries around the world.

During the Cold War,[1] the US–Europe partnership was the most important in the world in terms of its military significance, economic power, and – last but far from least – its global model for democracy and peaceful interaction. The US–EU relationship today is still crucially important: both are economic superpowers, possess significant military or "hard" power, and have used their economic strength as well as their domination of global culture to achieve vast amounts of "soft" power. Yet while the Cold War brought the two sides together with a common project and common enemy, in its aftermath a complex set of emerging threats and challenges has emerged. The US hoped to reap the benefits of the peaceful conclusion of the Cold War through the form of a reduced need to finance and staff its security efforts, but soon found that new risks and dangers had replaced the old tensions of the Cold War, demanding a different set of approaches and structures. How to deal with threats of global terrorism (in the form of 9/11 and Iraq) and policy responses to climate change divided the two sides under the Bush administration, and the Obama administration at times disappointed Europeans by its less assertive leadership on pressing global issues and its continuation of Bush-era targeted assassinations of suspected terrorists.

The arrival of the Trump administration has greatly exacerbated these differences, with President Trump proclaiming a policy of "America first," putting the NATO alliance into question, threatening a trade war with the EU, staking out very different positions on security issues (such as how to deal with Russia and Iran), pulling out of the Paris accord on climate change action, and downplaying the promotion of democracy around the world. Regardless of who occupies the White House in the future, however, it has become clear that Europe and the US no longer have quite the same relationship they enjoyed during the Cold War. After long assuming that they were on the same page when it came to universal issues such as democracy and capitalism, Americans and Europeans now find themselves often at loggerheads over many fundamental issues, undoubtedly reflecting a growing divergence of political-cultural values.

Besides its relationship with the US, the EU has many other global connections. Relations with its immediate geographic neighbors are crucially important to EU security and trade, and serve as a demonstration of EU soft power. Russia is the EU's closest big neighbor, and the EU sees the security and economic stability of Russia as vital, especially as it depends heavily on Russian energy supplies. However, it is also a troublesome neighbor, and the last decade has seen a worsening of EU–Russia relations in the wake of conflict in Ukraine, concerns about the lack of democracy under Vladimir Putin, Russian meddling in the domestic politics of member states, and resurgent Russian military power in the region and in the Middle East. Concerns about the erosion of democracy and human rights plague the EU's relationship with its other large neighbor, Turkey, as well. Farther afield, China, India, and Brazil enjoy relationships with the EU which are only growing in importance. China has dual significance, for while it is a huge external market for EU goods it is also a growing economic competitor for the bloc. Finally, the EU's relationships with countries of the global south are key figures in EU foreign policy. Here, however, EU priorities are driven by a combination of altruistic motives and self-interest: countries in Africa, the Caribbean, and Pacific deal with poverty, environmental issues, and security concerns which the EU through development aid has attempted to alleviate. At the same time, these countries also represent a major source of EU exports and supply key raw materials to Europe.

THE TRANSATLANTIC RELATIONSHIP

The alliance between the US and the EU cannot be underestimated. They are both economic superpowers and have among the most powerful military forces in the world. Furthermore, they dominate global culture – their corporations spearheading a communications and technology revolution that has given new meaning to the global impact of "the West." Residents of the US and EU are the wealthiest, healthiest, and best-educated people in the world; their leaders historically have agreed on the promotion of democracy and capitalism; and what one says and does matters a great deal not only to the other but to much of the world at large.

The transatlantic relationship was never an easy one, however. Before World War II, Americans were suspicious of the European way of life, wary of being pulled in to European conflicts, and critical of European colonialism. Meanwhile, Europeans cast nervous glances at the rising political, economic, and cultural influence of the US. After World War II, Europeans fell into an often reluctant subservience to American leadership, worrying about US foreign policy priorities but admitting their need for American economic investment and security guarantees. Privately, European governments might have criticized US policy, but publicly they largely acquiesced to US wishes. As Europe recovered from the war, however, Europeans became more self-reliant and increasingly conscious of their differences with the US, not only on policy issues, but on political and social norms and values.

As we have seen, the US has played a critical role in the development of the EU through both intentional policy and unintentional effects. Intentionally, the US made a signal contribution to the birth of the EU by supporting the economic reconstruction of postwar

Western Europe through the Marshall Plan, encouraging Europeans to work together in the Organisation for European Economic Cooperation, and providing a security umbrella that allowed Western Europe to concentrate its energy and resources on internal reorganization and reconstruction instead of external threats. American administrations also generally gave their blessing to European integration, understanding that it played an important role in building European peace and stability and fostering it as a political and economic partner of the US. At the same time, the US contributed unintentionally to European integration, by pursuing policies that have helped unite Europeans either in support of US policy or in opposition – for example, how best to deal with the Soviet threat during the Cold War, the Suez conflict, or the war in Vietnam. Nevertheless, US policy initiatives helped Europeans identify their weaknesses. For example, it was the feeble European responses to the crises in the Balkans in the 1990s that encouraged Europeans to work harder at developing common security policies.

The end of the Cold War saw a number of diplomatic initiatives reflecting US recognition of the new importance of the EU and the relative decline of the central role of NATO. In a December 1989 speech, US secretary of state James Baker spoke of the need for beefed-up economic and political ties and for stronger institutional and consultative links.[2] Negotiations commenced, leading to the November 1990 signature of the first bilateral agreement between the two, the Transatlantic Declaration. This pact committed the two sides to regular high-level contacts and called for cooperation in a variety of policy areas, including combating terrorism, drug trafficking, international crime, and preventing the spread of weapons of mass destruction.[3] Similarly, in late 1995 the two sides signed the New Transatlantic Agenda, agreeing to move from consultation to joint action aimed at promoting peace and democracy around the world, which would contribute to the expansion of world trade the improvement of transatlantic ties.

Yet the end of the Cold War also created new strains. Counting on a "peace dividend," the US hoped to reduce the cost and scope of its military and security efforts. However, new risks and dangers emerged which required new, and no less burdensome, approaches and structures. Any hopes among American leaders that the Community could take more of the responsibility for dealing with international crises were dashed by the divided European response to the 1990–1991 Gulf War and the absence of Community leadership in the conflict in the Balkans in the early 1990s. Economic matters also rose in significance with the European single market program and a growing economic competition between the US and EU (see Box 16.1).

Box 16.1 Global Frenemies? The US–EU Economic Relationship and Trade Tensions

The North Atlantic is the wealthiest and most important two-way economic street in the world. The EU and the US are each other's largest trading partners and the two economies account together for just under half of world gross domestic product and nearly a third of world trade flows. Indeed, whatever analysts claim about the rising economic power of China, it pales by comparison to the size and productivity of the EU–US nexus. Total US investment in the EU is three times higher than in all of Asia, and EU investment in the US is eight times more than that of India and China together.[4] The EU and US also control two of the key international currencies, the dollar and the euro, and lead the world in the development of new technology. Consider, too, the following realities:

- The EU and the US account for about one-fifth of each other's bilateral trade, they rank first and second in the world in share of foreign direct investment (FDI) and they are each other's biggest sources of FDI. In 2018 US FDI (stock) in the EU was $3.3 trillion (€2.96) while EU FDI (stock) was $2.6 trillion (€2.33).[5]
- While millions of Europeans work for US-owned corporations, the reverse has become true as well. Already by 2004 about as many Americans (nearly 4.4 million) worked for European companies as vice versa.[6] "Our multinationals are so thoroughly intertwined," said EU trade commissioner Pascal Lamy in 2003, "that some of them have forgotten whether their origins are European or American." In his view, the size and significance of the relationship had become such that it defined "the shape of the global economy as a whole."[7]

Throughout the Cold War, the balance rested firmly in favor of the US, which was the world's dominating economic superpower. But the rise of the European single market – together with all its related economic effects – has shifted the scales. Tellingly, the US had a large trade deficit with the EU – around $169 billion (€1.52) in 2019.[8]

Despite their economic ties, the EU and the US have nevertheless had a number of trade disputes over the last several decades, ranging from conflict over investment in Cuba in the early 1990s (the Helms–Burton Act, which allowed for foreign companies investing in Cuba to be sued in US courts) to the "banana wars" (involving preferential trade for former European colonies) of the late 1990s to different regulatory approaches toward internet giants such as Google, Twitter, and Facebook.[9] Under the Trump administration trade disputes have intensified. Angered at the US's negative trade balance with the EU, President Trump has accused the EU of unfair trade practices, including actions by the European Central Bank which purportedly weaken the euro against the dollar (thus hurting US exports). Consequently, in 2018 the administration slapped tariffs on European steel and aluminum and more recently announced tariffs on Airbus planes (a chief competitor with Boeing in the US) and 25 percent duties on French wine, Scotch and Irish whiskies, and cheese from across the EU.[10]

The terrorist attacks of September 2001 jolted the transatlantic relationship further, injecting new elements into the definition of security policy on both sides of the Atlantic: terrorism (especially when it involved suicide attacks) (1) could not be met with conventional military responses, (2) transcended national borders, (3) showed that US military power, while impressive, was not a guarantor of success in itself, and (4) revealed that Americans and Europeans had different definitions of both the causes of terrorism and the most effective responses. President Bush liked to argue that the terrorists had attacked the US because they "hated" America and were envious of its democratic record, and that violence should be met with force. Europeans were more inclined to look at the root causes of militant resentment – including US policy on the Arab–Israeli problem and the stationing of US troops in Saudi Arabia – and to design policy accordingly.

As the attacks on 9/11 prompted a massive outpouring of political and public sympathy in the EU, European leaders for their part hoped that the tragedy would herald a new era in US foreign policy, with an emphasis on multilateralism and diplomacy. Within months, however, it was clear that the Bush administration planned to pursue unilateral responses to terrorism. President Bush drew particular European criticism for his reference in January 2002 to the "axis of evil," meaning Iran, Iraq, and North Korea – a characterization that was dismissed by the French foreign minister as "simplistic."[11] The subsequent 2003 crisis over Iraq was a watershed in the transatlantic relationship. For the first time since 1945, several European governments, notably Germany and France, openly opposed US policy. American critics accused the EU of dithering and of trying to appease the regime of Saddam Hussein. US defense secretary Donald Rumsfeld dismissed Germany and France as "problems" and as "Old Europe," while arguing that the center of gravity had shifted eastward to "New Europe." Europeans responded by using unflattering Wild West metaphors to describe President George W. Bush.

Many wondered during the Bush presidency whether the US–EU relationship would ever be the same. But while the easy knee-jerk reaction was to focus on the policies of the Bush administration, others began to ask whether there were long-term structural differences in play. This point was vindicated to some degree by the election of Barack Obama. Although immediately before and after his election Obama enjoyed huge popularity in Europe (not least because of his symbolism as the "anti-Bush"), his administration's foreign policy proved a disappointment to some Europeans who had hoped that he might take a more active approach to the Arab–Israeli problem and to dealing with climate change. The Obama administration even stepped up the extremely controversial policy of targeted killings of suspected terrorists (most via drone strike) started under the Bush administration.

Yet despite these points of contention between Europe and the US under Obama, the election of President Trump can be said to represent a sea change in the transatlantic relationship. Very critical of multilateral institutions, President Trump asserted a foreign policy of "American first."[12] The Trump administration has largely rejected multilateral solutions to key issues: the US pulled out of both the Paris Climate Accord and the nuclear agreement with Iran; it actively sought warmer relations with Russia and rebuffed Europeans' attempts for a united strategy in dealing with Vladimir Putin; it cultivated ties with President Erdogan of Turkey, allowing it to invade Syria and make war on the Kurds who assisted the US in its fight against ISIS; it supported populist radical right and Euroskeptic leaders in EU member states; and downgraded mechanisms of global governance. Through all of these moves, President Trump largely pursued a go-it-alone approach. Certainly, differences in policy approaches have always characterized the US–EU relationship. Yet President Trump has gone beyond simple policy differences by putting into question bedrock principles of the relationship, for example by questioning the utility of NATO while demanding higher financial contributions from NATO members in much harsher language than his predecessors.[13] Moreover, although trade disputes are also not new to the US–EU relationship, the Trump administration has escalated trade tensions by slapping tariffs on steel and threatening a wider trade war, and President Trump has made no secret that he is skeptical of there being an EU at all. It would not be a stretch to suggest that US–EU relations have reached a new low point.

Having said this, we should not lose sight of the fact that whoever occupies the White House in the future, the US and Europe no longer have quite the same relationship they enjoyed during the Cold War. Buoyed by their economic power and new political influence over the last decade, Europeans have become more assertive and more willing to pursue their own interpretation of the most pressing international problems, and more aware of how they differ with the US on the solutions. As Angela Merkel of Germany has stated, "The times in which we could totally rely on others are to some extent over."[14] The US for its part has started to turn its attention more and more to other parts of the world and often sees the EU as more competitor than ally. Optimists argue that the transatlantic relationship is vital, that both sides need each other, and that cooperation is far preferable to disagreement. But pessimists wonder if the two sides can agree on critical issues, given their different values and their often contrasting views about the most serious international problems, their causes, and

PHOTO 16.1 Donald Trump with EU Leaders, 2017.
Source: © European Union, 2017, EC – Audiovisual Service.

their most promising solutions. After long assuming that they were on the same page when it came to universal issues such as democracy and capitalism, Americans and Europeans now find themselves often at loggerheads over many fundamental issues.

EXPLAINING US–EU DIFFERENCES

Historically, the US and the EU have largely agreed on policy and the relationship between the two has been close and productive.[15] But they have also often disagreed; such disagreements have become especially pronounced in the last several years. These disputes are indicative not just of Europeans' increasing willingness to resist following the American lead when the two disagree, but also of the extent to which the two bring different sets of values and goals to bear on their interpretations of the priorities of international relations.

So how can the differences be explained? One approach is to take the long view, i.e. the idea that Americans and Europeans have simply developed very divergent values – on religion, the proper role of government, individual versus the collective good, national identity, etc. – rooted in their different historical and political development. Consider these fundamental differences:

- *Contrasting attitudes toward patriotism and nationalism.* Minxin Pei considers the US "one of the most nationalist countries in the world," a belief which he concludes is based not on notions of ethnic superiority but on a belief in the ideals of American democracy.[16] Where most Americans are delighted to wear their patriotism on their sleeves, Europeans (at least until recently) tend to be more wary about pride in their country, in large part because they have had to live for so long with the war and conflict that can arise out of aggressive nationalism. Polls over the last several decades have amply demonstrated the divide between Europeans and Americans. To take one recent example, a 2019 YouGov-Cambridge Globalism Project survey found that while only 10 percent of British, 6 percent of French, and 5 percent of Germans answered that their country was "the best in the world," more than 37 percent of Americans agreed with this – far more than any other country in the survey.[17]

- *The role of religion.* Europeans and Americans have been diverging on the role of religion in their societies since well before the end of the Cold War. As a recent illustration, around half of all Americans in a 2019 Pew Center poll said that religion was very important in their daily lives, while only 22 percent of Western Europeans and 19 percent of Central and Eastern Europeans said the same.[18] Meanwhile, another Pew Center poll in 2011 found that regular church attendance was significantly higher in the US than in Europe, and that more than 50 percent of Americans believe that it is necessary to believe in God to have morals/good values, while only 20 percent of the British, 19 percent of Spaniards, and 15 percent of the French held this view.[19] Not surprisingly then, religion plays a prominent role in the public and private lives of Americans, as reflected in attitudes toward a wide range of issues, from abortion to the teaching of evolution to doctor-assisted suicide, and the expectation that presidential candidates must make public declarations of faith. Europe, by contrast, is a predominantly secular society in which religion plays only a marginal role.

- *The role of government.* Americans and Europeans have developed different views about the role that government should play in their lives. Where the majority of Americans feel that it is more important for government to provide them with the freedom to pursue individual goals, a strong majority of Europeans feel that it is more important for government to guarantee that no one is in need.[20] Not surprisingly then, Americans typically disagree that success in life is determined by forces outside our control and strongly agree that hard work is very important for success – attitudes that contrast strongly with most European countries.[21] The effects can be seen in views on welfare: Americans use it (more often than most realize) and value it, but Europeans make it more widely available and are more willing to be taxed at higher rates in order to receive more services. Tellingly, the US is, despite the Affordable Care Act, the only liberal democracy in the world that does not have universal health care, a concept that is taken for granted in every European state.

However, more recent history could also help explain growing US–EU frictions. While the Cold War brought the two sides together with a common project and common enemy, its conclusion changed the realities of the international system: the ideological competition of the superpowers has been replaced by a bewildering set of threats and challenges, including trade and economic competition, the pressures of globalization, the threats posed by China's rise and the reemergence of Russia, a wave of populist discontent in established democracies and the rise of regional strongmen, and searing debates over mass migration. Within this wider landscape, the relationship between the EU and the US has changed, not just because of how the two sides see and relate to each other, but also because of how they each see and relate to the rest of the world. In short, Europeans and Americans appear to simply *think differently* about how to approach global challenges (see Box 16.2). To be sure, the two sides are still deeply invested in each other, and both continue to look to each other for support and reassurance on critical international problems, but the transatlantic relationship has shifted and it is not clear where it is heading in the future.

Box 16.2 Are Americans from Mars and Europeans from Venus?

The debate about the state of transatlantic relations was given a controversial twist in 2002 with the publication of an essay by Robert Kagan, an American neoconservative political commentator.[22] Kagan argued that Europeans and Americans no longer share a common view of the world, and that while Europe has moved into a world of laws, rules, and international cooperation, the US believes that security and defense depend on the possession and use of military power. On major strategic and international questions, he wrote, "Americans are from Mars and Europeans are from Venus." This is not a transitory state of affairs, he concludes – it is likely to endure. Most European intellectuals feel that the two no longer share a "strategic culture" and that the US is dominated by a "culture of death." They argue that the US is less patient with diplomacy and sees the world as divided between good and evil, friends and enemies. Meanwhile, Europeans see a more complex global system and are more tolerant of failure, more patient, and prefer to negotiate and persuade rather than to coerce.

Kagan went on to argue that the differences do not arise naturally out of the character of Europeans and Americans, but are instead a reflection of the relative positions of the two actors in the world; their attitudes have been reversed as their roles have been reversed. When European states were the key global powers in the eighteenth and nineteenth centuries, and when nationalism colored their views of one another, they were more ready to use violence to achieve their goals. But now that Europeans and Americans have traded places, they have also traded perspectives. When the US was weak, argues Kagan, it used the strategies of the weak, but now that it is strong, it uses the strategies of power.

Kagan's arguments had a mixed response, with the majority seeing them as an accurate summary of the state of play, but with a minority suggesting otherwise. One perspective argued that Europeans had not stumbled upon a new approach to international relations in which force played only a limited role, but that Europeans have deliberately chosen to be militarily weak; Europe is not a continent of pacifists, but one where the "just" causes of war are actively debated and where there are different opinions about the role of military force.[23] Whatever the opinions about Kagan's thesis, however, it had the important effect of sparking a vigorous debate about the character and future of the transatlantic relationship.

ENLARGEMENT AND THE EU'S NEIGHBORHOOD

One of the most vital relationships the EU has is with its immediate neighbors, and one where EU soft power is most evident. Within three months of taking office in January 1989, US president George H.W. Bush was presciently describing Western Europe as an economic magnet that could pull Eastern Europe toward a new commonwealth of free nations, and the US encouraged the Community to take responsibility for coordinating Western economic aid to the East. From those beginnings, the EU has evolved into a club to which almost all its neighbors want access, either as fully paid-up members or through preferential access agreements. The impact on the promotion of democracy and capitalism throughout the region has been profound.[24]

The foundations were laid by trade and cooperation agreements between the Community and almost all Eastern European states, the provision of several billion dollars in loans through the European Investment Bank, the launching of several programs to help Eastern European social reform, and the creation in 1990 of the European Bank for Reconstruction and Development. Talk of the expansion of Community membership to the east followed in short order, leading to association agreements that allowed for the gradual expansion of free trade, provided for foreign policy coordination and cultural exchanges, and encouraged preparations for eventual EU membership.[25]

The expansion to twelve new member states in 2004–2007 was the logical conclusion to all these developments. However, since that time something of an "enlargement fatigue" has set in among existing EU members, driven by concerns about the economic costs of integrating poorer member states, absorbing new members into an EU whose decision-making procedures have reached their capacity, and sensitivity to Russia's perception that the EU is encroaching on its sphere of influence. A total of sixteen countries could theoretically qualify for membership in the EU, including Ukraine, which signed a new association agreement with the EU in June 2014 after preparations for implementing an earlier agreement in 2013 were suspended, under Russian pressure, by Ukraine (one element in the dramatic escalation of conflict there, see below). Five of these sixteen potential members – Albania, North Macedonia (after a conflict over its name was resolved with Greece[26]), Montenegro, Serbia, and Turkey – have been formally accepted as "candidate countries," meaning that membership has been agreed to in principle and negotiations on terms have begun. Meanwhile, Bosnia and Herzegovina and Kosovo have been officially designated as "potential candidates." Nevertheless, and perhaps underscoring enlargement fatigue, European leaders recently blocked the opening of accession negotiations for both North Macedonia and Albania. Led by Emmanuel Macron of France, they argued that the policy itself needed to be reformed before opening any serious talks with the two countries.[27] This position seems to have gotten some traction with the Commission, which is considering plans to considerably tighten entrance requirements for the club.[28] Another candidate country, Iceland, withdrew its request to be considered in 2015.

Whatever the prospects for more enlargement in the immediate future, the EU has been conscious of the need to reach out to its neighbors and to create a "circle of friends." In 1995 the EU initiated the Euro-Mediterranean Partnership – otherwise known as the Barcelona Process – aimed at strengthening political, economic, and social ties between the EU and twelve neighboring countries. In 2004, the European Neighbourhood Policy (ENP) was launched, targeted at the EU's sixteen closest neighbors: Algeria, Armenia, Azerbaijan, Belarus, Egypt, Georgia, Israel, Jordan, Lebanon, Libya, Moldova, Morocco, the Palestinian Authority, Syria, Tunisia, and Ukraine (Russia is the subject of a separate set of agreements; see below). The policy promotes a relationship that the EU describes as "privileged," with the view to increase democratization, prosperity, human rights, the rule of law, good governance, and sustainable and inclusive development.[29] As discussed in Chapter 15, the EU's new watchword is the "resilience" of states. Practically, this means that the EU has a more sober view of its ability to transform its neighborhood into a democratic one, at least in the short term. Until then, the overriding goal is in achieving stability and avoiding the kind of unrest that could spill over into the EU itself. The ENP is financially supported by the European Neighborhood Instrument (ENI) to the tune of about 15.5 billion euros during the 2014–2020 budget period. The ENI finances a wide variety of projects, including joint border security with western Balkan countries, public administration reform in Albania, entrepreneurship in Bosnia and Herzegovina, and environmental protection in Jordan.

Among the most controversial residents in the EU's neighborhood is Turkey. The Community agreed as long ago as 1963 that Turkish membership in the EU was possible,

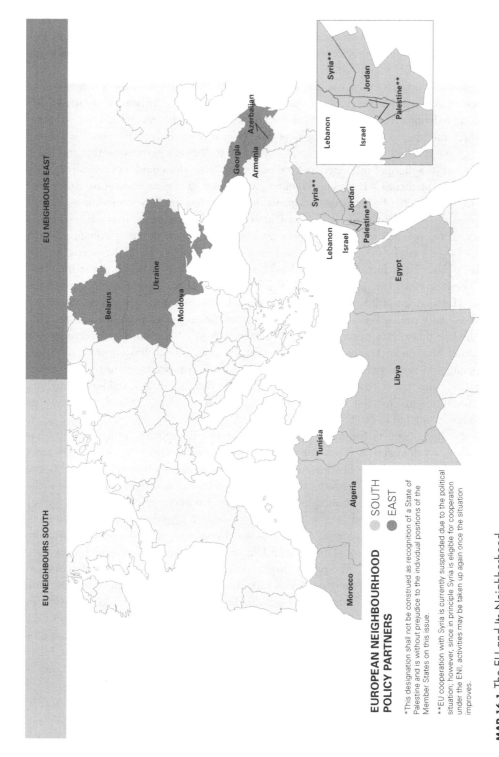

MAP 16.1 The EU and Its Neighborhood.

Source: © European Union, 2020; https://euneighbours.eu/en.

but Turkey has historically had a weak record on human rights, and it is big, poor, and predominantly Muslim, which raises troubling economic and social questions. There has also been a side debate about whether it is really European; since Europe ends at the Bosporus Strait, only a small part of Turkey is actually in Europe. Turkey has been an associate member since 1963 and applied for full membership in 1987; a customs union between the EU and Turkey came into force in December 1995; and Turkey was formally recognized in 2002 as an applicant country. Negotiations on Turkish membership in the EU opened in 2005 but were almost immediately tripped up by Turkey's refusal to open its ports to Greek Cyprus, human rights concerns, and its slow progress on changing its laws to correspond with EU law, all of which contributed to a near freezing of negotiations over entry into the EU. Since that time, the relationship between the EU and Turkey has continued along a contradictory and unclear trajectory. On the one hand, while the EU has continued to suffer economic problems, Turkey's economic growth until recently recorded impressive gains. Furthermore, as discussed in Chapter 4, progress toward membership was dangled as a carrot in getting Turkey to keep Syrian refugees in Turkey, thus helping to significantly alleviate pressure on EU member states. On the other hand, Turkey's economy has recently slowed precipitously, and Turkey's President Erdogan's increasingly authoritarian behavior, cozy relationship with Vladimir Putin, and aggressive military actions toward the Kurds has soured Turkey–EU relations. As a result of these red flags, EU priorities are focused on pre-serving a cordial, stable relationship with its huge Muslim neighbor. Turkey's prospects for EU membership remain dim.

THE EU'S ROCKY RELATIONSHIP WITH RUSSIA

Similarly, the EU's relationship with Russia has become increasingly troubled. As its closest big neighbor, the security and economic stability of Russia is viewed by the EU as crucial, and – despite EU criticism of Russian policy on the breakaway province of Chechnya – links between the two sides improved during the 1990s: Russia sought the respectability and economic opportunities that would come from a good relationship with the EU, while the EU looked for Russian support for eastern enlargement. Yet enlarge-ment was not met with enthusiasm in Russia, particularly as it included three former Soviet republics (Estonia, Latvia, and Lithuania); Russians worried about a new economic rift between a wealthy Europe and a relatively poor Russia and about the impact of enlargement on Russian exports to Eastern Europe. Russia was also displeased by the role of the EU in the outcome of the 2004 election in Ukraine, a portent of things to come.

The situation today has only worsened, with both sides needing each other but not trusting the other's motives. They share a common land border of 1,400 miles (2,250 kilometers), Russia is the EU's third largest trading partner (after the US and China), and the EU is reliant on Russia for energy supplies – about one-fifth of the EU's oil and one-quarter of its natural gas come from Russia, which especially affects several of the newer EU states such as Hungary, Slovakia, and the Czech Republic. But Russia's annexation of the Crimea and support of rebel groups in eastern Ukraine after the "Maidan" revolution in 2013–2014 heightened tensions, and in the wake of the downing of a Malaysia Airlines flight in July 2014 over rebel-held airspace the EU (along with the US) imposed sanc-tions. Still, despite obvious Russian violations of an accord worked out in Minsk in early 2015 meant to further negotiations between the Ukrainians and the rebels, attempts to widen EU sanctions have failed due to the resistance of several member states, including Hungary (whose president Viktor Orbán has developed a close relationship with Vladimir

PHOTO 16.2 A Frayed Relationship: German Chancellor Angela Merkel and Russian President Vladimir Putin.

Source: © European Communities, 2007, EC – Audiovisual Service.

Putin), the Czech Republic, and (at least for a while) Greece. A divide has thus opened up within the EU, preventing it from taking more concerted action vis-à-vis Russia. The March 4, 2018, poisoning of a former Russian spy Sergei Skripal and his daughter Yulia by suspected Russian agents further soured the relationship, with member states coordinating the expulsion of Russian diplomats. Yet calls from some quarters (most notably from a number of US politicians but also from Polish officials as well) to move more aggressively (i.e., arm the Ukrainians in their fight) have been rebuffed by many member states.

For its part, Russia is keenly aware of the international isolation it has provoked between it and the EU and most especially in the bilateral German–Russian relationship where Angela Merkel – once considered Vladimir Putin's closest friend in Europe – has distanced herself from the Russian leader.[30] Russia is also conscious that the EU is a crucial trading partner, accounting for 70 percent of its exports and the biggest source of foreign investment in Russian industry and infrastructure. So far Russia has clearly prioritized a "frozen" Ukraine conflict (much like previous conflicts in Georgia and Moldova) over improving EU–Russian relations, counting on its cultivation of friendships with Hungary and other EU states and its leverage in fossil fuel supply to force the EU to back down. There is some initial evidence this is working: in the summer of 2019 Russia was readmitted to the Council of Europe, Emmanuel Macron has recently suggested a new summit meeting to resolve the Ukraine crisis, and German firms are pressuring Angela Merkel to clear away obstacles to the final construction of the NordStream 2 pipeline from Russia to Germany.[31]

RELATIONS WITH BRIC COUNTRIES

Increasingly important to the EU are the BRIC countries – Brazil, Russia (discussed above), India, and China. Over the last ten years, they have all moved into the top ten EU trading partners. In particular, China has emerged as a serious global player, important to both the US and the EU. Over the centuries, Europe and China have had a long relationship, even if it has not always been a particularly good one. Contacts between the EU and China were thin before the 1980s (the first visit to China by a European commissioner was in 1975) and the relationship was set back by the events of Tiananmen Square in 1989. But relations improved in the mid-1990s, with a series of EU–China summits held between 1998 and 2002. Today, the EU is China's largest trading partner, and China is the EU's second-largest trading partner after the US.

Since 1998, the EU and China have held bilateral annual summits. At the 2013 summit the EU and China adopted the EU–China 2020 Strategic Agenda for Cooperation. Meant to significantly advance the EU–China relationship, the agreement spelled out key areas in which the two powers could strengthen their ties, such as security issues (fighting terrorism and ensuring maritime security), climate change and environmental protection, energy and agricultural development, and trade and investment. With respect to the last area, the goal is to negotiate and conclude a comprehensive EU–China investment agreement that will lead to the liberalization of investment and the removal of barriers for investors to each other's market.[32]

Unlike China's relationship with the US, EU–China relations are untroubled by the issue of Taiwan and military presence in East Asia. Still, the EU–China relationship has its challenges. The EU – like the US – is critical of China's human rights record, has serious concerns about China's authoritarian system, has accorded diplomatic contacts with individuals China sees as enemies (such as the Dalai Lama or other high-profile Chinese dissidents), and has seen eye to eye with the US on issues of human rights such as military intervention and peacekeeping in Kosovo, humanitarian intervention in Sudan, and other issues which China sees as encroaching upon state sovereignty (or as China deems these, "internal matters").

Brazil and India have also become much more important bilateral partners over the last decade and the EU's relationships with these countries are far less clouded by human rights or state sovereignty issues. The EU and Brazil – the EU's tenth largest trading partner and third largest destination for FDI – established diplomatic relations in 1960, but the establishment of a strategic partnership in 2007 deepened that relationship significantly. The EU–Brazil partnership really covers three overlapping institutional levels: direct cooperation between Brazil and the EU, bilateral strategic partnerships with EU member states, and the EU's relationship with Mercosur, the South American trade bloc, with includes Brazil.[33] Focusing on foreign policy issues, economic growth, climate change, sustainable energy, the fight against global poverty, and (of course) trade, the EU and Brazil hold annual summits and issue "joint action plans." At its February 2014 summit, the EU and Brazil agreed to work toward implementing a new joint action plan to enhance and develop the goals of the previous 2011–2014 plan. That plan included among other things concrete steps toward promoting human rights by enhancing the powers of the International Criminal Court, combatting sex trafficking, furthering cooperation in preventing the illicit sale and distribution of materials related to weapons of mass destruction, fighting terrorism and organized crime, and developing trade, investment, and business relations through the protection of intellectual property rights and the mutual fostering of public and private investment opportunities.[34]

Meanwhile, the EU and India – the EU's ninth-largest economic partner – have also seen a deepening of their economic and political relationship. In 2004 India became another of the

EU's "strategic partners." Their 2005 joint action plan (revised in 2008) called for developing cooperation on security issues (primarily terrorism), combatting global climate change, and working toward the eventual conclusion of a free trade agreement.[35] In addition, the EU has increased development funds to India to address its needs in health, sustainable agriculture, and education. Accordingly, the EU has pledged to fund fellowships for Indian students and professors through the "Erasmus Mundus" program (see Chapter 14) and to foster exchanges in secondary and vocational education.[36]

THE EU'S RELATIONSHIP WITH THE GLOBAL SOUTH

The long history of European colonialism has left behind a heritage of strong political and economic ties between EU states and their former colonies. A combination of factors fuel EU priorities, especially moral concerns about underdevelopment, poverty, and hunger, as well as self-interest: the global south accounts for around 10–12 percent of EU exports[37] and is the source of most of the EU's supply of key raw materials such as oil, rubber, copper, and uranium. But while claiming to be concerned about the plight of developing countries, the EU has avoided taking a lead on many of the security problems in its former colonies (such as Somalia and Rwanda), and its policies toward the developing world have not always had the desired results.[38]

Development aid is at the heart of the relationship.[39] The EU has become the chief source of official development assistance in the world, with its member states together accounting for around $84 million (€74.7) in 2017.[40] In addition to bilateral aid, the EU channels assistance through the European Development Fund (EDF), which provides grants and low-interest loans to seventy-nine countries under the African, Caribbean, and Pacific (ACP) program and the Overseas Countries and Territories program. Support from the EDF goes mainly to educational development, the building of infrastructure, the development and diversification of production, humanitarian aid, and long-term projects aimed at reducing poverty and protecting the environment. Money is not everything though; the real impact of aid depends on how resources are used and how well they are used. And in spite of being the world's largest source of aid, the EU still does not have as much influence on international development debates as the US, the World Bank, or the International Monetary Fund.

The EU has also negotiated a series of cooperative agreements with selected former colonies, mainly the non-Asian former colonies of the UK and France. These began with the Yaoundé Conventions (named for the capital of Cameroon, where they were signed), which gave eighteen former colonies of the original six European Economic Community member states preferential access to Community markets between 1963 and 1975. In return, the eighteen states allowed the Community limited duty-free or quota-free access to their markets. The accession of the UK to the Community in 1973 brought many former British colonies into the equation, so the Lomé Convention (named for the capital of Togo) was signed in 1975, raising the number of ACP states to forty-six and allowing ACP countries to export almost anything to the EU duty free.

Lomé III (1985–1990) shifted the focus of aid away from the promotion of industrial development and more toward self-sufficiency and food security. Lomé IV (1990–2000) included an attempt to push EU policy in new directions by adding a structural adjustment element to ACP aid; in other words, it encouraged economic diversification in the ACP states rather than simply providing project aid. This made the EU more like the International Monetary Fund or the World Bank as a significant financial actor in international economic relations.[41] Lomé IV also banned exports of toxic wastes between the EU and ACP countries, and included clauses aimed at promoting human rights and protecting tropical forests in ACP countries.

The ACP program may have resulted in the building of closer commercial ties between the EU and the ACP states – there was an overall increase in ACP exports to Europe – but there were many problems as well: few ACP countries saw economic growth (and in some, economic prospects actually worsened); imports to the EU from other parts of the world grew more quickly than those from ACP states; EDF funds took too long to be disbursed and were relatively small when divided up seventy-nine ways; too little attention was paid to the environmental implications of the focus on cash crops for export; and the program neither helped address the ACP debt crisis nor really changed the relationship between the EU and the ACP states.

In 1996 an intensive review of the ACP program was launched,[42] and negotiations opened in 1998 between the EU and the ACP states aimed at replacing the Lomé Convention with a more flexible structure based on a series of interregional free trade agreements between groups of ACP countries and the EU. The result was the Cotonou Agreement (named for the capital of Benin), which was signed in 2000 and expired in early 2020. Critics charge that Cotonou has been based on an abandonment of preferential trade agreements, that it has been less innovative and based more on following global trends, and that EU development aid policy has become more symbolic than substantive.[43] Today, however, the EU's relationship with ACP countries is even more challenging than when Cotonou was signed. China is now aggressively competing with the EU for investments and good relations with African states, refugees from Africa have been a contributing factor to the EU's migration crisis while adding to a significant brain drain in Africa, poverty and climate change need to be urgently addressed and yet impact the EU's agricultural export policies, and global trade tensions continue to mount. In addition, many former British colonies among ACP countries will no longer have a direct advocate in the form of the UK after Brexit, and an important source of funding for development aid will be lost. How to tackle these challenges in a post-Cotonou agreement is sticky as the Commission negotiates the new partnership, one which, according to the Commission, aims at "a more tailored approach to Africa, the Caribbean and the Pacific."[44]

QUESTIONS TO CONSIDER

1 Did the end of the Cold War signal a decisive shift in US–European relations? If so, why?
2 Americans and Europeans differ on what they see as the proper role of government. What historical factors might help explain this difference in political culture?
3 What have been the significant achievements of EU aid to the developing world? Has the EU done this to genuinely help economic development in the developing world or is its foreign aid simply a way to increase its economic foothold in many countries?

NOTES

1 A superb history of the Cold War is John Lewis Gaddis, *The Cold War: A New History* (New York: Penguin, 2007).
2 *New York Times*, "Upheaval in the East," December 13, 1989.
3 European Commission, *Transatlantic Declaration on EC–US Relations*, November 23, 1990 (Brussels: European Commission, 1991).

4 European Commission, "Trade Picture," at https://ec.europa.eu/trade/policy/countries-and-regions/countries/united-states/, accessed October 31, 2019.

5 Congressional Research Service, "US–EU Trade and Investment Ties: Magnitude and Scope," July 9, 2019, at https://fas.org/sgp/crs/row/IF10930.pdf, accessed October 31, 2019.

6 Figures quoted by Raymond J. Ahearn, *US–European Union Trade Relations: Issues and Policy Challenges* (Washington, DC: Congressional Research Service, 2005).

7 Pascal Lamy, speech before the Congressional Economic Leadership Institute, Washington, DC, March 4, 2003, European Commission, at http://trade.ec.europa.eu/civilsoc/meetdetails.cfm?meet=102.

8 Office of the United States Trade Representative, "European Union," at https://ustr.gov/countries-regions/europe-middle-east/europe/european-union, accessed October 31, 2019.

9 In October of 2015, the Court of Justice of the EU struck down a fifteen-year-old agreement between the US and EU known as "safe harbor" which allowed the flow of digital information between Europe and North America, with the explanation that the agreement did not provide sufficient privacy protections for European citizens. The biggest issues were the US's desire to allow American intelligence agencies access to European data, and the EU's insistence that Europeans should be able to bring legal cases in the US when their data is misused. Concerned about a possible negative ruling by the Court, the US and EU negotiated a new agreement in 2016 which provided a legal mechanism for companies to transfer personal data from the EU to the US. See Federal Trade Commission, "US–EU Safe Harbor Framework," at www.ftc.gov/tips-advice/business-center/privacy-and-security/US-eu-safe-harbor-framework, accessed October 31, 2019.

10 See Tim Hepher, Philip Blenkinsop, and David Lawder, "US Widens Trade War with Tariffs on European Planes, Cheese, Whisky to Punish Subsidies," Reuters Business News, October 2, 2019, at www.reuters.com/article/us-wto-aircraft/u-s-widens-trade-war-with-tariffs-on-european-planes-cheese-whisky-to-punish-subsidies-idUSKBN1WH0SI, accessed October 31, 2019.

11 CNN Late Edition with Wolf Blitzer, Interview with Colin Powell, February 17, 2002, at www.cnn.com/TRANSCRIPTS/0202/17/le.00.html, accessed April 28, 2020.

12 This hostility to multilateral institutions may have reached its most absurd heights when the Trump administration downgraded the diplomatic status of the EU's delegation to the US. See Steven Erlanger, "US Downgraded EU's Diplomatic Status (but Didn't Say Anything)," *New York Times*, January 8, 2019, at www.nytimes.com/2019/01/08/world/europe/eu-us-diplomatic-status.html, accessed January 10, 2019.

13 "Defend Me Maybe," *The Economist*, July 30, 2016, at www.economist.com/europe/2016/07/28/defend-me-maybe, accessed August 2, 2016.

14 Cited in "Donald Trump Makes It Hard for Europeans to Keep Their Cool," *The Economist*, June 1, 2017, at www.economist.com/europe/2017/06/01/donald-trump-makes-it-hard-for-europeans-to-keep-their-cool, accessed June 1, 2017.

15 For an overview of some of the major foreign policy issues historically dividing the US and EU, see Münevver Cebeci, *Issues in EU and US Foreign Policy* (New York: Lexington Books, 2011).

16 Minxin Pei, "The Paradoxes of American Nationalism," *Foreign Policy* 136 (May/June 2003): 30–37.

17 Cited in "US Still Outdoes All Other Countries for National Pride," *Guardian*, May 9, 2019, at www.theguardian.com/us-news/2019/may/07/us-outdoes-other-countries-national-pride, accessed October 31, 2019.

18 Laura Silver, "Where Americans and Europeans Agree – and Differ – in the Values They See as Important," Pew Research Center, October 16, 2019, at www.pewresearch.org/fact-tank/2019/10/16/where-americans-and-europeans-agree-and-differ-in-the-values-they-see-as-important/, accessed October 22, 2019.

19 Pew Global Attitudes Project, "The American–Western European Values Gap," www.pewresearch.org/global/wp-content/uploads/sites/2/2011/11/Pew-Global-Attitudes-Values-Report-FINAL-November-17-2011-10AM-EST1.pdf, accessed October 31, 2019.

20 Pew Global Attitudes Project, "The American–Western European Values Gap."

21 Laura Silver, "Where Americans and Europeans agree – and differ – in the values they see as Important."

22 Robert Kagan, *Of Paradise and Power: America and Europe in the New World* (New York: Knopf, 2003). This is an extended version of the original essay published in the journal *Policy Review* (June–July 2002).

23 Anand Menon, Kalypso Nicolaidis, and Jennifer Welsh, "In Defence of Europe: A Response to Kagan," *Journal of European Affairs* 2, no. 3 (August 2004): 5–14.

24 On the EU's efforts at democracy promotion, see Richard Youngs, ed., *The European Union and Democracy Promotion* (Baltimore, MD: Johns Hopkins University Press, 2010).

25 For details, see Graham Avery and Fraser Cameron, *The Enlargement of the European Union* (Sheffield: Sheffield Academic Press, 1998).

26 See Una Hajdari, "How a Name Change Opened the Door to NATO for Macedonia," *New York Times*, February 6, 2019, at www.nytimes.com/2019/02/06/world/europe/macedonia-nato.html, accessed February 10, 2019.

27 "At French Insistence, the Macedonians Are Left Out in the Cold," *The Economist*, October 26, 2019, at www.economist.com/europe/2019/10/26/at-french-insistence-the-macedonians-are-left-out-in-the-cold, accessed October 25, 2019.

28 See Michael Peel and Valerie Hopkins, "Brussels Opens Way for Member States to Halt EU Enlargement Talks," *Financial Times*, February 3, 2020, at www.ft.com/content/fec586c0-46ad-11ea-aeb3-955839e06441, accessed February 4, 2020.

29 On the EU's "neighborhood policy," see Richard G.G. Whitman and Stefan Wolff, eds., *The European Neighbourhood Policy in Perspective* (New York: Palgrave Macmillan, 2010).

30 There are some recent signs, however, that the relationship between Merkel and Putin is beginning to thaw. See "Merkel and Putin's Forced 'Rapprochement,'" *Euractiv*, January 14, 2020, at www.euractiv.com/section/global-europe/news/merkel-and-putins-forced-rapprochement/, accessed January 16, 2020.

31 See "A Thaw in EU–Russia relations is starting," *The Economist*, October 12, 2019, at www.economist.com/europe/2019/10/12/a-thaw-in-eu-russia-relations-is-starting, accessed October 26, 2019.

32 Delegation of the European Union to China, at https://eeas.europa.eu/delegations/china_en, accessed October 31, 2019.

33 Susanne Gratius, "Brazil and the European Union: From Liberal Inter-Regionalism to Realist Bilateralism," *Revista Brasileira de Política Internacional*, 61, no. 1 (2018), at www.scielo.br/scielo.php?script=sci_arttext&pid=S0034-73292018000100203, accessed October 29, 2019.

34 Delegation of the European Union to Brazil at https://eeas.europa.eu/delegations/brazil_en, accessed October 31, 2019.

35 Delegation of the European Union to India and Bhutan at https://eeas.europa.eu/delegations/india_en, accessed October 31, 2019.

36 European Commission, External Action DG, at http://eeas.europa.eu/india/index_en.htm.

37 See figures from European Commission, "Economic Partnerships," at https://ec.europa.eu/trade/policy/countries-and-regions/development/economic-partnerships/ and World Trade Organization, *International Trade Statistics*, 2018, at https://data.wto.org/.

38 Yves Bourdet, Joakim Gullstrand, and Karin Olofsdotter, eds., *The European Union and Developing Countries: Trade, Aid and Growth in an Integrating World* (Cheltenham: Edward Elgar, 2007).

39 On EU development aid and cooperation, see Paul Hoebink, *European Development Cooperation: In Between the Local and the Global* (Amsterdam: Amsterdam University Press, 2010).

40 European Commission, "International Cooperation and Development," at https://ec.europa.eu/europeaid/news-and-events/eu-remains-worlds-leading-donor-development-assistance-eu757-billion-2017_en, accessed July 31, 2019.

41 Carol Cosgrove and Pierre-Henri Laurent, "The Unique Relationship: The European Community and the ACP," in *The External Relations of the European Community*, edited by John Redmond (New York: St. Martin's, 1992).

42 For details, see Martin Holland, "Resisting Reform or Risking Revival? Renegotiating the Lomé Convention," in *The State of the European Union*, edited by Maria Green Cowles and Michael Smith (Oxford: Oxford University Press, 2001).

43 Karin Arts and Anna K. Dickson, *EU Development Cooperation: From Model to Symbol* (Manchester: Manchester University Press, 2004).
44 European Commission, "European Commission Ready to Start Negotiations for a New Ambitious Partnership with 79 Countries in Africa, the Caribbean and the Pacific," Press Release, June 22, 2018, at https://europa.eu/rapid/press-release_IP-18-3930_en.htm, accessed October 29, 2019.

BIBLIOGRAPHY

Ahearn, Raymond J., *US–European Union Trade Relations: Issues and Policy Challenges* (Washington, DC: Congressional Research Service, 2005).
Alcaro, Ricardo, John Peterson, and Ettore Greco, eds., *The West and the Global Power Shift: Transatlantic Relations and Global Governance* (New York and London: Palgrave, 2016).
Arts, Karin, and Anna K. Dickson, *EU Development Cooperation: From Model to Symbol* (Manchester: Manchester University Press, 2004).
Avery, Graham, and Fraser Cameron, *The Enlargement of the European Union* (Sheffield: Sheffield Academic Press, 1998).
Baldwin, Peter, *The Narcissism of Minor Differences: How America and Europe Are Alike* (New York: Oxford University Press, 2009).
Bourdet, Yves, Joakim Gullstrand, and Karin Olofsdotter, eds., *The European Union and Developing Countries: Trade, Aid and Growth in an Integrating World* (Cheltenham: Edward Elgar, 2007).
Bouris, Dmitris and Tobias Schumacher, eds., *The Revised European Neighbourhood Policy: Continuity and Change in EU Foreign Policy* (New York and London: Palgrave Macmillan, 2016).
Cebeci, Münevver, *Issues in EU and US Foreign Policy* (New York: Lexington Books, 2011).
CNN, Late Edition with Wolf Blitzer, Interview with Colin Powell, February 17, 2002, at www.cnn.com/TRANSCRIPTS/0202/17/le.00.html, accessed April 28, 2020.
Congressional Research Service, "US–EU Trade and Investment Ties: Magnitude and Scope," July 9, 2019, at https://fas.org/sgp/crs/row/IF10930.pdf, accessed October 31, 2019.
Cosgrove, Carol and Pierre-Henri Lauren, "The Unique Relationship: The European Community and the ACP," *The External Relations of the European Community*, edited by in John Redmond (New York: St. Martin's, 1992).
Delegation of the European Union to India and Bhutan, at https://eeas.europa.eu/delegations/india_en, accessed October 31, 2019.
Delegation of the European Union to Brazil, at https://eeas.europa.eu/delegations/brazil_en, accessed October 31, 2019.
Delegation of the European Union to China, at https://eeas.europa.eu/delegations/china_en, accessed October 31, 2019.
European Commission, External Action DG, at http://eeas.europa.eu/india/index_en.htm.
Economist, The, "Defend Me Maybe," July 30, 2016, at www.economist.com/europe/2016/07/28/defend-me-maybe, accessed August 2, 2016.
Economist, The, "Donald Trump Makes It Hard for Europeans to Keep Their Cool," June 1, 2017, at www.economist.com/europe/2017/06/01/donald-trump-makes-it-hard-for-europeans-to-keep-their-cool, accessed June 1, 2017.
Economist, The, "A Thaw in EU–Russia Relations Is Starting" October 12, 2019, at www.economist.com/europe/2019/10/12/a-thaw-in-eu-russia-relations-is-starting, accessed October 26, 2019.
Economist, The, "At French Insistence, the Macedonians Are Left Out in the Cold," October 26, 2019, at www.economist.com/europe/2019/10/26/at-french-insistence-the-macedonians-are-left-out-in-the-cold, accessed October 25, 2019.
Erlanger, Steven, "US Downgraded EU's Diplomatic Status (but Didn't Say Anything)," *New York Times,* January 8, 2019, at www.nytimes.com/2019/01/08/world/europe/eu-us-diplomatic-status.html, accessed January 10, 2019.

Euractiv, "Merkel and Putin's Forced 'Rapprochement,'" January 14, 2020, at www.euractiv.com/section/global-europe/news/merkel-and-putins-forced-rapprochement/, accessed January 16, 2020.

European Commission, *Transatlantic Declaration on EC–US Relations*, November 23, 1990 (Brussels: European Commission, 1991).

European Commission, "European Commission Ready to Start Negotiations for a New Ambitious Partnership with 79 Countries in Africa, the Caribbean and the Pacific," Press Release, June 22, 2018, at https://europa.eu/rapid/press-release_IP-18-3930_en.htm, accessed October 29, 2019.

European Commission, "Economic Partnerships," February 1, 2019, at https://ec.europa.eu/trade/policy/countries-and-regions/development/economic-partnerships/.

European Commission, "Trade Picture," at https://ec.europa.eu/trade/policy/countries-and-regions/countries/united-states/, accessed October 31, 2019.

European Commission, "International Cooperation and Development," at https://ec.europa.eu/europeaid/news-and-events/eu-remains-worlds-leading-donor-development-assistance-eu757-billion-2017_en, accessed July 31, 2019.

Federal Trade Commission, "US–EU Safe Harbor Framework," at www.ftc.gov/tips-advice/business-center/privacy-and-security/US-eu-safe-harbor-framework, accessed October 31, 2019.

Gaddis, John Lewis, *The Cold War: A New History* (New York: Penguin, 2005).

Gratius, Susanne, "Brazil and the European Union: From Liberal Inter-Regionalism to Realist Bilateralism," *Revista Brasileira de Política Internacional* 61, no. 1 (2018), at www.scielo.br/scielo.php?script=sci_arttext&pid=S0034-73292018000100203, accessed October 29, 2019.

Guardian, "US Still Outdoes All Other Countries for National Pride," May 9, 2019, at www.theguardian.com/us-news/2019/may/07/us-outdoes-other-countries-national-pride, accessed October 31, 2019.

Hajdari, Una, "How a Name Change Opened the Door to NATO for Macedonia," *New York Times*, February 6, 2019, at www.nytimes.com/2019/02/06/world/europe/macedonia-nato.html, accessed February 10, 2019.

Hanhimaki, Jussi, Benedikt Schoenborn, and Barbara Zanchetta, *Transatlantic Relations since 1945: An Introduction* (Abingdon: Routledge, 2012).

Hepher, Tim, Philip Blenkinsop, and David Lawder, "US Widens Trade War with Tariffs on European Planes, Cheese, Whisky to Punish Subsidies," Reuters Business News, October 2, 2019, at www.reuters.com/article/us-wto-aircraft/u-s-widens-trade-war-with-tariffs-on-european-planes-cheese-whisky-to-punish-subsidies-idUSKBN1WH0SI, accessed October 31, 2019.

Hoebink, Paul, *European Development Cooperation: In Between the Local and the Global* (Amsterdam: Amsterdam University Press, 2010).

Holland, Martin, "Resisting Reform or Risking Revival? Renegotiating the Lomé Convention," in *The State of the European Union*, edited by Maria Green Cowles and Michael Smith (Oxford: Oxford University Press, 2001).

Kagan, Robert, *Of Paradise and Power: America and Europe in the New World* (New York: Knopf, 2003).

Lamy, Pascal, Speech before the Congressional Economic Leadership Institute, Washington, DC, March 4, 2003.

McCormick, John, *Europeanism* (Oxford: Oxford University Press, 2010).

Menon, Anand, Kalypso Nicolaidis, and Jennifer Welsh, "In Defence of Europe: A Response to Kagan," *Journal of European Affairs* 2, no. 3 (August 2004): 5–14.

New York Times, "Upheaval in the East," December 26, 1989, Section 1, 17.

Office of the United States Trade Representative, "European Union," at https://ustr.gov/countries-regions/europe-middle-east/europe/european-union, accessed October 31, 2019.

Peel, Michael and Valerie Hopkins, "Brussels Opens Way for Member States to Halt EU Enlargement Talks," *Financial Times*, February 3, 2020, at www.ft.com/content/fec586c0-46ad-11ea-aeb3-955839e06441, accessed February 4, 2020.

Pei, Minxin, "The Paradoxes of American Nationalism," *Foreign Policy* 136 (May/June 2003): 30–37.

Pew Global Attitudes Project, "The American–Western European Values Gap," at www.pewresearch.org/global/wp-content/uploads/sites/2/2011/11/Pew-Global-Attitudes-Values-Report-FINAL-November-17-2011-10AM-EST1.pdf, accessed October 31, 2019.

Silver, Laura, "Where Americans and Europeans Agree – and Differ – in the Values They See as Important," Pew Research Center, October 16, 2019, at www.pewresearch.org/fact-tank/2019/10/16/where-americans-and-europeans-agree-and-differ-in-the-values-they-see-as-important/, accessed October 22, 2019.

Whitman, Richard G.G. and Stefan Wolff, eds., *The European Neighbourhood Policy in Perspective* (New York: Palgrave Macmillan, 2010).

World Trade Organization, *International Trade Statistics*, 2018, at https://data.wto.org/.

Youngs, Richard. ed., *The European Union and Democracy Promotion* (Baltimore, MD: Johns Hopkins University Press, 2010).

FURTHER READING

Ricardo Alcaro, John Peterson, and Ettore Greco, eds., *The West and the Global Power Shift: Transatlantic Relations and Global Governance* (New York and London: Palgrave, 2016).

> Analyzes factors which have led to tensions between the EU and US but argues that the two allies are still closely bound together, even in a time of great change in the international arena.

Dmitris Bouris and Tobias Schumacher, eds., *The Revised European Neighbourhood Policy: Continuity and Change in EU Foreign Policy* (New York and London: Palgrave Macmillan, 2016).

> An edited volume analyzing the European Neighbourhood Policy, including changes in the ENP since 2004, crises and conflicts in the region, and the effects of cooperation in issue areas such as immigration and energy.

Jussi Hanhimaki, Benedikt Schoenborn, and Barbara Zanchetta, *Transatlantic Relations since 1945: An Introduction* (Abingdon: Routledge, 2012).

> A good survey of the evolution of US–European relations since the end of World War II through 2012.

Robert Kagan, *Of Paradise and Power: America and Europe in the New World* (New York: Knopf, 2003).

> A now classic and controversial analysis by an American neoconservative, who argues that American and European views of the world are diverging, that they agree on little, and that they understand each other less and less.

John McCormick, *Europeanism* (Oxford: Oxford University Press, 2010).

> Argues that there is a core of values and beliefs – "Europeanism" – that binds Europe together and which stands in contrast to other areas of the world, including the US.

Peter Baldwin. *The Narcissism of Minor Differences: How America and Europe Are Alike* (New York: Oxford University Press, 2009).

> An assessment that runs counter to popular perceptions and argues that Europe and the US are much more similar than they think.

Conclusion

We cannot aim at anything less than the union of Europe as a whole, and we look forward with confidence to the day when that union will be achieved.
　　　　　　　　　—Winston Churchill, The Hague Congress, May 1948

Europe will not be made all at once, or according to a single plan. It will be built through concrete achievements which first create a de facto solidarity.
　　　　　　　　　—Robert Schuman, The Schuman Declaration, May 1950

That such an unnecessary and irrational project as building a European superstate was ever embarked on will seem in future years to be perhaps the greatest folly of the modern era.
　　　　　　　　　—Margaret Thatcher, *Statecraft: Strategies for a Changing World*, 2003

With the UK's departure from the EU, the European Union is facing what many consider to be the most existential period in its history. To be sure, pessimism has always colored the musings of those who keep an eye on European affairs. Even before the ink had dried on the Treaty of Paris, ranks of doubting Thomases wondered if the European experiment was viable. There was too much complicated history to resolve, they said, and keeping the French and the Germans at peace was too tall an order. Following Paris (signed by disappointingly few countries – six), skeptics took heart at the collapse of the European Defence Community and the European Political Community. Following Rome (signed by the same few countries), there was de Gaulle's veto of further enlargement, then the empty chair crisis, and then Western Europe was stung by the collapse of Bretton Woods and the energy crises of the 1970s.

Thereafter, Europe's trials and tribulations followed one upon another, chipping away at the foundations of European cooperation and fulfilling the warnings of the pessimists. There were the squabbles over the budget in the 1980s, the ongoing arguments over the Common Agricultural Policy, the divisions over the 1990–1991 Gulf War and the Balkans, the Exchange Rate Mechanism crisis, the Danish rejection of Maastricht, the resignation of the Commission, the Irish rejection of Nice, the Danish and Swedish rejection of the euro, and the French and Dutch rejection of the constitutional treaty. For Euroskeptics, the breakdown of this treaty especially cast a heavier pall over the entire future direction, confirmed the general collapse of confidence in Europe, and threatened to trigger strategic and institutional paralysis.

Nevertheless, it is true that Brexit is testing the EU like no other time before. The EU will lose the fifth-largest economy in the world and, along with France, the EU's leading military power. It will lose the second-largest contributor to the EU budget, its leading provider of financial services, and one of its largest intra-bloc trading partners. It will lose a moderating influence and crucial interlocutor in intra-EU disputes, for example in debates over markets v. regulation, monetary policy between eurozone and non-eurozone member states, or the EU's relationship with the US – one in which the UK has always played a bridging role. Beyond the concrete impacts of the UK's departure, however, its symbolism is also significant. As one analyst has suggested, "Brexit is a defeat, a rebellion against the concept that working together makes Europeans stronger."[1]

Brexit is far from the only challenge, however. Europe's share of the world population is falling, its citizens aging, its share of global GDP shrinking, and its currency confronting competition with those of both established (the US, the UK) and rising (China) powers. The COVID-19 global pandemic has furthermore heightened tensions between member states, strengthened the authoritarian hand of national leaders in Hungary and Poland, and put the future of the free movement of people within the EU in some doubt. Some ethnic nationalists within the EU, such as those in Catalonia, feel emboldened by Brexit, prompting fears of further dissolution and internal strife. The European public is on edge, tensions between member states lurk in the background, and anti-EU parties across the Union have gained in strength. How to balance security and freedom – most prominently in the EU's approach toward irregular migration – will continue to preoccupy the bloc, with no comprehensive agreement yet in sight. Meanwhile, the financial and debt crisis continues to reverberate within the EU: while some countries have stabilized, others – such as Greece – still continue to struggle, and a few of those who did not make for the biggest negative headlines in 2009–2010 now appear increasingly shaky (e.g., Italy). Even those who love the EU are nervous, critical of the trajectory it has taken. As the German-Croatian writer Jagoda Marinić has written, the wealth that the EU has helped to create has not benefitted all Europeans. Many see the EU as responsible for perpetuating this inequality, a "Europe of the rich." In response, she argues that those in the EU:

> must translate the ideals they espouse into policies that benefit citizens. When "freedom" is no longer a sufficient argument on its own, discontent begins to simmer. Europe can only become the love of Europeans again when we sense that it is about "our future."[2]

Yet therein lies hope and opportunity.

For even among many who criticize the EU, who see its flaws and who acknowledge its many failures, the contours of the EU's future may be difficult to discern, but that it should exist and move forward is not in question. Indeed, they see its achievements, as do would-be suitors in the EU's neighborhood. Europe has enjoyed the longest spell of general peace in its recorded history, and the divisions of the Cold War have all but faded into the mists of history. Moreover, the EU has transformed the lives of Europeans. It has meant freedom of movement, improved living and working conditions, growing gender equality, increased multilingualism and protection of minority languages, more productive farmers, the end of currency exchange in most of Europe, more corporate competition, deregulation and the breakup of national monopolies, more investment in the poorer parts of Europe, stronger protection of human rights, regional cooperation on crime, the end of the death penalty in Europe, more foreign study for students, cheaper and easier travel, an explosion of tourism, heightened consumer protection, European peacekeeping forces, improved food safety, cleaner air and rivers, greater protection for wildlife, and much more.

Moreover, while supporters of Brexit can point to potential gains from leaving the EU, in the transaction UK citizens will find some serious negative consequences. It will be much more difficult to work, study, and do business in Europe. They will face longer queues at airports, train stations, and ports for those traveling abroad. Access to the European health-care market and prescription drugs will be more difficult; consumer protection and social security rights will be limited, if not nonexistent.[3] UK economic and political power may suffer a blow, and its strength in international trade may weaken. Tensions on the Irish border could very well continue to grow, and Scotland has already indicated that it is considering another referendum on independence. Not surprisingly, the UK's experience with Brexit, rather than emboldening talk of "Frexit," "Nexit," or "Italeave" within the EU seems have to have sucked much of the wind out of these sails. Support for the EU has increased, especially among younger Europeans – the "E-Generation" who see their identity as equal parts their native country and "European."

Still, the EU is facing, much like the UK and the US, a kind of rebellion of the "left behind" in the EU – those with lower levels of education, low employment opportunities, and a belief that a globalized world is uprooting their traditions and ways of life. As has happened so many times before – but with greater depth and urgency – current events are illuminating future directions the EU could take.

Accordingly, in 2017 the Commission released its *White Paper on the Future of Europe*, in which it outlined five scenarios for the future of Europe, post-Brexit.[4] The scenarios it envisions are instructive.

"Carrying on." Under this scenario, the EU would work cautiously through its crises while continuing to move, albeit painstakingly, toward more economic integration and the further development of the single market. A more robust system of safeguarding against economic meltdown in its member states would be developed, both through the European Stability Mechanism and a more expanded and aggressive role for the European Central Bank. Schengen would persist but allowance made for member states to maintain target internal controls; external borders would continue to be the responsibility of individual member states. This might involve introducing greater discretion on the part of each member state when it can temporarily close its borders or otherwise introduce passport controls. Security and foreign policy would be deepened in some areas, but in others cooperation would be voluntary. This scenario of "muddling through" would not cause upheaval but it risks a slow erosion, especially as the EU gets tested in the next major crisis.

Nothing but the single market. Under this scenario, the EU-27 fail to agree on a further political deepening of Europe. Consequently, it focuses on deepening economic integration/ the single market. There would be no further agreements on migration, security, or defense, and policy in this area is increasingly ad hoc or achieved on a bilateral basis. Border checks would become more systematic and widespread, even if Schengen is not officially abolished. The free movement of workers and services would not be fully guaranteed. In terms of the single market, there might be greater harmonization of consumer, social, and environmental standards and unnecessary regulations further reduced. In essence, the EU would be rolled back, continuing to exist and function, but coming to resemble its 1960s and 1970s incarnation. This path would placate those who fear the EU but would disappoint, and possibly alienate, those strong supporters of Europe who wish for something bolder and more inspirational.

Those who want more do more. Under scenario three, the EU would become more decentralized, leaving it to member states to decide in which areas they wish to cooperate (and in which areas they don't). Replicating to some extent the path of the euro or Schengen, member states would have the possibility but would not be compelled to cooperate in a number of policy areas, such as security and defense, justice and home affairs, and economic matters (e.g., harmonization of tax rules or regulation of working conditions). These "coalitions of the willing" would certainly signal a less active Commission and European Parliament, with more power going to the Council of Ministers and European Council. This scenario echoes longstanding debates in the EU whether to pursue a future with "core" and "periphery" countries.

Doing less more efficiently. Under this fourth scenario, the EU agrees on vigorous joint action and the deepening of integration, but only in a few key areas. For example, it could – as in scenarios two and three – concentrate only on the single market. It could also focus on border management, crafting a single European asylum agency, reforming Dublin in the process. Moreover, it could focus on strengthening the euro, tightening further control over the fiscal management of member states. On the other hand, the bloc might largely abandon joint EU policy making in such areas as regional development, employment, or social policy. Instead of "core" countries, discussed in scenario three, this scenario envisions "core" policies. The chief challenge here, however, lies in finding consensus among the member states on just what those core policies should be.

Doing much more together. Under this final scenario, the EU would take a huge leap into more economic and political integration. Closer integration would mean a thoroughgoing Europeanization of various institutions and policy areas still left in national hands, most especially greater control over national economic and fiscal policy. New institutions might be created, with authority to decide budgets for the member states using the euro. Similarly, the post of finance minister for the eurozone could be created, giving the EU more control over national budgets. Along the same lines, powers for the European Central Bank would continue to increase, with the bank becoming the "lender of last resort" and the distinctions between it and the US Federal Reserve fully erased. The Schengen zone would continue intact, with few if any "temporary" controls implemented. Foreign policy would be further integrated, and a common asylum policy and authority agreed to: justice and home affairs would be thoroughly Europeanized. In short, the EU would continue much as before, but with even greater political and economic integration and increased powers for Brussels, a risky bet given that a sizable minority of EU citizens are implacably opposed to "more Europe."

What then is the takeaway from all of this? While predicting which of these scenarios is more likely to materialize is difficult, the discussions the Commission and European Parliament are currently having on this white paper are sure to impact both the general strategic plans outlined here as well as the specific policies each scenario would entail. Nonetheless, the fifth scenario seems highly unlikely in the present climate, while the second and fourth would each seem to have some serious flaws. Thus "carrying on" or "core Europe" may be the only realistic scenarios and may also provide enough institutional change to keep crises from overwhelming the EU. However, they are not without their own dangers, inasmuch as they might fail to inspire and to carry any momentum forward for the EU's future. Indeed, scenario three further risks creating a two-tiered EU which, while perhaps placating some Euroskeptics, might erode support in member states who feel they have become second-class citizens of the EU.

Above all, much more work needs to be done to bridge the gap between Europeans and the EU institutions. However large the democratic deficit actually is, it remains a potent psychological barrier to the efficiency of the EU, in part because it denies European citizens adequate involvement in European policy making – other than through the intermediary of their national governments – and in part because it discourages Europeans from taking an interest in European issues. Along with that concern, the EU must address the growing gap between those who feel they have benefitted from the EU and those who feel they have not. The EU's reputation (sometimes well earned) as a neo-liberal club which is a boon to the well-off and well-positioned must be addressed, and bolder initiatives undertaken for those left behind by globalization. And while there will always be Euroskeptics who would like nothing more than seeing the EU vanish, these still remain a distinct minority. Most European citizens have some degree of inner conflict regarding the EU's effect on their lives – clearly recognizing and cherishing many of the benefits it has brought, but nevertheless critical of institutions and policies which do not seem to work on their behalf. They want to see a strengthened EU, if not necessarily one which changes so many aspects of their lives that they feel threatened.

Whatever the future may hold and despite its many longstanding problems and its current challenges, the reality remains that the construction of the EU has been a unique achievement, and it has helped make Europeans on balance safer, happier, healthier, and wealthier. The journey's end may be hard to discern, and the future undoubtedly promises many more surprises, crises, and dramas, but there is surely no going back.

NOTES

1 Rosa Balfour, senior fellow at the German Marshall Fund, cited in Steven Erlanger, "Brexit is Here, and It's a Texas-Size Defeat for the EU," *New York Times*, January 29, 2020, at www.nytimes.com/2020/01/29/world/europe/brexit-brussels-eu.html?smid=nytcore-ios-share, accessed January 29, 2020.
2 Jagoda Marinić, "My Europe: The Continent I Love," December 5, 2018, at www.dw.com/en/my-europe-the-continent-i-love/a-43748741, accessed December 6, 2018.
3 On this, see Claus Hecking, "What Awaits Britons Abroad after Brexit," *Spiegel International*, October 8, 2019, at www.spiegel.de/international/europe/life-for-britons-abroad-after-brexit-a-1290488.html, accessed October 15, 2019; Adam Payne, "All the Rights British People Could Lose after Brexit," *Business Insider*, 31 May, 2018, at www.businessinsider.com/the-rights-british-people-could-lose-under-each-brexit-model-2018-5, accessed June 2, 2018.
4 European Commission, *White Paper on the Future of Europe. Reflections and Scenarios for the EU27 by 2025*, at https://ec.europa.eu/commission/sites/beta-political/files/white_paper_on_the_future_of_europe_en.pdf, accessed January 31, 2020.

BIBLIOGRAPHY

Erlanger, Steven, "Brexit is Here, and It's a Texas-Size Defeat for the EU," *New York Times*, January 29, 2020, at www.nytimes.com/2020/01/29/world/europe/brexit-brussels-eu.html?smid=nytcore-ios-share, accessed January 29, 2020.
European Commission, *White Paper on the Future of Europe. Reflections and scenarios for the EU27 by 2025*, https://ec.europa.eu/commission/sites/beta-political/files/white_paper_on_the_future_of_europe_en.pdf, accessed January 31, 2020.
Hecking, Claus, "What Awaits Britons Abroad after Brexit," *Spiegel International*, October 8, 2019, www.spiegel.de/international/europe/life-for-britons-abroad-after-brexit-a-1290488.html, accessed October 15, 2019.
Marinić, Jagoda, "My Europe: The Continent I Love," December 5, 2018, at www.dw.com/en/my-europe-the-continent-i-love/a-43748741, accessed December 6, 2018.
Payne, Adam, "All the Rights British People Could Lose after Brexit," *Business Insider*, May 31, 2018, www.businessinsider.com/the-rights-british-people-could-lose-under-each-brexit-model-2018-5, accessed June 2, 2018.

Glossary

Acquis communitaire   The collective laws and regulations adopted by the EU.

Agencification   The growth of semi-autonomous administrative bodies within the EU.

Assent procedure   The legislative process under which no new member state can join the EU without the support of a majority in the European Parliament.

Atlanticism   The belief of some European states that a close transatlantic relationship – particularly with regard to security matters – is preferable to the independent European foreign policy that others prefer.

Authority gap   The difference between what EU institutions would like to be able to do and what EU citizens and governments allow them to do.

Benelux   A collective term for Belgium, the Netherlands, and Luxembourg.

Bretton Woods system   A plan worked out at a 1944 meeting in Bretton Woods, New Hampshire, among representatives of forty-four countries. Based on US leadership, it was aimed at establishing international management of the global economy, free trade, exchange rate stability, low tariffs, and aid to war-damaged economies.

Brexit   The slang term given to the UK's exit from the European Union.

BRIC   The term given to Brazil, Russia, India, and China as emerging political and economic powers in the world.

Cohesion   The goal of ensuring that the development of the EU reduces the social and economic differences between its poorer and richer regions.

Common Agricultural Policy   An agricultural price support system incorporated into the Treaty of Rome that originally supported guaranteed prices to Community farmers for their produce but has since been reformed with a view to reducing payments.

Common Foreign and Security Policy   The process introduced by Maastricht under which the EU works toward agreeing on common foreign and defense policy positions.

Common market   See **Single market**.

Competence   A word that describes the authority of the EU in different policy areas. Thus, it has competence (authority) in the fields of agricultural and trade policy but not in tax policy or criminal justice matters.

Confederalism   An administrative system in which independent political units cooperate and pool authority on issues of mutual interest while retaining independence, sovereignty, and control of their own affairs.

Convergence criteria   The four requirements that EU member states must meet before being allowed to join the euro: controls on national deficits, public debt, consumer inflation, and interest rates.

Customs union   An arrangement under which a group of states agrees on a common external tariff on all goods entering the group from outside.

Deepening The argument that the EU should focus on consolidating integration among existing members before allowing new members to join. Although this seems to contradict arguments in favor of enlargement (see **Widening**), the two are now seen less as alternatives and more as two sides of the same coin.

Democratic deficit The gap between the powers of EU institutions and the ability of EU citizens to influence those institutions. In short, the public's perception of there being too little of a democratic nature in the way the officials of EU institutions (other than the European Parliament) are appointed, and too little direct accountability and sense of public responsibility among those institutions.

Dublin Regulation An EU law – first established in 1990 and modified in 2003, 2008, and 2013 – regulating which EU member state is responsible for processing an application for asylum.

Economic and monetary union The process by which the EU worked toward the goals of establishing fixed exchange rates and common monetary policies before adopting the single currency.

Eurocrat A nickname for EU bureaucrats, particularly those working in the European Commission.

Eurogroup The (informal) group of eurozone finance ministers who meet periodically to discuss matters relating to the euro.

European Monetary System A process launched in 1979 under which attempts were made to encourage exchange rate stability and to control inflation within the Community.

European Stability Mechanism The EU's emergency bailout fund for troubled member states, established in September 2012.

Europeanization The process by which national policies and government structures in the member states have been changed and brought into alignment by European laws and policies.

Euroskeptic Someone who is either opposed to European integration or critical of the nature, speed, or progress of integration.

Eurozone The group of EU member states that have adopted the euro.

Exchange Rate Mechanism An arrangement under the European Monetary System by which EU member states agreed to keep the value of their currencies relatively stable against those of the other EU member states.

Federalism An administrative arrangement in which two or more levels of government with independent powers over specified policy areas coexist. Each level is directly accountable to its citizens.

Fiscal compact The fiscal chapter of the Fiscal Stability Treaty, a revision to the Stability and Growth Pact, signed in March 2012. It compels member states to enshrine into law a balanced national budget and requires states to correct any budget imbalances upon threat of financial sanctions by the EU.

Free trade An arrangement by which the barriers to trade between two or more states are either reduced or removed.

Functionalism The theory that if states cooperate in selected functional areas (such as the management of coal and steel), the ties they build will compel them to cooperate in other areas as well.

Governance An arrangement in which laws and policies are made and implemented without the existence of a formally acknowledged set of governing institutions, but instead as a result of interactions involving states, institutions, interest groups, and other sources of influence.

Government   The exercise of influence and authority over a group of people, either through law or coercion. Also used to describe the body of officials and institutions that exercise that power.

Grexit   The slang term given to the possibility of Greece leaving the eurozone and readopting its old currency, the drachma.

Gross national product   The total value of all goods and services produced by a state, including the va lue of its overseas operations. (Gross domestic product is a measure that excludes the latter.) The basic measure of the absolute wealth of a state, sometime adjusted on a per capita basis (i.e., GNPCAP).

Harmonization   The goal of standardizing national legislation in EU member states in the interest of promoting competition and free trade. Involves removing legal and fiscal barriers to competition and free trade.

Intergovernmental conference   A summit meeting at which representatives of EU member states discuss and decide upon issues of broad strategic interest.

Intergovernmentalism   The phenomenon by which decisions are reached as a result of negotiation between or among governments. Usually applied to the work of the Council of Ministers and the European Council. Contrast with **Supranationalism**.

Internal market   See **Single market**.

Legitimation   The process by which a government converts its policies into generally acceptable means for achieving its objectives.

Liberal intergovernmentalism   The theory that regional integration proceeds mainly as a result of agreements and bargains among the participating governments, moved by the pressures of domestic politics.

Luxembourg Compromise   An arrangement worked out in 1966 following a crisis set off by Charles de Gaulle's concerns about the accumulation of powers by the European Commission. The "compromise" allowed member states to veto proposals when they believed their national interests were at stake.

Multilevel governance   A system in which power is shared among the different levels of government in the EU (supranational, national, subnational, and local) with considerable interaction among the levels.

Mutual recognition   An agreement that if a product or service can be lawfully produced and marketed in one EU member state, it must be allowed to be marketed in any other member state.

Nationalism   A belief that a state should be focused on a nation, and that national identity should be promoted through political action.

Neofunctionalism   A variation on the theme of functionalism, which argues that states are encouraged to cooperate by nonstate actors and that regional integration takes place through a process of spillover: cooperation in one area creates pressures that lead to integration in others.

Ordinary legislative procedure   Formerly known as the "codecision procedure," this is the legislative process under which the Council of Ministers cannot make a final decision on new laws without giving the European Parliament the opportunity for a third reading. Under the Treaty of Lisbon it was extended to almost all policy areas, making the European Parliament a co-legislature with the Council of Ministers.

People's Europe A program aimed at making the EU more real and accessible to its citizens.

Petersberg tasks A commitment by EU member states to focus the work of their military on humanitarian, rescue, peacekeeping, and other crisis management operations, including peacemaking.

Preliminary ruling A ruling by the European Court of Justice on the interpretation or validity of an EU law that arises in a national court case in one of the member states.

Qualified majority voting A system used with most votes taken in the Council of Ministers, whereby – instead of having one vote each – member states have different numbers of votes (based roughly on their population size). Under the Lisbon treaty, a revised "standard" QMV – used for most EU legislation in the European Council and Council of Ministers – requires 55 percent of member states representing 65 percent of the EU's population for a vote to pass.

Rapporteur An MEP in the European Parliament appointed by a committee to draw up a legislative recommendation from the committee to be submitted to a vote in the full EP.

Realism A theory often described as the "traditional" approach to the study of international relations; it dominated the study of that field from the 1940s to the 1960s. It argues that states are the key actors in the world system, that world politics is driven by a struggle for power among states, and that states place national interests, security, and autonomy at the top of their agendas.

Regional integration The process by which states voluntarily transfer authority to joint institutions, creating a common body of law and pooling responsibility in selected policy areas.

Schuman Plan The plan developed by Jean Monnet and Robert Schuman to coordinate the coal and steel industries of Europe. Announced to the public on May 9, 1950, it led to the creation of the European Coal and Steel Community.

Single market An area within which there is free movement of people, money, goods, and services. Also known as a "common market" or "internal market." The term can be applied to a single state (such as the US) or to a group of states that have removed the necessary barriers (such as the EU).

Social Charter The Charter of Fundamental Rights for Workers, agreed on in 1988 and promoting free movement of workers, fair pay, better living and working conditions, and related matters.

Sovereignty The right to own and control. In relation to states, the term is usually used to connote jurisdiction over a territory, but it can also refer to the rights of one person or group relative to those of another (for example, the sovereignty of the people over government).

Spillover An element of neofunctional theory that suggests that if states integrate in one area, the economic, technical, social, and political pressures for them to integrate in other areas will increase.

Spitzenkandidat The (disputed) method the European Parliament uses to nominate a Commission president through the selection of a candidate (*Spitzenkandidat*, "lead candidate" in German) for each political group in the European Parliament, with the group winning the largest percentage of the vote in European elections receiving the position.

Stability and growth pact An attempt launched in 1997 to encourage members of the eurozone to control borrowing and budget deficits.

State A community of individuals living within recognized frontiers, adhering to a common body of law, and coming under the jurisdiction of a common government. Also used to describe collectively the officials, laws, and powers of that government.

Structural funds Funds made available by the EU to promote regional development and economic and social cohesion. They include the European Regional Development Fund, the European Social Fund, the guidance element of the European Agricultural Guidance and Guarantee Fund, and the Cohesion Fund.

Subsidiarity The principle whereby the EU agrees to take action only in those policy areas that are best dealt with at the EU level rather than at the national or local level.

Supranationalism A view that emphasizes the common good or goals of the EU, as opposed to the separate interests of the member states. Decisions are made by a process or an institution that is independent of national governments. Often used to describe the work of the European Commission and the European Court of Justice. Contrast with **Intergovernmentalism**.

Trans-European networks Transport, energy, telecommunications, and other networks designed to integrate the EU and promote the mobility of its residents.

Transparency The process by which the documents, decisions, and decision-making processes of the EU are made more accessible and understandable to EU citizens.

Value-added tax A form of consumption tax used in European states and applied to any product whose form has been changed through manufacturing, thereby adding value (for example, steel used to construct a car).

Widening The argument that EU membership should be extended to other European states. Sometimes also used to describe the expansion of EU powers or policy interests. Can be contrasted with **Deepening**.

Chronology of the EU

APPENDIX 1

1944	July	Bretton Woods conference to plan postwar global economy
1945	May	Germany surrenders; World War II ends in Europe
	October	Creation of United Nations
1946	March	Winston Churchill makes "iron curtain" speech in Fulton, Missouri
	September	Churchill makes "United States of Europe" speech in Zurich
1947	March	Announcement of Truman Doctrine
	June	US Secretary of State George Marshall offers Europe aid for economic recovery
	October	General Agreement on Tariffs and Trade launched in Geneva
1948	January	Benelux customs union enters into force; GATT enters into force
	March	Treaty of Brussels signed by the UK, France, and Benelux states, creating Western Union
	April	Organisation for European Economic Cooperation founded
	May	Congress of Europe held in The Hague
	June	Soviet blockade sparks eleven-month Berlin airlift
1949	April	North Atlantic Treaty signed in Washington, DC
	May	Treaty of London signed, creating Council of Europe; formalization of division of Germany
1950	May	Schuman Declaration
	June	Opening of IGC to plan ECSC
	October	Publication of plan outlining European Defence Community
1951	April	Treaty of Paris signed, creating ECSC
1952	March	Nordic Council founded
	May	Six ECSC members sign draft treaty creating European Defence Community
	July	Treaty of Paris comes into force
1953	March	Plans announced for European Political Community
1954	May	French defeat in Indochina
	August	Collapse of plans for European Defence Community and European Political Community
	October	Protocol to Treaty of Brussels signed, creating Western European Union
	December	European Court of Justice issues its first ruling

1955	May	Western European Union comes into operation, headquartered in London; creation of Warsaw Pact
	June	Opening of IGC in Messina to discuss the next step in European integration
	December	Council of Europe adopts flag with twelve gold stars on blue background
1956	June	Negotiations open on creation of EEC and Euratom
	October	Soviet invasion of Hungary
	October–December	Suez crisis
1957	March	Treaties of Rome signed, creating Euratom and EEC
1958	January	Treaties of Rome come into force
	February	Treaty creating Benelux Economic Union signed in The Hague
	July	Conference in Stresa, Italy, works out details of Common Agricultural Policy
1960	January	Seven countries sign European Free Trade Association Convention in Stockholm
	May	EFTA comes into force
	November	Benelux Economic Union comes into force
	December	OEEC becomes Organisation for Economic Cooperation and Development
1961	February	First summit of EEC heads of government
	July	Ireland applies for EEC membership
	August	The UK and Denmark apply for EEC membership; construction begins on Berlin Wall
1962	April	Norway applies for EEC membership
	October	Cuban missile crisis
1963	January	De Gaulle vetoes UK membership of EEC; France and Germany sign Treaty of Friendship and Cooperation
	July	Yaoundé Convention signed between EEC and eighteen African countries
	September	Death of Robert Schuman
1965	April	Merger Treaty signed, establishing a single Commission and Council for the three European Communities
	July	France begins boycott of Community institutions (the empty chair crisis)
1966	January	Empty chair crisis ends with Luxembourg Compromise
1967	May	Second application for EEC membership from the UK, Denmark, and Ireland, followed by Norway in July
	June	Arab–Israeli War
	July	Merger Treaty comes into force
	November	Second veto by de Gaulle of UK membership of EEC
1968	July	Agreement on a common external tariff completes creation of EEC customs union

1969	April	Resignation of Charles de Gaulle
	December	EEC leaders meeting in The Hague agree on principle of economic and monetary union
1970	June	Membership negotiations with the UK, Denmark, Ireland, and Norway resume; concluded January 1972
1971	August	United States abandons gold standard; end of Bretton Woods system of fixed exchange rates
1972	April	Launch of the European exchange rate stabilization system (the "snake")
	May	European Social Fund becomes operational; Irish referendum approves EEC membership
	September	Norwegian referendum rejects EEC membership
	October	Danish referendum approves EEC membership
1973	January	The UK, Denmark, and Ireland join the Community, bringing membership to nine
	October	Yom Kippur War
1974	December	Community leaders decide to form European Council
1975	February	First Lomé Convention signed between EEC and forty-six ACP states
	March	First meeting of European Council in Dublin; creation of European Regional Development Fund
	June	UK referendum on continued EC membership; Greece applies to join Community; negotiations open July 1976
1977	March	Portugal applies to join Community; negotiations open June 1978
	July	Spain applies to join Community; negotiations open February 1979
	October	Court of Auditors holds its first meeting
1978	December	European Council establishes European Monetary System
1979	February	Court of Justice issues *Cassis de Dijon* ruling
	March	European Monetary System comes into operation; death of Jean Monnet
	June	First direct elections to European Parliament
1981	January	Greece joins Community, bringing membership to ten
1982	February	Greenland votes to leave the EEC; finally leaves February 1985
1983	December	Agreement on Common Fisheries Policy
1984	January	Free trade area established between EFTA and the Community
	June	Second direct elections to European Parliament; European Council resolves UK budget problem
1985	January	Jacques Delors begins first term as Commission president; introduction of European passports
	June	Publication of Commission white paper on the single market; signing of the Schengen agreement

1985	September	Opening of IGC on the single market
	December	European Council agrees to drawing up of Single European Act
1986	January	Portugal and Spain join Community, bringing membership to twelve
	February	Single European Act signed in Luxembourg
	May	Flag of EC flown for the first time
1987	April	Turkey applies to join Community; negotiations do not open until 2005
	July	Single European Act comes into force
1988	October	Court of First Instance created
1989	April	Delors report on economic and monetary union
	June	Third direct elections to European Parliament
	July	Austria applies to join Community
	September–December	Collapse of communist governments in Eastern Europe; fall of Berlin Wall (November)
	December	Adoption of the Social Charter by eleven EC member states
1990	June	Schengen agreement signed by Benelux states, France, and Germany; negotiations open on creation of European Economic Area
	July	Cyprus and Malta apply to join Community
	August	Iraqi invasion of Kuwait
	October	German reunification brings former East Germany into Community
	December	Opening of IGCs on economic and monetary union and on political union
1991	January	US-led invasion expels Iraq from Kuwait
	April	European Bank for Reconstruction and Development opens in London
	June	Outbreak of war in Yugoslavia
	July	Sweden applies to join Community
	December	Maastricht European Council agrees on draft Treaty on European Union; breakup of USSR
1992	February	Treaty on European Union signed in Maastricht
	March	Finland applies to join EU
	May	France and Germany announce creation of 35,000-member Eurocorps; Switzerland signs EEA membership agreement and applies to join EU
	June	Danish referendum rejects terms of Maastricht
	September	ERM crisis; UK and Italy suspend membership
	November	Norway applies again to join EU
	December	Swiss referendum rejects membership of EEA; Swiss application for EU membership suspended

1993	January	Single European market comes into force
	February	Membership negotiations open with Austria, Finland, and Sweden (and with Norway in April)
	May	Second Danish referendum accepts terms of Maastricht
	November	Treaty on European Union comes into force; European Community becomes one of three "pillars" of a new European Union
1994	January	European Economic Area enters into force
	March	Inaugural session of Committee of the Regions; Hungary applies to join the EU
	April	Poland applies to join the EU
	May	Opening of Channel Tunnel linking the UK and France
	June	Fourth direct elections to European Parliament; referendum in Austria favors EU membership
	October	Finnish referendum accepts EU membership
	November	Swedish referendum accepts EU membership; Norwegians again reject membership
1995	January	Austria, Finland, and Sweden join EU, bringing membership to fifteen; GATT replaced by the World Trade Organization
	March	Schengen agreement comes into force
	June	Romania and Slovakia apply to join EU
	July	Europol Convention signed
	October–December	Bulgaria, Estonia, Latvia, and Lithuania apply to join EU
	December	Dayton peace accords end war in Yugoslavia; European Council decides to call single currency the "euro"
1996	January	Czech Republic applies to join EU
	June	Slovenia applies to join EU
	December	Agreement on stability and growth pact
1997	June	European Council agrees on Treaty of Amsterdam
	July	Launch of Agenda 2000
	October	Treaty of Amsterdam signed
1998	March	Negotiations on EU membership opened with Cyprus, Czech Republic, Estonia, Hungary, Poland, and Slovenia
	June	Establishment of European Central Bank
1999	January	Official launch of the euro in eleven member states, which fix currency exchange rates relative to one another and to the euro
	March	Resignation of College of Commissioners following publication of report alleging fraud, mismanagement, and nepotism in Commission

1999	March–April	NATO air attacks on Kosovo
	May	Treaty of Amsterdam comes into force
	June	Fifth direct elections to European Parliament – record low voter turnout
2000	January	Negotiations on EU membership open with Bulgaria, Latvia, Lithuania, Malta, Romania, and Slovakia
	March	Launch of Lisbon Strategy
	June	Cotonou Convention signed between EU and ACP states
	September	Danish referendum rejects adoption of euro
	December	European Council agrees on Treaty of Nice
2001	February	Treaty of Nice signed
	March	Swiss referendum rejects EU membership
	June	Irish referendum rejects Treaty of Nice
	September	Terrorist attacks on the World Trade Center in New York and the Pentagon in Washington, DC
	December	Laeken European Council agrees to launch Convention on the Future of Europe
2002	January–March	Euro coins and notes begin circulating in twelve member states
	February	Opening of Convention on the Future of Europe
	July	Treaty of Paris expires
	October	Second Irish referendum accepts Treaty of Nice
2003	February	Treaty of Nice comes into force
	March	United States launches attack on Iraq despite French and German opposition
	July	Publication of draft treaty establishing a constitution for Europe
	March–September	Referendums in Czech Republic, Estonia, Hungary, Poland, Latvia, Lithuania, Malta, Slovakia, and Slovenia all approve EU membership; Swedish referendum rejects adoption of euro
	October	IGC opens on the draft European constitutional treaty
	December	European Council fails to reach agreement on constitutional treaty
2004	March	Terrorist bombings in Madrid
	May	Ten countries, mainly Eastern European, join the EU, bringing membership to twenty-five
	June	Sixth direct elections to European Parliament; European Council reaches agreement on constitutional treaty
	October	European leaders sign treaty on the European constitution
	November	Lithuania is first member state to endorse constitution

2005	February	Spain is first member state to hold referendum on constitution; approves constitution
	May	France rejects constitution in national referendum
	June	Netherlands rejects constitution in national referendum
	July	Terrorist bombings in London
	October	Negotiations on EU membership open with Croatia and Turkey
2007	January	Bulgaria and Romania join the EU, bringing membership to twenty-seven; Slovenia becomes the thirteenth country to adopt the euro
	March	Berlin Declaration marking fiftieth anniversary of the signing of Treaties of Rome
	August	Global economic crisis begins, with slowly evolving consequences for EU member states
	October	European Council agrees on new Lisbon Treaty to replace defunct constitutional treaty
2008	January	Cyprus and Malta adopt the euro
	June	Irish referendum rejects Lisbon treaty
2009	January	Slovakia adopts the euro
	February	Spain enters into economic recession
	October	New Irish referendum on Lisbon passes
	November	Lisbon treaty comes into force
2010	April	The downgrading of Greek government bonds to junk status prompts fears of the collapse of the Greek economy; the EU and IMF agree on a €110 billion ($147 billion) bailout of Greece
2011	January	Estonia adopts the euro
	October	Second bailout package, of €130 billion ($175 billion), from the EU for Greece; Spain's economic outlook worsens and international ratings agencies downgrade its credit rating
2012	March	Treaty on Stability, Coordination and Governance in the Economic and Monetary Union (fiscal compact) signed by all EU states except the UK and the Czech Republic; member states begin the ratification process
	June	European Council agrees to bank recapitalization through ESM, a €120 billion ($160 billion) "European Growth Pact," and a plan for an EU-wide banking union
	October	The European Council agrees to set a timetable for the set-up and legal foundations for a new eurozone bank regulator as part of the proposed EU Banking union
2013	February	EU leaders agree on budget package for 2014–20
	July	Croatia becomes the EU's twenty-eighth member state
	November	Georgia and Moldova sign association agreements with the EU. Ukraine turns down agreement and seeks closer ties to Russia. Demonstrations against President Yanukovych increase dramatically. He is ousted two months later

2014	January	Latvia adopts the euro
	May	Elections for the EP are held. Anti-EU/EU-skeptical parties win big
	July	After the shooting down of a Malaysian airliner in Ukraine, the EU and US impose sanctions on Russia over its involvement in the Ukraine crisis
	November	The single supervisory mechanism for banks enters into force
2015	January	Lithuania adopts the euro
	May	The Conservative party under David Cameron wins an absolute majority in UK parliamentary elections and promises an "in-out" referendum on EU membership before the end of 2017
	July	Greek voters reject a bailout proposal from the EU in a referendum; two weeks later the Greek parliament approves a new, harsher bailout offer from the EU
	September	The Council of the EU votes to relocate and redistribute 120,000 refugees across all member states
2016	June	52 percent of voters approve referendum in UK to leave the EU (Brexit)
	July	Theresa May becomes UK prime minister and begins negotiations for Brexit
	November	High Court in the UK rules that government cannot invoke Article 50 on leaving the EU without being authorized by Parliament
2017	March	Sixtieth anniversary of the signing of the Treaty of Rome
	April	After UK gives official notice on Article 50 (leaving the EU), EU leaders meet to discuss Brexit
	September	EU initiates ten initial projects for Permanent Structured Cooperation (PESCO)
	November	The European Council votes to relocate the European Banking Authority from London to Paris and the European Medicines Agency from London to Amsterdam
2018	October	Court of Justice rules that Polish legislation giving the government significant power over the composition and nature of the Polish Supreme Court is contrary to EU law
	November	Theresa May's plan for Brexit approved by EU member states
2019	April	Brexit postponed after May loses vote on Brexit in UK Parliament
	May	EP elections see some gains for populist, anti-EU parties but pro-EU parties secure a majority
	July	Theresa May resigns as prime minister after failing to pass a plan for Brexit acceptable to a majority in the UK Parliament
	November	European Parliament approves the 2019–2014 Commission
	December	Boris Johnson's Conservative Party wins a decisive majority in UK, ending the Brexit debate in the UK
2020	January	EU leaders sign Brexit withdrawal agreement; the UK officially exits the European Union at midnight, January 31st

APPENDIX 2

Sources of Information

For researchers on the EU, shortage of information is not a problem. Publishing on the EU has become a growth industry, and the flow of new books and journal articles matches both the EU's increasing powers and reach and its growing impact on global politics, economics, and public opinion. The challenge for the researcher lies less in finding material than in making sense of it all and in keeping up with rapidly changing developments. Rather than provide a lengthy bibliography that would quickly go out of date, this appendix provides a selective list of sources of information, which can be used as the foundation for a broader search. For online sources/websites (especially for the "Europa" website and for sites connected to EU institutions), it is especially important to remember that there are numerous secondary links from the main site. This means that just about any piece of information concerning "who is who" and how the EU functions can be found by carefully following all possible links from the main site.

ONLINE SOURCES

There are literally thousands of websites dealing with the EU, the most useful of which include the following:

Official EU Websites

- Europa: http://europa.eu. The official website of the EU and the most easily accessible for students to all kinds of official EU information. Especially interesting are sections dealing with the history and institutions.
- European Union Law: https://eur-lex.europa.eu/homepage.html. The website for EUR-Lex, the authoritative source on all EU laws. The site includes the official journal of the EU.
- European Commission: http://ec.europa.eu/index_en.htm
- Council of Ministers: www.consilium.europa.eu
- European Parliament: www.europarl.europa.eu
- European Court of Justice: http://curia.europa.eu
- European Central Bank: www.ecb.europa.eu/home/html/index.en.html
- Delegation of the European Commission to the US: www.euintheus.org/
- Delegation of the European Commission to Canada: https://eeas.europa.eu/delegations/canada_en

Academic Organizations for the Study of the EU

- Council for European Studies: https://councilforeuropeanstudies.org/?option=com_cont ent&view=article&id=11&Itemid=10
- European Union Studies Association: www.eustudies.org/
- University Association for Contemporary European Studies: www.uaces.org/
- London School of Economics: www.lse.ac.uk/
- European Law Institute: www.europeanlawinstitute.eu/about-eli/
- Jean Monnet Center, New York University: http://jeanmonnetprogram.org/
- University of Leiden, EU history site: www.hum.leiden.edu/history/eu-history

Sources of News on the EU

- *The Economist.* A weekly British news magazine that has news and statistics on world politics, including a section on Europe (and occasional special supplements on the EU): www.economist.com/
- BBC News Online: www.bbc.co.uk/news
- EUBusiness: www.eubusiness.com
- EUObserver: http://euobserver.com
- Euractiv: www.euractiv.com
- Euronews: www.euronews.com/european-affairs/european-news
- *Financial Times.* An English-language international newspaper, with extensive daily coverage of the EU: www.ft.com/home/us
- *Politico Europe.* Once known as *European Voice*, a weekly newspaper published in Brussels but acquired in 2014 by POLITICO: www.politico.eu/author/european-voice/

Publishers

The publishers that have developed the most comprehensive lists of books on the EU include Lynne Rienner, Oxford University Press, Palgrave Macmillan, Routledge, and Rowman and Littlefield. A search of their websites will reveal many useful sources on the EU.

Academic Journals

There are numerous political science, comparative politics, international relations, and area studies journals that deal with EU issues, among the most consistently useful of which are the following:

- *Common Market Law Review*
- *Comparative European Politics*
- *East European Politics*
- *Europe Asia Studies*
- *European Foreign Affairs Review*
- *European Journal of International Relations*
- *European Journal of Political Research*
- *European Union Politics*
- *Foreign Affairs*
- *International Organization*

- *Journal of Common Market Studies*
- *Journal of Contemporary European Research*
- *Journal of Contemporary European Studies*
- *Journal of European Integration*
- *Journal of Integration History*
- *Journal of European Public Policy*
- *Journal of European Social Policy*
- *Journal of Transatlantic Studies*
- *Parliamentary Affairs*
- *West European Politics*

EU INFORMATION CENTERS IN NORTH AMERICA

Most major university and college libraries in the US and Canada carry general information on the EU, but some also contain more specialized resources. Some are EU Depository Libraries and receive a wide range of EU publications. Others are EU Centers of Excellence and offer a wider selection of services and activities. For a complete listing, visit the websites of the European Commission offices in Washington, DC, and Ottawa (see above, under Official EU Websites).

Index

Made in United States
Cleveland, OH
18 January 2025

13572349R00190